A Practitioner's Guide to Executorship and Administration

The College of Law
of England and Wales

LIBRARY SERVICES

The College of Law, 133 Great Hampton Street, Birmingham, B18 6AQ
Telephone: 01483 216041   E-mail: library.brm@lawcol.co.uk

D1494060

Birmingham · Chester · Guildford · London · Manchester · York

A Practitioner's Guide to Executorship and Administration

Seventh Edition

John Thurston, LLB, Solicitor TEP

Tottel
publishing

Tottel Publishing Ltd, Maxwelton House, 41–43 Boltro Road, Haywards Heath, West Sussex, RH16 1BJ

ISBN 978 1 84766 111 1
© John Thurston 2009

British Library Cataloguing-in-Publication Data
A CIP Catalogue record for this book is available from the British Library.

Typeset by Columns Design Ltd, Reading, Berkshire

Printed and bound in Great Britain by M & A Thomson Litho Ltd, East Kilbride, Glasgow

Preface

This book is aimed at the busy professional, be they solicitor, accountant, legal executive or will draftsman. It is intended to provide a quick and easily digestible guide to the administration of estates of deceased persons.

Although some legal knowledge is assumed, I hope that it will also be of use to lay persons dealing with the estates of deceased persons.

Contents

Contents

Contents

Table of statutes

References in the right-hand column are to paragraph number. Paragraph references printed in **bold** type indicate where the Act is set out in part or in full.

xi

Table of statutes

Table of statutory instruments

References in the right-hand column are to paragraph number. Paragraph references printed in **bold** type indicate where the Statutory Instrument is set out in part or in full.

Table of statutory instruments

Table of cases

Chapter 1

Overview

1.1　　This chapter is intended for lay persons wishing to administer an estate themselves.

The first duty of the personal representatives or relatives of a deceased person is to register the death with Registrar of Births, Deaths and Marriages. Normally this is a formality, but in certain circumstances an inquest may be held.

The next stage is to secure the assets of the deceased and to begin to collect the information required to obtain a grant of probate or letters of administration to the estate of the deceased person. If the estate is large enough, consideration will have to be given to the funding of the inheritance tax due.

It will then be necessary to draft the oath, and if required the Inland Revenue account in order to obtain the grant of probate or letters of administration.

Once the grant has been obtained, it is then necessary to pay the debts and funeral expenses of the deceased. When all the liabilities have been met, the personal representatives can then distribute the assets to those with an entitlement under the will or intestacy rules.

Accounts will have to be prepared, and approved by the executors and the residuary beneficiaries where appropriate.

Chapter 2

Immediate post death procedure

REGISTERING THE DEATH

2.1   Usually professionals do not become involved in registering the deaths of clients, although it can happen, for example where there are no relatives. If there are no relatives, the person arranging for the disposal of the body can register the death. This should normally be done within five days of the death in the sub-district where the death occurred. It will be necessary to supply the following information:

(a)   the date and place of birth of the deceased;

(b)   date and place of death;

(c)   name and surname of the deceased;

(d)   maiden surname, if the deceased was a woman who had married;

(e)   date and place of birth;

(f)   occupation;

(g)   name and occupation of spouse, where the deceased was married or widowed;

(h)   name and occupation of civil partner, where the deceased was in a civil partnership or was a surviving civil partner;

(i)   usual address;

(j)   whether the deceased received a pension or allowance from public funds;

(k)   if the deceased was married or in a civil partnership, the date of birth of the surviving spouse or civil partner;

The only document required is the medical certificate giving the cause of death.

The Registrar will issue a certificate for burial or cremation and a certificate of notification of death for the Department of Work and Pensions, and on payment of a fee, a copy of the entry in the Register. Whether or not a professional is involved with the registration of the death, it is a good idea to obtain several copies of the death certificate as it may be necessary to produce such copies to any banks or building societies where the deceased had an account, and also to any life insurance companies where the deceased was insured.

INQUESTS

2.2   In certain circumstances the Registrar must report a death to the coroner, for example, if the deceased had not seen his doctor in the 14 days before death, or the cause of death was unknown or uncertain. The coroner is not obliged to hold an inquest in every case, although there are some situations where an inquest must be held, for example, if the death was violent or unnatural. In other cases, he has a discretion as to whether to order an inquest, but if he is satisfied that the death was due to natural causes, he can issue a certificate to the Registrar so that the death can be registered.

DISPOSAL OF THE BODY

2.3   Anyone can express a wish as to how they would like the disposal of his or her body to take place. The wish can be expressed either orally, or in a will, or in written document not contained in the will. Whilst most personal representatives will seek to comply with the wishes of the deceased, there is no obligation on them to do so. However, it should be noted that personal representatives are under a duty to dispose of the body.

It may be that the client has expressed a wish for his body to be used for medical research, in which case the nearest medical school should be contacted on the day of death, or next day. If this is not possible, arrangements should be made for the body to be kept in refrigerated storage. Unless the relatives have expressed a wish to the contrary, the medical school will pay the cost of a simple funeral.

If the deceased has expressed a wish to donate their organs, than the nearest hospital should be notified as soon as possible after death. Where the personal representatives are not close relatives of the deceased, they should consult them to ensure that they agree to the proposed donation.

The body or ashes may be interred in a churchyard with the consent of the incumbent, or in a cemetery maintained by a local authority. Usually a fee will be charged.

PAYING FOR THE FUNERAL

2.4   It may be that the deceased has entered into an arrangement to pay for his funeral during his lifetime. If this is not the case, then the person or persons arranging the funeral become personally liable to the undertaker for the cost of the funeral. However, reasonable funeral costs are the first charge on the estate, and many banks and building societies are prepared to release funds for this purpose before a grant has been obtained.

Occasionally there may be disputes as to the funeral arrangements. These are considered in more detail in **chapter 11**.

PRESERVING THE ASSETS

2.5   The executors or administrators, or the solicitors instructed by the executors or administrators should take possession of all relevant documents belonging to the deceased – share certificates, cheque books, passbooks, life insurance policies, land certificates and title deeds.

If the deceased left a house, which due to his death has become unoccupied, then the insurers should be notified. The house should also be secured, and relevant electricity, gas, water and telephone companies notified. The local authority should also be notified. If cold weather is expected, then steps should be taken to ensure that frozen pipes do not cause damage.

The personal representatives should also check the position with regard to insurance. Personal representatives now have wide powers of insurance under s 19 of the Trustee Act 1925 as amended by Trustee Act 2000. In particular, the position with regard to house insurance should be checked, as the premises or contents may not be covered if they are unoccupied.

THE WILL

2.6   Frequently the deceased will have told relatives about the existence of a will, and its whereabouts. If the deceased did not do so, then it will be necessary to conduct a search of his or her papers to see if there is a will, or correspondence containing any reference to a will.

Consideration should also be given to whether letters should be sent to all the solicitors' firms in the areas where the deceased was living at the date of death or has lived enquiring if they hold a will on behalf of the deceased. Advertisements can also be inserted in the Law Society's Gazette for lost wills. Most long-established firms of solicitors will hold wills executed many years ago where the testators must have died; it is possible that these testators executed later wills, but there is always a suspicion that these testators were regarded as having died intestate as the relatives were unaware of the existence of the will.

It is also possible to deposit wills at the Principal Registry. This facility is not used very much, but a search should be made for missing wills.

The beneficiaries may be keen to know the contents of the will, but personal representatives are under no duty to tell them. However, once the will has been proved, it becomes a public document and is available for inspection by all; therefore in most cases there is little point in the personal representatives refusing to disclose the contents of a will to the beneficiaries.

SOLICITORS AS PERSONAL REPRESENTATIVES OR INSTRUCTED TO ACT BY PERSONAL REPRESENTATIVES

2.7   The Solicitors' Code of Conduct requires solicitors to give information about costs and other matters and to operate a complaints-handling procedure in accordance with the Code.

Strictly, it is the executors or administrators who are the clients of the solicitor. However, it is clearly good and desirable practice to send a client care letter to the residuary beneficiaries under the will.

Can a beneficiary under the will who is not an executor or administrator request the solicitor to obtain a remuneration certificate? The answer is yes, but only in limited circumstances. An entitled third party is allowed to apply for a remuneration certificate. 'An entitled third party' means a residuary beneficiary, absolutely and immediately (and not contingently) entitled to an inheritance, where a solicitor has charged the estate for his professional costs for acting in the administration of the estate, and either:

(a)   the only personal representatives are solicitors (whether or not acting in a professional capacity); or

(b)   the only personal representatives are solicitors acting jointly with partners or employees in a professional capacity.

A solicitor dealing with an estate is not obliged to provide information about the estate to a beneficiary who is not a personal representative, but it is good practice to do so. Where the solicitor is sole executor, the solicitor should keep the beneficiaries informed about the administration of the estate.

A solicitor, who has been appointed an executor, cannot be forced to renounce the right to grant. However, the solicitor should consider whether it is the best interests of the estate not to renounce the right to grant. The solicitor may find it embarrassing to have to deal with beneficiaries who do not wish him to take out a grant.

Chapter 3

Collecting the required information

OVERVIEW

3.1   In order to obtain the grant, it is necessary to collect the following various pieces of information:

(a)   whether the deceased left a will;

(b)   full name and address of the deceased;

(c)   date of birth of the deceased;

(d)   names, addresses and occupations of the executors or administrators;

(e)   whether the deceased was survived by parents, brothers and sisters, spouse, children or grandchildren, and if so, how many;

(f)   whether the deceased was domiciled in England and Wales;

(g)   the National Insurance number of the deceased;

(h)   the income tax reference of the deceased;

(i)   the name and address of the tax district to which the deceased submitted returns;

(j)   the assets of the deceased;

(k)   the debts and liabilities of the deceased;

(l)   whether there is anyone for whom the deceased should have provided but failed to do so;

(m)   whether the deceased made *inter vivos* (lifetime) gifts in the seven years before death;

(n)   whether the deceased was a member of a pension scheme, and whether a lump sum was payable on retirement;

(o)   whether the deceased had taken out any life insurance policies;

(p)   whether the deceased was in receipt of an annuity, and if so, details.

Having ascertained the assets owned by the deceased, it will then be necessary to obtain valuations of the various assets. The procedure for the valuation of assets is set out below.

LAND

3.2   It is usual to obtain a valuation of any land within the estate from a qualified valuer.

SHARES

3.3   It is common to obtain a valuation from brokers, who can also be requested to check the number of shares held by the deceased.

The Stock Exchange also provides a pricing service; the email address is products@londonstockexchange.com. Subscribers can telephone 020 7797 3343.

BANKS AND BUILDING SOCIETIES

3.4   The executors should write to all banks and building societies where it is thought the deceased held accounts requesting details of all accounts, the amount standing to the credit of the account as at the date of death, the interest due to the date of death and the interest paid or credited to the account since the deceased's last tax return.

In the case of a large estate, it may be desirable to open an executors' account.

SOCIAL SECURITY BENEFITS/PENSIONS

3.5   Letters should be sent to the local office of the Department of Work and Pensions and to the Recovery from Estates, 'A' Wing, Government Buildings, Otley Road, Lawnswood, Leeds, LS16 5PU requesting details of any overpayments and/or underpayments.

PENSIONS

3.6   The deceased may have been a member of a pension scheme provided by his employer, or a member of a private scheme. The relevant scheme providers should be notified of the death, and asked to provide details of any overpayment or underpayment.

LIFE ASSURANCE POLICIES

3.7   The insurance company should be notified of the death, and the company should be asked to provide a note of the amount due under the policy. A claim form should also be requested.

IHMRC

3.8   The deceased's tax office should be notified of the date of death, as there may be a refund due to the estate where the deceased was employed. However, where the deceased was self-employed, additional tax may be due.

UNCLAIMED ASSETS

3.9   It is possible to search for lost assets in insurance companies, banks, building societies and National Savings. The searches can be made with the Unclaimed Assets Register (www.uar.co.uk), and for lost bank, building society and National Savings accounts, www.mylostaccount.org.uk.

Chapter 4

Types of grant

IS A GRANT NECESSARY?

4.1   Once the executors have collected the necessary information, the next stage is to apply for a grant of probate or letters of administration. The effect of a grant is to confer authority on the executors and administrators to deal with the estate of the deceased, and in the case of a grant of probate where there is a will appointing executors, it confirms that the will is valid.

However, it is sometimes possible to complete the administration of an estate without obtaining a grant. Frequently, spouses, civil partners and cohabitees own the home as joint tenants, and there may also be bank and building society accounts in the joint names of both spouses, civil partners or cohabitees. If everything is jointly owned, it will not be necessary to obtain a grant. The survivor will be entitled to all the jointly owned assets, and only needs to produce the death certificate to have the house or joint accounts transferred into their sole name.

If the deceased has only left a small amount of money invested in a building society account, then the building society can agree to release the money without the need for the production of a grant. This power can only be exercised where the amount in the account is less than £5,000. A similar provision applies to money invested with the National Savings Bank, Trustee Savings Bank, Savings Certificates or Premium Bonds. It may also be possible to obtain other moneys without the need for the production of the grant, for example, arrears of salary or money in bank accounts.

TYPES OF GRANT

4.2   There are various types of grant which can be obtained in order to administer the estate of a deceased person. They are:

(a)   grant of probate;

(b)   grant of letters of administration;

(c)   grant of letters of administration with the will annexed;

(d)   grant to the unadministered estate;

(e)   grant during the minority of an executor or administrator;

(f)   grants to attorneys;

(g)   grants where the deceased died domiciled outside England and Wales;

(h)   grant limited to certain property.

It is necessary to examine each of these grants in turn.

Grant of probate

4.3   A grant of probate will be obtained where the deceased left a will appointing executors who are able and willing to take out a grant. If there is a will, but no valid appointment of executors, for example because they have all predeceased the testator, then it is necessary to obtain a grant of letters of administration with the will annexed.

Whilst there is no limit on the number of persons who can be appointed executors, a grant will not be made out to more than four.

Strictly there are no restrictions on who can be appointed as an executor, and so a testator can appoint anyone, however undesirable they may be. However, a grant of probate will not be made to an infant; instead a grant will be made to another person, possibly the parents, for the use and benefit of the child. Such a grant will usually have a time limit, so that the infant can take a grant in his or her own right once he or she has attained the age of 18.

Grant of letters of administration

4.4   It is necessary to obtain a grant of letters of administration when the deceased did not leave a will, and died intestate.

The Non-Contentious Probate Rules (NCPR 1987) prescribe who is entitled to the grant; the order follows the order of entitlement to the estate under the intestacy rules. Rule 22(1) provides that the following are entitled:

(a)   the surviving spouse;

(b)   the children of the deceased or the issue of any deceased child who died before the deceased;

(c)   the father and mother of the deceased;

(d)   brothers and sisters of the whole blood and the issue of any deceased brother and sister of the whole blood who died before the deceased;

(e)   brothers and sisters of the half blood and the issue of any deceased brother and sister of the half blood who died before the deceased;

(f)   grandparents;

(g)   uncles and aunts of the whole blood and the issue of any deceased uncle and aunt of the whole blood who died before the deceased;

(h)   uncles and aunts of the half blood and the issue of any deceased uncle or aunt of the half blood who died before the deceased.

'Children' includes legitimate, illegitimate and adopted children.

Rule 22(2) provides that in default of any person having a beneficial interest in the estate, the Treasury Solicitor is entitled to a grant if he claims *bona vacantia* on behalf of the Crown.

Rule 22(3) provides that if all persons entitled to a grant under the foregoing provisions of the rule have been cleared off, a grant may be made to a creditor of the deceased or to any person who, notwithstanding that he has no immediate beneficial interest in the estate, may have a beneficial interest in the estate in the event of an accretion thereto.

If a person entitled to a grant dies, his or her personal representatives may be entitled to a grant. Rule 22(4) provides that subject to paragraph (5) of r 27, the personal representative of a person in any of the classes mentioned in paragraph (1) of this rule or the personal representative of a creditor of the deceased shall have the same right to a grant as the person whom he represents. However, if the spouse of the intestate has died without taking a beneficial interest in the whole estate of the deceased as ascertained at the time of the application for the grant, then the other persons entitled to the grant are to be preferred to the personal representatives of the deceased spouse. Rule 27(5) provides that unless a District Judge or Registrar otherwise directs, administration is to be granted to a person of full age entitled thereto in preference to a guardian of a minor, and to a living person entitled thereto in preference to the personal representative of a deceased person.

Grant of letters of administration with the will annexed

4.5   This grant can be obtained where there is a will, but there are no executors willing and able to prove the will. This might be for various reasons, for example:

(a)   all the executors appointed in the will have predeceased the testator;

(b)   all the executors have either predeceased the testator or are unwilling to take out a grant;

(c)   the will did not appoint any executors (this should not be the case if the will is professionally drawn).

In this situation, r 20 of the NCPR 1987 provides the order of priority to a grant is to be determined in accordance with the following order:

(a)   the executor (but subject to r 36(4)(d));

(b)   any residuary legatee or devisee holding in trust for any other person;

(c)   any other residuary legatee (including one for life) or where the residue is not wholly disposed of by the will, any person entitled to share in the undisposed of residue (including the Treasury Solicitor when claiming *bona vacantia* on behalf of the Crown) provided that:

    (i)   unless a District Judge or Registrar otherwise directs, a residuary legatee or devisee whose legacy or devise is vested in interest shall be preferred to one entitled on the happening of a contingency; and

    (ii)   where the residue is not in terms wholly disposed of, the District Judge or Registrar may, if he is satisfied that the testator has nevertheless disposed of the whole or substantially the whole of the known estate, allow a grant to be made to any legatee or devisee entitled to, or to share in the estate disposed of, without regard to the person entitled to share in any residue not disposed of by will;

(d) the personal representatives of any residuary legatee or devisee (but not one for life, or one holding in trust for any other person), or of any person entitled to share in any residue not disposed of by the will;

(e) any other legatee or devisee (including one for life or one holding in trust for any other person) or any creditor of the deceased, provided that, unless a District Judge or Registrar otherwise directs, a legatee or devisee whose legacy or devise is vested in interest shall be preferred to one entitled on the happening of a contingency;

(f) the personal representatives of any other legatee or devisee (but not one for life or one holding in trust for any other person) or any creditor of the deceased.

Rule 36 is concerned with grants to trust corporations. Rule 36(4)(a) provides that where a corporate body would, if an individual, be entitled to a grant but is not a trust corporation as defined in the rules, administration for its use and benefit, limited until further representation be granted, may be made to its nominee or to its lawfully constituted attorney. Rule 36(4)(d) provides that the provisions of paragraph (a) are not to apply where a body corporate is appointed executor jointly with an individual unless the right of the individual has been cleared off. 'Clearing off' is a process whereby the person or persons applying for a grant explain why those with a better right to a grant are not applying.

A person who is a beneficiary under a will, but is not entitled to take because he has witnessed the will, is not entitled to a grant (r 21, NCPR 1987).

Rule 20 covers three situations:

(a) where there is a complete disposal of the whole residuary estate;

(b) where there is a part disposal of the residuary estate;

(c) where there is no residuary gift in the will;

and there is no effective appointment of executors.

In the last situation, the person or persons entitled under the intestacy rules to the residuary estate will be entitled to the grant under this paragraph.

General points about letters of administration

4.6   Rule 27(4) of the NCPR 1987 provides that a grant of administration may be made to any person entitled thereto without notice to other persons entitled in the same degree. So if a parent dies intestate leaving five children, one child can obtain a grant of letters of administration without notice to the others. If a will appoints executors, then notice must be given to those not proving the will.

It may be that a minor and an adult are entitled to a grant. In this situation; r 27(5) provides that unless a Registrar otherwise directs, administration is to be granted to a person of full age entitled thereto in preference to a guardian of a minor.

The rules also provide that personal representatives of a deceased beneficiary are entitled to a grant just as if the beneficiary was still alive. If a living person is also entitled, then that living person must be given priority in preference to the personal representatives of a deceased person (r 27(5)). Thus if the deceased died intestate and a widower leaving three children, one of whom predeceased the intestate, the two surviving children have a better right to the grant than the personal representatives of the deceased child.

Rule 27(6) provides that a dispute between persons entitled to a grant in the same degree shall be brought by summons before a Registrar.

Grant to the unadministered estate

4.7   This grant is issued where part of the estate is unadministered, and the sole, or if the original grant was to more than one personal representative, the last surviving personal representative, has died. It should be noted that such a grant is not necessary where no original grant was obtained. If a sole executor has died without obtaining a grant, then a grant of letters of administration with the will annexed will be made. In this situation, the order of entitlement is governed by r 20 of the NCPR 1987. If the deceased died without leaving a will, then a simple grant of letters of administration to the next person entitled under r 22 of the NCPR will be made.

If a grant has been obtained, the order of entitlement to the grant depends on whether the deceased died leaving a will. If this was the case, it may be that the chain of executorship will apply. Section 7(1) of the Administration of Estates Act 1925 provides that the executor of the sole or last surviving executor of a testator is the executor of that testator. However, this only applies if the executor of the original testator proves the will of that testator. In addition, it does not apply if other executors survive, and prove the will. Section 7(2) provides that so long as the chain is unbroken, the last executor in the chain is the executor of every preceding testator. Section 7(3) provides that the chain of such representation is broken by:

(a)   an intestacy; or

(b)   the failure of the testator to appoint an executor; or

(c)   the failure to obtain probate of the will.

The chain of representation will not be broken by a temporary grant of administration where probate is subsequently granted.

If the chain of executorship does not apply, then the order of entitlement is governed by r 20 of the NCPR 1987 where the deceased left a will. If the deceased died intestate, the order of entitlement is governed by r 22 of the NCPR 1987.

Grant during the minority of an executor or administrator

4.8   It is to be hoped that no professionally drawn will would appoint an infant as an executor. However, it may be on intestacy that a minor is entitled to a grant. If a minor is entitled, then r 32 of the NCPR 1987 provides for the grant of letters of administration to the parents jointly or to the guardians of the infant. Such a grant will terminate when the infant attains 18. Rule 32(2) provides that a Registrar may, by order, assign any person as guardian of the minor.

Grants in case of mental incapacity

4.9   Due to the increase in longevity, there may be an increase in the number of grants under this category. An elderly couple where the husband dies intestate may leave a spouse entitled under the intestacy rules, but incapable of managing her affairs because of, for example, Alzheimer's disease. If the deceased had left a will appointing the spouse as executor, it is to be hoped that in this scenario at the very least a codicil would have been executed revoking the appointment of the spouse as executor, and appointing an adult child in his or her place, but this will not always happen.

If a person entitled to a grant is incapable of managing his affairs by reason of mental incapacity, r 35(2) of the NCPR 1987 provides that administration for his use and benefit may be granted in the following order of priority:

(a)   to the person authorised by the Court of Protection to apply for a grant;

(b)   where there is no person so authorised, to the lawful attorney of the incapable person acting under a registered enduring power of attorney or lasting power of attorney;

(c)   where there is no such attorney entitled to act, or if the attorney renounces administration for the use and benefit of the incapable person, to the person entitled to the residuary estate of the deceased.

Rule 35(1) of the NCPR 1987 provides that unless a Registrar otherwise directs, no grant shall be made in this situation unless all the persons entitled in the same degree as the incapable person have been cleared off. This would apply, for example, if the testator has appointed his wife and children as executors. If the wife is mentally incapable, then no grant will be made under r 35 until they have been cleared off; the children might renounce their right to the grant, or possibly might have predeceased the testator. It would also apply if the deceased had died intestate leaving three children. If one is mentally incapable, then no grant will be made under r 35 if the other children wish to take out a grant.

Rule 35(3) provides that where a grant is required to be made to not less than two administrators, and there is only one person competent and willing to take a grant under the rule, administration may be granted to such person jointly with any other person nominated by him, unless a Registrar otherwise directs. Rule 35(4) provides that notwithstanding the other provisions in the rule, administration for the use and benefit of the incapable person may be granted to such two or more other persons as the Registrar may by order direct.

Rule 35(5) provides that notice of an intended application under this rule must be given to the Court of Protection unless the application is made by the person authorised by the Court of Protection to apply for a grant.

It is also necessary to produce a medical certificate to the effect that the executor or administrator is mentally incapable. This is not required if the Court of Protection has authorised the applicant to apply for a grant, or the applicant is acting under an enduring power of attorney which has been registered (see Practice Direction, 16 November 2007). The effect is that if an application is made by an attorney acting under a registered lasting power of attorney, evidence of the incapacity of the donor must be lodged. This should confirm that the donor suffers from an impairment of, or disturbance in, the functioning of the mind or brain as a result of which he lacks capacity within the meaning of the Mental Capacity Act 2005 and is unable to make a decision for himself in relation to the application for grant of representation and subsequent administration of the estate. It should also confirm that the donor is unlikely to be able to make any decision for himself within a period of three months.

Grant to an attorney

4.10   An attorney can apply for a grant for the use and benefit of the donor under r 31 of the NCPR 1987. Such a grant will be limited until further representation is granted, or in such other way as the District Judge or Registrar may direct.

If the donor is an executor, notice of the application must be given to any other executor unless the District Judge or Registrar dispenses with such notice (r 31(2)).

Rule 31(3) provides that if the donor is mentally incapable, and the attorney is acting under an enduring power of attorney, the application has to be made under r 35 (see **para 4.9**).

Grants where the deceased died domiciled outside England and Wales

4.11   Rule 30(1) of the NCPR 1987 provides that where the deceased died domiciled outside England and Wales, a District Judge or Registrar may order that a grant, limited in such way as the District Judge or Registrar may direct, should be issued to any of the following persons:

(a)   to the person entrusted with the administration of the estate by the court having jurisdiction at the place where the deceased died domiciled; or

(b)   where there is no person so entrusted, to the person beneficially entitled to the estate by the law of the place where the deceased died domiciled or, if there is more than one person so entitled, to such of them as the District Judge or Registrar may so direct; or

(c)   if in the opinion of the District Judge or Registrar the circumstances so require, to such person as the Registrar may direct.

Rule 30(2) provides that a grant under paragraph (a) or (b) may be issued jointly with such person as the District Judge or Registrar may direct, if the grant is required to be made to not less than two administrators.

Rule 30(3) provides that without any order under r 30(1):

(a)   probate of any will which is admissible to proof may be granted:

   (i)   if the will is in the English or Welsh language, to the executor named therein; or

   (ii)   if the will describes the duties of a named person in terms sufficient to constitute him executor according to the tenor, to that person; and

(b)   where the whole or substantially the whole of the estate in England and Wales consists of immovable property, a grant in respect of the whole estate may be made in accordance with the law which would have been applicable if the deceased had died domiciled in England and Wales.

Grants limited to certain property

4.12   Where required it is possible to obtain a grant limited to certain property, for example settled land.

It is also common for authors to appoint literary executors to deal with the copyrights of their published work, and general executors to deal with the remainder of the estate.

Very occasionally, where the deceased is in business, whether as a sole trader, in a partnership or through the medium of a limited company, separate executors may be appointed to deal with the business assets and other assets.

These types of grant are rare, and therefore are not considered in detail in this book.

Grants to assignees

4.13   Rule 24(1) of the NCPR 1987 provides that where all the persons entitled to the estate of the deceased (whether under a will or on intestacy) have assigned their whole interest in the estate to one or more persons, the assignee or assignees shall replace, in the order of priority for a grant of administration, the assignor or, if there are two or more assignors, the assignor with the highest priority. Rule 24(2) provides that where there are two or more assignees, administration may be granted with the consent of the others to any one or more (not exceeding four) of them. The original instrument of assignment must be produced, and a copy lodged in the registry (r 24(3)).

NUMBER OF EXECUTORS

4.14   A testator can appoint as many executors as he or she likes, although if an excessive number were appointed, there must clearly be a doubt about the capacity of the testator! However, whilst in theory a testator can appoint as many executors as he likes, only four will be permitted to take out a grant. If more than four executors apply for a grant of probate, it will be granted to the first four to apply with power reserved to the others.

Rule 27(1) provides that where on an application for probate, power to apply for a like grant is to be reserved to such other of the executors as have not renounced probate, the oath must state that notice of the application has been given to the executor or executors to whom power is to be reserved. If power is to be reserved to the partners in a firm, notice is to be given to the partners by sending it to the firm at its principal or last known place of business (r 27(2)). Rule 27(3) provides that a District Judge or Registrar may dispense with giving notice if he is satisfied that the giving of such notice is impracticable or would result in unreasonable delay or expense.

A grant can be made to one executor, although the court has power to appoint another administrator under s 114(4) of the Supreme Court Act 1981 (SCA 1981). This should be contrasted with administrators where two have to be appointed if there is a life interest or a minority interest.

NUMBER OF ADMINISTRATORS

4.15   Under s 114(1) of the SCA 1981 the number of administrators is limited to four. If more than four persons are entitled, the grant will be made to the first four to apply. Thus if the deceased died intestate without a spouse, but leaving six children, the first four children to apply for a grant will be the persons to whom the grant is made.

A grant can be made to a single administrator, but this cannot be done if a minority or life interest arises under the intestacy, in which event the grant must be made to at least two persons or a trust corporation.

If a minority or life interest does arise under the intestacy rules, and one of two the administrators dies, it is not necessary to appoint another administrator.

Where a deceased died intestate leaving a spouse and children, the person with the best right to the grant is the spouse. It may be that a second administrator is required because there is a life interest, or because some or all of the children are under age. If one of the children is of age, that child can be appointed an administrator without leave under r 25(1). This provides that a person entitled in priority to a grant of administration, may without leave, apply for a grant with a person entitled in a lower degree, provided there is no other person entitled in a higher degree to the person to be joined, unless every other such person has renounced.

Rule 25(2) provides that an application must be to a Registrar or District Judge in order to obtain leave to join with a person entitled in priority to a grant of administration a person having no right or no immediate right thereto. It must be supported by an affidavit by the person entitled in priority, the consent of the person who has been proposed to join as an administrator and such other evidence as the District Judge or Registrar may direct.

No leave is required if the person to be joined is a trust corporation. Leave is also not required if r 32(3) or 35(3) apply. Rule 32 applies to grants to minors, and r 32(3) provides that in this situation where there is only one person competent and willing to take a grant, such person may, unless a District Judge or Registrar otherwise directs, nominate any fit and proper person to act jointly with him in taking the grant. Rule 35 applies to grants in cases of mental incapacity, and r 35(3) provides that where a grant is required to be made to not less than two administrators, and there is only one person competent and willing to take a grant, administration may be granted to such person jointly with any other person nominated by him, unless a District Judge or Registrar otherwise directs.

APPOINTMENT OF ADDITIONAL PERSONAL REPRESENTATIVES

4.16   Rule 26(1) of the NCPR 1987 provides that an application under s 114(4) of the SCA 1981 to add a personal representative shall be made to a Registrar and shall be supported by an affidavit by the applicant, the consent of the person proposed to be added as personal representative and such other evidence as the Registrar may require. Rule 26(2) provides that on any such application the Registrar may direct that a note shall be made on the original grant of the addition of a further personal representative, or he may impound or revoke the grant or make such other order as the circumstances of the case may require.

CAPACITY TO TAKE OUT THE GRANT

4.17   A testator can appoint anyone he wishes as executor even though that person may be completely undesirable as an executor. Similarly anyone entitled to a grant of letters of administration with or without the will under the NCPR 1987 can apply even though that person may have convictions for fraud, and be unsuitable as an administrator. It should be noted that it may be that there is a duty on administrators to disclose facts about their past which may mean that they are unsuitable to be administrators (see *Shephard v Wheeler [2000] 1 WTLR 1175*).

Whilst the general rule is that anyone can be appointed as an executor or administrator, there are rules preventing some types of applicant applying, or imposing restrictions on their right to apply.

A grant will not be made to an infant. Instead, a grant will be made for the use and benefit of the minor under r 32 (see **para 4.8** above).

A grant will not be made to a person who is incapable of managing his affairs by reason of mental disorder. Instead, a grant will be made for his use and benefit under r 35, NCPR 1987 (see **para 4.9** above).

A grant may be made to a person resident outside the jurisdiction.

A trust corporation is also entitled to a grant. Section 128 of the SCA 1981 provides that a trust corporation means the Public Trustee or a corporation either appointed by the court in any particular case to be a trustee or authorised by rules made under s 4(3) of the Public Trustee Act 1906 to act as custodian trustee.

RENUNCIATION

4.18   Acting as an executor and administrator can be an onerous task, and a person appointed as executor, who may have agreed to act as such, may not feel able to do so when the testator dies because of ill health.

Anyone appointed as an executor can renounce the right to take out a grant, as long as they have not intermeddled with the estate. Intermeddling means that the person has taken steps to administer the estate – it is an implied acceptance of the office of executor. A person entitled to apply for grant of letters of administration can also renounce even if that person has intermeddled with the estate as the authority of an administrator is derived from the grant.

It should be noted that acts of humanity or necessity will not constitute intermeddling. Thus arranging the funeral of the deceased, feeding the animals of the deceased, and preserving the property of the deceased will not amount to intermeddling.

Rule 37(1) provides that renunciation of probate by an executor shall not operate as renunciation of any right which he may have to a grant of administration in some other capacity unless he expressly renounces such right. A different rule applies to administrators. Rule 37(2) provides that no person who has renounced administration in one capacity may obtain a grant thereof in some other capacity.

Some testators appoint the members of firm of solicitors as executors. Rule 37(2A) of the NCPR 1987 provides that renunciation of probate or administration by members of a partnership:

(a)   may be effected; or

(b)   subject to paragraph (3), may be retracted by any two of them with the authority of the others and any such renunciation or retraction must recite such authority.

A renunciation of probate or administration may be retracted at any time with the leave of a District Judge or Registrar. However, if a grant has been made to some other person entitled in a lower degree, leave to retract a renunciation of probate will only be given in exceptional circumstances (r 37(3)).

Rule 37(4) provides that a direction or order giving leave under this rule may be made either by the Registrar of a district probate registry where the renunciation is filed or by a District Judge.

GRANT OF LETTERS OF ADMINISTRATION TO A PERSON NOT ENTITLED TO IT

4.19   The court has power to grant letters of administration to a person not strictly entitled to it. Rule 52 provides that an application for such a grant must be made to a District Judge or Registrar and must be supported by an affidavit setting out the grounds of the application.

INHERITANCE (PROVISION FOR FAMILY AND DEPENDANTS) ACT 1975

4.20   Occasionally, an applicant may wish to bring proceedings against an estate where no grant has been obtained, for example, if all the assets are jointly owned. In this situation, application can be made for the appointment of the Official Solicitor as administrator with his consent. However, in that situation, it may be possible to appoint another person to deal with the estate (see *Murphy v Murphy [2003] EWCA Civ 1862*). Another possibility is for potential claimants to apply for a grant of letters of administration pending suit.

Chapter 5

Procedure for obtaining the grant in straightforward cases

OVERVIEW

5.1   In the great majority of cases, there is no dispute about the validity of a will, or the fact that the deceased died intestate. In these cases, obtaining a grant of probate or letters of administration is straightforward. Challenges to the validity of wills are discussed in **chapter 11**.

DOCUMENTS REQUIRED TO BE SUBMITTED

5.2   In order to obtain a grant of probate or letters of administration, it is necessary to prepare and submit the following documents:

(a)   to the Probate Registry:

    (i)   oath for executors and administrators;

    (ii)   any will and codicils and two copies (see below);

    (iii)   a cheque for the fees payable to the Probate Registry;

    (iv)   such other affidavits as may be required;

    (v)   form D18 or IHT 421 – part of the Inland Revenue account;

The copies must be made in A4 size, from the original will after the oath has been sworn. The copies should not be stapled. The top and left margins should be clear so that the grant can be attached to it. If it is necessary to take the will apart in order to copy it, a letter should be sent to the Probate Registry informing the Registry that this was done and that the will has been restored to the same plight and condition that it was before it was copied and nothing of a testamentary nature was further attached or detached.

(b)   to the Capital Taxes Office:

    (i)   Inland Revenue account – this is not required in every case;

    (ii)   a cheque for any inheritance tax payable unless the Inheritance Tax Direct Payment Scheme is being used (see **para 5.7**).

WHERE TO APPLY

5.3   Application can be made to the Principal Registry, a district probate registry or a sub-registry. Registries have no territorial jurisdiction, and so an application can be made to a registry which operates in an area with which neither the deceased nor any beneficiary has any connection (rr 4(1) and 5(1), Non-Contentious Probate Rules 1987 (NCPR 1987)). The addresses and telephone numbers of all registries and sub-registries in England and Wales are set out in **appendix 4**.

APPLICATIONS BY SOLICITORS

5.4   Executors and administrators can employ a solicitor to make the application for a grant. Rule 4(2) of the NCPR 1987 provides that every solicitor through whom an application is made must give the address of his place of business in England and Wales.

APPLICATIONS BY LAY PERSONS

5.5   A lay person can apply for a grant without using a solicitor. Such applications are governed by r 5 of the NCPR 1987. Rule 5(2) provides that a personal applicant may not apply through an agent, whether paid or unpaid. In addition, any personal applicant must not be attended by any person acting or appearing to act as his adviser. Rule 5(3) provides that no personal application shall be proceeded with if:

(a)   it becomes necessary to bring the matter before the court by action or summons, unless a District Judge or Registrar so permits;

(b)   an application has already been made by a solicitor or probate practitioner on behalf of the applicant and has not been withdrawn; or

(c)   the District Judge or Registrar so directs.

Rule 5(4) provides that after a will has been deposited in a registry by a personal applicant, it may not be delivered to the applicant or to any other person unless there are special circumstances and the District Judge or Registrar so directs.

Rule 5(5) provides that a personal applicant must produce a certificate of the death of the deceased or such other evidence of the death as the District Judge or Registrar may approve.

Rule 5(6) provides that a personal applicant must supply all information necessary to enable the papers leading to the grant to be prepared by the registry.

Rule 5(7) provides that unless the District Judge or Registrar otherwise directs every oath or affidavit required on a personal application must be sworn or executed by all the deponents before an authorised officer.

Rule 5(8) provides that no legal advice must be given to a personal applicant by an officer of a registry and every such officer shall be responsible only for embodying in proper form the applicant's instructions for a grant.

TIME LIMITS

5.6   Rule 6(2) provides that except with the leave of a District Judge or Registrar, no grant of probate or of administration with the will annexed can be issued within seven days of the death of the deceased, and no grant of administration can be issued within 14 days of the death.

There is no other time limit for applications, although penalties may be imposed if the Inland Revenue account is not submitted within 12 months.

Rule 6(1) provides that a District Judge or Registrar shall not allow any grant to be issued until all enquiries which he may see fit to make have been answered to his satisfaction.

RAISING THE FUNDS TO PAY IHT

5.7   Inheritance tax is due six months after the end of the month of death unless due to the circumstances listed below there is a right to pay by instalments. The right to pay by instalments applies to:

(a)   land of any description, wherever situated;

(b)   a business or an interest in a business;

(c)   shares or securities in a company controlled by the deceased;

(d)   unquoted shares and securities not giving control if not less than 20 per cent of so much of the tax chargeable on the value transferred as is tax for which the person paying the tax attributable as mentioned in s 227(1) of the Inheritance Tax Act 1984 is liable (in the same capacity) consists of tax attributable to the value of the shares and securities or such other tax as may by virtue of s 227 be paid by instalments. This means that there is a right to pay by instalments if at least 20 per cent of the tax payable on the estate of the deceased is attributable to shares not giving any control or on other assets qualifying for instalments;

(e)   unquoted shares and securities in a company not controlled by the deceased if the Board are satisfied that the tax attributable to their value cannot be paid in one sum without undue hardship;

(f)   unquoted shares and securities in a company not controlled by the deceased if so much of the value transferred as is attributable to the shares exceeds £20,000; and either:

    (i)   the nominal value of the shares is not less than 10 per cent of the nominal value of all the shares of the company at the time of the transfer; or

    (ii)   the shares are ordinary shares and their nominal value is not less than 10 per cent of the nominal value of all ordinary shares of the company at that time;

(g)   woodlands.

The most important category is the first – land of any description. The other categories, apart from (g), are not so important as frequently the assets listed will qualify for 100 per cent business property relief.

If there is a right to pay by instalments, then the tax attributable to the property must be paid by ten equal yearly instalments. The election to do so is usually made in the Inland Revenue account. If the property is sold, then the IHT due in respect of that property must be paid.

Interest is due on the outstanding instalments except in the case of property qualifying for business property relief, agricultural property relief or timber. Whether or not interest is due on the outstanding instalments, it is always due if an instalment is paid late.

If there is no right to pay by instalments, then the tax due should be paid six months after the end of the month of death. If it is not paid, interest is due. It must also be paid before the grant is obtained. Possible methods of raising the tax are:

(a) building society accounts – if the deceased had any accounts with building societies, then they may be prepared to release the funds required to pay the IHT;

(b) banks – approach banks with which the deceased held accounts in order to see if they are prepared to release funds. It may be that the deceased held bank accounts as a joint tenant. If this is the case, no grant is required to enable the surviving joint tenant to access the money; all that is required is the production of the death certificate. A bank loan can be obtained. Obviously the bank will charge interest and an arrangement fee;

(c) the Inheritance Tax Direct Payment Scheme – most banks and building societies participate in this scheme. It is necessary to obtain a reference number by completing IHT 422 and sending it to the appropriate Capital Taxes Office, or by telephoning the Capital Taxes Office helpline. Once the amount of inheritance tax due has been ascertained, then form IHT 423 should be completed and sent to the relevant bank or building society;

(d) it may be possible to obtain payment of the moneys due under a life assurance policy without the need for a grant;

(e) it is possible to sell chattels before a grant has been obtained;

(f) if a deputy has been appointed by the Court of Protection to deal with the property of the deceased, the Court may be prepared to release funds in order to pay IHT;

(g) it is possible to use moneys invested with National Savings to pay inheritance tax. A letter should be obtained from National Savings as to the appropriate value of the relevant holdings, and this should be sent to the Pre-Grant Section of the Capital Taxes Office together with the Inland Revenue account;

(h)   it may be that the beneficiaries will have some spare cash which can be used to pay the inheritance tax. It will be cheaper to utilise this money rather than obtain a bridging loan from the bank.

If there is a possibility of a deed of variation or disclaimer, these can be entered into before the papers are submitted to the Inland Revenue. A deed of variation or disclaimer may reduce the inheritance tax payable. If the variation or disclaimer is in favour of a spouse, it may mean that no inheritance tax is payable because of spouse exemption.

LEAVE TO SWEAR DEATH

5.8   Rule 53(1) of the NCPR 1987 provides that an application to swear to the death of a person in whose estate a grant is sought may be made to a District Judge or Registrar, and shall be supported by an affidavit setting out the grounds of the application and containing particulars of any policies of insurance effected on the life of the presumed deceased, together with such further evidence as the District Judge or Registrar may require.

Chapter 6

Drafting the oath, and any other affidavits required to obtain a grant

OVERVIEW

6.1   In order to obtain a grant, personal representatives must submit an executors' or administrators' oath. It may also be necessary to submit, in the form of an affidavit, evidence with regard to the following issues:

(a)   if there is any doubt about compliance with the requirements of s 9 of the Wills Act 1837;

(b)   if there is any doubt about the date of the will – this will be important if there is more than one will, and it is necessary to determine which is the most recent;

(c)   if there are any circumstances casting doubt as to whether the testator knew and approved of the contents of the will. Normally, this is presumed, but if it appears that the testator was, for example, blind, it will probably be necessary for witnesses to swear affidavits confirming that the will was read to the testator before he signed it, and that he appeared to understand it. This may not be necessary if the attestation clause indicates that the will has been read over to the testator;

(d)   if the will contains alterations – there is a presumption that they were made after the will was executed, and are invalid. However, if it can be proved that they were made before the will was executed, then they are valid;

(e)   if it is apparent from the will that another document has been attached to the will, for example, if there is an indentation in the will which appears to have been made by a paperclip.

THE EXECUTORS' OR ADMINISTRATORS' OATH

6.2   When swearing the executor's or administrator's oath it is usual to use the printed forms supplied by Law Stationers, or word processed forms. The following points are common to all forms.

The name of the deceased

6.3   The true name of the deceased should be inserted.

It is not uncommon for people not to use a name, perhaps because they do not like it, and people sometimes change their surnames. In addition, sometimes

26

there are different spellings for a name – Alan can also be Allen or Allan. If this is the case, the true name should still be inserted, unless property is vested in the name of the deceased in a name other than the true name, or the will was executed in a name other than the true name, in which event it will be necessary to include the alias in the oath. It is also necessary to specify which part of the estate was held in the other name, or give any other reason for the inclusion of the name in the grant (r 9, NCPR 1987).

Order of names of applicants

6.4   The order should follow the order in the will.

If this is not done, the Probate Registry will treat that as an implied request to vary the order.

If the application is for a grant of letters of administration, then the order should follow the order of entitlement to the estate.

Dates of birth and death

6.5   It is necessary to insert the dates of birth and death of the deceased. If you are taking instructions from an elderly person who appears confused, the date of birth should be checked against the birth certificate of the deceased. The date of death should be obtained from the death certificate.

Domicile

6.6   It is important to state the correct domicile of the deceased. The significance of this is that it will be stated in the grant where the deceased was domiciled, and if it is England and Wales, Scotland or Northern Ireland, it will be recognised automatically in those jurisdictions without the need for resealing.

Everyone has a domicile of origin, which is usually determined by the domicile of the parents. It is also possible to acquire a domicile of choice by residing in a country with the intention of living there permanently. It should be noted that residence in another country, even if it is for a long period, will not give the person concerned a domicile of choice in that country if the person does not intend to remain there permanently.

The will and any codicil

6.7   The oath must specify how many documents are being proved, for example a will and two codicils. The will and any codicils must be marked; this means that the applicant and the person before whom the oath is sworn must sign those documents (r 10, NCPR 1987).

Rule 10(2) provides that the Registrar may allow a facsimile copy of the will to be marked or exhibited in lieu of the original document.

Settled land

6.8   Rule 8(3) of the NCPR 1987 requires that the oath shall state whether or not, to the best of the applicant's knowledge information and belief, there was land vested in the deceased which was settled previously to his death and not by his will and which remained settled land notwithstanding his death.

In the great majority of cases, the deceased will not have been entitled to settled land, or if they were, the settlement will have terminated on the death of the life tenant. Since the Trusts of Land and Appointment of Trustees Act 1996, it has not been possible to create a strict settlement governed by the Settled Land Act 1925.

If the deceased was entitled to settled land, and if the settlement continued after death, then a grant limited to the settled land in favour of the trustees of the settlement will be required.

Duty of personal representatives

6.9   The oath then requires that the personal representatives will administer the estate in accordance with the duties imposed by s 25 of the Administration of Estates Act 1925.

Certificates of value

6.10   If the estate of the deceased was within certain limits, then it is not necessary to deliver an Inland Revenue account.

If the estate is an excepted estate, then the gross estate must be stated as not exceeding the current nil rate band; if the deceased died before 1 August, then the figure to be inserted is the nil rate band for the previous tax year; the net value of the estate must be shown as not exceeding the net value of the estate rounded up to the next whole thousand.

If the estate of the deceased was outside these limits, then the gross and net estate can be ascertained from the Inland Revenue account.

The fee payable to the Probate Registry depends on the value of the net estate. If it is more than £5,000, it is £40 plus £1 for every office copy required.

GRANTS OF PROBATE

Non proving executors

6.11   If the will appoints more than one executor, it is common for some of the executors not to take out the grant. Instead, power is reserved to them to take out the grant if they wish to do so.

If there are executors who do not want to take out the grant, r 27(1) of the NCPR 1987 provides that the oath must state that notice of the application has been given to those to whom power is to be reserved. If the partners in a firm of solicitors have been appointed executors, r 27(2) provides that notice may be given to the partners by sending it to the firm at its principal or last known place of business.

Rule 27(3) provides that a District Judge or Registrar may dispense with the giving of such notice if he is satisfied that the giving of such a notice would be impracticable or would result in unreasonable delay or expense.

Change of name of applicant

6.12   It may be that an applicant for a grant of probate has changed his or her name; for example, a woman may have changed her name on marriage. If this is the case, the oath must state that there has been a change of name, and offer an explanation. If it is marriage which has caused the name change, then the oath should state 'Wendy June Wood in the will called Wendy June Swallow having changed her name on marriage'. (See *Tolley's Administration of Estates*, para C7.23).

GRANTS OF LETTERS OF ADMINISTRATION

6.13   The oath to lead to a grant of simple administration is very similar to that required to obtain a grant of probate. The differences are:

(a)   there is no reference to any will or codicil;

(b)   the oath must state in what manner all persons having a prior right to the grant have been cleared off;

(c)   the oath also states in what capacity the applicants are entitled to the grant.

Rule 22 of the NCPR 1987 prescribes the order of entitlement to a grant of letters of administration. An applicant for a grant must show how anyone higher up the order has ceased to be entitled. Thus no words of clearance are necessary if the application is by the spouse of the deceased as there is no one with a better right to the grant. If it is a child who is applying then the deceased should be described as a widow or widower.

If the deceased was unmarried at the date of death, but had been divorced, then the oath must state 'that the marriage between and was dissolved by the final decree of the Court in England and Wales dated the day of and the deceased did not thereafter remarry'. (See *Administration of Estates* (Tolley, 1997), para C9.43.)

If the application is made by persons other than the surviving spouse or children, the words 'or any other person entitled in priority to share in his/her estate by virtue of any enactment' must be added.

It is also necessary to state the capacity in which the applicant is claiming. It is only necessary to use the word 'lawful' if the application is by a surviving spouse, or an adopted child.

Grant of letters of administration with the will annexed

6.14   The major difference is that the oath will refer to any wills or codicils which the deceased left. In addition, the order of entitlement to the grant is determined by r 20 of the NCPR 1987. As with grants of simple administration, it is necessary to clear off anyone with a better right to the grant – to explain why they are not obtaining a grant. This might be because they were appointed executors in the will, but have renounced the right to a grant, or have predeceased.

Chapter 7

Drafting the Inland Revenue account

OVERVIEW

7.1   IHT 200 is being replaced by IHT 400, although HMRC will accept IHT 200s up to 9 June 2009.

It is not necessary to submit an IHT 400 if the estate is a low value estate or an excepted estate. For an estate to be excepted, the following conditions must be satisfied:

- the deceased died domiciled in the UK;

- the gross value of the estate does not exceed £1 million and the net chargeable value of the estate after deduction of liabilities and spouse or civil partner exemption and/or charity exemption only does not exceed the IHT threshold;

- if the estate includes any assets in trust, they are held in a single trust and the gross value does not exceed £150,000 (unless the settled property passes to a spouse or civil partner, or to a charity, in which case the limit is waived);

- if the estate includes foreign assets, their gross value does not exceed £100,000;

- if there are any specified transfers, their chargeable value does not exceed £150,000, and the deceased had not made a gift with reservation of benefit;

- no charge arises on the individual's death under any of the provisions relating to Alternatively Secured Pensions.

If the estate is an excepted estate, then it is necessary to submit an IHT 205 to the Probate Registry.

In addition, whenever an IHT 400 is delivered, an IHT 421 must be submitted to HMRC, even though no IHT is payable.

If it is necessary to submit an Inland Revenue account, then the relevant forms can be obtained from IR Capital Taxes, Ferrers House, PO Box 38, Castle Meadow Road, Nottingham, NG2 1BB, telephone 0845 302 0900, fax 0115 974 2432.

It is also possible to obtain the forms and leaflets via the internet – the address is www.hmrc.gov.uk.

The forms are also available on the computerised forms packages available commercially.

HMRC also produce some guidance notes. These are essential reading for anyone contemplating completing an IHT 400 or IHT 205.

The IHT 400 account is a summary of the all the property the deceased owned in his own right, any jointly owned property, and sometimes property in which the deceased had a life interest. The account calculates the total estate, deducts any debts due from the deceased and the funeral expenses, and then calculates the IHT. This sounds very simple, but if it is done manually, it can involve considerable calculations, and carrying figures from one page to another.

There are also supplementary schedules – IHT 402 to IHT 423 – which have to be completed. As the totals from these pages have to be inserted in IHT 400, it is probably best to start by completing the supplementary schedules. There is also a worksheet which has to be completed in order to calculate the inheritance tax due in more complicated cases.

Once the forms have been completed, if no tax is payable, the forms necessary to obtain the grant and the IHT 205 must be sent to the Probate Registry.

If tax is payable, the procedure is different. The IHT 400 and the supplementary pages, including IHT 421, should be sent to HMRC, together with the tax due.

HMRC will complete the IHT 421 and send it back. The IHT 421 and the papers required to obtain the grant of probate must then be submitted to the Probate Registry.

COMPLETION OF THE SUPPLEMENTARY SCHEDULES

7.2   The supplementary schedules are:

(a)   IHT 401 – domicile outside the UK;

(b)   IHT 402 – transfer of unused nil rate band;

(c)   IHT 403 – gifts and other transfers of value;

(d)   IHT 404 – jointly owned assets;

(e)   IHT 405 – houses, land, buildings and interests in land;

(f)   IHT 406 – bank and building society accounts;

(g)   IHT 407 – household and personal goods;

(h)   IHT 408 – household and personal goods donated to charity;

(i)   IHT 409 – pensions;

(j)   IHT 410 – life assurance and annuities;

(k)   IHT 411 – listed stocks and shares;

(l)   IHT 412 – unlisted stocks and shares and control holdings;

(m)   IHT 413 – business relief, business and partnership interests and assets;

(n)   IHT 414 – farms, farmhouses and land;

(o)   IHT 415 – interest in another estate;

(p)   IHT 416 – debts due to the estate;

(q)   IHT 417 – foreign assets;

(r)   IHT 418 – assets held in trust;

(s)   IHT 419 – debts owed by the deceased;

(t)   IHT 420 – National Heritage assets;

(u)   IHT 421 – probate summary;

(v)   IHT 422 – application for inheritance tax reference;

(w)   IHT 423 – Direct Payment Scheme – bank or building society account.

It is not proposed to go through each supplementary schedule or the main account in detail. The requirements of HMRC are clearly set out in the guidance notes, and readers are referred to those notes which are set out in **appendix 2**. However, it is hoped that the following comments will assist readers.

(The references to numbers are to the relevant questions or pages in IHT 400 or the schedules.)

IHT 400 – the will

7.3   25–26. It is quite common for a testator to move between making a will and death.

If the property given as the address of the deceased is not included as part of the estate in IHT 400, it is necessary to explain what has happened to the proceeds. Usually the explanation is quite simple – the deceased has moved.

27, 28. If there are specific gifts, then if they are included in IHT 400, the yes box should be ticked.

If the items of specific gifts have been the subject of lifetime gifts, then it is necessary to give details.

If the item has been sold, then details about the sale must be given, and say what the deceased did with the proceeds.

92, 93. If a spouse or civil partner exemption is claimed, the full name of the spouse, the date and country of birth and country of domicile must be given. It is also desirable to ask to see the marriage or civil partnership certificate to ensure that the deceased was in fact married or in a civil partnership.

If the surviving spouse or civil partner is not domiciled in the United Kingdom, then the spouse exemption is limited to £55,000 plus whatever is left of the nil rate band.

If a deed of variation reduces the amount of IHT payable, it can often be completed before the IHT 400 is drafted, and the IHT 400 can then be completed on the basis that it is in force.

101. Nominated assets must also be included in the form. This is where the deceased has made use of the ability to specify who is to have the money in an

account without having to comply with the requirements of the Wills Act 1837. This facility was at one time available for, *inter alia*, moneys invested with the Post Office Savings Bank, but is now limited to sums not exceeding £5,000 invested with industrial and provident societies, friendly societies and trades unions where the rules permit nomination.

Often pension schemes provide for the payment of a lump sum on death in service. Frequently, this lump sum is payable at the discretion of the trustees of the pension scheme as otherwise it would form part of the estate of the deceased for inheritance tax purposes. It is possible for the employee to request the trustees to pay the lump sum to a particular person, and whilst trustees do not have to comply with the request, frequently they will do so. These requests are sometimes incorrectly called nominations.

IHT 401 – domicile outside the UK

7.4   Every person has a domicile of origin, which is usually determined by the domicile of the parents. It is also possible to acquire a domicile of choice by residing in a country with the intention of permanently residing there.

There are special rules which apply for IHT purposes – if the deceased has lived in the UK for 17 out of the last 20 years, they will be deemed to be domiciled in the UK. In addition, the deceased will be deemed to have been domiciled in the UK if they were domiciled in the UK at any time in the three years before death. It should be stressed that these rules only apply for the purposes of inheritance tax, and it may be that for other purposes the deceased will not be domiciled here, for example, in order for an application to be made under the Inheritance (Provision for Family and Dependants) Act 1975, it must be proved that the deceased died domiciled in England and Wales. It is possible for a deceased to be domiciled here for inheritance tax purposes, but not for the purposes of an application under the 1975 Act.

Domicile is very significant – if the deceased was domiciled outside the UK, then any foreign property will not be subject to inheritance tax. If the deceased was domiciled in the UK, then all the assets of the deceased wherever situated will be subject to inheritance tax.

If the deceased was domiciled in the UK and owned foreign assets, it is necessary to complete IHT 417. If the deceased was domiciled elsewhere, then it is only necessary to complete the schedules applying to assets in this country in addition to IHT 401.

There have been several reported cases in recent years on the question of domicile.

In *F and S2 v IRC [2000] WTLR 505*, F was born in Iran, but qualified as an accountant in England, where he met and married F. On qualification, he returned to Iran, and ultimately set up a practice in Iran. For various reasons, he left Iran, and it was difficult for him to return.

H lived with F and his children in this country. He became a naturalised British citizen, although the statements on his application form were untrue. He needed a passport so that he could travel – his Iranian passport had expired.

It was held that he was not domiciled in England and Wales as the evidence was that he would have returned to Iran if it had been possible.

In *Executors of Robert Moore Deceased v IRC [2002] WTLR 1471*, D was an interior designer who worked in different countries. He was an American citizen, and he submitted income tax returns in the US, but not the UK. He was granted limited permission to stay in England in order to work. He also owned a residential property in London.

It was held that he was not domiciled in England and Wales.

In *Surveyor v IRC [2003] WTLR 111*, S had a UK domicile of origin, but he had worked in Hong Kong from 1986, had met his wife in Hong Kong, and had three children, all of whom had been born in Hong Kong.

In 1999 he was forced to relocate to Singapore due to a reorganisation by his employers. He subsequently resigned, and was looking for a job in Hong Kong.

It was held that S had acquired a domicile of choice in Hong Kong.

In *Allen v HMRC [2005] WTLR 937*, D had an English domicile of origin. Following her marriage in 1953, she always lived abroad because of her husband's work. Her husband retired in 1982, and they purchased a house in Spain. The deceased had been diagnosed with Parkinson's disease, and her visits to the UK were infrequent and short.

The deceased's husband died in 1996, and the deceased went to live with her half sister in the UK because of her declining health. At the suggestion of her half sister and her husband she bought a house next door as they were struggling to look after her.

At all times the deceased maintained the house in Spain, and visited it occasionally. She had no investments in the UK apart from an account here for everyday expenses.

It was held that she was domiciled in Spain at the date of death.

In *Mark v Mark [2005] UKHL 42*, it was held that it is possible to acquire a domicile of choice in the UK even though the presence of a person here was illegal.

IHT 402 – transfer of unused nil rate band

7.5   As practitioners will be aware, this form must be used when the personal representatives of a surviving spouse or civil partner are claiming to carry forward the unused nil rate band of a predeceased spouse or civil partner.

The draft guidance about this is set out in the **appendix 3**.

IHT 403 – gifts and other transfers of value

7.6   HMRC need to know about gifts during the lifetime of the deceased as these may affect the rate of inheritance tax payable on death, and in addition if the gift is large enough, or there has been a series of gifts, then the gift or gifts may be chargeable to inheritance tax. However, if the gift is fully covered by spouse or civil partner exemptions, small gifts exemption or annual exemption, it need not be included.

If normal expenditure out of the income exemption is claimed, presumably it need not be included if the payments are less than the annual exemption, and the deceased had not made any other gifts as the annual exemption will cover the payments. However, if it does exceed the annual exemption, it must be included, and an additional form completed showing the income and expenditure of the deceased.

Note that a gift has a wider meaning than the usual accepted meaning. When it comes to lifetime transactions, IHT is payable on the reduction in value of the donor's estate. It follows that transactions less than an absolute gift can give rise to a liability to IHT. So if a house is sold to a child at an undervalue, that can give rise to a charge to IHT as the parent's estate has been reduced in value.

4. In the past one good way of providing for children or grandchildren was to take out an endowment policy with a life insurance company, and make it subject to a declaration of trust in favour of children or grandchildren. The parents or grandparents would then continue to pay the premiums. Normally this will not have any IHT consequences as the premiums will come within the annual exemption or normal expenditure out of income exemption for IHT purposes.

5. The deceased may have been a life tenant, in which event they may be deemed to own all the underlying trust assets as far as IHT is concerned. If the deceased is deemed to own the trust assets, and has given up any part of the life interest, the deceased will be deemed to make a PET of whatever part of the underlying trust assets are given up. So if the life tenant surrenders 50 per cent of the life interest, and is deemed to own the trust assets, they will be deemed to make a PET of the underlying trust assets.

8–12 – gifts with reservation

7.7   These are ineffective as far as IHT is concerned; the donor will still be deemed to own the assets as far as IHT is concerned. So if parents give their house to a child, but continue living there, that is a gift with a reservation of benefit. If the parent dies within seven years of making the gift, it should be included as well. Similarly if a parent gives an antique to a child, but still uses the antique, then it must be included in his or her estate.

If parents give their house to a child, and pay the market rent, then the gift should be included on page 2.

If parents give their house to a child, continue living in the house so a benefit has been reserved, but then move out, the reservation of benefit ceases at that point. Page 2 should then be completed giving the value of the house at the date the reservation of benefit ceased. It should not be included on page 3.

Page 4. The pre-owned assets charge applies in general terms when the deceased has entered into an arrangement under which assets are not part of the deceased's estate, but nonetheless the deceased is still using them. In those circumstances, the deceased would have had to pay income tax on a notional benefit. It is possible to elect not to pay income tax, but for the asset to remain part of the deceased's estate.

Page 5. Chargeable gifts here are lifetime transfers to discretionary trusts, and since 22 March 2006, lifetime transfers to all trusts apart from trusts for disabled persons, and also to companies.

If the deceased has during his lifetime transferred assets to the trustees of a discretionary trust, or after 22 March 2006, to any trust apart from a trust for disabled persons, and also made other lifetime gifts within seven years of death, the amount transferred to the trustees within seven years of any other lifetime gift must be brought into account in order to determine the rate of tax.

This means that in order to determine to the rate of tax on a lifetime gift, it might be necessary to go back almost 14 years.

For example, Z creates a discretionary trust in 1996. He creates another discretionary trust in 2002, or makes a PET in that year. He dies in 2008.

As he has died within seven years of the creation of the 2002 discretionary trust, it will be necessary to recalculate the inheritance tax payable on that discretionary trust.

If it was a PET, then it will become chargeable for the first time as the deceased has not survived for seven years after making the gift.

In order to determine the rate of tax applying to the 2002 discretionary trust on death or the PET, it will be necessary to bring into account all lifetime transfers to discretionary trusts in the seven years prior to 2002. Accordingly, it will be necessary to bring into account the 1996 discretionary trust in order to determine the rate of tax that applies to the 2002 discretionary trust or PET.

IHT 404 –joint and nominated assets

7.8   There are two ways of holding property as co-owners – as joint tenants or as tenants in common. If co-owners are joint tenants, then the right of survivorship operates. This means that when one joint tenant dies, his or her interest automatically passes to the surviving joint tenant. If the co-owners are tenants in common, then if one dies his or her interest passes under his or her will, or if there is no will, under the intestacy rules to whoever is entitled to it.

All forms of property can be held as joint tenants or co-owners, so that there can be a joint tenancy or tenancy in common of land, houses, bank accounts and shareholdings.

Sometimes property is in joint names, but in fact it is all owned by one of the co-owners. This sometimes happens with bank or building society accounts which are opened in the joint names of a parent and child so as to facilitate the operation of the account because the parent is infirm. In this situation, the whole of the account will have to be included in the parent's IHT 400; it is unclear whether it should be included here or in IHT 406.

Even if there is an intention to give part of the money in an account to the other joint holder or holders, HMRC may argue that the whole account is part of the deceased's estate. In *Sillars and Deeprose v IRC [2004] WTLR 591*, D transferred a building society account into the joint names of her daughters and herself. She made various withdrawals from it, and her daughters did so on her behalf. Each included one third of the income in their income tax returns.

On D's death, it was argued that only one third of the account should be included in her estate for IHT purposes.

It was held that the deceased had a general power of appointment over the account, and therefore the whole amount was subject to IHT. There had also been a reservation of benefit as the deceased had made withdrawals from the account.

Frequently household goods will be jointly owned. If that is the case, do they go in the D10 or here? The answer is here.

IHT 405 – land, buildings and interests in land

7.9   This form must be completed if the deceased owned any land. It need not be completed if the deceased was entitled as a joint tenant or tenant in common to any land or house.

It is essential to obtain a valuation from a qualified valuer, and a copy of that valuation should be sent to tHMRC. On what basis should the valuer be asked to value the land or property? It should be the market value as at the date of death.

There is a question on page four of the form as to whether the personal representatives intend to sell the property within 12 months of death. If that is the case, in stable market conditions, HMRC will expect the sale price to be used as the market price as at the date of death.

IHT 406 – bank and building society accounts and National Savings and Investments

7.10   This is a new form. However, joint accounts should not be included here, and neither should accounts which are business assets – they should go in IHT 404 and IHT 413 respectively.

IHT 407 – household and personal goods

7.11   More often than not the household and personal goods will not have been sold before the personal representatives apply for the grant of probate or letters of administration.

If they have not been sold, then it is necessary to include the market value of all the household and personal goods as at the date of death. This is not the replacement cost, but what the personal representatives would receive for the assets if they were sold on the open market. For most personal representatives, this means what they would fetch if they were sold at auction.

If it is fairly standard furniture, then its value will be small. In some cases, it may even have a negative value in that it may be necessary to pay someone to take it away.

If the deceased left a motor car, then if it is necessary to include details of the make, exact model, year of registration and the registration number.

If the deceased left jewellery or antiques, then it will usually be necessary to obtain a valuation from a jeweller or specialist in antiques. In the view of the writer, the market value for items such as these is what they would fetch if sold by auction on the day of death.

IHT 409 – pensions

7.12 Pensions need to be included on this sheet if:

(a) the pension continues to be paid after death, in which event the value of the right to receive the pension must be included; note that it need not be included if the continuation is in the form of reduced payments to the surviving spouse of the deceased;

(b) if a lump sum is paid on the death of the deceased; if it payable at the discretion of the trustees of the pension fund, it will not be subject to IHT;

(c) if the deceased had made any changes to the pension arrangements in the two years before death.

There are also questions about alternative secured pensions. An alternative secured pension is for a person over 75. If that person or a dependant of that person dies, then what is left in the pension fund will be subject to IHT unless it goes to charity or a dependant relative.

A dependant is:

(a) the spouse or civil partner of the member; or

(b) a child of the member who was under the age of 23; or

(c) aged 23 or over and in the opinion of the scheme administrator was dependant on the member because of physical or mental impairment; or

There can also be IHT payable if there is a dependant's pension fund, and the dependant dies.

IHT 410 – life insurance and annuities

7.13 1. The deceased may have taken out a life policy. If this has not been made the subject of a declaration of trust in favour of children or grandchildren, then it will be part of the deceased's estate for inheritance tax purposes, and must be included here.

3. Spouses, civil partners or cohabitees may take out joint life policies which sometimes pay out on the death of the first spouse, civil partner or cohabitee, and sometimes on the death of the second spouse, civil partner or cohabitee.

If the policy pays out on the death of the first spouse, civil partner or cohabitee, then the proceeds will be part of the estate of the first spouse, civil partner or cohabitee, and should have been included under 1.

If the policy pays out on the death of the second spouse, civil partner or cohabitee, then the surrender value of the policy will be part of the estate of the first spouse, civil partner or cohabitee to die as far as inheritance tax is concerned, and should be included in IHT 404.

If it is the spouse or civil partner who is entitled to the policy, there will not be any inheritance tax implications as the spouse or civil partner exemption will apply provided the spouse or civil partner is domiciled in the United Kingdom.

If the spouse or civil partner is not domiciled in the United Kingdom, then the spouse or civil partner exemption is limited to £55,000 plus whatever is left of the nil rate band.

If the deceased had paid all the premiums on a joint life policy, then the deceased is in effect making a gift of one half of the premiums to the other person insured, and these payments should have been recorded in IHT 404. So if there is a joint life policy on the lives of both spouses, and the wife pays all the premiums, then that should be disclosed in IHT 404.

4. Sometimes people buy policies on other people's lives. The policy will not pay out on the death of the owner, but there will be a payout when the life assured dies.

If the deceased had bought a policy on the life of some other person, then the market or surrender value of that policy is part of their estate for inheritance tax purposes.

7. Most annuities terminate on the death of the person entitled to it. However, occasionally payments may be guaranteed for a minimum fixed period. If the deceased was entitled to an annuity with a guaranteed fixed minimum period, then if the deceased died before the expiry of that fixed minimum period, the capitalised value of the annuity will form part of the estate of the deceased for inheritance tax purposes.

If the surviving spouse or civil partner is entitled to the annuity, then it will not have any inheritance tax consequences because of the spouse or civil partner exemption, provided the surviving spouse or civil partner is domiciled in the United Kingdom.

10. An annuity is a gamble. If the person entitled to it lives for 20 or 30 years after having taken out the annuity, then it may be a good buy. On the other hand, if the person entitled to it dies six months after taking out the annuity, then it will be a very bad buy. On account of this, some annuities provide for the payment of a lump sum if the annuitant dies shortly after taking out the annuity. If that is the case, the lump sum will be part of the annuitant's estate for inheritance tax purposes.

Again, if the surviving spouse or civil partner is entitled to the lump sum, and is domiciled in the United Kingdom, then no inheritance tax will be payable on it. However, if the lump sum is payable to a cohabitee or children, then it will be subject to inheritance tax.

12. It was at one time quite a good way of providing for children or grandchildren for parents or grandparents to take out an endowment policy, and put it into trust for the benefit of children and grandchildren.

The initial declaration of trust was a PET, but if it was done when the policy was first taken out, it did not usually have any adverse inheritance tax consequences.

The parents or grandparents continue to pay the premiums due under the policy, and again frequently these did not have any inheritance tax consequences because each payment either came within the annual exemption or the normal expenditure out of income exemption for inheritance tax purposes.

If the deceased had taken out one of these endowment policies, and put it in trust for children and grandchildren, the answer to this question is yes. If the answer is yes, then details of the premiums paid must be included in IHT 403.

As a result of the changes to the taxation of trusts, the trust would now probably be a chargeable disposal as far as IHT is concerned, but it would not have any serious IHT consequences if the trust is created when the policy is first taken out, and the premiums were payable periodically as the value of the policy will not be very great.

14. This is concerned with the situation where parents have taken out a life insurance policy, and put it in trust for children or grandchildren. What happens if a child predeceases the parent?

In that situation, the surrender value of the policy will form part of the estate of the deceased child, and will have to be included in IHT 418 on the child's death.

IHT 411 – listed stocks and shares

7.14   If the price of the shares is 'xd', it means that a dividend was due at the date of death, but has not been paid. The net value of the dividend must be included in this form. If the price is quoted 'cum div', then it means that any future dividend is included in the price.

If the deceased died on a day when the Exchange was not open, then it is permissible to take the price on the last day the Exchange was open before the date of death or the next day the Exchange is open after the date of death.

It is common to ask brokers to value shares. Alternatively, information can be obtained from the Historic Price Service of the Stock Exchange; the email address is products@londonstockexchange.com. Subscribers can telephone 020 7797 3343.

Their address is Historic Price Service T/4, London Stock Exchange, Old Broad Street, London, EC2N 1HP.

Another method is to work out the value from a newspaper the day after the deceased died, or if the deceased died on a day when the Exchange was closed, the price on the last day when the Exchange was open or the price on the next day when it was open.

The value for IHT purposes is either one quarter up from the lower to the higher limit of the prices quoted, or halfway between the highest and lowest bargains recorded for the day, but excluding bargains at special prices.

It is also desirable to check the deceased's actual holding in the register of each company where the deceased owned shares as one can never be certain that share certificates have not been lost or mislaid. Brokers are usually able to check the deceased's holding.

IHT 412 – unlisted stocks and shares, and control interests

7.15   This is a new form. These shares will often qualify for 100 per cent business property relief provided that they are not subject to a contract for sale and have been owned for two years.

The guidance notes about completing IHT 400 suggest that these shares should be accurately valued. This seems to be unnecessary if the shares will qualify for 100 per cent business property relief.

IHT 413 – business and partnership interests and assets

7.16   The business interests of a sole trader or a partner will often qualify for 100 per cent business property relief provided the assets have been owned for two years and are not subject to a contract for sale. However, if there is a partnership agreement, and that gives the continuing partners a right to purchase the share of a deceased partner (an option), then this property relief is still available.

Problems with business property relief

7.17   The main problem with claims to business property relief is that it is not available if the business is a land holding or an investment business.

In *Stedman v IRC [2002] WTLR 1357*, S owned 85 per cent of the shares in a company which operated a residential homes park, provided services to the tenants, a country club, caravan storage, warehouse, shops (both let), fields let on a grazing licence and an insurance agency.

The question was whether the shareholding qualified for BPR. It would not do so if the business consisted wholly or mainly of holding investments. Only about 16 per cent of the net profit came from investment activities. On this basis it was held that the shareholding did qualify for BPR.

There has been an appeal, and the case confusingly changed its name. In *IRC v George [2003] WTLR 471*, it was held that the correct approach was that adopted by Lawrence Collins J in *Weston v IRC*, and that the questions to be asked were:

(a)   did the company have investments?

(b)   was it holding investments?

(c)   did its business consist wholly or mainly of holding investments (to be answered by first identifying the scope of the business, and then by comparing the investment with the non-investment activities)?

On this basis, it was held that the shares did not qualify for BPR.

There was an appeal to the Court of Appeal. In *IRC v George [2004] WTLR 75*, it was argued by the Revenue that the supply of services to the tenants under a contractual obligation in the lease was investment business.

The Court of Appeal rejected this approach. The court considered that it was a question of fact as to whether what was being carried on was an investment business. Whilst to a certain extent critical of the Special Commissioner, the court was not prepared to disturb the decision on the facts.

In *Re Clark (Executors of Clark Deceased) (2005) Taxation, 3 November*, D owned shares in T Clark & Son Ltd. This company had built residential and commercial properties, and owned about 100 residential properties which it maintained with its own workforce. It also managed and maintained 141 dwellings owned by the Clark family, and was paid a management fee.

It was held that the shares did not qualify for BPR. The Special Commissioner stated that there was a wide spectrum of activity which could be carried on with regard to the exploitation of land. At one end, merely granting a tenancy, to at the other end, sufficient activity to constitute a business.

Looking at the matter in the round, the shares did not qualify for 100 per cent BPR.

In *Philllips v HMRC [2006] UKSPC 00555*, the deceased owned shares in a company which made loans to other companies carrying on investment business. It was held that it was not an investment company, and so the shares qualified for 100 per cent BPR.

In *McCall v HMRC [2008] UKSPC 00678*, the deceased owned farmland which she had inherited from her husband, but it was used for grazing. She gradually lost mental capacity, and her son in law, Mr Mitchell, took over the organisation of the grazing. His evidence was that he had ensured that the fences surrounding the land were repaired. For the last few years of the deceased's life, the rental income had been paid into Mr and Mrs Mitchell's bank account, and had not been paid over to the deceased.

The local council classified the land as development land, on which basis the value was £5.8m, whereas the agricultural value was about £165,000. It was argued that the land qualified for business property relief.

It was held:

(a)   on the evidence, it was just about possible to say that Mr Mitchell was running a business;

(b)   the deceased could own the business even though it was being run by Mr Mitchell;

(c)   the business was really an investment business, and accordingly did not qualify for business property relief.

In *Vinton v HMRC [2008] UKSPC 00666*, the deceased was allotted one million shares in a company two days before she died. If this was a reorganisation of the shares, then they replaced the shares which she had owned for two years, and would qualify for business property relief. If it was a fresh allotment of shares, then the shares would not qualify for business property relief.

It was held that this was a fresh allotment of shares, and accordingly the new shares did not qualify for business property relief.

In *Trustees of the Nelson Dance Family Settlement v HMRC [2008] WTLR 891*, the deceased was a farmer and sole trader. He executed two declarations of trust in respect of some of his land and buildings. There was no question that the land qualified for agricultural property relief, but the land had development value, which did not qualify for agricultural property relief. It was argued that this development value qualified for business property relief, but HMRC argued that business property relief did not apply here as the business had not been transferred.

It was held that it did not matter that the business had not been transferred. All that was required was that there should be a reduction in the value of the business assets, which was the case here.

If there has been a lifetime gift of an asset which qualifies for business property relief, as with agricultural property relief, there is no problem if the donor survives for seven years after making the gift as it will then be exempt. However, if the donor does not survive for seven years after making the gift, then it will be chargeable to inheritance tax. However, business property relief will be available if the donee still has the business property the subject of the original gift, or if it has been sold, if it has been replaced with other property which qualifies for business property relief.

IHT 414 – agricultural property relief

7.18   The main problem with claims to agricultural property relief is whether it is available on a house. The test is, in effect, is it a house with some farmland attached, or is it part of a working farm? If it is a house with some farmland attached, then it will not qualify for agricultural property relief, but if it is part of a working farm, then it will qualify.

In *Dixon v IRC [2002] WTLR 17*, the deceased was the co-owner of a cottage, garden, garage, outhouses and damson orchard. The orchard was used at various times for grazing animals. The fruit was sold, but the proceeds were less than £50, and were not declared for income tax purposes.

On the death of the deceased, it was argued that the property qualified for 100 per cent APR.

It was held that whilst growing fruit and grazing were clearly agricultural activities, it was a matter of fact and degree as to whether the land was used for agriculture; here the property was used as a residence and garden.

It was also held that the house was not used for the purposes of agriculture.

In *Executors of John Sidney Higginson v IRC [2002] WTLR 1413*, D lived in a large lodge surrounded by 134 acres, including 63 acres of agricultural land. He farmed it until about 1985, but thereafter it was let. On his death, the farm was sold for £1,150,000, and of that figure, a small proportion was attributable to the farmland.

It was held that APR could not be claimed in respect of the farmland as the farmhouse was not 'of a character appropriate to the property'.

In *Lloyds TSB as Personal Representatives of Rosemary Antrobus Deceased v IRC [2002] WTLR 1435*, A lived in a house dating back to the Tudor period. It had six bedrooms. It was surrounded by 126 acres of freehold land and 6.54 acres of let land. A farmed the land, but the business was not commercially successful.

It was held that the farmhouse qualified for APR. It was appropriate for the activities carried out on the farm.

In *Rosser v IRC [2003] WTLR 1057*, D and her husband had owned a 41 acre holding in Wales. They gave 39 acres to their daughter, but retained two acres, a barn and a farmhouse. They continued to live on the farm, and eventually their daughter and her husband assumed responsibility for the farm.

D's husband died first, and a few weeks later D died.

It was argued that both the farmhouse and the barn qualified for APR, but HMRC determined that they did not.

On appeal, it was held that the farmhouse did not qualify for APR, but that the barn did.

The relevant statutory provision is s 115(2). This first refers to agricultural land, and later talks about farmhouses qualifying for APR. It had been argued that agricultural land included farmhouses, and therefore that the farmhouse here qualified for APR under this limb of the section.

The judge gave short shrift to this argument. It is correct that normally the word 'land' includes buildings as well, but this is all subject to contrary intention. The reference in the section to 'farmhouses' later on meant that the normal meaning was modified, and did not include buildings.

It had also been argued that the property included the land given away, but again this argument was rejected. The reality was that the farmhouse had become a retirement home. It was no longer a farmhouse.

In *Arnander and Executors of McKenna Deceased v HMRC [2006] UKSPC 00565*, DM and his wife CM purchased a farm in 1945, but they did not live in Rosteague House until 1978. DM maintained a flat in London as the couple had many interests.

In 1984 they began to farm the land attached to Rosteague House by employing contractors. DM employed an agent, and discussed farming issues with him. He also kept detailed accounts. DM and CM walked the farm frequently.

The acreage of the farmland surrounding Rosteague House was about 110 acres. The accommodation in Rosteague House was described in one of the sales particulars as: 'long hall, dining room, library, study, drawing room, flower room, main foyer and stairs, cloakroom, rear hall, kitchen, staff sitting room, back kitchen, seven bedrooms, three bathrooms, sewing room, laundry room, staff flat, detached lodge, cottage, music room, garage, gardens, range of outbuildings'.

On the death of DM and CM Rosteague House was not sold as a farmhouse.

HMRC refused the claim to APR on Rosteague House. On appeal, the Special Commissioner considered the following issues.

Is it a farmhouse?

7.18A   The Special Commissioner said:

> 'From those authorities I derive the following principles. That a farmhouse is a dwelling for the farmer from which the farm is managed (*Rosser*); that the farmer of the land is the person who farms it on a day-to-day basis rather then the person who is in overall control of the agricultural business conducted on the land (*Antrobus 2* and *Lindsay*); that the status of the occupier of the premises is not the test but the proper criterion is the purpose of the occupation of the premises (*Whiteford*); however, if the premises are extravagantly large for the purpose for which they are being used, or if they have been constructed upon some more elaborate and expensive scale, it may be that, notwithstanding the purpose of occupation, they should be treated as having been converted into something much more grand (*Whiteford*); and that the decision as to whether a building is a farmhouse is a matter of fact to be decided on the circumstances of each case and must be judged in accordance with ordinary ideas of what is appropriate in size, content and layout, taken in conjunction with the farm buildings and the particular area of farm being farmed (*Korner*).'

It was held that it was not a farmhouse.

If it was a farmhouse, was it of a character appropriate to the property?

7.18B   The Special Commissioner said:

> 'In my view it is not appropriate to compile an exclusive list of relevant factors which are to be considered in deciding whether a farmhouse is of a character appropriate to the agricultural land. The question is one of fact and degree and any factor could be relevant. No one factor is determinative but relevant factors in this appeal are: the historical associations; the size,

content and layout of the house; the farm outbuildings; the area being farmed and whether the house is proportionate to the land being farmed; the view of the educated rural layman; and the relationship between the value of the house and the profitability of the land.'

On the facts, it was held that the farmhouse was not of a character appropriate to the property.

Was it occupied for the purposes of agriculture?

7.18C   It was held that it was not.

Agricultural value.

7.19   Assuming that the farmhouse does qualify, how much of the value is subject to relief? APR operates by reducing the value transferred. This value is the agricultural value, which is the value on the assumption that the house is subject to a covenant that it can only be used for agricultural purposes. So it is not the full market value. On the other hand, it could be argued that it is not far short of the full market value as a purchaser would be prepared to pay this in the hope that the covenant would be released.

The issue has been litigated before the Lands Tribunal in a sequel to the *Antrobus* case. In *Lloyds TSB Private Banking plc v Twiddy [2005] WTLR 1535*, the deceased was the owner of a farmhouse. In previous proceedings it had been accepted that the farmhouse qualified for APR.

The issue to be decided in this case was the value of the farmhouse for the purposes of APR as it is the value subject to a covenant that it can only be used for agricultural purposes in perpetuity.

It was held that normally the agricultural value would be about 30 per cent less than the market value. However, if there were a lifestyle purchaser who would be prepared to accept a lower discount, it would be 15 per cent.

In *Pissidarou v Rosser (2005) EW Lands Tribunal TMA/4/2005*, the deceased had left a barn which qualified for 100 per cent APR. The agricultural value was £40,000, but there was a possibility of obtaining planning permission. If planning permission had been granted, the market value would have been £120,000. The District Valuer assumed that a purchaser would be prepared to pay one half of the difference between the agricultural value and the market value assuming planning permission had been granted, £80,000.

5. This could be very important. In order to qualify for APR, the land concerned must have been used for agricultural purposes. Often, there will be no doubt that the land has been used for agricultural purposes. However, in some situations, it may be doubtful whether the land has in fact been used for agricultural purposes. If that is the case, then considerable care needs to be taken in drafting the answer to this question.

6. This is also important. The form requires the personal representatives to give details of the extent of the deceased's involvement in the farm. It requires the personal representatives to state what actual tasks the deceased did, for

example, milking cows or feeding pigs. It also requires the personal representatives to state how much time the deceased spent each week on these tasks.

The significance of these questions is whether the deceased was still farming. If the deceased had ceased to farm, but there is a claim for APR in respect of the farmhouse, this will almost certainly not succeed as HMRC will argue that the house had ceased to be a farmhouse, and had become a retirement home. If it is a retirement home, then it will not qualify for APR.

17. If there is a lifetime gift of property, and the personal representatives wish to claim APR, this question must be answered.

If there has been a gift of land qualifying for agricultural or property relief, the gift will of course be a PET, and there is no problem if the donor survives for seven years after making the gift because it will then be exempt from inheritance tax. However, what is the position if the donor dies before the seven years have expired? Is it still possible to obtain APR? The answer is yes, provided the assets are still owned by the donee at the date of death of the donor, or if not, they have been replaced by other property.

IHT 415 – interest in another estate

7.20   This applies where the deceased was entitled to benefit from the estate of another person, but dies before the administration of the estate of the other person has been completed.

For example, I dies having left a will giving a legacy of £200,000 to J. J dies before the legacy of £200,000 has been paid to him.

In this situation, the right to receive the legacy of £200,000 will have to be included in the inheritance tax account of J.

Suppose G dies having left a will giving all her property to her only child H, but H dies before the administration of G's estate has been completed.

This is more complicated as it will be necessary to ascertain the likely value of the residuary estate that will form part of H's estate for inheritance tax purposes. The personal representatives of H will have to ask the personal representatives of G for details of the residuary estate as these will have to be included in the IHT 400 of H. This would also apply if H was entitled under the intestacy rules to the whole or part of G's estate.

Quick succession relief may be available on the death of the second person.

IHT 416 – debts due to the estate

7.21   If there are any debts due to the deceased, then they are of course part of the assets of the deceased as far as IHT is concerned.

Parents may lend money to a child to enable that child to purchase a house. If the loan is still outstanding when the parents die, then that loan is part of the surviving parent's estate as far as IHT is concerned.

Another situation where this form may have to be completed is where the deceased was carrying on business through the medium of a limited company. Sometimes dividends or earnings are left in the company as a loan from the directors to the company. In this situation, the loan account is part of the deceased's estate as far as IHT is concerned.

Another situation where it will be necessary to complete this form is where the deceased has lent money to the trustees of a trust who have used it to purchase a bond.

For example, C creates a discretionary trust for the benefit of children and grandchildren. C lends the trustees £500,000. The trustees buy a bond and surrender 5 per cent each year.

These surrenders may be used to repay the loan. Whatever is still outstanding on the loan must be included in IHT 400.

IHT 417 – foreign assets

7.22   If the deceased was domiciled in England and Wales at the date of death, then all the assets of the deceased wherever situated will be subject to inheritance tax.

If the deceased was not domiciled in England and Wales, then it is not necessary to fill in this form. Instead, the personal representatives should include in the other schedules all the assets of the deceased situated in England and Wales.

Occasionally, a deceased who is domiciled in England and Wales may have shareholdings in foreign companies, which will have to be included in this form. More frequently, the deceased may own or have an interest in a house in France, Spain or Portugal. If the deceased was domiciled in England and Wales and owned or had an interest in a house abroad, then the value of that house or interest must be included in this form.

Note that the rules about paying inheritance tax by instalments apply to foreign assets as well as assets situated in England and Wales. So if the deceased owned a house in France, then any inheritance tax payable on that can be paid by instalments over ten years.

The value of the asset should be shown in its foreign currency, with the English equivalent shown as well.

It may be that a tax similar to English inheritance tax will be payable on foreign assets in the country where it is situated. If that is the case, it may be possible to offset all or part of the foreign equivalent of inheritance tax against the English inheritance tax. This can only be done to the extent that inheritance tax is payable on the foreign asset. This is dealt with in the IHT 400 calculation.

If the deceased owned a house abroad, there will almost certainly be furniture in it. This is part of the estate of the deceased as far as inheritance tax is concerned. This should go in IHT 417.

IHT 418 – assets held in trust

7.23   The deceased may have been a life tenant under a will or settlement created prior to 22 March 2006, or after that date an immediate post death interest. If that is the case, then as far as inheritance tax is concerned, the deceased is deemed to have owned all the underlying trust assets, and they must be cumulated with the all the deceased's personal assets in order to determine the rate of tax.

The trust assets must therefore be included in IHT 418.

The personal representative of the deceased may be the same as the trustees of the settlement, so they will be able to obtain the information needed to complete the assets without any difficulty. If not, then they will have to ask the trustees of the life interest trust for the details.

If the deceased was within the class of beneficiaries entitled under a discretionary trust, then the members of the class are not entitled to anything as of right, and therefore the trust assets do not need to be included anywhere in IHT 400.

IHT 419 – debts owed by the estate

7.24   Debts owed by the deceased are clearly deductible in calculating the amount of the estate which is subject to inheritance tax.

If the deceased owed money for the supply of electricity, gas, water, etc, these are deductible in computing the amount of the deceased's estate which is subject to inheritance tax.

Such debts are deducted in IHT 400. In addition, reasonable funeral expenses and the cost of a tombstone are also deductible. Again these are deducted in IHT 400.

However, there are some debts which may not be deductible. There are anti-avoidance provisions concerned with artificial debts. It is essential that HMRC have these anti-avoidance provisions as otherwise it would be very easy to reduce an estate to nothing by creating artificial debts. It would be possible to make a large gift to a child. The child could then lend the same amount back to the deceased. On the death of the deceased, it would be possible to claim the loan as a debt due from the estate of the deceased if there were not the anti-avoidance rules concerned with artificial debts.

This form is designed to give information to the Revenue to enable them to determine if there are any artificial debts.

2. The Revenue will look very carefully at claims to deduct money owing to a close relative or friend.

4. If the deceased had guaranteed a bank loan to a child, then again the Revenue need to know about it.

If the guarantee has been called in, the deceased is in effect making a gift to the child of the amount the deceased had to pay.

5. If the deceased had made a gift to a person, and then borrowed money from that person, the Revenue will say that the debt is artificial and cannot be deducted from the estate of the deceased.

If the deceased and spouse had created NRB discretionary trusts, with power for the trustees to accept an IOU, and the deceased has made gifts to the spouse and the spouse dies first, then HMRC will say that the debt is artificial and cannot be deducted. It is artificial because the consideration for the IOU is in part assets which came from the deceased in the first place.

IHT 422, 423

7.25   This is a relatively new procedure for paying IHT.

If the deceased had an account with a bank or building society, most banks and building societies will let you have a cheque for whatever is in the account in order to pay IHT, or will transfer the money directly.

It is necessary to obtain a reference number from HMRC online, by telephoning the helpline, or submitting IHT 422. If advantage is to be taken of the direct transfer method, then IHT 423 should sent to the bank or building society with the reference number.

IHT 400

7.26   It is then necessary to transfer some of the figures from the schedules to IHT 400.

If there are no complications, then the IHT can be calculated on page 11 of IHT 400, but if there are complications, then it is necessary to calculate the IHT using separate calculation sheets.

Successive charges relief

7.27   Suppose a parent dies leaving all the assets to a child, and the child dies within five years of the parent.

It is possible to obtain relief on the child's death in respect of the IHT payable on the parent's estate.

The relief starts off at 100 per cent if death is within one year, and then gradually reduces by 20 per cent each year.

Double taxation relief

7.28   This applies if the deceased owned assets abroad, and was domiciled in the United Kingdom.

Those foreign assets will be subject to United Kingdom inheritance tax, but it may be that the equivalent of inheritance tax has been paid on those assets in the country where they are situated. If that is the case, it is possible to offset the foreign equivalent against the English inheritance tax payable in respect of those assets. However, the amount of deduction is limited to the amount of inheritance tax attributable to those assets.

For example, O dies leaving an estate of £800,000, which includes foreign assets worth £400,000. IHT paid on the estate is £200,000.

The IHT attributable to the foreign assets is £200,000 divided by £800,000 × £400,000 = £100,000.

If the foreign IHT is £110,000, only £100,000 is deductible.

IHT 421 – probate summary

7.29 Once the forms have been completed, if no tax is payable, the forms necessary to obtain the grant and IHT 421 must be sent to the Probate Registry. The Inland Revenue account should be sent to HMRC at the same time.

If tax is payable, the procedure is different. The IHT 400 and the supplementary pages, including IHT 421, should be sent to HMRC, together with the tax due, or if personal representatives are making use of the procedure for transmitting the IHT directly, send IHT 423 to the bank or building society.

HMRC will complete IHT 421, and send it back. The IHT 421 and the papers required to obtain the grant of probate must then be submitted to the Probate Registry.

IHT 205

7.30 This has to be produced in all cases now part from where the full IHT 400 has to be submitted.

VALUATION

7.31 The basic rule is that the value to be included is the market value at the date of death. If it is difficult to ascertain the value as at the date of death after making full enquiries, then an estimate can be included.

It is essential to use a professionally qualified valuer to value any house or land owned by the deceased at the date of death, and this must be an actual market value valuation.

If the estate includes jewellery or antiques or other valuable chattels, then these must be valued by someone who has expertise in the relevant area. It is suggested that a good basis for valuation is the price the item would have fetched if sold by auction on the day of death.

There have been some cases on valuation in recent years which may be of interest to readers.

In *Prosser v IRC [2002] WTLR 259*, the deceased left a cottage and garden. There was a possibility of obtaining planning consent for the garden. How was this to be valued for IHT purposes?

It was held that the normal practice was to assess the value of the land, and then add on an element for hope value. The land here had only minimal value. It was held that a purchaser would have paid an extra 25 per cent of the value assuming that planning consent was granted.

In *Personal Representatives of Bernard Everall Williams Deceased, IRC v Arkwright [2004] EWHC 1720*, Mr and Mrs W owned Ash Lane Farm as tenants in common. Mr W left his half share to his wife in his will, and within two years of his death, Mrs W and her daughters, the personal representatives, varied the will so as to give one half to the daughters.

The Revenue argued that the value transferred was one half of the vacant possession value of the house, whereas the personal representatives argued that it should be discounted because Mrs W had rights to occupy the land under the TLATA 1996, and also because it could not be sold without her consent. This was not in dispute.

The Commissioner held that the value had to be discounted because of the rights of the surviving spouse.

It was argued that s 171, IHTA applied. This provides that changes occurring in relation to a person's estate as a result of death must be taken into account in valuing the deceased's estate. However, the section does not apply if an interest terminates on death. The Commissioner held that the interest of the deceased did not terminate on death as it passed to his daughters under the deed of variation. The death did result in a change of value.

Section 161, IHTA is concerned with related property. It was held that s 161 did not apply to incorporeal shares in land as it talked about units or shares, and this was inappropriate when discussing incorporeal shares. However, if Mr W's share had been more than half, then s 161 might apply.

This case has been affirmed on appeal (*[2004] EWHC 1720, Ch*), but not as far as the Commissioner's findings on valuation were concerned. It was for the Lands Tribunal to decide the value of the half share.

HMRC have recently announced that they have received advice that the case may be wrong – see Revenue and Customs Brief 71/07.

In *HSBC Trust Co v Twiddy EW Lands Tribunal TMA/130/2005*, there was a mixed commercial and residential development valued as a whole at £4.15m. It was owned by various parties, and there was an agreement that it could only be sold if those holding a majority of the joint interests agreed.

It was necessary to value a 13/80 share in the development. The taxpayer's valuer suggested that there should be a 50 per cent deduction from the proportionate value of the entirety giving a value of £337,187. He also suggested that on an investment basis the value would be £366,800. The District Valuer suggested that an investment basis would be appropriate, and that the value was £520,200. The Lands Tribunal decided that the investment basis was correct, and assessed the value at £425,000.

In *St Clair-Ford v Ryder (HMRC Capital Taxes) (2006) EW Lands Tribunal TMA/215/2005*, the deceased was the tenant in common of a commercial property let to Woolworth plc. He owned a 50 per cent interest.

It was held that a 10 per cent discount was correct, although the Lands Tribunal accepted that a higher discount might be appropriate if there were complications.

In *Lloyds TSB Private Banking plc v Twiddy [2005] WTLR 1535*, the deceased was the owner of a farmhouse. In previous proceedings it had been accepted that the farmhouse qualified for APR.

The issue to be decided in this case was the value of the farmhouse for the purposes of APR as it is the value subject to a covenant that it can only be used for agricultural purposes in perpetuity.

It was held that normally the agricultural value would be about 30 per cent less than the market value. However, if there were a lifestyle purchaser who would be prepared to accept a lower discount, it would be 15 per cent.

In *Pissidarou v Rosser (2005) EW Lands Tribunal TMA/4/2005*, the deceased had left a barn which qualified for 100 per cent APR. The agricultural value was £40,000, but there was a possibility of obtaining planning permission. If planning permission had been granted, the market value would have been £120,000. The District Valuer assumed that a purchaser would be prepared to pay one half of the difference between the agricultural value and the market value assuming planning permission had been granted.

Chapter 8

Post grant procedure

OVERVIEW

8.1   Once the grant has been obtained, then the personal representatives should register the grant with banks and building societies where the deceased held accounts, and with the registrars of any companies in which the deceased held shareholdings. If it is known that the shares may be sold, or transferred to a beneficiary in the near future, then the personal representatives may not register the grant, but instead submit it on a transfer.

It will be necessary to withdraw the moneys held in any bank or building society accounts, and it may also be necessary to sell other assets in order to pay the debts of the deceased. The debts may include liability for income tax and capital gains tax.

Once the personal representatives are satisfied that all debts have been settled, they must distribute the assets to those entitled to them under the will or intestacy.

REGISTERING THE GRANT

8.2   The original grant or an office copy should be sent to the bank, building society, insurance company or registrar of the company together with the pass book, policy or share certificate as appropriate, with a request for the forms required to close the account or to obtain payment if appropriate and not already obtained.

If a bank has provided some form of borrowing facility to pay the inheritance tax due, then the bank should be requested to transfer the balance from any current or deposit account to pay off the loan.

Any moneys not required to settle debts should be placed on deposit pending distribution to the beneficiaries.

SALE OF ASSETS

8.3   With many estates the moneys withdrawn from bank and building society accounts will be enough to pay all the deceased's debts. If this is not the case, it will be necessary to sell some if not all the deceased's assets in order to pay the debts. It may also be necessary to sell assets in order to pay any legacies and to effect a distribution to the beneficiaries.

Section 39 of the Administration of Estates Act 1925 (AEA 1925) confers wide powers of sale on personal representatives for the purposes of the administration, or during a minority of any beneficiary, or the subsistence of any life interest, or until the period of distribution arrives.

The authority of personal representatives as far as personalty is concerned is joint and several, so that one can withdraw moneys in a bank or building society account. However, frequently banks and building societies will insist on all the personal representatives signing all the forms required to withdraw money.

If the personal representatives have been registered as proprietors of shares, it will be necessary for all of them to sign the stock transfer form.

As far as land is concerned, all the personal representatives must sign any transfer or other document. Section 2(2) of the AEA 1925 provides that where there are two or more personal representatives, a conveyance of real estate or contract for such conveyance is not to be made without the concurrence therein of all such personal representatives without an order of the court. However, if not all the executors have proved the will, and power has been reserved to the other executors, then the proving executors can execute the conveyance or enter into a contract on their own.

Theoretically, the personal representatives can sell whichever of the deceased's assets they wish. However, they should have regard to the following factors:

(a)   any direction in the will – usually the personal representatives are directed to pay the debts from the residuary estate;

(b)   the wishes of the residuary beneficiaries – they may prefer assets to be transferred to themselves rather than sold, and the proceeds divided. This is particularly so if the stock market or housing prices are depressed (or rapidly increasing!);

(c)   if the residuary estate is insufficient to pay off the debts, the AEA 1925 prescribes the order as to which class of gifts is to bear the debts;

(d)   if there is a specific gift, the subject of the specific gift should not be sold unless it is absolutely necessary;

(e)   if it is necessary to raise money urgently, for example to repay a loan from a bank, the speed of sale. Quoted shares are relatively easy to sell, but land or houses may be difficult in some market conditions.

Inheritance tax will have been paid on the market value of the deceased's assets. If land is sold within four years of the date of death, or quoted shares are sold within one year of the date of death for less than the market value as at the date of death, then that lower value can be substituted for inheritance tax purposes, and a refund of inheritance tax obtained. If more than one shareholding is sold, then the prices and death values must be aggregated together to ascertain if there has been an overall loss.

Capital gains tax must also be considered. The personal representatives of the deceased will be deemed to have acquired the assets of the deceased at market value as at the date of death. If they sell the assets for more than the market value at the date of death, there is a potential liability to capital gains tax. For more details about capital gains tax on death, see **chapter 14**.

PAYMENT OF DEBTS – SOLVENT ESTATES

Secured debts – mortgages

8.4   Frequently the deceased's assets will include a house or other residence, which may be in the sole name of the deceased, or jointly owned by spouses or cohabitees. The house may be mortgaged, and that mortgage may be linked to some form of life insurance, so that on the death of the deceased the loan is repaid.

If that is not the case, then s 35(1) of the AEA 1925 provides that where the deceased by his will disposes of an interest in property, which at the time of his death is charged with the payment of money, whether by way of legal mortgage, equitable charge or otherwise, and the deceased has not by will or other document signified a contrary intention, the interest so charged is primarily liable for the payment of the charge. Thus in the absence of any direction to the contrary, if there is a specific gift of a house subject to a mortgage, the beneficiary will take the house subject to the mortgage.

What constitutes a direction to the contrary? Section 35(2) provides that such a contrary intention shall not be deemed to be signified:

(a)   by a general direction for the payment of debts or of all the debts of the testator out of his personal estate, or his residuary real and personal estate, or his residuary real estate; or

(b)   by a charge of debts upon any such estate; unless such intention is further signified by words expressly or by necessary implication referring to all or some part of the charge.

Thus clear words should be used to indicate which beneficiary is to bear the burden of any charge.

The best way is to include a specific direction as to whether the mortgage is to be discharged from the residuary estate, or to be borne by the beneficiary.

However, the court will take into account surrounding circumstances in deciding whether or not a contrary intention has been displayed. In *Re Estate of David Ross Deceased [2004] EWHC 2559*, R executed a home-made will giving his apartment and the contents to his fiancée. He gave the residue to his fiancée and his brothers.

He had purchased the apartment with the aid of a mortgage linked to an endowment policy, which had been charged to the lender. However, the original lender was taken over by another lender, which did not take assignments of life policies. R was not aware of this change.

Shortly before he died he increased the premiums to take account of a projected shortfall.

It was held that whilst the will did not show any contrary intention displacing s 35, the court could take into account the surrounding circumstances, and held that it was the intention of the deceased that the apartment should pass free of mortgage.

Unsecured debts

8.5   Part II of the First Schedule to the AEA 1925 prescribes the order in which the assets of the deceased are to be applied in payment of the debts of the deceased where the estate of the deceased is solvent. The order is:

(a)   property of the deceased undisposed of by will, but subject to the retention thereout of a fund sufficient to meet any pecuniary legacies;

(b)   property of the deceased not specifically devised or bequeathed but included (either by specific or general description) in a residuary gift, subject to the retention out of such property of a fund sufficient to meet any pecuniary legacies, so far as not provided for as aforesaid;

(c)   property of the deceased specifically appropriated or devised or bequeathed (either by a specific or general description) for the payment of debts – 'I give Greenacre to A and I direct that my debts shall be paid from it';

(d)   property of the deceased charged with, or devised or bequeathed (either by a specific or general description) subject to a charge for the payment of debts – 'I give all the money in my account with Z Building Society to B subject to the payment of my debts therefrom';

(e)   the fund, if any, retained to meet pecuniary legacies;

(f)   property specifically devised or bequeathed, rateably according to value;

(g)   property appointed by will under a general power, including the statutory power to dispose of entailed interests, rateably according to value.

There are some omissions from the list – property the subject of a *donatio mortis causa*, and nominated property. Presumably they would come at the end of the list if it was necessary to resort to them for the payment of the debts. Such property is rarely met in practice.

The order is slightly odd in that logically property within categories (c) and (d) should come before the property within categories (a) and (b). It is clearly open to a testator to specify expressly that property within these categories should be used to pay the debts before other property. If this is not done, the courts may be prepared to find an implied intention to vary the order; this will be the case if there is a residuary gift in favour of another beneficiary.

Paragraph 8(a) provides that the order may be varied by the will of the deceased. It is very common for the order to be varied in professionally drawn wills – the usual provision is that the debts should be paid from the residuary estate.

Marshalling

8.6   The order laid down in Part II of the First Schedule to the AEA 1925 does not bind a creditor, who can enforce the debt owed to him or her against any part of the estate of the deceased. Another possibility is that the personal representatives of the deceased might resort to property higher up the order in order to satisfy the debts when there was no need to do so. For example, property the subject of a specific gift might be used to pay the debts when the residuary estate has not been exhausted. In this situation, the personal representatives must compensate the disappointed specific beneficiary out of the property which should have been used to pay the debts.

Income tax

8.7   Income tax arises in three contexts: the period up to the date of death, the administration period, and the position of the beneficiaries.

The period up to the date of death

8.8   With regard to the period up to the date of death, the Inspector of Taxes for the district in which the deceased made a tax return should be notified of the death by the personal representatives. It will probably be necessary for the personal representatives to complete a tax return or repayment claim up to the date of death. Some inspectors will accept a statement of the income up to the date of death. If all the deceased's income was taxed at source, a refund may be due, particularly if the deceased died early in the tax year having not used much of the personal allowance. On the other hand, if the deceased had untaxed income, or was a higher rate taxpayer, more may be due.

It can be difficult sometimes to establish the income of the deceased; it can be particularly difficult with regard to the state pension unless personal representatives obtain the figures quickly as the relevant government department destroys the pension records shortly after death.

It may be necessary to complete income tax returns for earlier years as well. HMRC can go back six years if the deceased has been guilty of neglect, wilful default or fraud; any such back assessment must be made within three years of the year of death.

The administration period

8.9   In almost every estate the personal representatives will receive income during the administration period, which is the period from the date of death until the residuary estate is ascertained. Frequently, this income will have been taxed at source, for example interest or dividends, and if that is the case, no more tax will be payable. If all the income accruing to the personal representatives has been taxed at source, no more tax will be due as personal representatives only pay basic rate tax. However, if the income has not been taxed at source, for example rental income from properties forming part of the assets of the deceased, then the personal representatives will have to complete a tax return, and pay the tax due.

As far as income tax is concerned, the crucial date for determining if the income should be taxed as part of the income of the deceased or as the income of the personal representatives depends on the date it is received or credited. If it is received or credited before the date of death, it is the income of the deceased. If it is received or credited after the date of death, it is the income of the personal representatives.

Note that a different rule applies for inheritance tax. All interest accrued to the date of death must be included in the IHT 400 account, and will be subject to both inheritance tax and income tax. It is possible to obtain relief against this double taxation.

Note that if the deceased was a life tenant, the income may have to be apportioned in order to ascertain which beneficiary is entitled to it. If the life tenant is entitled to it, then it will be taxed as part of the income of the life tenant. In addition, the income due before the date of death will be treated as capital for IHT purposes.

The beneficiaries

8.10   Ultimately the beneficiaries will be entitled to the income.

The rules as to entitlement to income are considered in more detail later. In general the rules are:

(a)   a beneficiary entitled to a pecuniary legacy is not usually entitled to interest from the date of death;

(b)   if there is a specific bequest, and the assets the subject of the specific bequest produce an income, then the beneficiary is entitled to the income from the date of death. For example, if the specific bequest is of a house which is let, the beneficiary will be entitled to the rent as from the date of death;

(c)   all other income will belong to the residuary beneficiaries.

Capital gains tax

8.11   As with income tax, it is necessary to consider CGT in three contexts – the period up to the date of death, the administration period, and the position of the beneficiaries.

The period up to the date of death

8.12   It may be that the deceased has incurred a liability for CGT in the tax year of death. The personal representatives must settle that liability; the deceased is entitled to the full annual exemption for CGT for the year of death. There may also be a liability for CGT in respect of earlier tax years.

If the deceased incurred a loss, that loss can be carried back and set off against any gains incurred in the three previous tax years. It cannot be carried forward, and set off against gains made by the personal representatives.

The administration period

8.13 The personal representatives are deemed to acquire the assets of the deceased at market value as at the date of death; this is usually the value for IHT purposes. If the personal representatives sell any of the assets at more than the market value at the date of death, there is a potential liability for CGT on the gain. However, they are entitled to the full annual exemption available to private individuals for the tax year of death, and for two subsequent years. If CGT is payable, the rate is 18 per cent.

If the personal representatives sell quoted shares within 12 months of death, or land within four years of death for less than the probate value, then they can elect to substitute that lower value for the probate value for IHT purposes. In this situation the reduced value also becomes the value at which the personal representatives will be deemed to have acquired the land or shares for CGT purposes, so that loss relief cannot be claimed. Whether the estate is small or large, the IHT relief should be claimed if the personal representatives do not have any gains against which to offset the loss – its benefit will then be lost – and since 6 April 2008, it should always be claimed because the rate of IHT is much higher than the 18 per cent CGT rate.

PAYMENT OF DEBTS – INSOLVENT ESTATES

8.14 The number of estates which prove to be insolvent is relatively small, but as practitioners may encounter them, the relevant provisions are considered here.

What assets are available?

8.15 If a person is made bankrupt in his or her lifetime, there are various statutory provisions under which gifts made by the bankrupt prior to the bankruptcy can be set aside. Similar provisions operate if the deceased's estate proves to be insolvent. These provisions are contained in Schedule 1 to the Administration of Insolvent Estates of Deceased Persons Order 1986.

Secured creditors

8.16 Secured creditors are in a strong position if the estate is insolvent. They can rely on their security under s 285(4) of the Insolvency Act 1986, and if the security proves to be inadequate, then they can prove in the bankruptcy for the balance under r 6.109 of the Insolvency Rules 1986 (SI 1986/1925).

Under rr 6.96–6.119, a secured creditor can value his security, and prove for the balance in the bankruptcy. If this is done, then the receiver can redeem the security at the value placed on the security by the secured creditor.

The secured creditor also has a further course of action open to him – if he voluntarily surrenders his security for the general benefit of creditors, he may prove for his whole debt, as if it were unsecured (r 6.109(2)). There must be very few situations where a secured creditor would wish to surrender their security.

Unsecured creditors

8.17   Any 'bankruptcy debt' can be proved in bankruptcy proceedings. Section 382(1) of the Insolvency Act 1986 provides that a bankruptcy debt in relation to a bankrupt means *inter alia* any debt or liability to which he is subject to at the commencement of the bankruptcy or may become subject after the commencement of the bankruptcy (including after his discharge from bankruptcy) by reason of any obligation incurred before the commencement of the bankruptcy.

There are various types of creditors – preferred, ordinary and deferred.

All ordinary debts rank equally. If the assets of the deceased are insufficient to pay them in full, then they abate rateably.

Deferred debts include a loan made by the spouse of the deceased; it is immaterial that the lender was not the spouse of the deceased at the date the loan was made (s 329 of the Insolvency Act 1986).

Most debts are classed as ordinary debts now if not deferred debts.

Joint tenancies

8.18   The Enterprise Act has inserted a new section into the Insolvency Act 1986, s 421A. This applies if the deceased was a joint tenant immediately before death, and within five years of death, application is made for an insolvency administration order. The court has a wide discretion about what type of order to make, but it can order the surviving joint tenant to make good the value lost to the estate. The court is required to assume that the interests of the deceased's creditors outweigh all other considerations.

PROTECTION OF THE PERSONAL REPRESENTATIVES

8.19   Before distributing the estate to the beneficiaries, the personal representatives need to be satisfied that all the debts have been paid, and all liabilities met. In the great majority of estates, this does not cause any problem. However, in some estates, it may be difficult for the personal representatives to be certain that there are no further liabilities. In view of this, there are various statutory provisions which protect the personal representatives. These are:

(a)   Personal representatives can protect themselves against claims of which they are unaware by means of advertisements under s 27 of the Trustee Act 1925 (TA 1925). Advertisements must be inserted in the *London Gazette*, and in a newspaper circulating in the district in which any land owned by the deceased is situated. The trustees must also give such other notices as would have been directed by a court of competent jurisdiction in an action for administration. The notice must require any person interested to send notice of claims to the personal representatives within the time specified in the notice, not being less than two months. The personal representatives must also make all the searches which an intending purchaser would make or be advised to make. At the expiration of the specified period, the personal representatives can distribute the estate only having regard to claims of which they had notice. Any disappointed claimant, ie a claimant outside the time limit, may follow the property, or any property representing the same, into the hands of a beneficiary. It should be noted that s 27 only protects personal representatives and trustees from liability for claims of which they are unaware. Personal representatives are also probably not protected from claims of which they are aware, but may be without foundation.

(b)   Section 48(1) of the Administration of Justice Act 1985 provides that where:

   (i)   any question of construction has arisen out of the terms of a will or a trust; and

   (ii)   an opinion in writing given by a person who has a ten-year High Court qualification, within the meaning of s 71 of the Courts and Legal Services Act 1990, has been obtained on that question by the personal representatives or trustees under the will or trust, the High Court may, on the application of the personal representatives or trustees and without hearing argument, make an order authorising those persons to take such steps in reliance on the said opinion as are specified in the order.

   Subsection (2) provides that the High Court shall not make an order if it appears that a dispute exists which would make it inappropriate for the court to make the order without hearing argument.

   There is a similar provision in the Standard Provisions of the Society of Trust and Estate Practitioners; the qualification period is reduced to five years.

(c)   Section 26 of the TA 1925 deals with the situation where personal representatives or trustees are liable for any rent or on any other covenant contained in a lease. If the personal representatives or trustees satisfy all liabilities under the lease or grant up to the date of the conveyance, and where necessary set apart a sufficient fund to answer any future claim that may be made in respect of any fixed and ascertained sum which the lessee agreed to lay out on the demised property, the personal representatives or trustees may then safely distribute the assets.

Section 26(1A) provides that where a personal representative or trustee has entered or may be required to enter into an authorised guarantee agreement within the Landlord and Tenant (Covenants) Act 1995 with respect to any lease comprised in the estate of a deceased testator or intestate or a trust estate:

'(a)   he may distribute the residuary real and personal estate of the deceased testator or intestate, or the trust estate, to or amongst the persons entitled thereto–

(i)   without appropriating any part of the estate of the deceased, or the trust estate, to meet any future liability (or, as the case may be, any liability) under any such agreement, and

(ii)   notwithstanding any potential liability of his to enter into any such agreement; and

(b)   notwithstanding any such distribution, he shall not be personally liable in respect of any subsequent claim (or, as the case may be, any claim) under any such agreement.'

If a personal representative or trustee has entered into such an agreement, he must have satisfied all liabilities under it which may have accrued and been claimed up to the date of distribution. The lessor has the right to follow the assets into the hands of the persons amongst whom the assets may have been distributed.

(d)   Illegitimate, legitimated, and adopted children are entitled to share in a gift to children just as if they are legitimate children, subject to any contrary intention.

Section 45 of the Adoption Act 1976 provides:

(i)   a trustee or personal representative is not under a duty, by virtue of the law relating to trusts or the administration of estates, to enquire, before conveying or distributing any property, whether any adoption has been effected or revoked if that fact could affect entitlement to the property;

(ii)   a trustee or personal representative shall not be liable to any person by reason of a conveyance or distribution of the property made without regard to any such fact if he has not received notice of the fact before the conveyance or distribution;

(iii)   this section does not prejudice the right of a person to follow the property, or any property representing it, into the hands of another person, other than a purchaser, who has received it.

There is now no protection as regards illegitimate children and so personal representatives must rely on advertisements under s 27 of the TA 1925 to protect them from claims by unknown children of the deceased.

(e)   There is always a possibility that an application for financial provision will be made under the Inheritance (Provision for Family and Dependants) Act 1975. The time limit for beginning proceedings under the Act is six months from the date of the grant, but the court can grant leave to applicants to begin proceedings outside this time limit. In order to protect personal representatives, s 20(1) of the Act provides that a personal representative of a deceased person is not liable for having distributed any part of the estate of the deceased after the end of the period of six months from the date on which representation with respect to the estate of the deceased was first taken out on the ground that he ought to have taken into account the possibility that the court might permit the making of an application for an order under s 2 of the Act after the end of that period.

Under the Civil Procedure Rules, a claimant has four months in which to serve any proceedings. It is possible that a claimant could begin proceedings just before the expiry of the six-month period, not tell the personal representatives about the claim and then serve them just before the four-month period has expired. Section 20 would not protect the personal representatives in that situation, although s 27 advertisements might.

(f)   In certain circumstances, it is possible to apply for rectification of a will under s 20 of the Administration of Justice Act 1982. The time limit for such applications is six months from the date of the grant, and the court can extend that time limit if they so wish. However, as with applications out of time under the Inheritance (Provision for Family and Dependants) Act 1982 personal representatives are protected if they delay distribution until six months after the date of the grant.

The point made above about service also applies to applications for rectification.

(g)   If the trustees have been unable to ascertain who is entitled, application can be made to the court for directions.

(h)   If the trustees have made all reasonable enquiries, but have not been able to identify all possible beneficiaries, application can be made to the court for a *Benjamin* order authorising the distribution of the assets in a certain manner. This procedure could be used if, for example, a possible beneficiary is almost certainly dead, for example, a member of the RAF who was certified by the Air Ministry to have died in January 1943 having failed to return from a bombing raid over Germany (*Re Green's Will Trusts [1985] 3 All ER 455*).

(i)   As a last resort money can be paid into court.

In the long term, the Limitation Act 1980 (LA 1980) may protect personal representatives. Section 21(1) of the LA 1980 provides that no period of limitation prescribed by the Act shall apply to an action by a beneficiary under a trust, being an action:

(a)   in respect of any fraud or fraudulent breach of trust to which the trustee was a party or privy; or

(b)   to recover from the trustee trust property or the proceeds of trust property in the possession of the trustee, or previously received by the trustee and converted to his use.

8.19 *Post grant procedure*

Section 22 provides that subject to s 21(1) and (2) of the LA 1980:

(a)   no action in respect of any claim to the personal estate of a deceased person or to any share or interest in any such estate (whether under a will or on intestacy) shall be brought after the expiration of 12 years from the date on which the right to receive the share or interest accrued; and

(b)   no action to recover arrears of interest in respect of any legacy, or damages in respect of such arrears, shall be brought after the expiration of six years from the date on which the interest became due.

If no period of limitation is specified in the LA 1980, then the doctrine of laches will apply. The idea behind this doctrine is that a potential claimant must not delay in bringing an action; the court will take into account various factors like hardship and the balance of justice before deciding if an action is barred by laches.

In a recent case, *Davies v Sharples [2006] WTLR 839*, T died in 1938. He left a will which created trusts. The trustees paid money out in error which was discovered many years later.

It was held that this was an action for breach of trust as the administration of the estate had been completed many years ago. It was also held that the limitation period did not start to run until the beneficiaries who had lost out should have realised that they had a cause of action. They had begun the proceedings within six years of when they could reasonably have discovered the breach.

In *Fea v Roberts [2005] EWHC 2186*, a solicitor dealing with the winding up of a trust paid over £100,000 to a person, R, who was not entitled to it. The solicitor did not check to see if the person was entitled to the money. Eight years later the person who was entitled to the money claimed it.

R was sued to recover the money paid under a mistake of fact. The solicitor accepted that he had been negligent in failing to check the identity of the beneficiary.

R pleaded the Limitation Act. It was held that time did not start to run until the solicitor became aware of the error, and so the proceedings were not barred under the Limitation Act. R also pleaded that he had thought that the money came from the estate of an uncle, and had altered his position because of this. This argument was rejected.

It will often be the case that the personal representatives will not be in a position to make a distribution to the beneficiaries for some time after the grant has been obtained. The personal representatives will then be able to take advantage of the protection afforded to them by s 20 of the Inheritance (Provision for Family and Dependants) Act 1975. However, some beneficiaries will not be prepared to wait six months or ten months as suggested above after the date of the grant for a distribution. In what circumstances is it safe for the personal representatives to make a distribution within the six or ten month period? It may be safe in the following circumstances:

(a)   whilst personal representatives can never be completely certain that a claim under the 1975 Act will not be lodged, there are estates where the personal representatives are virtually certain that there will not be a claim;

(b)   it may be clear that the claim will only affect a small part of the estate. The remainder can then be safely distributed, although it would be prudent to retain a generous amount to meet the claim;

(c)   if the applicant agrees;

(d)   if the beneficiary gives the personal representatives an indemnity. The difficulty with the indemnity is that unless it is secured, it may prove to be worthless;

(e)   if the personal representatives and the residuary beneficiaries are the same persons;

(f)   if the court agrees (it might be difficult to arrange a hearing within six months of the date of the grant).

Chapter 9

Powers of the personal representatives

OVERVIEW

9.1   Certain powers are conferred on personal representatives and trustees; these powers are frequently modified in wills, and the common variations are detailed in this section.

Most of the powers apply to personal representatives and trustees; in any event personal representatives frequently become trustees – they may be expressly appointed trustees by the will, or they may become trustees because minors are entitled under the will and cannot give a valid receipt for capital money.

ADVANCEMENT

9.2   Section 32 of the Trustee Act 1925 (TA 1925) empowers trustees to advance capital to a beneficiary.

When does the power of advancement arise?

9.3   Section 32(2) of the TA 1925, as amended by the Trusts of Land and Appointment of Trustees Act 1996, provides that the section does not apply to capital money arising under the Settled Land Act 1925. Thus the trustees of a strict settlement have no power to advance capital to a beneficiary under s 32.

Section 32(1) of the TA 1925 gives the trustees wide powers to apply the capital for the advancement or benefit of a beneficiary. The beneficiary may be absolutely or contingently entitled, the contingency, for example, could be attaining a specified age or some other such contingency. It is immaterial that the interest of the beneficiary is liable to be defeated by the exercise of a power of appointment or revocation, or to be diminished by the increase of the class to which he belongs.

There is a proviso to s 32(1) of the TA 1925 limiting the powers of the trustees. Only one-half of the presumptive share of a beneficiary can be advanced, and when the beneficiary becomes absolutely and indefeasibly entitled, the advancement must be brought into account. In addition, if there is a beneficiary with a prior or life interest, an advancement cannot be made without the consent of that person in writing.

What is meant by 'advancement or benefit'?

9.4   This phrase has been given a wide meaning. In *Pilkington v IRC [1964] AC 612*, Lord Radcliffe said at page 635 that it meant 'any use of money which will improve the material situation of the beneficiary'. It has been held to include even the payment of a donation to a charity (*Re Clore's Settlement Trust [1966] 2 All ER 272*), and also payments to a beneficiary which will result in a saving in tax (*Re Moxon's Will Trust [1958] 1 All ER 386*).

It is also possible to exercise the power of advancement in order to resettle trust funds. Furthermore, there is no objection to the exercise of the power if other persons benefit incidentally (*Pilkington v IRC [1964] AC 612*).

It is possible that a resettlement may infringe the equitable rule that trustees must not delegate (of course statute has now conferred some powers of delegation). However, in Pilkington's case, Viscount Radcliffe said at pages 638–639:

> 'I am unconvinced by the argument that the trustees would be improperly delegating their trust by allowing the money raised to pass over to new trustees under a settlement conferring new powers on the latter. In fact I think the whole issue of delegation is here beside the mark. The law is not that trustees cannot delegate; it is that trustees cannot delegate unless they have authority to do so. If the power of advancement which they possess is so read as to allow them to raise money for the purpose of having it settled, then they do have the necessary authority to let the money pass out of the old settlement into the new trusts. No question of delegation of their powers or trusts arises. If, on the other hand, their power of advancement is read so as to exclude settled advances, *cadit quaestio*.'

The statutory power in s 32 of the TA 1925 is wide enough to permit the resettlement of trust funds, but a discretionary trust may not be permissible (see Parker and Mellows, *Modern Law of Trusts* (7th edition, Sweet & Maxwell) pages 623–624).

Resettlements can fall foul of the perpetuity rules, but with settlements coming into existence after 15 July 1964 the 'wait and see' rule will apply so that the resettlement will only be invalid if it becomes clear that the perpetuity rules will be infringed. It should be noted that for perpetuity purposes the resettlement is treated as being contained in the original settlement.

Prior interests

9.5   An advancement cannot be made unless the person with a prior interest consents. Thus if there is a life tenant, no advance can be made to the remainderman unless the life tenant consents.

What is the position of discretionary beneficiaries? It is clear that they do not have any prior interest within the meaning of the section, and so their consent to an advancement is not necessary (*Re Harris' Settlement (1940) 162 LT 358*). However, a beneficiary with a protected interest does have a prior interest, and will not forfeit it by giving consent (*Re Hastings-Bass [1975] Ch 25, Re Shaw's Settlement [1951] Ch 833*). It should be noted that the court has no power to dispense with the consent required by s 32.

In *Henley v Wardell (1988) Times, 29 January*, a power of advancement was subject to an uncontrolled discretion, but it was still necessary to obtain the consent of the life tenant before it could be exercised.

Money advanced for a particular purpose

9.6   If trustees advance money for a particular purpose, it will not be necessary for the trustees to ensure that it is applied for that particular purpose if they have grounds for thinking that this will be done. However, if money has been advanced in previous years for a particular purpose, and the trustees are aware that it was not applied for that particular purpose, the trustees must then ensure that any further advance is so applied (*Re Pauling's Settlement Trust [1964] Ch 303*).

Common alterations

9.7   It is common to include variations which:

(a)   permit the personal representatives to advance the whole of the capital;

(b)   dispense with the requirement that the advance should be brought into account, or give the trustees a discretion as to whether the advance should be brought into account;

(c)   dispense with consents of beneficiaries with prior interests;

(d)   if there is a life interest, power to advance capital to the life tenant.

APPROPRIATION

9.8   Section 41 of the Administration of Estates Act 1925 (AEA 1925) authorises personal representatives to appropriate any part of the real or personal estate, including things in action, of the deceased in the actual state or condition or state of investment thereof at the time of appropriation in or towards satisfaction of any legacy bequeathed by the deceased. Thus if a beneficiary has a legacy of £10,000, the personal representatives can satisfy that legacy by transferring shares worth £10,000 to the beneficiary.

If the asset is worth more than the legacy, it is probable that personal representatives cannot use s 41 of the AEA 1925. Instead, they can sell the asset to the beneficiary. In addition, there is some doubt as to whether a personal representative who is also a beneficiary can make use of s 41 of the AEA 1925.

There are various limitations on the power of appropriation. An appropriation must not be made so as to affect prejudicially any specific devise or bequest (s 41(1)(i)). If the beneficiary is absolutely entitled, the appropriation can only be made with the consent of that beneficiary. If the legacy is settled, the appropriation can only be made with the consent of the trustees, or the person for the time being entitled to the income (s 41(1)(ii)).

If the person whose consent is required cannot give it because he is an infant, or incapable of managing his own affairs by reason of mental disorder within the meaning of the Mental Health Act 1983, the consent can be given by his parents or parent, testamentary or other guardian, or deputy, or, if, in the case of an infant, there is no such parent or guardian, by the court on the application of his litigation friend. It is not necessary to obtain consent on behalf of a person who may come into existence after the time of appropriation, or who cannot be found or ascertained at that time (s 41(1)(iii)). However, s 41(5) of the AEA 1925 provides that the personal representatives in making the appropriation shall have regard to the rights of any person who may thereafter come into existence, or who cannot be found or ascertained at the time of appropriation, and of any other person whose consent is not required by the section. Furthermore, if there is no deputy acting for a person lacking capacity, and the appropriation is of an investment authorised by law or by the will, if one exists, of the deceased for the investment of money subject to the trust, no consent is required on behalf of the person lacking capacity (s 41(1)(iv)). In similar circumstances, no consent is required if there is no trustee of a settled legacy, and there is no person of full age entitled to the income (s 41(1)(v)).

An appropriation made under s 41 binds all persons interested in the property whose consent is not required by the section (s 41(4)).

Assume that a beneficiary has a legacy of £20,000. The personal representatives can satisfy that legacy by transferring to the beneficiary land to the value of £20,000. If the land is worth more than the legacy, this cannot be done. Instead, the personal representatives can sell the asset to the beneficiary. If the asset is the subject of a specific devise to another beneficiary, appropriation cannot be made. If the residuary beneficiaries are entitled to the land, they are bound by any appropriation made by the personal representatives.

Valuation

9.9   Section 41(3) provides that the personal representatives may ascertain and fix the value of the respective parts of the real and personal estate and the liabilities of the deceased as they may think fit, and shall for that purpose employ a duly qualified valuer where necessary. Thus an executrix cannot value shares in an unquoted company herself, and then appropriate them in her favour at that valuation (*Re Bythway (1911) 104 LT 411*).

The date for the valuation of the assets could be very important in a volatile market. The Act does not provide any guidance, but the question was decided in the case of *Re Collins [1975] 1 WLR 309*, where it was held that the relevant date was the date of appropriation, and not the date of death. Thus if prices are rising, the beneficiary will want the appropriation to be made as soon as possible, whereas if they are dropping, the beneficiary will want the appropriation to be delayed.

Intestacy

9.10   Section 41(9) specifically provides that the section applies whether the deceased died intestate or not.

In *Kane v Radley-Kane [1999] Ch 274*, James Radley-Kane died intestate in May 1994 leaving a widow, the first defendant, and three sons. The widow was, in fact, the step-mother of the three sons.

The deceased owned 36 per cent of the ordinary shares in a company called Shiredean Limited, which were valued for probate purposes at £50,000. The net value of the deceased's estate was £93,000. Letters of administration were granted to the widow, and she regarded herself as entitled to the whole estate under the intestacy rules.

In January 1997 the shares in Shiredean were sold for £1,131,438.

The claimant, one of the sons, issued proceedings claiming that the appropriation of the shares by the widow in her own favour was invalid.

It was held that this was the case. However, the judge stated that if the assets had been equivalent of cash, for example government stock, then the appropriation would have been valid.

Trustees and powers of appropriation

9.11   Section 41 applies only to personal representatives, and does not apply to trustees, who have the following powers of appropriation:

(a)   if there are separate trusts of separate property, the trustees can appropriate assets to the value of the separate amounts given;

(b)   if there is a trust for sale, and there is nothing in the trust instrument to indicate that an appropriation should not be made, the trustees may make an appropriation.

Normally any adult beneficiaries must agree.

For a fuller discussion, see Parker and Mellows, *Modern Law of Trusts* (7th edition, Sweet & Maxwell) page 632.

Stamp duty

9.12   Stamp duty is not payable in respect of an instrument giving effect to an appropriation in or towards satisfaction of a general legacy, provided that the instrument is duly certified as coming within the appropriate category of the schedule to the regulations. Since 1 December 2003, stamp duty only applies to share transfers.

With regard to stamp duty land tax, it is clear that where a person takes a property under the will or intestacy of a deceased person, stamp duty land tax is not payable whether or not the property is subject to a charge. In such a case, no certificate is required. However, if the beneficiary provides other consideration than the assumption of a charge, stamp duty land tax may be payable. For example, if a beneficiary agrees to take a house in satisfaction of a legacy, but also pays to the executors the difference between the legacy and the market value of the house, stamp duty land tax may be payable.

BUSINESSES

Sole traders

9.13   The personal representatives can continue the business, but only for the purpose of selling it, and only for a year. The personal representatives are personally liable for debts they incur, but there is a right of indemnity from the estate. This right takes priority over the rights of the creditors if the business is being run in order to sell it. However, if the business is being run under a power in the will, the personal representatives have the right of indemnity in preference to the beneficiaries but not the creditors.

If the personal representatives hold the residue on trust for sale with power to postpone the sale, then they can delay sale for as long as they want, subject to their duty to obtain the best possible price.

The personal representatives can only use the assets employed in the business at the date of death; these could prove to be insufficient.

Common variations

9.14   It is common to include clauses which provide for the following:

(a)   to run the business as long as the personal representatives like;

(b)   to use other assets;

(c)   to appoint a manager;

(d)   indemnity.

Partnerships

9.15   The death of a partner automatically dissolves a partnership, unless the partnership agreement provides that on the death of a partner the partnership continues.

There is no need to give the personal representatives of a partner extra powers to run the business, but it should be done in the case of a small partnership as all the other partners may die or retire leaving the personal representatives as the personal representatives of a sole trader.

Companies

9.16   The testator may have shares in a company which will pass to the personal representatives. The company will continue to trade as before, and so there is no need for any extra powers, apart perhaps from empowering the personal representatives to give warranties on a sale.

CHARGING CLAUSES

9.17 The traditional rule is that trustees are not entitled to profit from a trust and are entitled only to reasonable expenses. However, the Trustee Act 2000 (TA 2000) has substantially changed the law. Section 29 contains provisions entitling a trustee who is a trust corporation, or acts in a professional capacity, to remuneration. Section 29(1) provides that a trustee who:

(a)   is a trust corporation; but

(b)   is not a trustee of a charitable trust;

is entitled to receive reasonable remuneration out of the trust funds for any services that the trust corporation provides on behalf of the trust.

A professional trustee is similarly entitled. Section 29(2) provides that a trustee who:

(a)   acts in a professional capacity; but

(b)   is not a trust corporation, a trustee of a charitable trust or a sole trustee;

is entitled to receive reasonable remuneration out of the trust funds for any services that he provides on behalf of the trust.

All the other trustees must agree in writing that he may be remunerated for the services. Note that a sole trustee cannot charge.

Section 28(5) defines what is meant by acting in a professional capacity. A trustee acts in a professional capacity if he acts in the course of a profession or business which consists of or includes the provision of services in connection with:

(a)   the management or administration of trusts generally or a particular kind of trust; or

(b)   any particular aspect of the management or administration of trusts generally or a particular kind of trust;

and the services he provides to or on behalf of the trust fall within that description.

Section 29(3) of the TA 2000 defines reasonable remuneration. In relation to the provision of services by a trustee, it means such remuneration as is reasonable in the circumstances for the provision of those services on behalf of that trust by that trustee. If the trustee in an institution, authorised under the Banking Act 1987, and provides the services in that capacity, reasonable remuneration will be the institution's reasonable charges for the provision of such services. Section 29(4) of the TA 2000 provides that a trustee is entitled to remuneration even if the services in question are capable of being provided by a lay trustee.

A trustee who has been appointed as an agent of the trustees, or nominee or custodian under the powers conferred by Part IV of the TA 2000 or the trust instrument, is also entitled to remuneration under s 29 (s 29(6)).

Section 29(5) of the TA 2000 provides that a trustee is not entitled to remuneration under s 29 if any provision about his entitlement to remuneration has been made:

(a)   by the trust instrument; or

(b)   by any enactment or any provision of subordinate legislation.

It has always been the case that trustees were entitled to the reimbursement of expenses. Section 31(1) of the TA 2000 confirms this position by providing that a trustee is entitled to be reimbursed out of the trust funds or may pay out of the trust fund expenses properly incurred when acting on behalf of the trust. Section 31(2) provides that the section applies to a trustee who has been authorised under a power conferred by Part IV or the trust instrument:

(a)   to exercise functions as an agent of the trustees; or

(b)   to act as a nominee or custodian;

as it applies to any other trustee.

Section 28 contains provisions dealing with the situation where there is a charging clause. Section 28(1) provides that subsections (2)–(4) apply to a trustee if:

(a)   there is a provision in the trust instrument entitling him to receive payment out of trust funds in respect of services provided by him on behalf of the trust; and

(b)   the trustee is a trust corporation or is acting in a professional capacity.

Section 28(2) provides that the trustee is to be treated as entitled under the trust instrument to receive payment in respect of services even if they are services which are capable of being provided by a lay trustee. Section 28(6) provides that a person acts as a lay trustee if he:

(a)   is not a trust corporation; and

(b)   does not act in a professional capacity.

Section 15 of the Wills Act 1837 provides that a gift to an attesting witness or the spouse or civil partner of an attesting witness is void. Section 28(4) provides that any payments to which the trustee is entitled in respect of services are to be treated as remuneration for services and not as a gift for the purposes of s 15 of the 1837 Act. This means that a trustee or a trustee's spouse or civil partner who are not beneficiaries can safely witness the will.

Section 34(3) of the Administration of Estates Act 1925 (AEA 1925) lays down the order in which the assets are to be applied in payment of the debts of the deceased. Again, s 28(4) applies so that any payments to which the trustee is entitled in respect of services are to be treated as remuneration for services and not as a gift.

Section 33(2) of the TA 2000 provides that nothing in ss 28 or 29 is to be treated as affecting the operation of:

9.17 *Powers of the personal representatives*

(a) s 15 of the Wills Act 1837; or

(b) s 34(3) of the Administration of Estates Act 1925 in relation to any death occurring before the commencement of ss 28 or 29.

Section 30 of the TA 2000 deals with the remuneration of trustees of charitable trusts. Section 30(1) provides that the Secretary of State may make regulations for the remuneration of trustees of charitable trusts who are trust corporations or act in a professional capacity. Section 30(2) provides that the power under subsection (1) includes power to make provision for the remuneration of a trustee who has been authorised under a power conferred by Part IV or the trust instrument:

(a) to exercise functions as an agent of the trustees; or

(b) to act as a nominee or custodian.

Section 30(3) of the TA 2000 provides that regulations under the section may:

(a) make different provisions for different cases;

(b) contain such supplemental, incidental, consequential and transitional conditions as the Secretary of State considers appropriate.

Section 30(4) of the TA 2000 provides that the power to make regulations under the section is exercisable by statutory instrument which will be subject to annulment in pursuance of a resolution of either House of Parliament. At the time of writing, no such regulations have been made.

If there is an express charging clause, a trustee of a charitable trust who is not a trust corporation is only entitled to receive payment for services which are capable of being provided by a lay trustee:

(a) if he is not a sole trustee; and

(b) to the extent that a majority of the other trustees have agreed that it should apply to him (s 28(3)).

Section 33(1) of the TA 2000 provides that ss 28, 29, 31 and 32 apply in relation to services provided or (as the case may be) expenses incurred on or after their coming into force on behalf of a trust whenever created.

These provisions also apply to personal representatives (s 35(1) and (2)).

Remuneration to which a personal representative would be entitled under ss 28 or 29 is to be treated as an administration expense for the purposes of s 34(3) of the TA 2000. It is also to be treated as an administration expense for the purposes of any provision giving reasonable administration expenses priority over the preferential debts listed in Schedule 6 to the Insolvency Act 1986 (s 35(3)). Section 35(4) provides that nothing in subsection (3) is to be treated as affecting the operation of the provisions mentioned in paragraphs (a) and (b) of that subsection in relation to any death occurring before the commencement of s 35.

Notwithstanding the Act, an express charging clause should still be inserted in a trust instrument or will as a sole executor cannot charge. Even if there are other executors, then they might not agree that the other professional executors can charge.

COMPOUNDING LIABILITIES

9.18   Section 15(f) of the Trustee Act 1925 empowers personal representatives or two or more trustees to, *inter alia*, 'compromise, compound, abandon, submit to arbitration, or otherwise settle any debt, account, claim, or thing whatever relating to the testator's or intestate's estate or to the trust'.

Notwithstanding the wide power conferred by the section, before compromising a claim, the trustees must be satisfied that it is in the best interests of the trust – in effect, it is the best deal which could be obtained.

THE POWER TO DELEGATE – COLLECTIVE DELEGATION

9.19   Before 1925 there was no doubt that a trustee could delegate his powers. In *Speight v Gaunt (1883) 22 Ch D 727*, Jessel MR said at pages 739–740:

> 'It seems to me that on general principles a trustee ought to conduct the business of the trust in the same manner that an ordinary prudent man of business would conduct his own, and that beyond there is no liability or obligation on the trustee ... If the investment is an investment made on the Stock Exchange through a stockbroker, the ordinary course of business is for the investor to select a stockbroker in good credit and in a good position, having regard to the sum to be invested, and to direct him to make the investment – that is, to purchase on the Stock Exchange of a jobber or another broker the investment required.'

The Trustee Act 1925 (TA 1925) contained various provisions concerning delegation by trustees.

The Trustee Act 2000 substantially changes the law. Sections 21, 23 and 30 of the TA 1925 are repealed. Instead, Part IV of the 2000 Act contains a comprehensive code dealing with the appointment of agents, nominees and custodians.

The TA 2000 is based on the recommendations of the Law Commission. Traditionally, the law has permitted trustees to delegate administrative decisions, but not fiduciary duties. The Law Commission considered that this distinction was out of date, and that the distinction ought to be between the administrative powers and distributive powers. It is possible to delegate administrative powers; it is not possible to delegate distributive powers.

Section 11(1) of the TA 2000 provides that trustees may authorise any person to exercise any or all of their delegable functions as their agent. Section 11(2) defines the trustees' delegable functions. These are any function other than:

(a)   any function relating to whether, or in what way, any assets of the trust should be distributed;

(b)   power to decide whether any fees or other payment due to be made out of the trust funds should be made out of income or capital (this is a decision about the distribution of assets);

(c)   any power to appoint a person to be a trustee of the trust; or

(d)   any power conferred by any other enactment or the trust instrument which permits the trustees to delegate any of their functions or to appoint a person to act as nominee or custodian.

Section 11(2) does not apply to charitable trustees. Instead, s 11(3) provides that in the case of a charitable trust, the trustees' delegable functions are:

(a)   any function consisting of carrying out a decision that the trustees have taken;

(b)   any function relating to the investment of assets subject to the trust (including, in the case of land acquired as an investment, managing the land and creating or disposing of an interest in the land);

(c)   any function relating to the raising of funds for the trust otherwise than by means of profits of a trade which is an integral part of the carrying out of the trust's charitable purpose;

(d)   any other function prescribed by an order made by the Secretary of State.

Section 11(4) of the TA 2000 provides that for the purposes of subsection (3)(c) a trade is an integral part of carrying out a trust's charitable purpose if, whether carried on in the UK or elsewhere, the profits are applied solely to the purposes of the trust and either:

(a)   the trade is exercised in the course of the actual carrying out of a primary purpose of the trust; or

(b)   the work in connection with the trade is mainly carried out by beneficiaries of the trust.

Section 12 of the TA 2000 deals with the question of who may be appointed as an agent. The trustees can appoint one of their number, but they cannot appoint a beneficiary, even if the beneficiary is a trustee. If two or more persons are appointed as agents, they must exercise their functions jointly. A person may be appointed to act as the agent of the trustees even though he is also appointed to act as the nominee or custodian of the trustees.

Section 13 of the TA 2000 deals with linked functions. Section 13(1) provides that a person who is authorised under s 11 to exercise a function is subject to any specific duties or restrictions attached to the function. The Act then goes on to provide as an example that a person who is authorised under s 11 to exercise a general power of investment is subject to the duties under s 4 in relation to that part. This applies whatever the terms of the agency. Section 13(2) provides that a person who is authorised under s 11 to exercise a power which is subject to a requirement to obtain advice is not subject to the requirement if he is the kind of person from whom it would have been proper for the trustees, in compliance with the requirement, to obtain advice. Thus if the trustees delegate the power of investment to a person who would normally give advice about investments, that person need not himself obtain further advice.

Section 11(1) of the Trusts of Land and Appointment of Trustees Act 1996 imposes a duty on trustees to consult beneficiaries and give effect to their wishes. Section 13(3) of the TA 2000 provides that subsections (4) and (5) apply to a trust to which s 11(1) of the 1996 Act applies. Subsection (4) provides that the trustees may not under s 11 authorise a person to exercise any of their functions on terms that prevent them from complying with s 11(1) of the 1996 Act. Subsection (5) provides that a person who is authorised under s 11 to exercise any function relating to land subject to the trust is not subject to s 11(1) of the 1996 Act. Thus trustees must still consult and give effect to the wishes of the beneficiaries even if they do delegate their powers.

Section 14(1) of the TA 2000 provides that the trustees may authorise a person to exercise functions as their agent on such terms as to remuneration and other matters as they may determine. This gives the trustees a wide discretion about the terms on which an agent is employed, but it is subject to various limitations. Section 14(2) provides that the trustees may not authorise a person to exercise functions as their agent on any of the terms mentioned in subsection (3) unless it is reasonably necessary for them to do so. The terms mentioned in subsection (3) are:

(a)   a term permitting the agent to appoint a substitute;

(b)   a term restricting the liability of the agent or his substitute to the trustees or any beneficiary;

(c)   a term permitting the agent to act in circumstances capable of giving rise to a conflict of interest.

Asset management

9.20   Section 15 of the TA 2000 deals with asset management. Section 15(1) provides that the trustees may not authorise a person to exercise any of their asset management functions as their agent except by an agreement which is in, or is evidenced in, writing. Section 15(2) provides that the trustees may not authorise a person to exercise any of their asset management functions as their agent unless:

(a)   they have prepared a statement (known as a policy statement) that gives guidance as to how a function should be exercised; and

(b)   the agreement under which the agent is to act includes a term to the effect that he will secure compliance with:

   (i)   the policy statement; or

   (ii)   if the policy statement is revised or replaced under s 22, the revised or replacement policy statement.

Section 15(3) provides that the trustees must formulate any guidance given in the policy statement with a view to ensuring that the functions will be exercised in the best interests of the trust.

Section 15(4) provides that the policy statement must be in, or evidenced in, writing.

Section 15(5) provides that the asset management functions of trustees are their functions relating to:

(a)   the investment of assets subject to the trust;

(b)   the acquisition of property which is to be subject to the trust; and

(c)   managing property which is subject to the trust and disposing of, or creating or disposing of an interest in, such property.

Section 16(1) provides that the trustees of a trust may:

(a)   appoint a person to act as their nominee in relation to such of the assets of the trust as they determine; and

(b)   take such steps as are necessary to secure that those assets are vested in a person so appointed.

An appointment under the section must be in, or evidenced in, writing, and the section does not apply to any trust having a custodian trustee or in relation to any assets vested in the official custodian for charities (s 16(2) and (3)).

Custodians

9.21   Section 17 of the TA 2000 confers on trustees the power to appoint custodians. Section 17(1) provides that the trustees of a trust may appoint a person to act as a custodian in relation to such assets of the trust as they have determined. Section 17(2) provides that a person is the custodian in relation to assets if he undertakes safe custody of the assets or of any documents or records concerning the assets. Section 17(3) provides that an appointment under the section must be in, or evidenced in, writing. Section 17(4) provides that the section does not apply to any trust having a custodian trustee or in relation to any assets vested in the official custodian for charities. Section 39(1) provides that 'custodian trustee' has the same meaning as in the Public Trustee Act 1906.

Section 18 deals with investments in bearer securities. Section 18(1) provides that if trustees retain or invest in securities payable to bearer, they must appoint a person to act as a custodian of the securities. This does not apply if the trust instrument contains a provision which permits the trustees to retain or invest in securities payable to bearer without appointing a person to act as a custodian (s 18(2)). Section 18(3) provides that an appointment under the section must be in, or evidenced in, writing. Section 18(4) provides that the section does not apply to any trust having a custodian trustee or in relation to any securities vested in the official custodian for charities. Note that s 25(2) provides that s 18 does not impose a duty on a sole trustee if that trustee is a trust corporation.

Who can be appointed?

9.22   Section 19(1) of the TA 2000 deals with the question of who may be appointed as nominees or custodians. Section 19(1) also provides that a person may not be appointed under ss 16, 17 or 18 as a nominee or custodian unless one of the relevant conditions is satisfied.

Section 19(2) provides that the relevant conditions are that:

(a)   the person carries on business which consists of or includes acting as a nominee or custodian; or

(b)   the person is a body corporate which is controlled by the trustees; or

(c)   the person is a body corporate recognised under s 9 of the Administration of Justice Act 1985.

Section 19(3) provides that the question of whether a body corporate is controlled by trustees is to be determined in accordance with s 840 of the Income and Corporation Taxes Act 1988.

Section 19(4) provides that the trustees of a charitable trust which is not an exempt charity must act in accordance with any guidance given by the Charity Commission concerning the selection of a person for appointment as a nominee or custodian under ss 16, 17 or 18. This guidance has been published, and is available on the Charity Commission website.

Section 19(5) provides that subject to subsections (1) and (4), the persons whom the trustees may appoint as a nominee or custodian under ss 16, 17 or 18 include:

(a)   one of their number, if that one is a trust corporation; or

(b)   two (or more) of their number, if they are to act as joint nominees or joint custodians.

It will be recalled that s 16 of the TA 2000 deals with the power of trustees to appoint nominees.

Frequently, professionals are appointed as trustees along with lay trustees. It appears that a sole professional trustee cannot be appointed as s 19(5)(b) requires two to be appointed.

Section 19(6) provides that the trustees may under s 16 appoint a person to act as their nominee even though he is also:

(a)   appointed to act as their custodian (under ss 17 or 18 or any other power); or

(b)   authorised to exercise functions as their agent under s 11 or any other power.

As already mentioned, s 17 deals with the power of trustees to appoint custodians, whilst s 18 deals with the power of trustees to retain or invest in securities payable to the bearer. Section 19(7) provides that the trustees may under those sections appoint a person to act as their custodian even though he is also:

(a)   appointed to act as their nominee (under s 16 or any other power); or

(b)   authorised to exercise functions as their agent (under s 11 or any other power).

Terms of appointment

9.23   Section 20 of the TA 2000 deals with the terms of appointment of nominees and custodians. Section 20(1) provides that the trustees may appoint a person to act as a nominee or custodian on such terms as to remuneration and other matters as they may determine. Section 29 contains further provisions dealing with the remuneration of a trustee who has been appointed as agent, nominee or custodian (see **para 9.17** above). Section 32(1) applies if a person other than a trustee has been:

(a)   authorised to exercise functions as an agent of the trustees; or

(b)   appointed to act as a nominee or custodian.

Section 32(2) provides that the trustees may remunerate the agent, nominee or custodian out of the trust funds for services if:

(a)   he is engaged on terms entitling him to be remunerated for those services; and

(b)   the amount does not exceed such remuneration as is reasonable in the circumstances for the provision of the services by him on behalf of that trust.

Section 32(3) provides that the trustees may reimburse the agent, nominee or custodian out of the trust funds for any expenses properly incurred by him in exercising functions as an agent, nominee or custodian.

Section 20(2) provides that the trustees may not appoint a person to act as a nominee or custodian on any of the terms mentioned in subsection (3), unless it is reasonably necessary for them to do so. The terms mentioned in subsection (3) are:

(a)   a term permitting the nominee or custodian to appoint a substitute;

(b)   a term restricting the liability of the nominee or custodian or his substitute to the trustees or to any beneficiary;

(c)   a term permitting the nominee or custodian to act in circumstances capable of giving rise to a conflict of interest.

Section 20 is subject to ss 29–32.

Review

9.24   For the whole of the time that the agent, nominee or custodian continues to act for the trust, the trustees must keep under review the arrangements under which the agent, nominee or custodian acts, and how those arrangements are being put into effect. If circumstances make it appropriate to do so, the trustees must consider whether there is a need to exercise any power of intervention that they have, and if they consider there is a need to exercise such a power, they must do so (s 22(1), TA 2000).

Section 22(4) of the TA 2000 provides that a power of intervention includes:

(a)   a power to give directions to the agent, nominee or custodian; and

(b)   a power to revoke the authorisation or appointment.

If the trustees have authorised an agent to exercise asset management functions, the duty under s 22(1) includes, in particular:

(a)   a duty to consider whether there is any need to revise or replace the policy statement made for the purposes of s 15;

(b)   if they consider that there is a need to revise or replace a policy statement, a duty to do so; and

(c)   a duty to assess whether the terms of the policy statement are being complied with.

Section 22(3) provides that s 15(3) and (4) apply to the revision or replacement of a policy statement under s 22 as they apply to the making of a policy statement under that section. Section 15(3) requires that the trustees must formulate any guidance given in the policy statement with a view to ensuring that the functions will be exercised in the best interests of the trust. Section 15(4) provides that the policy statement must be in, or evidenced in, writing.

Liability of trustees

9.25   Section 23(1) of the TA 2000 provides that a trustee is not liable for any act or default of the agent, nominee or custodian unless he has failed to comply with the duty of care applicable to him, under paragraph 3 of Schedule 1:

(a)   when entering into the arrangement under which the person acts as agent, nominee or custodian; or

(b)   when carrying out his duties under s 22.

The duty of care is defined in s 1. A trustee must exercise such care and skill as is reasonable in the circumstances, having regard in particular:

(a)   to any special knowledge or experience that he has or holds himself out as having; and

(b)   if he acts as trustee in the course of a business or profession, to any special knowledge or experience that it is reasonable to expect of a person acting in the course of that kind of business or profession.

Paragraph 3(1) of Schedule 1 provides that the duty of care applies to a trustee:

(a)   when entering into arrangements under which a person is authorised under s 11 to exercise functions as an agent;

(b)   when entering into arrangements under which a person is appointed under s 16 to act as a nominee;

(c)   when entering into arrangements under which a person is appointed under ss 17 or 18 to act as a custodian;

(d)   when entering into arrangements under which, under any power conferred by the trust instrument, a person is authorised to exercise functions as an agent or is appointed to act as a nominee or custodian;

(e)   when carrying out his duties under s 22.

Paragraph 3(2) provides that for the purposes of paragraph 3(1), entry into arrangements under which a person is authorised to exercise functions or is appointed to act as a nominee or custodian includes, in particular:

(a)   selecting a person to act;

(b)   determining any terms on which he is to act; and

(c)   if a person is being authorised to exercise asset management functions, the preparation of a policy statement under s 15.

Section 23(2) provides that if a trustee has agreed a term under which the agent, nominee or custodian is permitted to appoint a substitute, the trustee is not liable for any act or default of the substitute unless he has failed to comply with the duty of care applicable to him, under paragraph 3 of Schedule 1:

(a)   when agreeing that term; or

(b)   when carrying out his duties under s 22 in so far as they relate to the use of the substitute.

Section 24 deals with the effect of trustees exceeding their powers. If trustees exceed their powers in authorising a person to exercise a function of theirs as an agent, or in appointing a person to act as a nominee or custodian, the authorisation or appointment is still valid.

General

9.26   Section 25(1) of the TA 2000 provides that a sole trustee can exercise all the powers described above.

Section 26 provides that the powers conferred by the Act on trustees to appoint agents, nominees and custodians are in addition to powers conferred on trustees otherwise than by the Act. However, powers can be restricted or excluded by the trust instrument or by any enactment or any provision of subordinate legislation. It is uncertain whether the powers can be extended.

It is provided by s 27 that the provisions about appointing agents, nominees and custodians apply in relation to trusts whether created before or after the commencement of the Act.

DELEGATION BY INDIVIDUAL TRUSTEE

9.27   Section 5 of the Trustee Delegation Act 1999 has substituted a new s 25 in the Trustee Act 1925. Section 25(1) provides that notwithstanding any rule of law to the contrary, a trustee may, by power of attorney, delegate the execution or exercise of all or any of the trusts, powers and discretions vested in him as trustee either alone or jointly with another person or persons.

A delegation under s 25(1) commences with the date of execution of the power if the instrument makes no provision as to the commencement of the delegation, and lasts for 12 months or any shorter period specified by the instrument creating the power (s 25(2)).

Section 25(3) provides that the persons who may be donees of a power of attorney under the section include a trust corporation.

Section 25(6) sets out a form which can be used. If a donor uses this form, or a form to the like effect but expressed to be made under s 25(5), it operates to delegate to the person identified in the form as the donee of the power the execution and exercise of all the trusts, powers and discretions vested in the donor as trustee (either alone or jointly with any other person or persons) under the trust so identified.

The donor must give written notice of the giving of the power to:

(a)   each person (other than himself), if any, who under any instrument creating the trust has power (whether alone or jointly) to appoint a new trustee; and

(b)   each of the other trustees, if any.

The written notice must specify:

(a)   the date on which the power comes into operation;

(b)   its duration;

(c)   the donee of the power;

(d)   the reason why the power is given;

(e)   where some only are delegated, the trusts, powers and discretions delegated.

The notice must be given within seven days of the giving of the power (s 25(4)).

Failure to comply with subsection (4) does not invalidate any act done or instrument executed by the donee in favour of a person dealing with the donee of the power.

What happens if the donee of the power commits a breach of trust? Section 25(7) provides that the donor of the power is liable for the acts or defaults of the donee in the same manner as if they were the acts or defaults of the donor.

Section 25(8) provides that for the purpose of executing or exercising the trusts or powers delegated to him, the donee may exercise any of the powers conferred on the donor as trustee by statute or by the instrument creating the trust. This includes the power, for the purpose of the transfer of any inscribed stock, himself to delegate to an attorney power to transfer, but not including the power of delegation conferred by this section.

Section 25(9) provides that the fact that it appears from any power of attorney given under s 25, or from any evidence required for the purposes of any such power of attorney or otherwise, that in dealing with any stock the donee of the power is acting in the execution of a trust shall not be deemed for any purpose to affect any person in whose books the stock is inscribed or registered with any notice of the trust.

Section 25(10) provides that s 25 applies to a personal representative, tenant for life and statutory owner as it applies to a trustee. However, the written notice as required by s 25(4) must be given:

(a)   in the case of a personal representative, to each of the other personal representatives, if any, except any executor who has renounced probate;

(b)   in the case of a tenant for life, to the trustees of the settlement and to each person, if any, who together with the person giving the notice constitutes the tenant for life; and

(c)   in the case of a statutory owner, to each of the persons, if any, who together with the person giving the notice constitute the statutory owner and, in the case of a statutory owner by virtue of s 23(1)(a) of the Settled Land Act 1925, to the trustees of the settlement.

Readers are reminded that s 7 of the Trustee Delegation Act 1999 preserves the two trustees rule so that if land is to be sold, delegation to a sole co-trustee does not mean that the sole co-trustee can give a valid receipt for capital money. Thus if spouses are holding the legal estate on trust for themselves, and one grants a power of attorney under s 25 to the other, the donee of the power cannot give a valid receipt for capital money.

DELEGATION TO BENEFICIARY WITH AN INTEREST IN POSSESSION

9.28   Section 9 of the Trusts of Land and Appointment of Trustees Act 1996 has extended the powers of trustees to delegate, although it is a limited power.

Section 9(1) provides that trustees of land can delegate any of their functions by power of attorney. The attorney must be a beneficiary of full age, and must also be entitled to an interest in possession in land subject to the trust. The power must be given by all the trustees jointly, and may be revoked by one or more of them, unless expressed to be irrevocable and to be given by way of security. If another person is appointed trustee, the power is revoked, although the death of any of the original appointors will not cause a revocation. Similarly, if an appointor ceases to be a trustee for any reason, the power will not be revoked (s 9(3)).

The delegation can be for any period or can be indefinite (s 9(5)), but an enduring power cannot be used (s 9(6)) for the purposes of delegation of their functions under s 9(1).

Section 9(4) provides that if the attorney ceases to be a person beneficially entitled to an interest in possession in land, and is the sole attorney, the power is revoked. If there is more than one attorney, the power is still exercisable by the other beneficiaries, provided that the functions delegated to them are specified to be exercised by them jointly and not separately, and they continue to be beneficially entitled to an interest in possession in the land in question.

Section 9(7) provides that the beneficiaries to whom functions have been delegated under s 9(1) are in the same position as trustees with the same duties and liabilities. However, they are not regarded as trustees for any other purpose, including in particular any enactment permitting the delegation of functions by trustees or imposing requirements relating to the payment of capital money. So if a beneficiary to whom powers have been delegated sells the land, the proceeds of sale must be paid to at least two trustees.

The TA 2000 has inserted s 9A into the Trusts of Land and Appointment of Trustees Act 1996. This provides that the duty of care under s 1 of the TA 2000 applies to trustees of land in deciding whether to delegate any of their functions under s 9. If the trustees of land delegate any of their functions under s 9, and the delegation is not irrevocable, while the delegation continues, the trustees:

(a) must keep the delegation under review;

(b) if circumstances make it appropriate to do so, must consider whether there is a need to exercise any power of intervention that they have; and

(c) if they consider that there is a need to exercise such a power, must do so (s 9A(3)).

Section 9A(5) provides that the duty of care under s 1 of the TA 2000 applies to the carrying out of any of these duties by trustees. 'Power of intervention' includes:

(a) a power to give directions to the beneficiary; and

(b) a power to revoke the delegation.

Section 9A(6) provides that a trustee of land is not liable for any act or default of the beneficiary, or beneficiaries, unless the trustee fails to comply with the duty of care in deciding to delegate any of the trustees' functions under s 9 or in carrying out any duty under subsection (3).

Section 9(2) provides protection for persons dealing with the attorney. It provides that if a person deals with the attorney in good faith, the attorney shall be presumed to have been a person to whom the function could be delegated unless that other person has knowledge at the time of the transaction that he was not such a person.

Subsequent purchasers of land are also protected if the person dealing with the attorney makes a statutory declaration before or within three months after completion of the purchase that they dealt in good faith and did not know that the attorney was a person to whom the functions could not be delegated.

The section applies to trusts where a beneficiary has a life interest, and also to co-ownership, but there is little point in using it where the trustees and beneficiaries are the same. In the great majority of co-ownership situations the beneficiaries and trustees will be the same person. This is considered in the next section.

DELEGATION BY TRUSTEE WHO IS ALSO BENEFICIALLY INTERESTED

9.29   Section 1(1) of the Trustee Delegation Act 1999 provides that the donee of an ordinary or an enduring power of attorney or lasting power of attorney can exercise the trustee functions of the donor in relation to:

(a)   land;

(b)   capital proceeds of a conveyance of land; or

(c)   income from land.

It is immaterial whether the donor is a sole trustee or a joint trustee (s 1(2)(b)). However, the donor must have a beneficial interest in the land, proceeds or income when the act is done.

Thus if spouses hold land on trust for themselves as joint tenants, and one executes a power of attorney in favour of a child, that child will be able to exercise the trustee functions of the parent, and will be able to give a valid receipt for capital money if the land is sold. Note that s 7 preserves the two trustee rule so that if one spouse grants a power of attorney to the other and becomes mentally incapable, that spouse cannot give a valid receipt for capital money.

Section 1(1) can be excluded by the instrument which created the power of attorney, and has effect subject to the terms of that instrument (s 1(3)).

What is the position if the donee of the power does an act which would be a breach of trust if committed by the donor? Section 1(4) provides that the donor will be liable in this situation. However, the donor is not liable by reason only that the function is exercised by the donee. Section 1(4) is subject to any contrary intention expressed in the trust instrument, and has effect subject to the terms of such an instrument (s 1(5)).

Section 1(6) provides that the fact that it appears that, in dealing with any shares or stock, the donee of a power of attorney is exercising a function by virtue of s 1(1) does not affect with any notice of any trust a person in whose books the shares are, or stock is, registered or inscribed.

If the donee of a power of attorney is acting under (a) a statutory provision or (b) a provision in the instrument (if any) creating a trust, under which the donor of the power is expressly authorised to delegate the exercise of all or any of his trustee functions by power of attorney, he is acting under a trustee delegation power, and is not to be regarded as exercising a trustee function by virtue of s 1(1). Thus the attorney cannot usually delegate again.

Section 1 applies only if the donor of the power has a beneficial interest in the land. How can a purchaser from the attorney be certain that this is the case? Section 2 provides that an appropriate statement is, in favour of a purchaser, conclusive evidence that the donor of the power had a beneficial interest in the property at the time of doing the act. An 'appropriate statement' means a signed statement made by the donee:

(a)   when doing the act in question; or

(b)   at any other time within the period of three months beginning with the day on which the act is done;

that the donor has a beneficial interest in the property at the time of the donee doing the act (s 2(3)). If the appropriate statement is false, the donee is liable in the same way as he would be if the statement were contained in a statutory declaration.

Section 10(2) of the Powers of Attorney Act 1971 provides that a general power of attorney in the form set out in Schedule 1 to that Act, or a similar form, does not confer on the donee of the power any authority to exercise functions of the donor as trustee. Section 3 of the Trustee Delegation Act 1999 provides that s 10 of the 1971 Act is now subject to s 1 of the 1999 Act.

INSURANCE

9.30   Section 19 of the TA 1925 conferred on trustees a power to insure the trust property. The TA 2000 has replaced the original s 19 with a new section. The substituted s 19 provides that a trustee may insure any property which is subject to the trust against risk of loss or damage due to any event. The premiums may be paid out of the trust funds (s 19(1)). Section 19(5) provides that 'trust funds' means any income or capital funds of the trust.

Special rules apply to property held on a bare trust. Section 19(3) provides that property is held on a bare trust if it is held on trusts for:

(a)   a beneficiary who is of full age and capacity and absolutely entitled to the property which is subject to the trust; or

(b)   beneficiaries each of whom is of full age and capacity and who (taken together) are absolutely entitled to the property subject to the trust.

If property is held on a bare trust, the beneficiary or each of the beneficiaries may direct that any property specified in the direction is not to be insured, or that it is only to be insured on such conditions as may be specified (s 19(2)). If such a direction is given, the power to insure ceases to be a delegable function for the purposes of s 11 of the TA 2000 (power to employ agents).

Section 34(3) provides that the amendments made by the section apply in relation to trusts whether created before or after the commencement of the Act.

Section 20 deals with the application of any trust money. It is to be regarded as capital money, and under s 20(4) it may be applied by the trustees in rebuilding, reinstating, replacing or repairing the property lost or damaged, but any such application by the trustees shall be subject to the consent of any person whose consent is required – by the instrument, if any, creating the trust – to the investment of money subject to the trust. If it is a settlement within the Settled Land Act, any such application of the money is subject to the provisions of that Act.

Section 20(5) preserves the rights of third parties to require the insurance money to be applied in rebuilding, reinstating, replacing or repairing the property lost or damaged. Mortgagees, lessors and lessees may have the right to insist on rebuilding or reinstatement.

Possible amendments

9.31   It is common to make the following variations to the power:

(a)   s 19 does not impose any duty on the trustees to insure; such a duty could be imposed. However, this could cause difficulties if, for example, they hold property in an area prone to flooding and cannot obtain insurance. Trustees who fail to insure when they could do so are probably guilty of a breach of the duty of care;

(b)   the trustees may be given an express discretion as to whether insurance money should be used to reinstate the settled property.

INVESTMENT

9.32   The TA 2000 has substantially amended the law with regard to investment.

Section 3(1) provides that subject to the provisions of Part II of the Act, a trustee may make any kind of investment that he could make if he were absolutely entitled to the assets of the trust. Subsection (2) provides that the power under subsection (1) is called 'the general power of investment'. Section 3(3) provides that the general power of investment does not permit a trustee to make investments in land other than in loans secured on land. However, s 8 does contain a power to invest in land. Section 8 is discussed below.

There are provisions concerned with the powers of trustees to make loans secured on land. Section 3(4) provides that a person invests in a loan secured on land if he has rights under any contract under which:

(a)   one person provides another with credits; and

(b)   the obligation of the borrower to repay is secured on land.

'Credit' is given a wide meaning in s 3(5), where it is defined as including any cash loan or other financial accommodation. Section 3(6) provides that cash includes money in any form.

The general power of investment is subject to various restrictions. Section 4 lays down the standard investment criteria. Section 4(1) provides that in exercising any power of investment, a trustee must have regard to the standard investment criteria. This duty applies whether or not the powers under the Act are being exercised, and so it applies to trustees who invest under an express investment clause in a will or settlement. Section 4(2) provides that a trustee must from time to time review the investments of the trust and consider whether, having regard to the standard investment criteria, they should be varied. Section 4(3) provides that the standard investment criteria, in relation to a trust, are:

(a) the suitability to the trust of investments of the same kind as any particular investment proposed to be made or retained and of that particular investment as an investment of that kind; and

(b) the need for diversification of investments of the trust in so far as is appropriate to the circumstances of the trust.

A trustee is also under a duty to obtain advice, whether investing under the Act, or an express power of investment. Section 5(1) provides that before exercising any power of investment, a trustee must obtain and consider proper advice about the way in which, having regard to the standard investment criteria, the power should be exercised. The duty to obtain and consider advice also applies when trustees are reviewing the investments of the trust. Section 5(2) provides that a trustee must obtain and consider proper advice about whether, having regard to the standard investment criteria, the investments should be varied. Section 5(3) provides that a trustee need not obtain such advice if he reasonably concludes that in all the circumstances it is unnecessary or inappropriate do so. If the trust fund is large, trustees cannot reasonably claim it is inappropriate. On the other hand, if the trust fund is under £100 it would be reasonable for a trustee to conclude that it was unnecessary and inappropriate. 'Proper advice' is defined in s 5(4) as the advice of a person who is reasonably believed by the trustee to be qualified to give it due to his ability and practical experience of financial and other matters relating to the proposed investment.

The general power of investment is in addition to powers conferred on trustees otherwise than by the Act, but it is subject to any restriction or exclusion imposed by the trust instrument or by any enactment or any provision of subordinate legislation (s 6(1)). Section 6(2) provides that for the purposes of the Act, an enactment or a provision of subordinate legislation is not to be regarded as being, or as being part of, a trust instrument.

What effect do ss 3, 4, 5 and 6 have on existing trusts? Section 7(1) provides that they apply to trusts whether created before or after the commencement of the Act. However, there are various exceptions to this provision.

Section 7(2) provides that no provision relating to the powers of a trustee contained in a trust instrument made before 3 August 1961 is to be treated (for the purposes of s 6(1)(b)) as restricting or excluding the general power of investment. This means that trustees of a trust made before 3 August 1961 have the general power of investment.

Section 7(3) provides that a provision contained in a trust instrument made before the commencement of Part II which:

(a) has effect under s 3(2) of the Trustee Investments Act 1961 as a power to invest under that Act; or

(b) confers power to invest under that Act;

is to be treated as conferring the general power of investment on a trustee.

This means that if trustees are authorised to invest under the Trustee Investments Act 1961, they now have the general powers of investment as a trustee.

It should be noted that Part II of Schedule 2 to the Act contains provisions dealing with the investment of the proceeds of sale of settled land.

Acquisition of land

9.33   Part III of the Act contains default powers for trustees to acquire freehold and leasehold land.

Section 8(1) provides that a trustee may acquire freehold or leasehold land in the UK:

(a)   as an investment;

(b)   for occupation by a beneficiary; or

(c)   or any other reason.

Section 8(2) provides that 'freehold or leasehold land' means:

(a)   in relation to England and Wales, a legal estate in land;

(b)   in relation to Scotland:

    (i)   the estate or interest of the proprietor of the *dominium utile* or, in the case of land not held on feudal tenure, the estate or interest of the owner; or

    (ii)   a tenancy; and

(c)   in relation to Northern Ireland, a legal estate in land, including land held under a fee farm grant.

Generally, the Act applies to personal representatives administering an estate according to the law as it applies to a trustee carrying out a trust for beneficiaries (s 35(1)). However, the definition of a beneficiary under s 8(1)(b) is to be read as a reference to the person who under the will of the deceased or under the law relating to intestacy is beneficially interested in the estate. This provision is necessary as otherwise a creditor might come within the definition of a beneficiary.

Section 9(a) provides that the powers conferred by Part III are in addition to powers conferred on trustees otherwise than by that part. This means that if the trustees already have power to invest in land under the will or settlement, they do not need to make use of the powers contained in the Act. However, if the will or settlement specifically prohibits the trustees from investing in land, then they cannot do so. Section 9(b) provides that the powers conferred by the Act are subject to any restriction or exclusion imposed by the trust instrument or by any enactment or any provision of subordinate legislation.

Section 10 contains provisions dealing with existing trusts. Section 10(1) provides that Part III of the Act does not apply in relation to a trust of property which consists of or includes land which is settled land (despite s 2 of the Trusts of Land and Appointment of Trustees Act 1996). Nor does it apply to a trust to which the Universities and Colleges Estates Act 1925 applies.

Subject to this, Part III applies to trusts whether created before or after its commencement (s 10(2)).

Section 8(3) provides that for the purpose of exercising his functions as a trustee, a trustee who acquires land under this section has all the powers of an absolute owner in relation to the land.

Section 6(3) of the Trusts of Land and Appointment of Trustees Act 1996 provides that trustees of land have the power to acquire land under the power conferred by s 8 of the Trustee Act 2000.

Section 6(5) provides that in exercising the powers conferred by the section, the trustees must have regard to the rights of the beneficiaries. Section 6(6) provides that the powers conferred by the section shall not be exercised in contravention of, or of any order made in pursuance of, any other enactment or any rule of law or equity.

Section 6(7) states that the reference to an order in subsection (6) includes an order of any court or of the Charity commissioners. Section 6(8) provides that where any enactment other than s 6 confers on trustees authority to act subject to any restriction, limitation or condition, trustees of land may not exercise the powers conferred by s 6 to do any act which they are prevented from doing under the other enactment by reason of the restriction, limitation or condition. Section 6(9) (inserted by the Trustee Act 2000) provides that the duty of care under s 1 of the Trustee Act 2000 applies to trustees of land when exercising the powers conferred by this section.

General duties with regard to investment

9.34   The duty of care applies to a trustee:

(a)   when exercising the general power of investment conferred on him by the trust instrument;

(b)   when carrying out a duty to which he is subject under ss 4 or 5 (duties relating to the exercise of a power of investment or to the review of investments) (Schedule 1, paragraph 1).

Section 1 defines the duty of care. A trustee must exercise such care and skill as is reasonable in the circumstances, having regard in particular:

(a)   to any special knowledge or experience that he has or holds himself out as having; and

(b)   if he acts as trustee in the course of a business or profession, to any special knowledge or experience that it is reasonable to expect of a person acting in the course of that kind of business or occupation.

Express powers of investment

9.35   Most, if not all, professionally drawn wills and settlements contain an express investment clause; frequently these will authorise the trustees to invest the trust funds as if they were the absolute owners. It has now been established that this means what it says – trustees can invest in appropriate investments (*Re Harari's Settlement Trusts [1949] 1 All ER 430*).

There is also some doubt about the meaning of the word 'invest'. Is it confined to assets which yield income, or does it include assets which are purchased in the hope that they will show large capital gains? There are some old cases where it has been held that assets purchased in the hope that they will increase in value are not 'investments'. However, in *Marson v Morton [1986] 1 WLR 1343*, a tax case, Sir Nicolas Browne-Wilkinson said at page 1350, 'But in my judgment in 1986 it is not any longer self-evident that unless land is producing income it cannot be an investment'.

Even though trustees may have wide powers of investment, it should be remembered that trustees are still subject to s 4 of the TA 2000, and the general duties imposed on trustees with regard to investment.

Express power to lend money on mortgage

9.36   Express investment powers frequently include a power to lend money to a beneficiary. The trustees may also be empowered not to charge any interest, and to make the loan without any security. Even though the express power may be very wide, the trustees must still have regard to the duties imposed by s 4 of the TA 2000. Thus it would normally be wrong for trustees to lend all the trust money on mortgage, although there may be exceptional circumstances where this is justified. Furthermore, trustees are under a duty to hold the balance fairly between the life tenant and the remainderman, and whilst a mortgage may satisfy the needs of a life tenant for income, there will be little capital appreciation to satisfy the needs of the remainderman. A mortgage where the amount of capital to be repaid and the rate of interest are both linked to other currencies as in *Multiservice Bookbinding Ltd v Marden [1979] Ch 84* may satisfy both the remainderman and the life tenant, but equally could disappoint depending on currency movements – unless carefully drafted, such a mortgage may not be permitted.

An unsecured loan to a beneficiary may be unfair to the remainderman as it may never be repaid. On the other hand, an interest free loan to the remainderman, or a loan at a low rate of interest to a beneficiary, may be unfair to the life tenant.

THE POWER OF MAINTENANCE

9.37   Section 31 of the TA 1925 contains a power of maintenance. This authorises the trustees to apply the whole of the income of a trust fund for the maintenance, education or benefit of a beneficiary.

When does s 31 apply?

9.38   Section 31 clearly applies to vested gifts, where the beneficiary will be entitled to the income, but in the case of a contingent interest s 31(3) states that it applies to a contingent interest only if the limitation or trust carries the intermediate income of the property.

Which contingent gifts carry the intermediate income? The law in this area is quite complicated, but the following gifts will carry the intermediate income:

(a)   a contingent or future specific devise or bequest of real or personal property – 'I give Blackacre to A if he becomes a doctor', or 'I give Blackacre to A after B has qualified as a doctor';

(b)   a contingent residuary devise of freehold land;

(c)   a specific or residuary devise of freehold land to trustees upon trust for persons whose interests are contingent or executory (s 175 of the Law of Property Act 1925);

(d)   contingent bequest of residuary personalty (*Re Adams [1893] 1 Ch 329*).

A contingent pecuniary legacy – 'I give £10,000 to A if he qualifies as a doctor' – does not normally carry interest until the time when it is payable. However, in the following situations, the gift will carry the intermediate income:

(a)   if the donor has shown an intention that the income should be applied for the maintenance of the beneficiary;

(b)   if the testator is the parent of the beneficiary, or stands in loco parentis to the beneficiary, the testator has not made any other provision for the beneficiary, the gift is directly to the beneficiary, and the condition to be satisfied is attaining an age no greater than 18;

(c)   if the testator has directed that the legacy should be set aside for the benefit of a beneficiary.

Section 31(3) provides that the section also applies to a future or contingent legacy by the parent of, or by a person standing *in loco parentis* to, the legatee, if and for such period as, under the general law, the legacy carries interest for the maintenance of the legatee. This is very similar to (b) above.

How is the power exercisable?

9.39   Section 31(1), TA 1925 provides that the trustees may, at their sole discretion, pay to the beneficiary's parent or guardian, if any, or otherwise apply for his benefit or towards his maintenance, education or benefit, the whole or such part, if any, of the income of that property as may, in all the circumstances, be reasonable, whether or not there is:

(a)   any other fund applicable for the same purpose; or

(b)   any person bound by law to provide for his maintenance or education.

What factors should the trustees take into account in deciding whether or not to exercise their discretion?

9.40   There is a proviso to s 31 of the TA 1925 which requires trustees to have regard to the following matters in deciding whether or not to apply the income for the maintenance, education or benefit of a beneficiary. These are as follows:

(a)   the age of the infant;

(b)   the requirements of the infant;

(c)   the circumstances of the case;

(d)   other income applicable for the same purpose;

(e)   if the income of more than one fund is applicable for the maintenance, education or benefit of the infant, a proportionate part only of the income of each fund shall be so paid or applied.

The effect of that proviso is to impose an objective test on the trustees, and to remove some of their discretion.

Entitlement at 18

9.41   A beneficiary who does not attain a vested interest at 18 is entitled to the income until he either attains a vested interest or dies, or until the failure of his interest (s 31(1)(ii), TA 1925).

Thus if there is a gift to a beneficiary contingent on the beneficiary attaining 30, and s 31 applies, the beneficiary will be entitled to the income at the age of 18, although he will not be entitled to the capital until the age of 30.

What happens to any income which is not applied for the benefit of the beneficiaries?

9.42   If any of the income is not applied for the maintenance, education or benefit of the beneficiary, it must be accumulated and invested. It must then be paid to a beneficiary who:

(a)   attains the age of 18 years, or marries under that age, and his interest in such income during his infancy or until his marriage is a vested interest; or

(b)   on attaining the age of 18 years or on marriage under that age becomes entitled to the property from which such income arose in fee simple, absolute or determinable, or absolutely, or for an entailed interest (s 31(2)).

Note that under (b) a beneficiary must become absolutely entitled to personalty, or have an entailed interest; a beneficiary with a conditional or determinable interest in personalty will not be entitled to the accumulated income on attaining 18 or on marriage. The position is different if the subject matter of the gift is land. 'Absolute' means complete beneficial ownership and dominion over property. It does not include an interest which can be destroyed at any time by the exercise of a power or the fulfilment of a condition with the consequence that the property must be retained by the trustees until the power or condition is spent (*Re Sharp's Settlement Trust [1972] 3 WLR 765* at page 769).

Section 31(2)(ii) provides that in any other case the trustees shall, notwithstanding that such person had a vested interest in such income, hold the accumulations as an accretion to the capital of the property from which such accumulations arose, and as one fund with such capital for all purposes. If such property is settled land, such accumulations are to be held upon the same trusts as if the same were capital money arising from the settled land.

The receipt of a married infant is a good discharge.

Class gifts

9.43   If there is a contingent class gift, the trustees are entitled to treat the share of each potential beneficiary separately, and to apply the income of each potential beneficiary's share for the maintenance of that beneficiary even if one or more beneficiary has satisfied the contingency (*Re Holford [1894] 3 Ch 30*). If a beneficiary dies without satisfying the contingency, any accumulated income accrues to the other beneficiaries as capital.

Express power of maintenance and prohibition on benefiting settlor

9.44   In *Fuller v Evans [2000] 1 All ER 636*, the settlor created an accumulation and maintenance settlement for the benefit of his children. The trustees had power to provide for the maintenance and education of the children. Clause 12 of the settlement prohibited the trustees from exercising their power in such manner that the settlor would or might become entitled either directly or indirectly to any benefit in any manner or in any circumstances whatsoever. There was a divorce, and the settlor agreed to pay for the children's maintenance and school fees. The trustees were concerned that if they exercised their power of maintenance, they would indirectly benefit the settlor, and would infringe clause 12 of the settlement. It was held that if the trustees did exercise their power of maintenance, they would not infringe clause 12.

Common variations

9.45   It is common to make the following variations to the statutory power of maintenance:

(a)   the trustees are given a complete discretion as to whether the income should be applied for the maintenance, education or benefit of a beneficiary;

(b)   the entitlement to income may be postponed to an age greater than 18.

POWERS WITH REGARD TO MINORS

9.46   Personal representatives and trustees cannot pay the income or hand the capital to a minor, but there are various exceptions to this rule. They are:

(a)   under s 21 of the Law of Property Act 1925, a married infant has power to give a valid receipt for all income but not capital. As an infant has to be 16 years of age to marry, this is a very limited exception as it can only apply for two years;

(b)   s 31 of the Trustee Act 1925 authorises trustees to apply income for the maintenance of an infant beneficiary. Such payments are to be made to the parent or guardian of the child. Section 32 authorises the advancement of a maximum of one-half of the capital;

(c)   payment into court. Section 63(1) of the Trustee Act 1925 provides that trustees, or the majority of trustees, having in their hands or under their control money or securities belonging to a trust, may pay the same into court. Section 63(2) provides that the receipt of the proper officer shall be a sufficient discharge to trustees for the money or securities so paid into court;

(d)   the will or trust instrument may authorise payment to the infant or to the guardian or parent of the child;

(e)   s 42 of the Administration of Estates Act 1925 applies where the will does not appoint trustees, and the infant is absolutely entitled. The personal representatives can then appoint a trust corporation or two or more individuals not exceeding four (whether or not including the personal representatives) to be trustees.

Note that s 42 only applies if the will does not appoint trustees, and the infant must be absolutely entitled;

(f)   s 41 of the Administration of Estates Act 1925 enables personal representatives to appropriate any asset in satisfaction of any legacy if the beneficiaries agree. In the case of an infant beneficiary, the consent can be given by the parent or guardian of the infant.

POWER OF TRUSTEES TO GIVE RECEIPTS

9.47   Section 14(1) of the TA 1925 provides that the receipt in writing of a trustee for any money, securities, investments or other personal property or effects payable, transferable, or deliverable to him under any trust or power shall be a sufficient discharge to the person paying, transferring, or delivering the same and shall effectually exonerate him.

Section 14(2) provides that the section does not, except where the trustee is a trust corporation, enable a sole trustee to give a valid receipt for:

(a)   the proceeds of sale or other capital money arising under a trust of land;

(b)   capital money arising under the Settled Land Act 1925.

It is not possible to displace this section by a provision in the trust deed.

Note that a sole personal representative can give a valid receipt for capital; see **para 8.3**.

SALE

The powers

9.48   Trustees have extensive powers to sell trust property. If the trust property consists of land, it will be a Settled Land Act settlement, or a trust for sale, or a trust of land. As a result of the Trusts of Land and Appointment of Trustees Act 1996 (TLATA 1996), it has not been possible since 1 January 1997 to create Settled Land Act settlements, although those created before that date remain in existence. If it is a Settled Land Act settlement, the tenant for life can sell the property (s 38(1) of the Settled Land Act 1925 (SLA 1925)), although the purchase price will have to be paid to at least two trustees or a trust corporation (s 94(1), SLA 1925). If it is a trust of land or trust for sale, the trustees have the power to sell the trust property (s 6(1), TLATA 1996), although again the purchaser must pay the purchase price to at least two trustees or a trust corporation (s 27(2) of the Law of Property Act 1925).

Section 8(1) of the TLATA 1996 provides that s 6 of the 1996 Act can be excluded, and s 8(2) provides that if any consent is required for the exercise of the power, the power may not be exercised without that consent. Section 10(1) of the TLATA 1996 provides that if the consent of more than two persons is required for the exercise by the trustees of any function relating to land, a purchaser need only satisfy himself that the consent of any two has been obtained. However, purchasers dealing with trustees of land held on charitable, ecclesiastical or public trusts must ensure that all appropriate consents have been obtained (s 10(2), TLATA 1996)).

It should be noted that the provisions of the 1996 Act apply to all trusts whenever created, apart from land which is settled land or land to which the Universities and Colleges Estates Act 1925 applies (s 1, TLATA 1996).

The 1996 Act provides that trustees are also under a duty to consult the beneficiaries of full age and beneficially entitled to an interest in possession in the land so far as practicable (s 11(1)). They must give effect to the wishes of those beneficiaries so far as consistent with the general interest of the trust; if there is a dispute, the views of the majority by value prevail (s 11(1)). The duty to consult can be excluded, and will not normally apply to a trust created before the TLATA 1996 came into force (1 January 1997), or to a trust created or arising under a will made before 1 January 1997 (s 11(2)), or in the case of a transfer to all the beneficiaries if they are of full age and capacity and absolutely entitled.

Suppose that T1 and T2 are the trustees of a settlement under which A is the life tenant. T1 and T2 are under a duty to consult A about the operation of the trust. If A wants any land in the trust to be sold, T1 and T2 must give effect to those wishes unless advised by a valuer that it would be best not to sell the land until the next year.

Section 18(1) of the TLATA 1996 provides that ss 10 and 11 of the Act do not apply to personal representatives. A sole personal representative can sell and give a valid receipt for capital.

Chattels may also be subject to an express trust with a power of sale, or it may be implied, for example, under s 33 of the Administration of Estates Act 1925 when a person dies intestate. In the case of other property, for example stocks and shares, it is probable that there is an implied power of sale.

Section 16 of the TA 1925 provides that where trustees are authorised by the trust instrument or by law to pay capital money subject to the trust, they can raise such money by the sale or mortgage of all or any part of the trust property for the time being in possession.

Section 212 of the Inheritance Tax Act 1984 provides that a person liable for IHT other than the transferor or the transferor's spouse has power to sell the property for the purpose of paying the IHT.

Method of sale

9.49 Section 12 of the Trustee Act 1925 confers a wide discretion on the trustees as to the mode of sale. It provides that where a trustee has a duty or power to sell property, he may sell or concur with any other person in selling all or any part of the property, either subject to prior charges or not, and either together or in lots, by public auction or by private contract, subject to any such conditions respecting title or evidence of title or other matter as the trustee thinks fit, with power to vary any contract for sale, and to buy in at any auction, or to rescind any contract for resale and to resell, without being answerable for any loss.

Section 12(2) provides that a trust or power to sell or dispose of land includes a trust or power to sell or dispose of part thereof, whether the division is horizontal, vertical, or made in any other way.

Duty of trustees

9.50 It is the duty of trustees to obtain the best possible price for trust property (*Buttle v Saunders [1950] 2 All ER 193*). Thus although trustees have a wide discretion as to the mode of sale, they should choose the method which is likely to yield the best price.

Protection of purchasers of land

9.51 Section 16 of the TLATA 1996 contains provisions for the protection of purchasers. It does not apply if the title is registered.

Section 16(1) provides that a purchaser of land which is or has been subject to a trust need not be concerned to see that any requirement imposed on the trustees by ss 6(5), 7(3) or 11(1) has been complied with. Section 6(5) provides that, in exercising the powers conferred by the section, the trustees must have regard to the rights of the beneficiaries. Section 7 is concerned with the partition of the land subject to a trust, and provides that before exercising their powers, the trustees must obtain the consent of the beneficiaries. Section 11(1) imposes a duty on trustees to consult the beneficiaries.

Section 16(2) provides that if trustees convey land and contravene s 6(6) or (8), but the purchaser from the trustees has no actual notice of contravention, the contravention does not invalidate the conveyance. Section 6(6) provides that the powers conferred by s 6 must not be exercised in contravention of, or of any order made in pursuance of, any enactment or any rule of law or equity. Section 6(8) provides that where any enactment other than s 6 confers on the trustees authority to act subject to any restriction, limitation or condition, trustees of land may not exercise the powers conferred by s 6 to do any act which they are prevented from doing under the other enactment by reason of the restriction, limitation or condition.

Section 16(3) provides that where the powers of the trustees of land are limited:

(a)   the trustees must take all reasonable steps to bring the limitation to the notice of any purchaser of the land from them; but

(b)   the limitation does not invalidate any conveyance by the trustees to a purchaser who has no actual notice of the limitation.

Section 16(2) and (3) do not apply to land held on charitable, ecclesiastical or public trusts.

Section 16(4) provides that where land which is subject to the trust is conveyed by the trustees to persons believed by them to be beneficiaries absolutely entitled to the land and of full age and capacity, the trustees must execute a deed declaring that they are discharged from the trust in relation to the land. If they fail to do so, the court may make an order requiring them to do so. Section 16(5) provides that a purchaser of land to which a deed under subsection (4) relates is entitled to assume that, as from the date of the deed, the land is not subject to the trust unless he has actual notice that the trustees were mistaken in their belief that the land was conveyed to beneficiaries absolutely entitled to the land under the trust and of full age and capacity.

POWER TO CONVEY THE LAND TO BENEFICIARIES

9.52   Section 6(2) of the TLATA 1996 permits the trustees to convey the land to the beneficiaries if they are all of full age and capacity, even if the beneficiaries have not required the trustees to do so. The beneficiaries must do whatever is necessary to ensure that the land vests in them, for example, they must get themselves registered as proprietors of the land. If the beneficiaries fail to do so, the court may make an order requiring them to do so.

POWER TO PARTITION LAND

9.53   The trustees have power to partition the land under s 7 of the TLATA 1996 where the beneficiaries (a) are of full age and absolutely entitled in undivided shares to land subject to the trust, and (b) agree to the partition. The trustees may provide for the payment of any equality money by way of mortgage or otherwise.

Where a share in the land is affected by an incumbrance, the trustees may either give effect to it, or provide for its discharge from the property allotted to that share as they think fit (s 7(4)).

If a share in land is absolutely vested in a minor, the provisions of s 7 apply as if he were of full age, except that the trustees may act on his behalf and retain land or other property representing his share in trust for him (s 7(5)).

ARE TRUSTEES UNDER A DUTY TO EXERCISE POWERS OF APPOINTMENT?

9.54   There may be an express power in a will or settlement authorising a person to appoint the property amongst the members of a class of beneficiaries.

If there is a discretionary trust, the trustees have a discretion as to which member of the class of beneficiaries they benefit, and in what proportions.

The cases distinguish between trust or fiduciary powers and bare or ordinary powers as the duties owed by the person holding the power depend on whether it is a trust power or bare or ordinary power. It can be very difficult to decide if a power is a trust power or an ordinary power. The distinction between trustee powers and bare powers is to a large extent irrelevant if the power is held by a trustee as the trustee will owe duties to the beneficiaries because they are trustees.

Duties of donees with a trust power of appointment

9.55   If it is a trust power, or the power is held by trustees, then the trustees owe duties to the beneficiaries.

That does not mean that the trustees must exercise the power. However, they cannot sit back and do nothing.They must consider whether to exercise the power. They may decide not to exercise the power, and there is little the beneficiaries can do about that. They may decide to benefit one member of the class of beneficiaries excluding all the others. It could be very difficult to challenge that, but what they cannot do is to refuse to exercise the power.

It would be difficult for the court to make an order that they should exercise the power – how would a court enforce it? So if a person with a trustee power refuses to exercise it, the court will not normally order them to exercise it. The court may remove the trustees, and appoint new ones, or it may exercise the power of appointment itself. The court may also invite the beneficiaries to agree on a scheme of distribution.

Trustees of discretionary trusts

9.56   Trustees of a discretionary trust have a discretion as to which member or members of the class they benefit. What duties are trustees under with regard to this discretion?

They cannot ignore it. They must consider whether or not to exercise the power. If they do take into consideration all relevant factors and decide not to exercise the discretion, the courts will not intervene. However, if the trustees do nothing, then the court will intervene.

Chapter 10

Completion of the administration

OVERVIEW

10.1   Once the personal representatives have settled all the liabilities including the liability for income tax, capital gains tax or inheritance tax, then they can distribute the assets to the beneficiaries. Often this is the easy stage in administering an estate, but there can be problems.

TIME LIMIT FOR COMPLETING THE ADMINISTRATION OF THE ESTATE

10.2   Section 44 of the Administration of Estates Act 1925 (AEA 1925) provides that a personal representative is not bound to distribute the estate of the deceased before the expiration of one year from the date of death.

If there are few assets in the estate, it should be possible to distribute them within the year. However, in more complicated estates, the personal representatives may struggle to complete the administration within a year; it may take several years.

WHO IS ENTITLED?

10.3   Personal representatives are under a duty to distribute the assets of the deceased to the correct persons, and if they do not do so, they may be personally liable to the disappointed beneficiaries.

In the great majority of cases, there is no problem with regard to this. However, even in apparently straightforward cases, caution may be desirable.

Gifts to children

10.4   Where a gift is made in a will to children or grandchildren, it will include legitimate, legitimated, illegitimate, adopted children, and in the case of a man, children conceived before death but not born until after death. It will not usually include stepchildren.

The same rule applies if the deceased died intestate, although it is clear that stepchildren cannot take on the intestacy of a stepparent.

It may be difficult for personal representatives to ascertain the exact number of children and grandchildren. Some protection is afforded to personal representatives as regards adopted and legitmated children (see **para 8.19**). However, this protection does not extend to illegitimate children, and so personal representatives must rely upon advertisements under s 27 of the Trustee Act 1925 (TA 1925) (see **para 8.19**) for protection against claims by unknown children of the deceased. As stated in **para 8.19**, s 27 advertisements probably do not protect personal representatives from claims of which they are aware, but may not be correct. So if a man dies intestate, and leaves no spouse or parents, then brothers and sisters will be entitled to the estate. However, if it comes to the notice of the personal representatives that the deceased might have fathered a child, then s 27 advertisements probably do not protect the personal representatives, and they must make enquiries about these children.

If there is any doubt about paternity, then it may be that DNA analysis will have to be used to determine fatherhood.

It may be desirable to check birth certificates, particularly with adopted children, as frequently there is a confusion in lay minds between fostering and adoption. However, even a birth certificate is not conclusive evidence as to parentage – it merely raises a presumption. In *Duckett v Backhurst [2006] WTLR 1729*, FKC was registered as the mother of PMD. It was alleged that this was incorrect, and that MP was the mother.

It was stated that if parentage were disputed, then the law was:

(a)   the burden of proof lies upon the one who seeks to establish that person's entitlement by reference to their parentage;

(b)   the standard or proof is on the balance of probabilities;

(c)   a birth certificate is *prima facie* evidence of its contents;

(d)   the presumption in (c) can be displaced by other evidence;

(e)   the exercise is for the court to decide on the balance of probabilities whether the presumption had been displaced, bearing in mind that evidence of appropriate quality is required, and if it has been displaced, to decide whether other evidence, supportive of it, has reinstated, again on the balance of probabilities, the accuracy of its contents.

On the evidence, it was held that MP was the mother.

Frequently gifts in wills to grandchildren, or the children of a named person, will specify that it is only the children or grandchildren living at the date of death of the testator who are to take. If that is not the case, personal representatives must have regard to the class closing rules. These close the class, and are necessary because otherwise it might be impossible to complete the administration of the estate. A gift to all my grandchildren would be very hard to operate if there were no class closing rules – the gift would have to remain open until the personal representatives were certain that there would be no more grandchildren. However, even with class closing rules, the gift may have to remain open for years. If there is a gift to all my grandchildren, and there are grandchildren living at the date of death, then those living at that date or *en ventre sa mère* take. If there are no such grandchildren, then the class remains open indefinitely.

Portions

10.5   There is a rule against double portions. What is a portion? It is a gift made by a father or person *in loco parentis* to a child, which is made for the purpose of establishing the child in life, or of making a permanent provision for him. If the will of the father or person *in loco parentis* to the child contains a legacy or gift of residue to that child, there is a presumption that the legacy or gift of the residue is satisfied by the portion either wholly or in part. This is all subject to contrary intention.

In *Casimir v Alexander [2001] WTLR 939*, L provided the finance to enable his daughter S to purchase a house as a residence for L, S and her children. He made a will in June 1985 appointing S as his executor. The will contained a specific bequest of all his furniture, and the residuary estate was given in different proportions to S, her two brothers, C and T, and any grandchildren living at the date of L's death.

L died in 1990. C commenced proceedings alleging that S had exerted undue influence in order to persuade L to purchase the house in her name. He also alleged that if the purchase had been a gift, it should be brought into account on the distribution of the residuary estate.

Both these allegations were dismissed.

The evidence showed that L had intended to make a gift, and also that this gift should not be brought into account on the distribution of the residuary estate.

In *Race v Race [2002] WTLR 1193*, MR and JR were brother and sister. Their father executed a will providing that JR could live in a public house for the rest of her life, and that the proceeds should then be treated as part of the residue, which was to be divided equally between MR and JR.

Subsequently, the father gave the public house to JR.

It was held that both gifts were portions, and that the one adeemed the other. A portion was defined as a gift intended to establish a child in life, or make some provision for him. It was distinguished from a gift or present.

Deceased beneficiaries

10.6   Normally if a beneficiary predeceases a testator, the gift to that beneficiary lapses. However, there are the following exceptions to this rule:

(a)   wills frequently contain an express substitution clause;

(b)   s 33 of the Wills Act 1837 (WA 1837) provides that if a child or remoter issue of the testator predeceases leaving issue the issue will take the share their parent would have taken had he or she survived. Section 33(1) provides that where:

    (i)   a will contains a devise or bequest to a child or remoter descendant of the testator; and

(ii) the intended beneficiary dies before the testator, leaving issue; and

(iii) issue of the intended beneficiary are living at the testator's death;

then, unless a contrary intention appears by the will, the devise or bequest shall take effect as a devise or bequest to the issue living at the testator's death.

Section 33(2) provides that where:

(a) a will contains a devise or bequest to a class of persons consisting of children or remoter descendants of the testator; and

(b) a member of the class dies before the testator leaving issue; and

(c) issue of that member are living at the testator's death;

then, unless a contrary intention appears by the will, the devise or bequest shall take effect as if the class included the issue of its deceased member living at the testator's death.

Section 33(3) provides that issue shall take under this section through all degrees, according to their stock, in equal shares if more than one, any gift or share which their parent would have taken and so that no issue shall take whose parent is living at the testator's death and so capable of taking.

Section 33(4) provides that for the purposes of the section:

(a) the illegitimacy of any person is to be disregarded; and

(b) a person conceived before the testator's death and born living thereafter is to be taken to have been living at the testator's death.

Note that there is no contingent entitlement under the section. If it applies, the issue of a deceased beneficiary are entitled even though they may be very small children.

If the deceased died intestate, then the children of the deceased are entitled on the statutory trusts. Section 47(1)(i) of the AEA 1925 defines these as in trust, in equal shares if more than one, for all or any children or child of the intestate, living at the death of the intestate, who attain the age of 18 years or marry under that age or enter into a civil partnership. If any child of the intestate predeceases the intestate leaving issue living at the death of the intestate, the issue are entitled provided they attain the age of 18 years or marry under that age or enter into a civil partnership. The issue take through all degrees, according to their stocks, in equal shares if more than one, the share their parent would have taken if living at the death of the intestate. In addition, no issue can take whose parent was living at the death of the intestate and so capable of taking.

Thus if a child of the intestate has predeceased the intestate leaving three children, those children will take the share their parent would have taken had he or she survived. Each grandchild must attain 18 or marry under that age in order to take; if one does not, then his or her share will accrue to his or her brothers and sisters.

Construction of wills

10.7   It is to be hoped that if the will has been professionally drafted there will not be any problems with regard to interpretation. However, if there are problems, the following approaches can be adopted:

(a)   if all the affected beneficiaries are of full age and capacity, they could be asked to agree to one particular interpretation. If they are not of full age and capacity because they are minors, and the amount of money or property involved is small, then the parents may be asked to agree to a compromise on their behalf with suitable indemnities to the personal representatives. If the amount of assets or money involved is large, then it may be that the beneficiaries should have independent advice;

(b)   make use of s 48 of the Administration of Justice Act 1985 (AJA 1985).

Section 48(1) of the AJA 1985 provides that where:

(i)   any question of construction has arisen out of the terms of a will or a trust; and

(ii)   an opinion in writing given by a person who has a ten-year High Court qualification, within the meaning of s 71 of the Courts and Legal Services Act 1990, has been obtained on that question by the personal representatives or trustees under the will or trust, the High Court may, on the application of the personal representatives or trustees and without hearing argument, make an order authorising those persons to take such steps in reliance on the said opinion as are specified in the order.

Subsection (2) of the AJA 1985 provides that the High Court shall not make an order if it appears that a dispute exists which would make it inappropriate for the court to make the order without hearing argument;

(c)   in certain circumstances it is possible to apply for rectification of a will. Section 20(1) of the AJA 1982 provides that if a court is satisfied that a will is so expressed that it fails to carry out the testator's intentions, in consequence of:

(i)   a clerical error; or

(ii)   a failure to understand his instructions;

it may order the will to be rectified so as to carry out his intentions.

Section 20(2) provides that an application for an order under the section shall not, except with the leave of the court, be made after the end of the period of six months from the date on which representation with respect to the estate of the deceased is first taken out. In deciding if leave should be granted, the courts apply the same principles as they would in deciding whether to grant leave for an application out of time under the Inheritance (Provision for Family and Dependants) Act 1975.

Rule 55(1) of the NCPR 1987 provides that an application for an order that a will be rectified by virtue of s 20(1) of the AJA 1982 may be made to a District Judge or Registrar, unless a probate action has been commenced. Rule 55(2) provides that the application must be supported by an affidavit, setting out the grounds of the application, together with such evidence as to the testator's intentions and as to whichever of the following matters as are in issue:

(a)   in what respects the testator's intentions were not understood; or

(b)   the nature of an alleged clerical error.

Rule 55(3) provides that unless otherwise directed, notice of the application must be given to every person having an interest under the will whose interests might be prejudiced, or such other person who might be prejudiced, by the rectification applied for and any comments in writing by any such person must be exhibited to the affidavit in support of the application.

Rule 55(4) provides that if the District Judge or Registrar is satisfied that, subject to any direction to the contrary, notice has been given to every person mentioned in paragraph (3) above, and that application is unopposed, he may order that the will be rectified accordingly.

Missing beneficiaries

10.8   It is sometimes difficult to trace missing beneficiaries. This is particularly true of the person who has died intestate in their eighties without a spouse or children, but with many brothers and sisters. In such a situation it may be wise to take out a missing beneficiary indemnity policy. In all cases where this is a possibility, ask the insurance company what enquiries they require to be made before they will issue the policy. Subject to this:

(a)   make enquiries of the living relatives;

(b)   make use of the various search facilities available through the internet;

(c)   advertise in appropriate newspapers and other publications;

(d)   employ enquiry agents, or tracing agencies;

(e)   distribute the estate to those entitled as if the missing beneficiary had died without issue having first obtained an indemnity from the persons to whom the estate is distributed. Ideally, the indemnity should be secured by a charge over property. The disadvantage of this is that it might be difficult to enforce the indemnity, particularly if it is not supported by a charge, but this may be the easiest and cheapest solution if the value of the assets involved is small;

(f)   apply to the court for an order to distribute the estate on the basis that a beneficiary is dead. These orders are known as *Benjamin* orders.

Divorce and decrees of dissolution

10.9   The divorce of the testator does not automatically revoke a will. Instead, any gift to the former spouse lapses, and any appointment of the former spouse as executor or trustee also lapses. Section 18A of the Wills Act 1837 (WA 1837) provides:

'(1) Where, after a testator has made a will, an order or decree of a court of civil jurisdiction in England and Wales dissolves or annuls his marriage or his marriage is dissolved or annulled and the divorce or annulment is entitled to recognition in England and Wales by virtue of Part II of the Family Law Act 1986, –

(a) provisions of the will appointing executors or trustees or conferring a power of appointment, if they appoint or confer the power on the former spouse, shall take effect as if the former spouse had died on the date on which the marriage is dissolved or annulled, and

(b) any property which, or an interest in which, is devised or bequeathed to the former spouse shall pass as if the former spouse had died on that date.'

Section 18A(2) of the WA 1837 provides that subsection (1)(b) is without prejudice to any right of the former spouse under the Inheritance (Provision for Family and Dependants) Act 1975.

If the testator has given the spouse a life interest with remainder to the children, then if the testator and his spouse are divorced, the effect is to accelerate the interest in remainder, so that the children will be absolutely entitled even though the former spouse is still alive at the date of death of the testator.

Similar rules now apply to civil partnerships.

Marriage

10.10 Marriage revokes any existing wills of the testator and the testatrix. However, s 18(3) of the WA 1837 provides that where it appears from a will that at the time it was made the testator was expecting to be married to a particular person and that he intended that the will should not be revoked by the marriage, the will is not revoked by marriage to that person. Thus if the testator marries someone else, then the will will be revoked by the marriage not contemplated by the will.

Section 18(4) deals with a will where one provision, but not the whole will, is expressed in expectation of marriage to a particular person, and that the testator intends that provision should not be revoked by the marriage. It provides that where it appears from a will that at the time it was made the testator was expecting to be married to a particular person and that he intended that a disposition in the will should not be revoked by his marriage to that person:

(a) that disposition shall take effect notwithstanding the marriage; and

(b) any other disposition in the will shall take effect also, unless it appears from the will that the testator intended the disposition to be revoked by the marriage.

Thus where only one provision in a will is expressed to be made in expectation of marriage to a particular person, and it is clear that the testator intended that that provision should not be revoked by the marriage, then normally the whole will will not be revoked by the marriage.

Intestacy

Total intestacy

10.11   This is dealt with in s 33 of the Administration of Estates Act 1925. This section imposes a trust, and gives the personal representatives power to sell all the assets. The personal representatives must then pay the funeral, testamentary and administration expenses and the debts of the deceased.

If a minority or life interest arises under the intestacy, then the personal representatives can invest the assets in accordance with the Trustee Act 2000.

Section 33(1) of the Administration of Estates Act 1925 (AEA 1925) imposes a trust in the case of a person who dies intestate. It provides that on the death of a person intestate as to any real or personal estate, such estate shall be held in trust by his personal representatives with the power to sell it – with power to postpone such sale and conversion for such period as the personal representatives, without being liable to account, may think proper.

Section 33(2) provides that out of the ready money of the deceased (so far as not disposed of by his will, if any) and any net money arising from disposing of any other part of his estate (after payment of costs), the personal representatives must pay all such funeral, testamentary and administration expenses, debts and other liabilities as are properly payable thereout, having regard to the rules of administration contained in that Part of the AEA 1925. Having done that, the personal representatives are then required to set aside a fund sufficient to provide for any pecuniary legacies bequeathed by the will, if any.

Section 33(3) directs that during the minority of any beneficiary, or the subsistence of any life interest, the money, or so much thereof as may not have been distributed, may be invested under the Trustee Act 2000.

Section 33(5) of the AEA 1925 provides that the income of so much of the real and personal estate of the deceased as may not be disposed of by his will, if any, or may not be required for administration purposes, may as from the death of the deceased be treated and applied as income. If necessary, the income must be apportioned between the life tenant and the remainderman. This applies however the estate is invested.

Partial intestacy

10.12   Section 33 of the AEA 1925 clearly contemplates that the section will apply to a partial intestacy, as subsection (2) refers to setting aside a fund for any pecuniary legacies bequeathed by the will. However, s 49(1) of the AEA 1925 provides that 'where any person dies leaving a will effectively disposing of part of his property, this Part of this Act shall have effect as respects the part of his property not so disposed of …' The Part referred to is Part IV, whereas s 33 is in Part III. Notwithstanding the apparent conflict between the two sections, it is considered that a court would impose a trust under s 33(1) in a partial intestacy.

What is the position if the will imposes an express trust? It may be that the terms of the trust imposed by the will are identical to the statutory implied trust, in which event there is no problem. However, the terms may differ, in which event it is probable that the terms of the express trust will prevail.

Order of entitlement

10.13   The AEA 1925 as amended prescribes the order of entitlement. The order is as follows:

(a)   If the intestate left a spouse or civil partner who survived the intestate by 28 days, and issue, then the surviving spouse is entitled to the personal chattels [see below for a definition of 'personal chattels'], a statutory legacy of £250,000 free of death duties and costs, but with interest thereon at the rate of 6 per cent and a life interest in one half of the residue.

The remainder of the estate (one half of the residuary estate and the interest in reversion after the death of the surviving spouse or civil partner) is held on the statutory trusts for the issue. The statutory trusts are discussed below.

(b)   If the deceased left a spouse and no issue, but did leave a parent or brother and sister of the whole blood, or issue of a brother or sister of the whole blood, if the spouse or civil partner survives for 28 days after the death of the intestate, the surviving spouse or civil partner is entitled to the personal chattels, a statutory legacy of £450,000 free of death duties and costs, but with interest thereon at the rate of 6 per cent, and one half of the residue.

Note that if the deceased and his or her spouse were involved in divorce proceedings, they are still married until the decree absolute is granted.

Section 55(1)(x) of the AEA 1925 defines personal chattels as 'carriages, horses, stable furniture and effects (not used for business purposes), motor cars and accessories (not used for business purposes), garden effects, domestic animals, plate, plated articles, linen, china, glass, books, pictures, prints, furniture, jewellery, articles of household or personal use or ornament, musical and scientific instruments and apparatus, wines, liquors, and consumable stores', but does not include any chattels used at the death of the intestate for business purposes, or money or security for money.

It should be noted that assets used for business purposes, money and security for money are not included. However, it can include very large items, as well as small but valuable items.

The other half of the residue is held on trust:

(i)   where the intestate leaves one parent or both parents (whether or not brothers or sisters of the intestate or their issue also survive) in trust for the parent absolutely or, as the case may be, for the two parents in equal shares absolutely;

      (ii) where the intestate leaves no parent, on the statutory trusts for the brothers and sisters of the whole blood of the intestate.

(c)   If the intestate leaves no issue and no parent or brother and sister of the whole blood or issue of a brother and sister of the whole blood, the surviving spouse is entitled to the whole estate provided he or she survives the testator by 28.

(d)   If the deceased did not leave a spouse or civil partner, then the order of entitlement is:

       (i) the issue on the statutory trusts;

      (ii) the parents in equal shares if more than one;

     (iii) brothers and sisters of the whole blood on the statutory trusts;

     (iv) brothers and sisters of the half blood on the statutory trusts;

      (v) the grandparents, and if more than one in equal shares;

     (vi) the uncles and aunts of the whole blood;

    (vii) the uncles and aunts of the half blood;

   (viii) the Crown or the Duchy of Lancaster or the Duke of Cornwall as *bona vacantia.*

Where there is a possibility that the beneficiaries might be under age, then the residuary estate is directed to be held on the statutory trusts. Section 47(1) of the AEA 1925 defines these trusts as:

'(i) in trust, in equal shares if more than one, for all or any children or child of the intestate, living at the death of the intestate, who attain the age of eighteen years or marry under that age, or enter into a civil partnership, and for all or any of the issue living at the death of the intestate who attain the age of eighteen years or marry or enter into a civil partnership under that age of any child of the intestate who predeceases the intestate, such issue to take through all degrees, according to their stocks, in equal shares if more than one, the share which their parent would have taken if living at the death of the intestate, and so that no issue shall take whose parent is living at the death of the intestate and so capable of taking.'

Thus if an intestate died without a spouse, leaving two children and three grandchildren – the children of a child who predeceased him – the residuary estate will be divided into three parts. Each of his two children will be entitled to a part, provided he or she has attained the age of 18, marrying under that age or entered into a civil partnership; if not it will be held in trust until the contingency is satisfied. The grandchildren will be entitled to the third share their parent would have taken, subject to them attaining the age of 18, marrying under that age or entering into a civil partnership.

If one of the children fails to satisfy the contingency, then his or her share goes to swell the share of the others.

The surviving spouse or civil partner has the right to redeem the life interest. Section 47A(1) of the AEA 1925 provides where a surviving spouse or civil partner is entitled to a life interest in part of the residuary estate, and so elects, the personal representative shall purchase or redeem the life interest by paying the capital value thereof to the tenant for life, or the persons deriving title under the tenant for life, and the costs of the transaction. Thereupon the residuary estate of the intestate may be dealt with and distributed free from the life interest. Regulations have been made as to the calculation of the capital value (Intestate Succession (Interest and Capitalisation) Order 1977 (SI 1977/1491 as amended by the Intestate Succession (Interest and Capitalisation) (Amendment) Order 2008, SI 2008/3162).

The election must be made within 12 months of the date of the grant, although the court has power to extend that time limit in certain circumstances (s 47(3)). The tenant for life must give notice to the personal representatives other than himself or herself, or if he or she is the sole personal representative, the Senior Registrar of the Family Division of the High Court. Rule 56(1) provides that where a surviving spouse or civil partner who is the sole or sole surviving personal representative of the deceased is entitled to a life interest in part of the residuary estate and elects under s 47A of the AEA 1925 to have the life interest redeemed, he may give written notice of the election to the Senior District Judge in pursuance of subsection (7) of that section by filing a notice in Form 6 in the Principal Registry or in the district probate registry from which the grant issued. Rule 56(2) provides that where the grant issued from a district probate registry, the notice shall be filed in duplicate. Rule 56(3) provides that a notice filed under this rule shall be noted on the grant and the record and shall be open to inspection.

Under the Intestates' Estates Act 1952 (IEA 1952) a surviving spouse or civil partner has the right to acquire the matrimonial home. Paragraph 1 of the Second Schedule provides that where the residuary estate of the intestate comprises an interest in a dwelling-house in which the surviving spouse or civil partner was resident at the time of the intestate's death, the surviving spouse or civil partner may require the personal representative, in exercise of the power conferred by s 41 of the AEA 1925 (and with due regard to the requirements of that section as to valuation) to appropriate the said interest in the dwelling-house in or towards satisfaction of any absolute interest of the surviving spouse in the real and personal estate of the intestate. Under paragraph 1(2) the right is not exercisable where the interest is:

(a)   a tenancy which at the date of the death of the intestate was a tenancy which would determine within the period of two years from that date; or

(b)   a tenancy which the landlord by notice given after that date could determine within the remainder of that period.

'Absolute interest' in the real and personal estate includes a reference to the capital value of a life interest which the surviving spouse has elected to have redeemed (para 1(4), IEA 1952).

Paragraph 1(5) provides that where part of a building was, at the date of the death of the intestate, occupied as a separate dwelling, that dwelling shall be treated as a dwelling-house for the purposes of the schedule.

Paragraph 2 provides that where:

(a) the dwelling-house forms part of a building and an interest in the whole of the building is comprised in the residuary estate; or

(b) the dwelling-house is held with agricultural land and an interest in the agricultural land is comprised in the residuary estate; or

(c) the whole or part of the dwelling was at the time of the intestate's death used as a hotel or lodging house; or

(d) a part of the dwelling-house was at the time of the intestate's death used for purposes other than domestic purposes;

the right conferred by paragraph 1 of the Schedule is not exercisable unless the court, on being satisfied that the exercise of that right is not likely to diminish the value of assets in the residuary estate (other than the interest in the dwelling-house) or make them more difficult to dispose of, so orders.

The right must be exercised within 12 months of the date of the grant by the surviving spouse giving notice to the other personal representatives. The court can extend the period of 12 months. If the spouse is the sole personal representative, then a spouse wishing to exercise the right should obtain the consent of the other beneficiaries if of full age and capacity, or arrange for the appointment of another administrator, or apply to the court.

Once given the notice is irrevocable except with the consent of the personal representatives. If the spouse is uncertain whether to give the notice, he or she can require the personal representatives to obtain a valuation of the house. The date for valuing the house is the date of appropriation (*Re Collins [1975] 1 WLR 309*).

The dwelling-house must not be sold during the period of 12 months after that date of the grant except with the consent of the surviving spouse unless it is necessary to do so in the course of administration owing to want of other assets.

Paragraph 5(1) provides that where the surviving spouse is one of two or more personal representatives, the rule that a trustee may not be a purchaser of trust property shall not prevent the surviving spouse from purchasing out of the estate of the intestate an interest in a dwelling-house in which the surviving spouse was resident at the time of the intestate's death.

Paragraph 5(2) provides that the power of appropriation under s 41 of the AEA 1925 includes a power to appropriate an interest in a dwelling-house in which the surviving spouse was resident at the time of the intestate's death partly in satisfaction of an interest of the surviving spouse in the real and personal estate of the intestate and partly in return for a payment of money by the surviving spouse to the personal representative. So if the house is worth more than the surviving spouse's entitlement, the surviving spouse can pay the difference between the market value and the surviving spouse's entitlement.

Entitlement to income or interest

10.14   It is highly unlikely that the personal representatives will be able to distribute the assets within a day or so of death, and so the law prescribes rules as to entitlement to income or interest. The entitlement varies according to the type of gift.

Specific gifts

10.15   If there is a specific gift in a will, then the beneficiary is entitled to all the income accruing since the date of death. Thus if there is a specific gift of a house which is let, the beneficiary is entitled to the rental income accruing since the date of death.

Note that it may be necessary to apportion the income if a payment relates to the period before and after death, and is made after death as the residuary beneficiaries are entitled to the income due up to the date of death. An example may be of help:

(a)   specific gift of shares in Z plc to A;

(b)   the company pays a dividend every six months on in respect of the period up to 1 September and the period up to 1 March;

(c)   the testator dies on 1 August.

The dividend payment due on 1 September will have to be apportioned as one month relates to the period after death, and five months to the period before death.

Note that if the testator had died on 2 September no apportionment of the 1 September dividend would have been required as the dividend related to the period before death even though it may not have been paid until after death.

Other legacies and bequests

10.16   Other legacies do not carry interest until the time when they are due. As from that date, they bear interest at 4 per cent per annum. When is a legacy due? The normal rule is that a legacy is due for payment one year after the date of death, but there are the following exceptions to this rule:

(a)   there may be a specific direction in the will as to the payment of interest or income;

(b)   the terms of the gift may indicate that interest is not to be paid until a later date. If there is a pecuniary legacy to a child contingent on attaining 25, interest will not be payable until the child has attained 25;

(c)   the following gifts will carry interest as from the date of the testator's death:

    (i)   where the legacy is to the testator's infant child or child to whom he stands *in loco parentis*. It is immaterial that the legacy is absolute, contingent or deferred, although if the legacy is contingent, then the contingency must be on attaining the age of 18. In addition, the will must make no other provision for the maintenance of the child (*Re Pollock [1943] Ch 338*);

(ii)　where the legacy is to an infant, and the testator has shown an intention to provide for the maintenance of the child. There must not be any other provision for the maintenance of the child, and it is immaterial that the child is not the testator's or one to whom the testator stood *in loco parentis*, or that the gift is contingent (*Re Churchill [1909] 2 Ch 431*);

(iii)　where the will contains an immediate legacy payable to a creditor of the testator in satisfaction of a debt (*Re Rattenberry [1906] 1 Ch 667*);

(iv)　where the legacy is immediate and charged on realty (*Turner v Buck (1874) LR 18 Eq 301*), but not if the realty is given on trust for sale.

Interest should be paid gross to a beneficiary. Tax should be deducted from other income.

The residue

10.17　The residuary beneficiaries are entitled to all the interest and income accruing to the personal representatives, whether or not there interests are immediate, contingent or deferred. There is one exception – a deferred or deferred contingent gift of residuary personalty.

Burden of pecuniary legacies

10.18　Out of which property should the pecuniary legacies be paid?

It is to be hoped that a professionally drawn will will include a direction as to which assets are to bear the pecuniary legacies. The normal direction is that they should be paid out of the residuary estate.

If there is no such direction, then it is possible that the pre-1925 rules still apply. These state that the pecuniary legacies must be paid out of residuary personalty. Residuary realty did not have to bear the burden. The reason for this rule was historical: originally the realty did not vest in the personal representatives, and therefore was not available to satisfy the pecuniary legacies. However, the rule was easily displaced as if there was a mixed residuary gift of personalty and realty, then the rule did not apply, although the residuary personalty had to be used first.

If there was a partial intestacy, then s 33(2) of the AEA 1925 provides that after payment of costs funeral testamentary and administration expenses and other liabilities, the personal representatives must set aside a fund sufficient to provide for any pecuniary legacies bequeathed by the will of the deceased.

Ademption of specific gifts

10.19   Section 24 of the Wills Act 1837 provides that every will shall be construed, with reference to the real and personal estate comprised in it, to speak and take effect as if it had been executed immediately before the death of the testator, unless a contrary intention appears.

Thus as far as the property the subject matter of the gift is concerned, s 24 provides that the will speaks from the death of the testator. However, it is very easy to displace the section. A gift of 'my piano' will be construed as meaning the piano owned by the testator at the date of the will rather than one owned at the date of death. This means that if the testator sells the piano and buys another after having made the will, the gift will fail, and the beneficiary will receive nothing.

However, if the gift had been generic, then s 24 will apply, and the gift will include the property owned at the date of death and not the date of the will. Thus a gift of all my golfing equipment will include the golfing equipment owned by the testator at the date of death.

Specific gifts of shares in companies, be they small or large, can cause difficulties if the company is taken over, and the shareholders receive shares or shares and cash. Are the beneficiaries entitled to these shares? The answer is no, unless the change is nominal, and the shareholding is in substance intact.

A draftsman drafting a will including a gift of shares in a company may wish to include a provision dealing with what happens if the company is taken over or amalgamates with another.

IHT CORRECTIVE ACCOUNT

10.20   It may be necessary to file a corrective account, for example if assets or liabilities unknown to the personal representatives come to light. Alternatively, HMRC may be prepared to accept a letter, particularly if it is only a minor amendment.

IHT CLEARANCE

10.21   If the personal representatives consider that no tax is payable, they should complete form D19, and submit it to the Capital Taxes Office.

If IHT is payable, once the personal representatives are certain that all IHT due has been paid, they can apply to the Capital Taxes Office for a clearance certificate.

Alternatively, practitioners may rely on the letter from HMRC stating that on the information given, there are no further queries, but HMRC must be notified if any other assets come to light.

COSTS

10.22 The Solicitors' Code of Conduct means that solicitors must give adequate costs information to the personal representatives. It is also desirable that this information is given to the residuary beneficiaries if they are not the personal representatives.

There is no uniform method of charging for administering an estate. Some firms charge solely according to the hours spent on the administration, whereas others also include a mark up or a percentage value element.

In *Jemma Trust Co Ltd v Liptrott [2003] WTLR 235*, the question to be decided was whether solicitors are entitled to include an additional element calculated according to the value of the estate. At first instance, it was held that it was wrong to include such an additional element. This has been reversed on appeal.

It was suggested that the appropriate percentages would be:

(a)   £1m – 1.5 per cent;

(b)   £4m – 0.5 per cent;

(c)   £8m – 0.16 per cent;

(d)   £12m – 0.08 per cent.

It was also made clear that it would not be right to include an additional charge according to the value of every estate.

If the major asset in the estate is the matrimonial home worth £750,000, and the surviving spouse is entitled to it, it would be wrong to charge an hourly rate, and then add 1.5 per cent of the value of the house.

It was also made clear that the correct procedure was for the solicitors to agree the costs or basis for charging at the outset.

Most wills direct that the costs of administering the estate should be paid from the residuary estate. In the great majority of estates, all the costs incurred will be chargeable against the residuary estate, but problems can arise. Two situations where this may happen are:

(a)   where there is a gift to a beneficiary who cannot be found;

(b)   where there is a dispute about ownership of a chattel which is the subject matter of a specific gift.

One method of dealing with a missing beneficiary is to take out a missing beneficiary indemnity policy. In *Re Evans (Deceased), Evans v Westcombe [1999] 2 All ER 777*, David Kenneth Evans married Helene Evans in 1945. There were two children of the marriage, the defendant who was born in 1946, and the plaintiff who was born in 1949. The parties separated shortly after the plaintiff's birth, but they were not divorced until 1973.

The plaintiff and defendant continued to live with their mother, but the childhood of the plaintiff and the defendant was not happy. The mother favoured the plaintiff, while the father and his parents favoured the defendant. As a result, the plaintiff had no contact with the defendant from 1962 until 1994.

David Kenneth Evans died intestate in 1987. Under the intestacy rules, the plaintiff and the defendant were entitled to his estate.

The defendant instructed solicitors to deal with the administration of the estate. An advertisement was inserted in the News of the World, but no further enquiries were made about whether the plaintiff was dead or alive. In 1989, a missing beneficiary policy was effected with Sun Alliance Insurance Group, and the estate was distributed to the defendant. The estate included a freehold property at Follend Road, Garnent, and this was vested in the defendant.

The plaintiff received payment from the insurance policy, but challenged the following items of expenditure:

(a)   a bill for work completed after the administration period;

(b)   the insurance premium paid to Sun Alliance Insurance Group;

(c)   the bill for the original administration of the estate;

(d)   the sum of £500 sought to be charged by the defendant as an estimate of expenditure of various items to do with the administration of the estate.

It was held that (b), (c) and (d) were proper expenses, but (a) was disallowed.

It was also held that the plaintiff was entitled to unpaid interest at the rate of 8 per cent. However, it was argued that the defendant should be removed from liability to account for interest because of s 61 of the Trustee Act 1925. It was held that the defendant should be relieved from liability to interest to the extent that the claim could not be satisfied out of the proceeds of the sale of the Follend Road property.

It was made clear by the judge that if there were a missing beneficiary, the correct way to proceed was to obtain a missing beneficiary indemnity policy as this would be cheaper than applying to the court for leave to distribute assets on the basis that a beneficiary was dead.

However, it may be that if the executors, administrators or beneficiaries do not make full disclosure of all relevant facts to solicitors employed to deal with the administration of the estate, so that proper enquiries are not made, the premium may not then be properly chargeable. Some beneficiaries may be deliberately vague about the whereabouts of other beneficiaries who have not been heard of for some years knowing full well that they will benefit if those beneficiaries cannot be found. In that situation, if the beneficiary later claims his or her entitlement, the premium may not be chargeable against the estate.

In addition, presumably all that the brother recovered from the insurers was one half of the net residuary estate after payment of all the expenses, including the indemnity insurance premium.

The daughter received far more than she was entitled to – the brother's half share. Should the daughter have not reimbursed the premium?

If there is a small legacy to a missing beneficiary, it would clearly be unreasonable for the personal representatives to spend a large amount of the residuary estate in a fruitless search for the missing beneficiary. It may be that the most appropriate way of dealing with that problem is to transfer the residuary estate to the residuary beneficiaries with suitable indemnities for the personal representatives.

With regard to (b), in *Re Estate of Cara Prunella Clough-Taylor [2003] WTLR 15*, D left a chattel to A. B removed the chattel after D's death claiming that D had given the chattel to him during her life. It was held that the executors were not obliged to begin proceedings to recover the chattel unless it was at the expense of A. However, they could assign the cause of action to A.

This decision is clearly correct as an asset the subject of a specific gift is at the risk of the specific beneficiary from the moment of death. If the chattel had been removed before death, it may be that the decision would have been the same. If the chattel had been part of the residuary estate, then the personal representatives are under a duty to take reasonable steps to recover the chattel. If all the residuary beneficiaries are of full age and capacity, then they should be consulted as to what is to be done to recover the chattel. If they are not, then the personal representatives must decide what is reasonable. Clearly this must have some regard to the value of the chattel. If the chattel is only worth £50, then it is not worth spending much money in an attempt to recover the asset. If it is worth £50,000, then clearly it is worth spending more money to recover it.

DISTRIBUTION

10.23   Once the personal representatives are satisfied that they have taken account of all debts and liabilities of the deceased, and taken advantage of any protection available to then (see **para 8.19**) they can begin to distribute the assets. It should be possible to pay the pecuniary legacies and transfer assets the subject of a specific gift at an early stage in the administration. It should also be possible to make an interim distribution to the residuary beneficiaries.

A bankruptcy search should be made against beneficiaries before distribution, and if the death occurred more than five years before distribution, then further enquiries must be made in order to ascertain whether the beneficiary was bankrupt before that date.

ESTATE ACCOUNTS

10.24   There is no set form for the accounts, but the aim should be to make them easily understandable by lay personal representatives and residuary beneficiaries, and to this end should be as simple as possible. The following guidelines may help:

(a)   if the estate comprises only a few assets, and the residuary beneficiaries are absolutely entitled, then simple accounts showing receipts and payments will suffice. However, it should clearly distinguish between income and capital, and the tax year to which income relates as the beneficiaries will have to include any income to which they are entitled in their income tax return for the relevant year.

Note that the crucial date for determining liability for income tax is the date when it is received or credited (see **paras 8.7– 8.10**). However, all interest due up to the date of death must be included in the IHT account, even though it may not be paid until after death;

(b) in larger estates, the following accounts may have to be prepared:

  (i) a statement setting out the name of the deceased, the date of the will, if any, the date of the grant and summarising the main provisions of the will;

  (ii) capital account – showing the value of the assets at the date of death, and the sale price if the assets have been sold;

  (iii) liabilities and expenses – showing the debts incurred by the deceased, the funeral, administration and testamentary expenses;

  (iv) income account – showing the income received since the date of death, the tax year, and the beneficiary entitled to it;

  (v) distribution account – showing the entitlement of the various beneficiaries.

Receipt and discharge

10.25 Normally a specific monetary legatee will be asked to sign a receipt for the legacy. If there is a specific bequest of a chattel or land, then the beneficiary should be asked to sign an acknowledgment.

It is common to request the personal representatives and residuary beneficiaries to sign the accounts.

POWER OF APPROPRIATION

10.26 There is a statutory power of appropriation under s 41 of the AEA 1925. This authorises personal representatives to appropriate any part of the real or personal estate, including things in action, of the deceased in the actual state or condition or state of investment thereof at the time of appropriation in or towards satisfaction of any legacy bequeathed by the deceased. Thus if a beneficiary has a legacy of £10,000, the personal representatives can satisfy that legacy by transferring shares worth £10,000 to the beneficiary.

If the asset is worth more than the legacy, it is probable that personal representatives cannot use s 41. Instead, they can sell the asset to the beneficiary. In addition, there is some doubt as to whether a personal representative who is also a beneficiary can make use of s 41.

There are various limitations on the power of appropriation. An appropriation must not be made so as to affect prejudicially any specific devise or bequest (s 41(1)(i)). If the beneficiary is absolutely entitled, the appropriation can only be made with the consent of that beneficiary. If the legacy is settled, the appropriation can only be made with the consent of the trustees, or the person for the time being entitled to the income (s 41(1)(ii)).

If the person whose consent is required cannot give it because he is an infant, or incapable of managing his own affairs by reason of mental disorder within the meaning of the Mental Health Act 1983, the consent can be given by his parents or parent, testamentary or other guardian, or receiver, or, if, in the case of an infant, there is no such parent or guardian, by the court on the application of his next friend. It is not necessary to obtain consent on behalf of a person who may come into existence after the time of appropriation, or who cannot be found or ascertained at that time (s 41(1)(iii)). However, s 41(5) provides that the personal representatives in making the appropriation shall have regard to the rights of any person who may thereafter come into existence, or who cannot be found or ascertained at the time of appropriation, and of any other person whose consent is not required by the section. Furthermore, if there is no deputy acting for a person suffering from mental disorder, and the appropriation is of an investment authorised by law or by the will, if any, of the deceased for the investment of money subject to the trust, no consent is required on behalf of the person suffering from mental disorder (s 41(1)(iv)). In similar circumstances, no consent is required if there is no trustee of a settled legacy, and there is no person of full age entitled to the income (s 41(1)(v)).

An appropriation made under s 41 of the AEA 1925 binds all persons interested in the property whose consent is not required by the section (s 41(4)).

Assume that a beneficiary has a legacy of £20,000. The personal representatives can satisfy that legacy by transferring to the beneficiary land to the value of £20,000. If the land is worth more than the legacy, this cannot be done. Instead, the personal representatives can sell the asset to the beneficiary. If the asset is the subject of a specific devise, appropriation cannot be made. If the residuary beneficiaries are entitled to the land, they are bound by any appropriation made by the personal representatives.

VALUATION

10.27   Section 41(3) of the AEA 1925 provides that the personal representatives may ascertain and fix the value of the respective parts of the real and personal estate and the liabilities of the deceased as they may think fit, and shall for that purpose employ a duly qualified valuer where necessary. Thus an executrix cannot value shares in an unquoted company herself, and then appropriate them in her favour at that valuation (*Re Bythway (1911) 104 LT 411*).

The date for the valuation of the assets could be very important in a volatile market. The Act does not provide any guidance, but the question was decided in the case of *Re Collins [1975] 1 WLR 309*, where it was held that the relevant date was the date of appropriation, and not the date of death. Thus if prices are rising, the beneficiary will want the appropriation to be made as soon as possible, whereas if they are dropping, the beneficiary will want the appropriation to be delayed.

INTESTACY

10.28   Section 41(9) of the AEA 1925 specifically provides that the section applies whether the deceased died intestate or not.

In *Kane v Radley-Kane [1999] Ch 274*, James Radley-Kane died intestate in May 1994 leaving a widow, the first defendant, and three sons. The widow was, in fact, the step-mother of the three sons.

The deceased owned 36 per cent of the ordinary shares in a company called Shiredean Limited, which were valued for probate purposes at £50,000. The net value of the deceased's estate was £93,000. Letters of Administration were granted to the widow, and she regarded herself as entitled to the whole estate under the intestacy rules.

In January 1997, the shares in Shiredean were sold for £1,131,438.

The claimant, one of the sons, issued proceedings claiming that the appropriation of the shares by the widow in her own favour was invalid.

It was held that this was the case. However, the judge stated that if the assets had been equivalent of cash, for example government stock, then the appropriation would have been valid.

What would have been the position if the widow had obtained another valuation of the shares on the day of appropriation, or shortly before, and the value had been £50,000? It is possible that the appropriation might have been valid.

The widow could also have asked the sons to agree to the appropriation; presumably they would have refused if they had any idea about the likely sale price of the shares.

Another possibility would have been for the widow not to have taken out the grant. The sons would then have been entitled, and they might or might not have appropriated the shares into the name of the widow.

Another possibility, albeit expensive, would have been to apply to the court for permission for the widow to appropriate in her favour.

A surviving spouse can also elect to take the matrimonial home in satisfaction of their statutory legacy or a capitalised life interest or both. The date for valuing the house is the date of appropriation, and the right must be exercised within 12 months of the date of issue of the grant of administration.

Transferring the assets

10.29   The personal representatives may have to sell all the assets of the deceased, but this is unusual, and it is more common for the personal representatives to transfer the assets of the deceased to the beneficiaries entitled to them. The formalities required for this are:

(a)   Chattels – frequently no formalities will be required. Ownership can be simply transferred by delivery. However, in the case of some chattels, there may be further requirements. If a car is transferred, for example, it will be necessary to notify DVLC about the change of registered keeper.

(b)   Bank and building society accounts – if these were in joint names, all that is necessary is to produce the death certificate.

   If the account was not in joint names, then it is difficult to transfer the account. Unless use is made of the Administration of Estates (Small

Payments) Act 1965, it will be necessary to produce the grant, and complete the forms required by the bank or building society in order to close the account. It will also be necessary to submit the passbook.

(c) Shares – the personal representatives may have submitted the grant to the Registrar. If not, it will have to be submitted together with the appropriate transfer form. If the appropriate certificate on the back of the form is completed, no stamp duty should be payable.

(d) Land – title already registered – if the deceased was solely entitled, the personal representatives can be registered as proprietors of the land, but usually they will not apply for registration as either the land will be sold, or will be vested in a beneficiary.

If the land is sold, the purchaser will have to produce at least a certified copy of the grant.

If the personal representatives assent to the property vesting in a beneficiary, the following documents will have to be lodged with the Land Registry:

(i)   Form AS1 or TR1, or if the transfer only relates to part of the land on the title, AS3 or TP1;

(ii) the grant or an official copy or a certified copy;

(iii) Form AP1;

(iv) the fee.

If the deceased was a joint tenant, the following must be submitted to the Land Registry:

(i)   the original death certificate or written confirmation by a conveyancer of the fact of the death which should include the full name of the deceased, the date and place of death and either the date of birth or the age at death of the deceased; or

(ii) the original grant of representation; or

(iii) a certificate given by the conveyancer that he holds the original or an official copy of such grant of representation; and

(iv) Form AP1. There is no fee payable.

It is clear that no stamp duty land tax is payable if a surviving joint tenant is absolutely entitled to a property not subject to any charge. However, the position if the property is subject to a charge is not clear as this is not covered by paragraph 3A of Schedule 3 to the Finance Act 2003. Paragraph 3A provides:

'(1) The acquisition of property by a person in or towards satisfaction of his entitlement under or in relation to the will of the deceased person, or on the intestacy of a deceased person, is exempt from charge.

(2)   Subparagraph (1) does not apply if the person acquiring the property gives any consideration for it, other than the assumption of secured debt.

(3)   In this paragraph–

"debt" means an obligation, whether certain or contingent, to pay a sum of money either immediately or at a future date, and

"secured debt" means debt that, immediately after the death of the deceased person, is secured on the property.'

Schedule 4, paragraph 8 to the Finance Act 2003 provides that the assumption of existing debt by a purchaser is chargeable consideration, and it could be argued that a surviving joint tenant is a purchaser assuming an existing debt, and that therefore stamp duty land tax is payable. However, in the view of the writer, stamp duty land tax is not payable as the vesting occurs by operation of law, and as far as joint tenants who are absolutely entitled are concerned, the survivor is already liable on the charge, and is not assuming any further debt.

If the deceased was a tenant in common, a restriction would have been entered on the register. This will be removed if the Registrar is satisfied that the other person or persons in whom the legal estate is vested is solely entitled to the property.

(e)   Land – if the title is unregistered – if the personal representatives intend to sell the land, then they need do nothing, although the purchaser will have to register the title.

If they assent to the land vesting in a beneficiary, then it will have to be registered. The appropriate assent should be used, and this should be submitted to the Land Registry with From FR1, the usual pre-registration documents and the grant or an official copy or a certified copy.

If the deceased was a joint tenant in equity, then the personal representatives need take no further action as the right of survivorship operates.

If the deceased was a trustee holding on trust for himself as a tenant in common, the legal estate would have been vested in the deceased as a joint tenant, and therefore the right of survivorship operates as far as the legal estate is concerned. If a new trustee is appointed, s 40 of the Trustee Act 1925 normally operates to vest any land in the new trustees. This is not an occasion of compulsory registration.

Chapter 11

Problems with wills and other disputes

OVERVIEW

11.1 The validity of a will may be challenged because the deceased did not have capacity to make it, or on the ground of non-compliance with the formal requirements, or on the ground that the testator did not know and approve of the contents of the will. Each possible ground of challenge will be considered in turn.

CAPACITY

11.2 A testator must normally be over 18 to make a valid will, although there are exceptions for soldiers, sailors and airmen.

The testator must also have the requisite mental capacity. This means that the testator must be able to understand three issues:

(a) that he is making a will, which will only come into effect on death;

(b) he has some idea of the persons he should be benefiting in his will;

(c) he has some idea of the extent of his property. It is not necessary to know down to the last penny.

Normally testators must possess this capacity at the date of execution of the will, but under the rule in *Parker v Felgate* a will can be valid if the testator had capacity at the time he gave instructions for a will, even if he did not have capacity at the time he came to execute the will, provided that the will is in accordance with the instructions given by the testator.

There are two rebuttable presumptions that assist those wishing to prove wills – if the will is rational, there is a presumption that the testator had capacity. In addition, if the testator had capacity, there is a presumption that that capacity continued.

If the capacity of the testator to make the will is challenged, then it may be necessary to obtain medical reports as to the capacity of the testator to execute a will.

Recent cases on capacity are considered below.

In *Clancy v Clancy [2003] WTLR 1097*, T had three children. She made a will in 1995 benefiting two of her children, I and L, but in November 1999 she gave instructions for a new will solely in favour of E. A draft was sent to her in December.

On 17 March 2000, T was admitted to hospital, and terminal cancer was diagnosed. On 24 March, she telephoned the solicitor to confirm that she approved the will. The solicitor attended the hospital on 28 March, and the will was duly executed. T was very weak, and probably could not have made decisions about her will. However, she would have been able to understand that the will she was signing was in accordance with her draft.

It was held that the will was valid, applying *Parker v Felgate*.

A donor making large gifts which will impact on the will must have a clear understanding of what they are doing and the effect on the will.

In *Padgham v Rochelle [2003] WTLR 71*, the beneficiaries under a will applied to set aside a lease of a farm granted by the deceased to his son shortly before his death. The lease was highly beneficial to the son.

The deceased was elderly, had had no independent advice about the grant of the lease, and had not been advised about the effect of the grant of the lease on the value of the property.

The lease was set aside.

In *Vatchet Tchilingirian v Ruby Ouzounian [2003] WTLR 709*, AO had one daughter, R, who had two sons by her first marriage, and a daughter by her second, AR.

She made a will in 1993 in effect giving her estate to her three grandchildren. She then made wills solely benefiting AR. Unbeknown to the solicitors who drafted two of the later wills, R had completed a questionnaire concerning these.

There was evidence that AO had begun to show signs of dementia and confusion.

It was held that she lacked the capacity to make the last three wills. In addition, it was held that she did not have the necessary knowledge and approval for the last three wills. R had filled in the questionnaire, and the contents of the wills had not been explained to her.

It was also alleged that undue influence had been used to persuade AO to alter her will. It was stated that undue influence involved findings that the testator did know and understand what she was doing when making the relevant will, but was coerced into making it. As it had been held that the AO did not have the necessary knowledge and approval to make the later wills, a finding of undue influence would be inconsistent.

In *Hoff v Atherton [2005] WTLR 99*, T was suffering from mild to moderate dementia when she made a will in June 1994 substantially benefiting A, a neighbour and close friend. This will was substantially different from earlier wills.

It was held that the 1994 will was valid. The evidence was that T appreciated the extent of her assets, and knew what was in the will.

It had been suggested that it should be pointed out to a testatrix when a will was substantially different from an earlier will. The Court of Appeal rejected this argument.

In *Sharp v Adam [2006] WTLR 1059*, T suffered from secondary progressive multiple sclerosis. He was divorced, but had two daughters. He owned a successful stud farm. Although one of the daughters lived in America, he was in contact with both of them.

In 2001, he executed a will disinheriting his two daughters, and giving the bulk of his estate to two employees, S and B, who had run the stud farm under his direction for some years. When he executed the will, he could not speak and communicated through his carer by means of nods. A solicitor drafted the will, and arranged for T's general practitioner to be present when the will was executed. The general practitioner considered that T had capacity to make the will.

The validity of the will was challenged. There was conflicting expert evidence as to whether T had capacity. It was held that he did not have capacity.

In *Re Estate of Ellen Jane Wilkes [2006] WTLR 1097*, T had five children who all survived her. She had suffered from hearing problems since 1979, and had two strokes in 1992. As a result of the strokes, she required 24-hour care. One of her children, George, saw her frequently, and looked after her when the carers were on holiday or not on duty.

George took T to see a solicitor in December 1994. T stated that she wished to leave her estate to George. There was no discussion about the size of her estate, or what other children she had. George left the room at some point. T executed the will in April 2005.

The validity of the will was challenged. There was evidence from a consultant geriatrician that T had widespread brain damage at the time of the execution of the will.

However, independent witnesses gave evidence that at the time T executed the will, she could recall the names and dates of birth of all her children and grandchildren, enter into meaningful conversations, and complete newspaper bingo competitions. Two witnesses stated that she had told them that she wanted George to have her house, which was by far the largest asset in her estate. Her GP also gave evidence to the effect that he considered that T had capacity at the time the will was executed.

It was held that the will was valid.

In *Re Estate of Peter Francis Barker-Benfield [2006] WTLR 1141*, T executed a will shortly before he died in favour of his daughter by a previous marriage. The validity of the will was challenged on the basis that he did not have the capacity to make a will. There was an earlier home-made will which did not have an attestation clause, but appeared to have been witnessed by two people.

T had also transferred properties into the name of his wife two months before his death.

There was evidence that he was suffering from delirium when he made his last will.

It was held that the onus of proving that T had capacity when he executed his last will was on the daughter. She had not discharged that burden, and so the will was invalid.

It was also held that the transfers to his wife were not tainted with undue influence. There was no presumption of undue influence in transactions between spouses, and whilst T was dependent on his wife, and therefore susceptible to influence, there was no evidence that she had exercised undue influence. She had objected to T's suggestion that he wanted to leave all his property to his daughter.

On the facts, the home-made will had been properly executed.

In *Re Estate of Dorothy Loxston [2006] WTLR 1567*, T died aged 98. She made two wills, one in 1990 benefiting the claimant and other beneficiaries, and another in 2003 benefiting mainly R who had worked for her in the six years before her death providing friendship, companionship and domestic help. Although R said that she had not facilitated the making of the 2003 will, it was held that the evidence was to the contrary.

It was stated that the test for capacity to make a will was that the testator must:

(a)   be able to understand the nature of the act of making a will;

(b)   know which persons he should consider as possible beneficiaries;

(c)   be able to understand the extent of the property of which he is disposing;

(d)   not be subject to any disorder of the mind as shall 'poison his affections, pervert his sense of right, or prevent the exercise of his natural faculties'; and

(e)   have the mental capacity to make decisions which take into account the relevant property, persons and circumstances and arrive at a 'rational, fair and just' testament.

The evidence was that when T made the 2003 will, she was not capable without assistance of taking into account all the people she might want to benefit. T therefore lacked testamentary capacity.

It was also held that T knew and approved of the contents of the will, and was not subject to undue influence.

In *Kostic v Chaplin [2007] EWHC 2298, Ch*, the testator believed that there was an international conspiracy of dark forces against him in which his wife, mother and sister were implicated. He left a will giving his entire estate to the Conservative Party.

It was held that these delusions meant that he did not have the capacity to make a will.

In *Ledger v Wootton [2007] EWHC 813, Ch*, the testatrix made a will benefiting some of her children, but cutting out others. A grant of probate was obtained to that will on her death, but its validity was challenged on the ground that the testatrix did not have capacity to make the will. The medical evidence was that the testatrix had a long history of mental illness.

It was held that once a real doubt was raised, the onus was on the propounders of wills to prove that the deceased had capacity, and that this person had not been discharged in this case.

Norris J summarised the law as follows:

'5. The principles of law which underlie my approach to the question of capacity may be stated as follows:

(a)   the burden is on the propounder of the will to establish capacity;

(b)   this remains the case even if the propounder has already obtained a grant in common form: see *Halsbury's Laws of England* (4th ed) vol 17(2) paragraph 269 n 6;

(c)   where a will is duly executed and appears rational on its face, then the court will presume capacity;

(d)   an evidential burden then lies on the objector to raise a real doubt about capacity;

(e)   once a real doubt arises there is a positive burden on the propounder to establish capacity;

(f)   the key authority on the nature of capacity remains *Banks v Goodfellow (1870) LR 5 QB 549* and in particular the familiar passage at p 565 which I will forbear repeating;

(g)   it is well to remember that the context of the passage was a case in which the testator (who made his will in 1863) had formerly been of unsound mind. He had been confined to the county lunatic asylum in 1841. When discharged he acquired the fixed delusion that a man called Alexander pursued and molested him, which persisted notwithstanding Alexander's death. He believed he was pursued by visible evil spirits. He suffered from epileptic fits. But he was capable of managing his financial affairs, and gave coherent instructions for a will at the same time as those for a lease, and at the taking of an account of rent due. The jury found for his will. The question for the court was whether the delusions under which the testator laboured were fatal to testamentary capacity:

"in other words, whether delusions arising from mental disease, but not calculated to prevent the exercise of the faculties essential to the making of a will, or to interfere with the consideration of the matters which should be weighed and taken into account on such an occasion, and which delusions had in point of fact no influence whatever on the testamentary disposition in question, are sufficient to deprive the testator of testamentary capacity and to invalidate a will" (*ibid* p 555);

(h)   it was in this context that the court pronounced the rule that the testator:

> "shall be able to comprehend and appreciate the claims to which he ought to give effect; and, with a view to the latter object, that no disorder of the mind shall poison his affections, pervert his sense of right, or prevent the exercise of his natural faculties – that no insane delusion shall influence his will in disposing of his property and bring about a disposal of it which, if the mind had been sound, would not have been made; if insane suspicion, or aversion, take the place of natural affection; if reason and judgement are lost, and the mind becomes a prey to insane delusions calculated to interfere with and disturb its functions, and to lead to a testamentary disposition, due only to their baneful influence – in such a case it is obvious that the condition of the testamentary power fails."

From this passage it may be collected that there must be a causal connection between the delusion and the disposition effected by the will, and that this is a question for the jury upon the whole of the evidence;

(i)   from a later passage at p 570 it may be collected what is the proper approach:

> "no doubt, where the fact that the testator has been subject to any insane delusion is established, a will should be regarded with great distrust, and every presumption should in the first instance be made against it. Where insane delusion has once been shown to have existed, it may be difficult to say whether the mental disorder may not possibly have extended beyond the particular form or instance in which it has manifested itself. It may be equally difficult to say how far the delusion may not have influenced the testator in particular disposal of his property. And the presumption against a will made under such circumstances becomes additionally strong where the will is one in which natural affection and the claims of near relationship have been disregarded";

(j)   in that last passage the court appears to have had in mind the principle expressed in *Harwood v Baker (1840) 3 Moore 282* at p 297:

> "that in all cases the party propounding the will is bound to prove, to the satisfaction of the court, that the paper in question does contain the last will and testament of the deceased, and that this obligation is more especially cast upon him when the evidence in the case shows that the mind of the testator was generally, about the time of its execution, incompetent to the exertion required for such a purpose.'"

In *Blackman v Man [2008] WTLR 389*, the husband of the testatrix had died in 1971, and her only son had died in 1974. The claimants were nephews and nieces of the testatrix, and challenged the validity of a will made in 1994 giving her residuary estate to the defendants, who were friends.

There was evidence that the deceased became confused in about 1994, but she obtained a will instruction form from Barclays Bank, and completed it herself. There was no direct evidence of the mental state of the testatrix in 1994.

It was held that the will was valid. The court held that too much reliance should not be placed on the evidence of medical witnesses who had not seen the testatrix in 1994.

It was also held that the testatrix did not have to be fully aware of the value of the assets at the time she executed her will. It was sufficient that she knew she had a substantial property portfolio of which to dispose.

There were no facts surrounding the execution of the 1994 will to arouse suspicion about her knowledge and approval of the will.

It was also argued that the costs of the claimants should be paid out of the estate as it was the testatrix's own actions in using a bank's will writing service which had caused the litigation. It was held that this was not sufficient justification for ordering the claimants' costs to be paid from the estate.

In *Scammell v Farmer [2008] EWHC 1100, Ch*, the testatrix made a will in 1995 substantially benefiting the claimants. In 2003, she executed another will substantially benefiting the defendant. The validity of this will was challenged by the claimants. There was evidence that the testatrix had the early stages of dementia. There was also evidence that the defendant had been instrumental in securing the execution of the 2003 will. The defendant had also destroyed the 1995 will and any copy.

It was argued that the test of capacity under the Mental Capacity Act 2005 should be applied in order to decide if the testatrix had capacity to make a will. This was rejected by a judge as he did not feel that this test was appropriate when considering wills, and in addition as the will was executed in 2003, it would be retrospective legislation.

On the facts, it was held that the testatrix did have capacity to make the will.

It was also held that the circumstances surrounding the execution of the will were suspicious, but that the defendant had discharged the burden of proving that the testatrix knew and approved of the contents of the will.

It was also held that the testatrix was not coerced into making the will.

A solicitor had prepared the 2003 will. The judge referred to the 'golden rule' as laid down by Templeman J in *Kenward v Adams*:

> 'When a solicitor is drawing up a will for an aged testatator or one who has been seriously ill it should be witnessed or approved by a medical practitioner, who ought to record his examination of the testator and his findings. That was the golden if tactless rule … Other precautions were that if there was an earlier will it should be examined, and any proposed alterations should be discussed with the testator.'

The judge also referred to *Cattermole v Prisk* where Norris J observed:

'This "golden rule" provides clear guidance as to how, in relevant cases, disputes can be avoided, or minimised (with the material relevant to the determination of the dispute contemporaneously recorded and preserved). The "golden rule" is not itself a touchstone of validity and is not a substitute for the established tests of capacity and of knowledge and approval that I have summarised in the two preceding paragraphs.'

It was held that there had been no breach of the 'golden rule'.

In *Re Baker (Deceased), Baker v Baker [2008] WTLR 565*, the deceased cohabited with Mrs Hazel for some years. He had a daughter, the claimant, with whom he had a good relationship.

Mrs Hazel had sold her own house, and lived with the deceased in his house. The proceeds of the sale of Mrs Hazel's house were used to fund the lifestyle of Mrs Hazel and the deceased. It was held that the sale of Mrs Hazel's house had caused her some anxiety, but that the deceased had reassured her by saying that he would take care of her and that their assets belonged to them both.

The deceased died on 27 April 2005. He executed a will prepared five days before he died by his brother under which he gave Mrs Hazel his estate absolutely provided she survived him by 28 days, but if she did not then his estate was to be divided between the claimant and the daughter of Mrs Hazel. A mirror image will was prepared for Mrs Hazel, but although it was dated with the same date as the deceased's will, it was clear that it had not been signed on that day. Mrs Hazel became his sole beneficiary.

There was evidence that before he died the deceased and Mrs Hazel had discussed the possibility of mutual wills under which they gave everything to each other, but then divided the residue between the claimant and the daughter of Mrs Hazel.

It was held that there was real doubt as to whether the deceased had testamentary capacity or knew and approved of the contents of the will. Accordingly, the burden of proof was on Mrs Hazel to prove that the deceased did have capacity and approved of the contents. She had not discharged that burden, and so the will was not admitted to probate.

Mrs Hazel had also argued that when she sold her own house, the deceased had told her that he would leave all his estate to her, and that she had acted to her detriment relying upon that promise. It was held that there was no evidence that the deceased had made such promise.

Mrs Hazel also claimed under the Inheritance (Provision for Family and Dependants) Act 1975 that she was either a person maintained by the deceased, or that they had been living together in the same household as husband and wife for two years up to the date of death of the deceased. It was held that this was the case, and it was ordered that Mrs Hazel should be given a life interest in the deceased's house or the proceeds of sale.

FORMALITIES

11.3   Section 9 of the Wills Act 1837 (WA 1837) as amended provides:

'No will shall be valid unless –

(a)   it is in writing, and signed by the testator, or by some other person in his presence and by his direction; and

(b)   it appears that the testator intended by his signature to give effect to the will; and

(c)   the signature is made or acknowledged by the testator in the presence of two or more witnesses present at the same time; and

(d)   each witness either –

   (i)   attests and signs the will; or

   (ii) acknowledges his signature,

in the presence of the testator (but not necessarily in the presence of any other witness), but no form of attestation shall be necessary.'

At its simplest all that is required is that the testator should execute the will in the presence of two witnesses, who should then sign the will in the presence of the testator.

If the will was professionally drawn, then the person responsible for drawing up the will should have ensured compliance with the formalities, and if they have not done so, there is the possibility that they may be liable for negligence.

Note the following points.

Writing

11.4   Whilst a will is normally written, typed or printed on paper, the only requirement under the WA 1837 is that it should be in writing, so it could be written on other media.

Signature

11.5   The WA 1837 does not define what is meant by a signature. Anything the testator intends to be his signature will suffice, for example a thumbprint.

Signatures by persons other than the testator

11.6   There is no requirement that the testator should sign the will. Another person can do it on his behalf as long as that person signs in the presence of, and at the request of the testator. This means that a blind person, or a person who cannot sign his or her name, can make a will.

Position of signature

11.7   Normal practice is for the testator to sign the will at the end. However, a signature in another place will be effective as long as the testator intended it to give effect to the will.

Witnesses

11.8   The testator must sign the will in the presence of two witnesses, who must then sign the will in the presence of the testator.

Anyone who can comprehend the procedure can witness a will, and so a child of mature years can act as a witness. A blind person cannot witness a will.

Acknowledgement of signatures

11.9   It is also possible for the testator and the witnesses to acknowledge a signature made in private. Clearly an express acknowledgement will be effective, but it has also been held that protests by a witness that the will was invalid amount to an acknowledgement of that witness's signature.

Attestation clause

11.10   It is not essential for the validity of a will that it should contain an attestation clause. However, it is desirable that a will should contain one, as on the death of the testator there is a rebuttable presumption that there had been compliance with the formal requirements of the WA 1837 if there is one.

If there is no attestation clause, then it may be necessary to lodge affidavit evidence from the witnesses or other persons present at the date of execution as to compliance with the formalities of the WA 1837.

Rule 12(1) of the Non-Contentious Probate Rules 1987 (NCPR 1987) provides that where a will contains no attestation clause, or the attestation clause is insufficient, or where it appears to the District Judge or Registrar that there is doubt about the due execution of the will, he must before admitting it to proof require an affidavit as to due execution from one or more of the attesting witnesses. If no attesting witness is conveniently available, an affidavit from any other person who was present when the will was executed should be lodged. Having considered the evidence, if the District Judge or Registrar is satisfied that the will was not duly executed, he must refuse probate and mark the will accordingly.

Rule 12(2) provides that if no affidavit can be obtained in accordance with paragraph (1), the District Judge or Registrar may accept evidence on affidavit from any person he may think fit to show that the signature on the will is in the handwriting of the deceased, or of any other matter which may raise a presumption in favour of due execution of the will. If he thinks fit he may require that notice of the application be given to any person who may be prejudiced by the will.

Rule 12(3) provides that a District Judge or Registrar may accept a will for proof without evidence if he is satisfied that the distribution of the estate is not thereby affected.

In *Sherrington v Sherrington [2005] EWCA Civ 326*, a solicitor made a will in favour of his third wife. The validity of the will was challenged by the children of previous marriages.

Peter Gibson LJ said:

> '41. To similar effect was Lord Penzance in *Wright v Rogers (1869) LR 1 PD 678* at page 682. In this case the survivor of the attesting witnesses of a will, which was signed by the testator and the witnesses at the foot of an attestation clause, gave evidence a year later that the will was not signed by him in the presence of the testator. Lord Penzance said at page 682 that the question was whether the court was able to rely on the witness's memory. He continued:
>
> > "The court ought to have in all cases the strongest evidence before it believes that a will, with a perfect attestation clause, and signed by the testator, was not duly executed, otherwise the greatest uncertainty would prevail in the proving of wills. The presumption of law is largely in favour of the due execution of a will, and in that light a perfect attestation clause is a most important element of proof. Where both the witnesses, however, swear that the will was not duly executed, and there is no evidence the other way, there is no footing for the court to affirm that the will was duly executed."
>
> 42. It is not in dispute that if the witnesses are dead, the presumption of due execution will prevail. Evidence that the witnesses have no recollection of having witnessed the deceased sign will not be enough to rebut the presumption. Positive evidence that the witness did not see the testator sign may not be enough to rebut the presumption unless the court is satisfied that it has "the strongest evidence", in Lord Penzance's words. The same approach should, in our judgment, be adopted towards evidence that the witness did not intend to attest that he saw the deceased sign when the will contains the signatures of the deceased and the witness and an attestation clause. That is because of the same policy reason, that otherwise the greatest uncertainty would arise in the proving of wills. In general, if a witness has the capacity to understand, he should be taken to have done what the attestation clause and the signatures of the testator and the witness indicated, viz that the testator has signed in their presence and they have signed in his presence. In the absence of the strongest evidence, the intention of the witness to attest is inferred from the presence of the testator's signature on the will (particularly where, as in the present case, it is expressly stated that in witness of the will, the testator has signed), the attestation clause and, underneath that clause, the signature of the witness.'

In *Channon v Perkins [2006] WTLR 425*, DC executed a will which largely benefited his partner, PO. It appeared to have been properly executed. His partner also executed a will on the same day with the same witnesses. The witnesses had no recollection of witnessing the wills. PO could not recall what happened when the wills were signed.

It was held that the will was valid. There was a presumption that a will which appeared to have been properly executed was valid, and strong evidence was required to rebut that presumption.

In *Re Estate of Rosetta Elsie Knight Papillon (Deceased), Murrin v Matthews [2008] WTLR 269*, the deceased had been born and brought up in England. Her second husband was a French Canadian, and on her marriage to him, she had moved to Canada. When he died, he left all his property to her.

She returned to England, and made a will dividing her residuary estate between her children or grandchildren. She later revoked that will.

When she died ten years later, the defendant, who was the daughter of the deceased, obtained a grant of letters of administration to the estate of the deceased.

The claimant, whose mother was a sister of the deceased's second husband, then produced a will which she claimed had been sent to her. Although the signature on the will appeared to be genuine, no address was given for either of the witnesses, and they could not be traced. The will also showed that it had been drafted by someone who was not English born, and whose first language was not English. In addition, it contained errors similar to those made by the claimant in other documents.

It was held that it was probable that this will had not been validly executed, and should not be admitted to probate.

In *Re Estate of Freda Walters Deceased [2008] WTLR 339*, the deceased made a will in 1953 giving all her assets to her husband provided he survived her by three months, but if he did not then all her assets went to her daughters in equal shares.

In 1988, the deceased executed a new will creating a nil rate band discretionary trust with grandchildren as the beneficiaries, the residuary estate to be divided between her daughters and grandchildren. In 1998, she signed a codicil giving one of the daughters a life interest in one third of the residue.

The 1988 will was prepared by a grandson, who was about to be admitted as a solicitor. There was evidence of an oral agreement to create mutual wills.

The husband argued that the codicil was invalid as it had not been signed by the deceased in the presence of the two witnesses. It was also argued that the agreement about mutual wills was unenforceable because it was not in writing.

It was held:

(a)   there was evidence of an oral agreement to create mutual wills, but this did not have to be in writing as the deceased had directed her executors to convert her estate into cash;

(b)   there was a presumption of due execution, and on a balance of probabilities the codicil had been validly executed by the deceased;

(c)   the codicil republished the 1988 will, and both should be admitted to probate.

In *Re Estate of Donald John Dickson Deceased [2002] WTLR 1395*, D had two children by his first marriage, and four as a result of his relationship with the plaintiff. There was evidence that this relationship was stormy. D made a will leaving everything to the plaintiff, and continued to make declarations that he had done so.

The original will was in the possession of D, and there was evidence that he was meticulous with regard to his paperwork.

On D's death, the will could not be found.

It was held that the presumption that a will last known to be in the possession of the testator had been revoked had been rebutted in this case.

In *Rowe v Clarke [2006] WTLR 347, [2005] EWHC 3068*, B had a homosexual relationship with R, and made a will in his favour. A copy was sent to R's mother. The relationship between B, who had a history of alcoholism, and R was stormy. The will was kept in a filing cabinet, but this was later disposed of and the contents were kept in a wardrobe.

When B died, the will could not be found. His brother, K, came to the house, and wanted B's possessions. K obtained a grant of letters of administration to B's estate.

R applied for revocation of the grant on the basis that there was a valid will.

It was argued that the presumption that a will last known to be in the possession of the deceased which could not be found after death had been revoked by the testator applied.

Mark Herbert QC, sitting as a Deputy Judge, rejected the view that K had found the will and destroyed it. This left two possibilities – either B had destroyed the will with the intention of revoking it, or he had accidentally destroyed it without any intention to revoke it. It was held that the latter was the correct conclusion, and so a copy will could be proved.

In *Rowe v Clarke [2007] WTLR 373*, a sequel to the previous case, it was held that if litigation is caused by the state in which the deceased left his papers, the costs of both parties should be ordered to be paid out of the estate. As this was the case here, then the costs of both parties came out of the estate.

In *Nicholls v Hudson [2007] WTLR 341*, the testator, who had been married three times, made a will in 1992 benefiting his four children. He gave the daughters of his second marriage copies of the will. When he died, his third wife was unable to find the will after a cursory search. About a year after the death of the testator, the wife obtained a grant of letters of administration to his estate, sold the matrimonial home, and spent the proceeds.

A daughter of the second marriage applied to revoke the grant of letters of administration on the basis that the 1992 will was valid.

There was no dispute about the capacity of the testator or performance or validity of the 1992 will. On the evidence, it was held that the testator had not destroyed the 1992 will with the intention of revoking it.

In *Wren v Wren [2006] EWHC 2243, Ch*, the claimant alleged that his father had told him that he had made a will leaving his house to him. After he died, the will could not be found.

The defendant, the other son of the deceased, alleged that because there was no will, his father had died intestate.

The claimant searched the house, and found a copy of a will under some floorboards together with some other papers.

There was evidence from attesting witnesses tending to support the validity of the will, and also evidence that the deceased was a hoarder of papers.

It was held that a copy of the will could be proved.

In *Re Estate of Zofia Wictoria Zielinski [2007] WTLR 1655*, the deceased, who was eccentric, demanding, forbidding and very formal, executed a will in December 2001 dividing her residuary estate between her daughter and her son. In July 2002, the deceased executed a transfer of her house to herself and her daughter, who lived with her.

The daughter obtained a grant of probate to a will made in July 2001 on the basis that the December 2001 will had been revoked by destruction or the making of a subsequent will which had also been revoked.

The son of the daughter applied for revocation of the grant of probate of the July 2001 will. The daughter accepted that the grant should be revoked, but contended that the December 2001 will had been revoked.

It was held that whilst there was a presumption that a will last known to be in the possession of a testator or testatrix which could not be found after death was presumed to have been revoked, on the facts of this case, the presumption had been rebutted.

It was also held that the transfer of the house to the deceased and her daughter was tainted by undue influence, and would be set aside.

KNOWLEDGE AND APPROVAL

11.11   A testator must know and approve of the contents of a will. Normally, there is a presumption that this is the case, but the presumption does not apply in the following circumstances:

(a)   where the testator is blind or illiterate or the will was signed by another person on behalf of the testator. In these cases, the will should be read to the testator before he executes it, and the attestation clause altered to indicate that this has been done. If this is not done, affidavit evidence will be required;

(b)   where there are suspicious circumstances, for example, it would be seen as suspicious where the draftsman was a major or sole beneficiary under a will. It does not mean that the beneficiary cannot take under the will, but it will be necessary for the beneficiary to dispel the doubt. The beneficiary must prove that the testator knew and approved of the contents of the will.

Rule 13 of the NCPR 1987 provides that before admitting to proof a will which appears to have been signed by a blind or illiterate testator, or which for any other reason raises doubts as to the testator having had knowledge of the contents of the will at the time of its execution, the District Judge or Registrar must satisfy himself that the testator had such knowledge.

ALTERATIONS AND OBLITERATIONS TO THE WILL

11.12   The words in a will may have been altered or obliterated by the testator.

If it is an alteration, the rules are:

(a)   if it can be proved that the alteration was made before the will was executed, the alteration will be valid. It will be necessary to produce evidence from the attesting witnesses or other persons present when the will was executed. If a codicil to the will has been executed confirming the original will, then the alteration will be valid;

(b)   if the alteration has been signed or initialled by the testator and two witnesses, then it will be upheld. The witnesses need not be the same persons as originally witnessed the will;

(c)   if neither of the above apply, then the alteration will be invalid, and the original wording will be admitted to probate.

If it is an obliteration, then the rules are:

(a)   if it can be proved that the obliteration was made before the will was executed, it will be valid. If a codicil to the will has been executed confirming the original will, then again the obliteration will be valid;

(b)   if the obliteration has been initialled by the testator and the witnesses, then it will be upheld. The witnesses need not be the same persons as originally witnessed the will;

(c)   if (a) and (b) do not apply, then if the original wording is apparent, that wording will be admitted to probate. 'Apparent' means that the original wording can be read by natural means without the use of artificial aids;

(d)   if (a), (b) and (c) do not apply, probate will be granted with a blank if the testator intended to revoke the wording;

(e)   if (a), (b), (c) and (d) do not apply, extrinsic evidence will be admissible to prove the original contents. This evidence may be a copy of the original will, or the testator's instructions to the draftsman.

In unusual circumstances, the doctrine of conditional revocation may apply. If the testator obliterates the amount of a legacy in a will, and substitutes another figure, that substitution may be invalid. If it is, extrinsic evidence will be admissible to as to the original amount as the testator's revocation was conditional on the validity of the substitution.

Rule 14(1) of the NCPR 1987 provides that where there appears in a will any obliteration, interlineations or other alteration which is not authenticated in the manner prescribed by s 21 of the WA 1837, or by the re-execution of the will or by the execution of a codicil, the District Judge or Registrar shall require evidence to show whether the alteration was present at the time the will was executed and shall give directions as to the form in which the will is to be proved. These provisions do not apply to any alteration which appears to the District Judge or Registrar to be of no practical importance.

Rule 11(1) provides that where the District Judge or Registrar considers that in any particular case a facsimile copy of the original will would not be satisfactory for purposes of record, he may require an engrossment suitable for facsimile reproduction to be lodged.

Rule 11(2) provides that where a will:

(a) contains alterations which are not to be admitted to proof; or

(b) has been ordered to be rectified by virtue of s 20(1) of the Administration of Justice Act 1982;

there shall be lodged an engrossment of the will in the form in which it is to be proved. Such engrossment must reproduce the punctuation, spacing, and division into paragraphs of the will and must follow continuously from page to page on both sides of the paper.

INCORPORATION OF DOCUMENTS IN A WILL

11.13 It is possible for a document to be incorporated in a will if the document is in existence at the date of the will, is referred to in the will as an existing document and can be easily identified.

Rule 14(3) of the NCPR 1987 provides that if a will contains any reference to another document in such terms as to suggest that it ought to be incorporated in the will, the District Judge or Registrar must require the document to be produced and may call for such evidence in regard to the incorporation of the document as he may think fit.

DOUBT AS TO DATE OF WILL

11.14 Rule 14(4) of the NCPR 1987 provides that where there is doubt as to the date on which a will was executed, the District Judge or Registrar may require such evidence as he thinks necessary to establish the date.

LOST OR DAMAGED WILLS

11.15 Sometimes a will cannot be found after death. In this situation, a copy may be admitted to probate.

There is a presumption that a will last known to have been in the possession of the testator has been revoked if it cannot be found after death. It is necessary to rebut this presumption.

Rule 54(1) of the NCPR 1987 provides that subject to paragraph (2) below, an application for an order admitting to proof a nuncupative will, or a will contained in a copy or reconstruction thereof where the original is not available, must be made to a District Judge or Registrar.

Rule 54(2) provides that in any case where a will is not available owing to its being retained in the custody of a foreign court or official, a duly authenticated copy of the will may be admitted to proof without the order referred to in paragraph (1) above.

Rule 54(3) provides that an application under paragraph (1) above shall be supported by an affidavit setting out the grounds of the application, and by such evidence on affidavit as the applicant can adduce as to:

(a)   the will's existence after the death of the testator or, where there is no such evidence, the facts on which the applicant relies to rebut the presumption that the will has been revoked by destruction;

(b)   in respect of a nuncupative will, the contents of that will; and

(c)   in respect of a reconstruction of a will, the accuracy of that reconstruction.

The District Judge or Registrar may require additional evidence in the circumstances of a particular case as to due execution of the will or as to the accuracy of the copy will, and may direct that notice be given to persons who would be prejudiced by the application (r 54(4)).

OTHER MATTERS AFFECTING THE VALIDITY OF A WILL

11.16   There are other factors which may affect the validity of a will, but are rarely encountered in practice. A will will be invalid if the testator was induced by fraud or undue influence to execute a will. It will also be invalid if the testator was forced to execute it against his will.

Disputes about funeral arrangements

11.17   Occasionally there are disputes about the funeral arrangements for the deceased. These disputes sometimes reach the courts.

In *Buchanan v Milton [1999] 2 FLR 844*, the deceased was born in Australia of Aboriginal parents. He was adopted very shortly after his birth, and brought up in England. He did return to Australia for a month when he was 23, but he did not enjoy the experience and returned to England. He died intestate leaving a child, H.

H's mother and his adoptive mother wanted him to be cremated, but his natural mother wanted him to be returned to Australia for burial there. His natural mother applied to be appointed as administrator in place of H. The application was made under s 116 of the Supreme Court Act 1981 on the basis that there were special circumstances justifying the displacement of an administrator. If the natural mother were appointed the administrator, she could decide on the funeral arrangements.

It was held that the special circumstances in s 116 could include all relevant circumstances. However, the application was refused.

In *Fessi v Whitmore [1999] 1 FLR 767*, the parents of a child lived in Nuneaton. They separated, and the father went to live in Wales with the child. The child was killed very shortly thereafter. The child had been very close to his paternal grandfather. The father wanted the ashes scattered in Wales; the mother wanted them scattered near those of the paternal grandfather at Nuneaton.

It was held that the ashes should be scattered at Nuneaton.

In *Re Blagdon Cemetery (2002) Law Society Gazette, 16 May*, the son of the petitioners had been killed in an industrial accident, and buried where they lived. They moved to another part of the country, and wanted their son's body to be exhumed and reburied where they now lived. Their petition was granted.

In *Re Christ Church Harwood (2002) Law Society Gazette, 16 May*, the young daughter of the petitioners died. They wanted to incorporate an engraved photographic image of the deceased in the memorial. The petition was granted.

In *Re Crawley Green Road Cemetery, Luton [2001] WTLR 1269*, S's ashes were interred in consecrated ground in Luton. S's wife moved to London, and wanted the ashes to be interred in a cemetery where she now lived.

It was stated that there was a presumption against exhumation, but it could be ordered if there were medical grounds justifying exhumation. In this case, there were no medical grounds.

However, the family were humanists, and there had been a humanist funeral service. They had not appreciated that the ashes were being interred in consecrated ground. It would be contrary to the European Convention on Human Rights to refuse exhumation.

In *Leeburn v Derndorfer and Plunkett [2004] WTLR 867* (a decision of the Supreme Court of Victoria), L, D and P were the children of the deceased, who was cremated, and his executors. Sometime after his death, D and P arranged for his ashes to be interred in a cemetery. Over two years later, L applied for an order that the ashes should be disinterred, and that he should be given one third.

It was held:

(a) the personal representatives of a deceased person had the right to decide about the disposal of the body;

(b) the action by the defendants bound the plaintiff;

(c) once a body had been buried, it became part of the realty;

(d) ashes could be owned and divided;

(e)   in view of the delay, and various other factors, the application was refused.

In *Re West Norwood Cemetery (2005) Times, 20 April*, SS died in 1992, and was buried in a cemetery plot granted to one of her sons, PS. Her other children and her husband, DS, all contributed to the purchase of the plot. When DS died, the children apart from PS arranged for his ashes to be interred in the same plot. PS did not agree with this, and it was probable that the signature of PS on the burial form had been forged.

It was held that as the family had contributed to the purchase of the plot on the understanding that DS would also be interred in the plot, there was a constructive trust, and it would be wrong for the ashes to be disinterred.

In *Re Mangotsfield Cemetery (2005) Times, 26 April*, SW and HS married, and had a son who died in infancy. SW purchased a burial plot, and the ashes of the son were interred there. SW and HS were divorced, and HS remarried. On her death HS's husband arranged for her ashes to be buried in the plot believing it to be hers.

It was held that the ashes should not be disinterred.

In *Lewisham Hospital Trust v Abdul Sada Hamuth [2007] WTLR 309*, the deceased made a will appointing the first defendant as his executor. The will contained a wish that the deceased should be cremated. The family of the deceased wanted him to be buried in the family burial plot. There was a dispute about the validity of the will.

The NHS Trust sought a declaration that it was lawfully in possession of the body, and that it could make arrangements to dispose of it.

It was held that the NHS Trust was lawfully in possession of the body, and could arrange for its disposal.

In *Hartshorne v Gardner [2008] WTLR 837*, the deceased was killed in a road accident. He was not married, and did not have any children. Accordingly, his parents, who were divorced, were entitled to a grant of letters of administration to his estate. Unfortunately, the parents could not agree about the funeral arrangements. His father wanted the deceased to be buried in Kington, whereas his mother wanted him to be cremated in Worcester.

The deceased had fallen out with his mother some time before death, and had been living and working in Kington. He had a brother, fiancee and friends living there.

It was held that the most important consideration was that the body be disposed of with all proper respect and decency and, if possible, without further delay. In addition, it was also relevant to consider any factors reflecting the wishes of the deceased, and the reasonable wishes and requirements of the surviving family and friends.

In the light of all these factors, it was held that burial in Kington was the appropriate funeral.

Disinherited stepchildren

11.18 Another problem faced by practitioners quite frequently is the disinherited stepchildren. This usually arises when both parties have been married before, and have children from a previous relationship. They may make wills giving everything to each other, with a gift in default to their respective children. The survivor then changes his or her will excluding the children of the first spouse to die, and giving all his or her assets to his or her own children. What can the excluded stepchildren do in this situation?

The following courses of action are open to the disappointed stepchildren:

(a) check to ensure that the testator had capacity to make a will;

(b) check to ensure that the testator knew and approved of the contents of the will;

(c) check to see if there was any agreement to enter into mutual wills;

(d) check for any possibility of a claim under the Inheritance (Provision for Family and Dependants) Act 1975;

(e) check to see if there is any room for the application of the equitable doctrine of proprietary estoppel;

(f) check to ensure compliance with s 9 of the Wills Act 1837.

Capacity

11.19 If a medical report was obtained at the time the testator executed the will confirming that the testator had capacity, then there is very little which can be done to challenge the will under this head.

If that is not the case, then further enquiries should be made as to whether the deceased was mentally capable at the time the will was made.

For further discussion of this aspect, see **para 11.2** above.

Knowledge and approval

11.20 Normally knowledge and approval are presumed if the testator had capacity to make the will, but there are some situations where there is no such presumption. One of these situations is where the draftsman of the will is a major beneficiary. In this case, it will be necessary for the beneficiary to prove that the deceased knew and approved of the contents of the will.

For further discussion of this aspect, see **para 11.11** above.

Mutual wills

11.21 It may be that the parties have agreed to make mutual wills, and if there is such an agreement, then the surviving party will be bound by the agreement. However, the mere fact that the parties have made mirror image wills giving each other absolute interests with the residue split equally between their respective children does not mean that mutual wills have been created.

If there is an agreement to create mutual wills, the effect is that the survivor gets a life interest in the property of the first one to die. The survivor may also be limited to a life interest in their own property – a life interest in a car?

In *Re Goodchild (Deceased), Goodchild v Goodchild [1997] 3 All ER 63*, Dennis and Joan Goodchild had a successful business. Their only child, the first plaintiff in these proceedings, worked in the business. They made mirror image wills giving their estate to each other, but if they did not survive each other by 28 days, Gary was entitled. Joan died first, and Dennis inherited all her property under her will. Dennis then married Enid, and died less than two months later. It was argued that Dennis and Joan had executed mutual wills. Gary also claimed to be entitled to claim under the Inheritance (Provision for Family and Dependants) Act 1975.

It was held that in order for the doctrine of mutual wills to apply, there had to be a contract in law between the two testators that both wills would be irrevocable and remain unaltered. The judge at first instance had held that there was no evidence of any such agreement, and his decision was upheld on appeal.

However, it was held that Gary was entitled to succeed under the 1975 Act as he was barely able to meet his financial requirements from his existing income. It was held that there was a moral obligation on Dennis to leave Gary property he had received from Joan, and Gary was awarded £185,000.

In *Birch v Curtis [2002] 2 FLR 847*, H and W had both been married before. They made wills in 1986. W died first, and H remarried. He subsequently made further wills. On his death, W's children alleged that where H and W had agreed to make wills in a certain format, the doctrine of mutual wills applied. It was held that this was not the case.

Inheritance (Provision for Family and Dependants) Act 1975

11.22   It is possible that the disinherited stepchildren might have a claim under the Inheritance (Provision for Family and Dependants) Act 1975.

However, there are two major hurdles which must be overcome. The first is that the stepchildren will have to prove that they come within the category of persons entitled to claim – usually the appropriate category will be children of the family. The second hurdle is that it will be necessary for the children to prove that reasonable financial provision has not been made for their maintenance.

With regard to the first issue, s 1(1) of the 1975 Act prescribes the persons entitled to claim. They include:

'(a)   any person (not being a child of the deceased) who, in the case of any marriage or civil partnership to which the deceased was at any time a party, was treated as a child of the family in relation to that marriage'.

This applies where the deceased had married someone with children from a previous relationship, and treated those children as his or her own. Note that it does not matter whether the marriage ended either by divorce or the death of the other party sometime earlier. If there was a child of the other party to the marriage, and the deceased treated the child as a child of the family, the child will still be able to claim, even though the marriage ended in divorce or the death of the parent of the child.

What test is applied to decide if the applicant is a child of the family? In *Re Leach Deceased [1985] 2 All ER 754*, Slade LJ said at page 762:

> 'I can see no reason why even an adult applicant who has at all material times been an adult person may not be capable of qualifying under that subsection, provided that the deceased has, as wife or husband (or widow or widower) under the relevant marriage, expressly or impliedly, assumed the position of parent towards the applicant, with the attendant responsibilities and privileges of that relationship.'

Maintenance does not necessarily mean subsistence level. Regard must be had to the standard of living enjoyed by the applicant prior to the death, and it can include the provision of luxuries (*Re Borthwick Deceased [1949] 1 All ER 472*). In *Re Christie Deceased [1979] 1 All ER 546*, it was defined as:

> 'Reasonable financial provision for the applicant in the sense that of such financial provision as it would be reasonable in all the circumstances of the case for the applicant to receive for the maintenance of his way of life and well-being, his health and financial security and well-being, the health and financial security of his immediate family for which he is responsible' (page 550).

Even if the stepchildren can prove that they come within the category of those entitled to claim, if they are otherwise adequately provided for, stepchildren stand little chance in succeeding in a claim under the 1975 Act.

There are also guidelines which the court must consider in deciding whether or not reasonable financial provision has been made for an applicant, and if reasonable financial provision has not been made for an applicant, what order should be made. If the applicant is a child of the family of the deceased, the court must have regard:

(a)   to whether the deceased had assumed any responsibility for the applicant's maintenance and, if so, to the extent to which and the basis upon which the deceased had assumed responsibility and to the length of time for which the deceased discharged that responsibility;

(b)   to whether in assuming and discharging that responsibility the deceased did so knowing that the applicant was not his own child;

(c)   to the liability of any other person to maintain the applicant.

Similar rules apply to civil partnerships.

Proprietary estoppel

11.23   What happens if the parties agree to make mutual wills, and the survivor then does something which prevents the implementation of the mutual wills? In this scenario, the court may impose a constructive trust.

In *Healey v Brown [2002] WTLR 849*, H and W owned the matrimonial home as beneficial joint tenants. H had a son by a previous marriage, PB, and W had a niece, JH. They executed mutual wills under which their interest in the house went to JH, and the residue to PB. W died first, and H transferred the property into the joint names of himself and PB. On his death, JH claimed that she was entitled to the property absolutely.

It was held that any contract between H and W was unenforceable because of non-compliance with s 2 of the Law of Property (Miscellaneous Provisions) Act 1989. However, equity would impose a constructive trust so that JH was entitled to one half of the property.

The doctrine of proprietary estoppel may also be relevant. If promises have been made to a stepchild, and the stepchild has acted to his or her detriment relying on the promise, the estate of the person making the promise may not be allowed to refuse to implement the promise.

In *Campbell v Griffin [2001] WTLR 981*, C, who had spent part of his childhood in a children's home, became Mr and Mrs A's lodger. Initially, this had been a commercial arrangement, but gradually Mr and Mrs A came to regard C as their son. He helped with domestic chores, and towards the end of Mr and Mrs A's life became a carer. Both Mr and Mrs A made promises to him that he would have a home for life.

It was held that the doctrine of proprietary estoppel applied, and C was awarded £35,000 from the proceeds of the sale of the house (about £160,000).

The court held that once it was proved that promises had been made, and that there has been conduct by the applicant of such a nature that inducement may be inferred, then there is a presumption of reliance.

In *Jiggins v Brisley [2003] WTLR 1141*, H and W were tenants of a council flat. They decided to purchase it with the benefit of the statutory discount, and one of their sons, B and his wife P, provided the purchase price and the costs. It was the understanding of the parties that H and W would live in the house during their joint lives, and that it would then pass to B and P.

In 1992 or 1993, H and W were asked to transfer the flat into the name of P, but they refused, although assurances were given in 1993 that the flat would be left to them on the death of the survivor. As a result of these assurances, B and P spent money on repairs to the flat.

B died in 2000, and H died shortly thereafter. W then changed her will so that P received a legacy of £20,000 with the residue going to her grandchildren.

It was held that no constructive trust had arisen when the flat was first purchased, but the doctrine of proprietary estoppel was applied, and the personal representatives of W held the flat on trust for P.

Section 9, Wills Act 1837

11.24 It is probably worth checking with witnesses if the will has been validly executed. This of course will not apply if it is clear that the will has been executed in the presence of a solicitor.

Chapter 12

Standing searches, caveats, citations and applications for an order to attend for examination or for a subpoena to bring in a will

OVERVIEW

12.1   In the great majority of probates there is no dispute about the validity of the will or the construction of the will. If there are any, they are frequently resolved without reference to the court.

There are various precautionary steps which are commonly taken in the initial stages of any probate dispute. They are:

(a)   standing searches – this procedure is used if a relative or any other person wishes to be notified of the issue of a grant;

(b)   caveats – these are lodged if someone wishes to challenge the issue of a grant;

(c)   citations – this is where someone is cited to take out a grant.

Rule 43(1) of the NCPR 1987 provides that any person who wishes to be notified of the issue of a grant may enter a standing search for the grant by lodging at, or sending by post to, any registry or sub-registry a notice in Form 2.

Rule 43(2) provides that a person who has entered a standing search will be sent an office copy of any grant which corresponds with the particulars given on the completed Form 2 and which was:

(a)   issued not more than 12 months before the entry of the standing search; or

(b)   issued within a period of six months after the entry of the standing search.

It is possible to renew the standing search by written application made within the last month of the original period.

CAVEATS

12.2   Rule 44 of the NCPR 1987 enables anyone to enter a caveat. Rule 44(1) provides that any person who wishes to show cause against the sealing of a grant may enter a caveat in any registry or sub-registry, and the District Judge or Registrar must not allow any grant to be sealed if he has knowledge of an effective caveat. However, a grant can still be issued on the day on which the caveat is entered.

Rule 44(2) provides that any person wishing to enter a caveat (the caveator) or a solicitor or probate practitioner on his behalf, may effect entry of a caveat:

(a) by completing Form 3 in the appropriate book at any registry or sub-registry; or

(b) by sending by post at his own risk a notice in Form 3 to any registry or sub-registry. The the proper officer must provide an acknowledgement of the entry of the caveat.

The caveat is effective for a period of six months, and can be renewed by lodging a written application within the last month of the period of six months. Subsequent renewals are also permissible.

An index of caveats is maintained. Whenever anyone applies for a grant, the registry or sub-registry at which the application is made must cause a search of the index to be made. The appropriate District Judge or Registrar must be notified of the entry of a caveat against the sealing of the grant for which application has been made (r 44(4)).

Rule 44(5) provides that where a person other than the caveator claims to have an interest in the estate a warning in Form 4 may be issued against the caveat. The person warning must state his interest in the estate of the deceased, and the caveator must be required to give particulars of any contrary interest in the estate. The warning or a copy must be served on the caveator forthwith.

Rule 44(6) provides that a caveator who has no interest contrary to that of the person warning, but who wishes to show the cause against the sealing of a grant to that person, may within eight days of service of the warning upon him (inclusive of the day of service), or at any time thereafter if no affidavit has been filed under paragraph (12), issue and serve a summons for directions.

Rule 44(7) provides that on the hearing of any summons for directions the District Judge or Registrar may give a direction for the caveat to cease to have any effect. Rule 44(8) provides that any caveat in force when a summons for directions is issued shall remain in force unless a direction has been given under paragraph (7) or until it is withdrawn under paragraph (11).

Rule 44(10) provides that a caveator having an interest contrary to that of the person warning may within eight days of the service of a warning upon him (inclusive of the day of service) or at any time thereafter if no affidavit has been filed under paragraph (12) enter an appearance in the nominated registry by filing Form 5. The caveator must serve on the person warning a copy of Form 5 sealed with the seal of the court.

Rule 44(11) provides that a caveator who has not entered an appearance to a warning may at any time withdraw his caveat by giving notice at the registry or sub-registry at which it was entered, and the caveat thereupon ceases to have effect. Where the caveat has been so withdrawn, the caveator must forthwith give notice of withdrawal to the person warning.

Rule 44(12) provides that if no appearance has been entered by the caveator, or no summons has been issued by him under paragraph (6), the person warning may at any time after eight days of service of the warning upon the caveator (inclusive of the day of service) file an affidavit in the nominated registry as to such service. The caveat then ceases to have effect provided that there is no pending summons under paragraph (6).

Rule 44(13) provides that unless a District Judge or, where application to discontinue a caveat is made by consent, a Registrar, by order made on summons otherwise directs, any caveat in respect of which an appearance to a warning has been entered is to remain in force until the commencement of a probate action.

If a probate action is commenced, the senior District Judge must give notice of the action to every caveator other than the plaintiff in the action in respect of each caveat that is in force upon being advised by the court concerned of the commencement of a probate action (r 45(1)). If a caveat is entered subsequent to the commencement of a probate action, the senior District Judge must give notice to that caveator of the existence of the action (r 45(2)). Unless a District Judge by order made on summons otherwise directs, the commencement of a probate action operates to prevent the sealing of a grant until application for a grant is made by the person shown to be entitled to it by the decision of the court in such action (r 45(4)). This does not prevent the issue of a grant of administration pending suit under s 117 of the Supreme Court Act 1981.

CITATIONS

12.3   Rule 46(1) of the NCPR 1987 provides that any citation may issue from the Principal Registry or a district probate registry. It must be settled by a District Judge or Registrar before being issued.

Rule 44(2) provides that every averment in a citation, and such other information as the Registrar may require, shall be verified by an affidavit sworn by the person issuing the citation ('the citor'). In special circumstances the District Judge or the Registrar may accept an affidavit sworn by the citor's solicitor or probate practitioner.

Rule 46(3) provides that the citor must enter a caveat before entering a citation. Unless a District Judge by order made on summons otherwise directs, any caveat in force at the beginning of the citation proceedings, unless withdrawn pursuant to paragraph (11) of r 44, remains in force until application for a grant is made by the person shown to be entitled thereto by the decision of the court in such proceedings. Upon such application any caveat entered by a party who had notice of the proceedings ceases to have effect.

Rule 46(4) requires every citation to be served personally on the person cited unless the District Judge or Registrar, on cause shown by affidavit, directs some other mode of service, which may include notice by advertisement.

Rule 46(5) provides that every will referred to in a citation must be lodged in a registry before the citation is issued, except where the will is not in the citor's possession and the District Judge or Registrar is satisfied that it is impracticable to require it to be lodged.

Rule 46(6) provides that a person who has been cited to appear may, within eight days of service of the citation upon him (inclusive of the day of such service), or at any time thereafter if no application has been made by the citor under paragraph (5) of r 47 or paragraph (2) of r 48, enter an appearance in the registry from which the citation issued by filing Form 5. A copy of Form 5 sealed with a seal of the registry must be served on the citor.

Rule 47 deals with citations to accept or refuse or to take a grant. Rule 47(1) provides that a citation to accept or refuse a grant may be issued at the instance of any person who would himself be entitled to a grant in the event of the person cited renouncing his right thereto.

Rule 47(2) provides that where power to make a grant to an executor has been reserved, a citation calling on him to accept or refuse a grant may be issued at the instance of the executors who have proved the will or the survivor of them or of the executors of the last survivor of deceased executors who have proved.

Rule 47(3) provides that a citation calling on an executor who has intermeddled in the estate of the deceased to show cause why he should not be ordered to take a grant may be issued at the instance of any person interested in the estate at any time after the expiration of six months from the death of the deceased. However, no citation to take a grant can be issued whilst proceedings as to the validity of the will are pending.

Rule 47(4) provides that a person cited who is willing to accept or take a grant may, after entering an appearance, apply *ex parte* by affidavit to a District Judge or Registrar for an order for a grant to himself.

Rule 47(5) sets out what happens if the time limited for appearance has expired, and the person cited has not entered an appearance. If the citation has been issued at the instance of any person who would himself be entitled to a grant in the event of the person cited renouncing his right to the grant, the citor may apply for an order for a grant to himself.

If the citation has been to an executor to whom power has been reserved, the citor may apply to a District Judge or Registrar for an order that a note be made on the grant that the executor in respect of whom power was reserved has been duly cited and has not appeared and that all his rights in respect of the executorship have wholly ceased.

If the citation is to someone who has intermeddled in the estate, the citor may apply to a District Judge or Registrar by summons (which must be served on the person cited) for an order requiring such person to take a grant within a specified time or for a grant to himself or to some other person specified in the summons. Intermeddling is taking active steps in the administration of the estate, but it does not include acts of humanity like feeding the animals belonging to the deceased.

Rule 47(6) provides that an application under r 47(5) must be supported by an affidavit showing that the citation was duly served.

Rule 47(7) sets out what happens if the person cited has entered an appearance but has not applied for a grant under paragraph (4), or has failed to prosecute his application with reasonable diligence. If the citation has been issued at the instance of any person who would himself be entitled to a grant in the event of the person cited renouncing his right to the grant, the citor may apply by summons to a District Judge or Registrar for an order for a grant to himself.

If the citation has been to an executor to whom power has been reserved, the citor may apply to a District Judge or Registrar for an order striking out the appearance and for the endorsement on the grant of a note that the executor in respect of whom power was reserved has been duly cited and that all his rights in respect of the executorship have wholly ceased.

If the citation is to someone who has intermeddled in the estate, the citor may apply to a District Judge or Registrar for an order requiring the person cited to take a grant within a specified time or for a grant to himself or to some other person specified in the summons.

The summons must be served on the person cited.

Rule 48 deals with citations to propound a will. Rule 48(1) provides that a citation to propound a will shall be directed to the executors named in the will and to all persons interested thereunder, and may be issued at the instance of any citor having an interest contrary to that of the executors or such other persons.

Rule 48(2) provides that if the time limited for appearance has expired, the citor may:

(a)   in the case where no person has entered an appearance, apply to a District Judge or Registrar for an order for a grant as if the will were invalid and such application shall be supported by an affidavit showing that the citation was duly served; or

(b)   in the case where no person who has entered an appearance proceeds with reasonable diligence to propound the will, apply to a District Judge or Registrar by summons, which shall be served on every person cited who has entered an appearance, for such an order as is mentioned in paragraph (a).

APPLICATION FOR AN ORDER TO ATTEND FOR EXAMINATION OR FOR SUBPOENA TO BRING IN A WILL

12.4   Section 122(1) of the Supreme Court Act 1981 (SCA 1981) provides that where there are reasonable grounds for believing that any person has knowledge of any document which is or purports to be a testamentary document, the High Court may, whether or not any legal proceedings are pending, order him to attend for the purpose of being examined in open court. Section 122(2) provides that the court may:

(a)   require any person who is before it, in compliance with an order under subsection (1) to answer any question relating to the document concerned; and

(b)   if appropriate, order him to bring in the document in such manner as the court may direct.

Section 122(3) provides that any person, who having been required by the court to do so under this section, fails to attend for examination, answer any question or bring in any document is guilty of contempt of court.

Section 123 provides that where it appears that any person has in his possession, custody or power any document which is or purports to be a testamentary document, the High Court may, whether or not any legal proceedings are pending, issue a subpoena requiring him to bring in the document in such manner as the court may in the subpoena direct.

Rule 50(1) of the NCPR 1987 provides that an application under s 122 of the SCA 1981 for an order requiring a person to attend for examination may, unless a probate action has been commenced, be made to a District Judge or Registrar by summons which shall be served on every such person.

Rule 50(2) provides that an application under s 123 of the SCA 1981 for the issue by a District Judge or Registrar of a subpoena to bring in a will must be supported by an affidavit setting out the grounds of the application, and if any person served with the subpoena denies that the will is in his possession or control he may file an affidavit to that effect in the registry from which the subpoena issued.

Chapter 13

Inheritance tax

DEATH ESTATE

13.1   Section 4(1) of the Inheritance Tax Act 1984 (ITA 1984) provides that on the death of any person tax shall be charged as if, immediately before his death, he had made a transfer of value and the value transferred by it had been equal to the value of his estate immediately before his death. Thus inheritance tax is payable on the value of all the property comprised in the estate of a deceased person.

The rate of tax is determined by cumulating all the PETS and *inter vivos* or lifetime chargeable transfers (transfers to trustees of all trusts apart from trusts for disabled persons within s 89, IHTA 1984 since 22 March 2006) in the seven years preceding the date of death. If they amount to more than the nil rate band, the whole of the estate is taxable at 40 per cent; if less, the unused part of the nil rate band can be offset against the death estate, and only the balance will be taxable at 40 per cent.

Assume that T dies leaving an estate of £612,000. Assuming that there have been no *inter vivos* gifts, IHT will be payable on £612,000 – the nil rate band for 2008/2009 of £312,000 = £300,000 at 40 per cent = £120,000.

If the deceased had made *inter vivos* or lifetime gifts on the seven years before death amounting to £400,000, the nil rate band would have been absorbed by these gifts, and so the whole death estate would have been taxable at 40 per cent.

POTENTIALLY EXEMPT TRANSFERS

13.2   Since 22 March 2006, a potentially exempt transfer is a transfer of value:

(a)   which is made by an individual on or after 18 March 1986; and

(b)   which, apart from this section, would be a chargeable transfer (or to the extent to which, apart from this section, it would be such a transfer); and

(c)   to the extent that it constitutes either a gift to another individual or a gift into a disabled trust or a gift into a bereaved minor's trust on the coming to an end of an immediate post death interest (s 3A, ITA 1984).

Gifts to individuals are thus PETS. If the donor survives for seven years, no IHT is payable. If the donor dies within the seven years, IHT is payable. However, tapering relief may operate to reduce the amount of IHT payable (s 7(4), ITA 1984). The amount of relief is:

PET within 0–3 years of death	100 per cent of IHT payable – no reduction
3–4	80 per cent
4–5	60 per cent
5–6	40 per cent
6–7	20 per cent

Note that tapering relief only reduces the amount of IHT payable; it does not reduce the value for IHT purposes, nor does it affect the value for cumulation purposes.

RATE OF TAX

13.3   There are two rates of tax applicable to the death estate at the moment – nil or 40 per cent. The nil rate band limit for 2008/2009 is £312,000.

In order to determine the rate of tax on death, the PET must be cumulated with:

(a)   all *inter vivos* or lifetime chargeable transfers made in the seven years preceding the PET; and

(b)   previous PETs provided they are within seven years of death.

If a PET was made more than seven years before death, the PET is ignored for all IHT purposes.

Examples

13.4   ae = annual exemption

(i)	2000	*inter vivos* or lifetime chargeable transfer
	2001	PET
	2006	PET
	2009	death

It will be necessary to calculate the IHT payable on the 2006 PET.

It will have to be cumulated with the 2000 *inter vivos* or lifetime chargeable transfer, but not the 2001 PET as this was more than seven years before death.

(ii)	2006	*inter vivos* chargeable transfer £131,000
	2008	PET £231,000
	2009	death

No IHT will be payable on the *inter vivos* chargeable transfer as it is within the nil rate band.

How much of the nil rate band is left to offset against the 2008 PET?

Nil rate band (2009/10)		£325,000
Deduct 2006 *inter vivos* chargeable transfer	£131,000	
Less ae × 2 (if not used in one year, the annual exemption or balance of the annual exemption can be carried forward to next year)	£6,000	£125,000
		£200,000
2008 PET		£231,000
Less ae × 2		£6,000
		£225,000
Less balance of nil rate band		£200,000
		£125,000
IHT at 40 per cent =		£50,000

(iii)	2004 PET		£431,000
	2009 death		
	PET		£431,000
	Less a e × 2		£6,000
			£425,000
	Less nil rate band		£325,000
			£100,000
	IHT at 40 per cent =		£40,000

4–5 years: 60 per cent of tax payable $\qquad £40,000 \times \dfrac{60}{100} \qquad$ £24,000

Note that the rates of IHT payable are the rates in force at the date of death, unless they have increased. The value on which IHT is payable in the case of a PET is the value at the date of the gift; thus the value is frozen. Even if the donor is not likely to survive for seven years, it is thus still a good idea to give away assets which may increase in value.

It may be possible to insure against the donor dying within seven years of the PET.

GIFTS WITH RESERVATION OF BENEFIT

13.5 Be careful not to infringe the rules relating to gifts with reservation of benefit – otherwise the PET will be ineffective as far as saving IHT is concerned.

Section 102 of the Finance Act 1986 applies where an individual disposes of any property by way of gift and either:

(a) possession and enjoyment of the property are not *bona fide* assumed by the donee at or before the beginning of the relevant period; or

(b)   at any time in the relevant period the property is not enjoyed to the entire exclusion, or virtually to the entire exclusion, of the donor and of any benefit to him by contract or otherwise.

The effect of these provisions is that such a gift is ineffective as far as IHT is concerned; at the date of death the donor will still be deemed to own the property. Furthermore, the original gift is still a PET. However, the donee still owns the property for other purposes, and so there will be no free uplift to market value for CGT purposes.

If the donor releases the reserved benefit, it will be deemed to be a PET as from the date when the reservation was released.

The Finance Act 1999 inserted special provisions dealing with land. Section 102A applies where an individual disposes of an interest in land by way of gift on or after 9 March 1999. Section 102A(2) provides that at any time in the relevant period when the donor or spouse enjoys a significant right or interest, or is party to a significant arrangement, in relation to the land:

(a)   the interest disposed of is referred to (in relation to the gift and the donor) as property subject to a reservation; and

(b)   s 102(3) and (4) above shall apply.

Section 102A(3) provides that subject to subsections (4) and (5), a right, interest or arrangement in relation to land is significant for the purposes of subsection (2) if (and only if) it entitles or enables the donor to occupy all or part of the land, or to enjoy some right in relation to all or part of the land, otherwise than for full consideration in money or money's worth.

Subsection (4) provides that a right, interest or arrangement is not significant for the purposes of subsection (2) if:

(a)   it does not and cannot prevent the enjoyment of the land to the entire exclusion, or virtually to the entire exclusion, of the donor; or

(b)   it does not entitle or enable the donor to occupy all or part of the land immediately after the disposal, but would do so were it not for the disposal of the interest.

Subsection (5) provides that a right or interest is not significant for the purposes of subsection (2) if it was granted or acquired before the period of seven years ending with the date of the gift.

Thus if a parent grants a lease of his house to himself, and then gives the freehold to a child, the donor will be deemed to have reserved a benefit, and the house will form part of the donor's estate on death. However, if the lease is granted on the same terms as a lease between strangers, then no benefit will have been reserved in the gift of the freehold.

What is the position if the parents execute a declaration of trust declaring that they hold the property on trust for themselves and their children? The declaration of trust will be a PET, but the reservation of benefit provisions will not apply if:

160

(a)   the parents and the children occupy the land; and

(b)   the parents do not receive any benefit, other than a negligible one, which is provided by or at the expense of the children for some reason connected with the gift.

Thus both the parents and the children must occupy the house. If the children do not do so, then the parents will be deemed to have reserved a benefit. The parents must not receive any collateral benefit. Thus if the child has a 50 per cent interest in the property, the child must not bear more than 50 per cent of the running expenses of the home. If they do bear more than 50 per cent, the reservation of benefit provisions will apply.

If a child moves out, the parents will have to provide full consideration to prevent the application of the reservation of benefit rules.

EXEMPTIONS AND RELIEFS APPLYING ON DEATH

13.6   It may be possible to claim the following exemptions and reliefs:

(a)   The spouse or civil partner exemption. If the spouse or civil partner of the deceased succeeds to the property, the spouse exemption will apply. Section 18(1) of the ITA 1984 provides that a transfer of value is an exempt transfer to the extent that the value transferred is attributable to property which becomes comprised in the estate of the transferor's spouse or civil partner, or, so far as the value transferred is not so attributable, to the extent that the estate is increased.

Note that the spouse or civil partner exemption only applies if the donee spouse or civil partner is domiciled in the United Kingdom. If the donee spouse or civil partner is not domiciled in the United Kingdom, then the spouse exemption is limited to £55,000. This means that an amount equal to the nil rate band plus £55,000 can be given to a spouse not domiciled here without incurring any liability for IHT.

(b)   Gifts of excluded property. No IHT is payable in respect of gifts of excluded property. Excluded property comprises the following:

  (i)   property situated outside the UK if the person beneficially entitled to it is an individual domiciled outside the UK (s 6(1)).

  Note that both conditions must be satisfied for property to be treated as excluded as property – the property must be situated outside the UK, and the person beneficially entitled to it must be domiciled outside the UK. If a person is domiciled in the UK, then all the assets of that person wherever situated will be subject to IHT. If a person is not domiciled in the UK, then it is only the assets in this country which will be subject to IHT;

  (ii)   a reversionary interest unless:

    —   it has at any time been acquired (whether by the person entitled to it or by a person previously entitled to it) for a consideration in money or money's worth; or

> — it is one to which the settlor or his spouse or civil partner is or has been beneficially entitled (s 48(1));

(iii) s 48(3) of the ITA 1984 provides that where property comprised in a settlement is situated outside the UK:

> — the property (but not a reversionary interest in the property) is excluded property unless the settlor was domiciled in the UK at the time when the settlement was made; and

> — s 6(1) applies to a reversionary interest in the property, but does not otherwise apply in relation to that property.

Thus normally there is no charge to IHT on any transfers of reversionary interests.

(c) Charities and political parties. Gifts to charities and political parties are exempt.

(d) Business property relief and agricultural property relief. Business property relief operates to reduce the value of the property by 100 per cent in the following cases:

(i) property consisting of a business or an interest in a business;

(ii) shares in or securities of a company which are unquoted and which (either by themselves or together with other such shares or securities owned by the transferor) gave the transferor control of the company immediately before the transfer;

(iii) any unquoted shares in a company.

Relief of 50 per cent is available on the following:

(i) shares in or securities of a company which are quoted and which (either by themselves or together with other such shares or securities owned by the transferor) gave the transferor control of the company immediately before the transfer;

(ii) any land, or building, machinery or plant which, immediately before the transfer, was used wholly or mainly for the purposes of a business carried on by a company of which the transferor then had control or by a partnership of which he was then a partner;

(iii) any land or building, machinery or plant which, immediately before the transfer, was used wholly or mainly for the purposes of a business carried on by the transferor and was settled property in which he was then beneficially entitled to an interest in possession (s 105(1), ITA 1984).

Shares are quoted if they are quoted on a recognised stock exchange (s 105(1ZA), ITA 1984).

Section 106 provides that property is not relevant business property in relation to a transfer of value unless it has been owned by the transferor for the two years immediately preceding the transfer.

Section 116 of the ITA 1984 permits the value of agricultural property to be reduced by 100 per cent if:

(i)   the interest of the transferor in the property immediately before the transfer carries the right to vacant possession or the right to obtain it within the next 24 months; or

(ii)   it is notwithstanding the terms of the tenancy valued at an amount broadly equivalent to vacant possession value; or

(iii)   the interest of the transferor in the property immediately before the transfer does not carry the right to vacant possession within 24 months because the property is let on a tenancy beginning on or after 1 September 1995 (see ESC F17).

In other cases the relief is 50 per cent.

Section 117 provides that relief is not available unless:

(i)   it was occupied by the transferor for the purposes of agriculture throughout the period of two years ending with the date of transfer; or

(ii)   it was owned by him throughout the period of seven years ending with that date and was throughout that period occupied (by him or another) for the purposes of agriculture.

A farmer who is an owner-occupier will qualify for 100 per cent relief if he has owned the land for two years.

If the land is let, it will still qualify for 100 per cent relief if the owner has owned it for seven years and can recover possession within 24 months, or the tenancy was granted after 1 September 1995.

(e)   Loss on sale relief. This applies if quoted shares or land are sold for less than the market value at the date of death. It is considered more fully at **para 14.1**.

LIABILITY FOR IHT

13.7   This section deals with who is liable to pay any inheritance tax due to the Inland Revenue.

Lifetime chargeable transfers

13.8   These are usually lifetime transfers to the trustees of any trust apart from a trust for disabled persons. Inheritance tax may have been paid when the transfer was first made, and if the settlor dies within seven years of the transfer, then the inheritance tax has to be recalculated using the death rate. If this calculation results in more tax being payable, the primary liability falls on the transferee trustees, but if they do not satisfy the liability within 12 months of death, then the personal representatives of the deceased become liable for the tax. Although it is uncertain, it would seem only right that the personal representatives should be able to recover the tax from the transferee trustees if they should be bearing the burden.

Potentially exempt transfers

13.9   If the donor dies within seven years of making a gift, the primary liability for any inheritance tax due falls on the donee. However, as with lifetime chargeable transfers, if the donee does not pay within 12 months of the tax becoming due, then it becomes the liability of the personal representatives. Again, although it is not absolutely certain, it seems that the personal representatives should be able to recover the tax from the donee if they should be bearing the burden.

The death estate

13.10   Section 200(1) of the ITA 1984 provides that the persons liable for tax on the value transferred by a chargeable transfer made on the death of any person are:

(a)   so far as the tax is attributable to the value of property which either:

(i)   was not immediately before the death comprised in a settlement; or

(ii)   was so comprised and consists of land in the UK which devolves upon or vests in the deceased's personal representatives;

(b)   so far as the tax is attributable to the value of property which, immediately before the death, was comprised in a settlement, the trustees of the settlement;

(c)   so far as the tax is attributable to the value of any property, any person in whom the property is vested (whether beneficially or otherwise) at any time after the death, or who at any such time is beneficially entitled to an interest in possession in the property;

(d)   so far as the tax is attributable to the value of any property which, immediately before the death, was comprised in a settlement, any person for whose benefit any of the property or income from it is applied after death.

BURDEN OF IHT

13.11   Which beneficiary has to bear the burden of inheritance tax? Normally the inheritance tax payable on the free estate of the deceased is a testamentary expense, and is payable out of the residuary estate.

Inheritance tax due in respect of property situated abroad is usually borne by the foreign property.

If property passes by survivorship, any inheritance tax due is normally borne by the survivor or survivors.

It is of course open to testators to direct that the burden of inheritance tax should fall on particular beneficiaries to the exclusion of others. The personal representatives must give effect to this direction, but it does not affect HMRC, who can take proceedings against whoever is liable for the tax.

TIME FOR PAYMENT

13.12   Inheritance tax is due in respect of the death estate six months after the end of the month of death. If it is not paid then, interest is due.

It is possible to elect to pay the inheritance tax due in respect of certain property by instalments over ten years; for a fuller description of the property to which the instalment option applies, see **para 5.7**.

INLAND REVENUE CHARGE

13.13   Section 237(1) of the ITA 1984 provides that a charge in respect of unpaid inheritance tax is imposed on:

(a)   any property to the value of which the value transferred is wholly or partly attributable; and

(b)   where the chargeable transfer is made by the making of a settlement or is made under Part III of the Act, any property comprised in the settlement.

Section 237(2) provides that where the chargeable transfer is made on death, personal or moveable property situated in the UK which was beneficially owned by the deceased immediately before his death and which vests in his personal representatives is not subject to the charge. 'Personal property' includes leaseholds.

The charge does not bind the purchasers of land in England and Wales unless it was registered as a land charge or, in the case of registered land, protected by notice on the register.

Position where there are gifts in a will to exempt beneficiaries and non-exempt beneficiaries

13.14   Section 41 of the ITA 1984 provides that notwithstanding the terms of any disposition:

(a)   none of the tax on the value transferred shall fall on any specific gift if or to the extent that the transfer is exempt with respect to the gift; and

(b)   none of the tax attributable to the value of the property comprised in the residue shall fall on any gift of a share of residue if or to the extent that the transfer is exempt with respect to the gift.

Whilst the theory behind this section is correct – a gift which would otherwise be exempt should not bear its own tax – it has caused difficulties in its application to mixed gifts of residue to exempt beneficiaries and non-exempt beneficiaries.

Part residue going to exempt beneficiaries, part to non-exempt

13.15   For example, suppose a will contains the following residuary gift: 'I give half of my residuary estate to my son and half to the RSPCA.'

There are two ways of dealing with this gift:

(a)   the son's share could be grossed up so that the son receives the same amount as the charity;

(b)   all the inheritance tax is paid form the son's share so that the son receives less than the charity.

According to *Re Ratcliffe* [1999[STC 262 it is a question of the construction of the will as to which method should be adopted, and in that particular case it was held that method (b) was the correct way of dealing with it.

Specific gift to exempt beneficiary, residue to non-exempt beneficiary

13.16   Section 42(1) of the ITA 1984 defines a specific gift as any gift other than a gift of residue or of a share of residue.

If there is a specific gift in a will to an exempt beneficiary, like the spouse or a charity, then the value of the specific gift does not bear any inheritance tax, but the residue bears tax at whatever rate is appropriate.

If a will contains a specific legacy of £400,000 to the spouse, that will be exempt because of the spouse exemption. If the residue of £500,000 goes to the children, then the balance of that after deducting the nil rate band will be chargeable to inheritance tax at 40 per cent.

Specific gift to non-exempt beneficiary bearing its own tax, residue to exempt beneficiary

13.17   No inheritance tax will be payable on the residue, and the value of the non-exempt gift will be subject to inheritance. Thus if the specific gift is worth £712,000, inheritance tax at 40 per cent will be payable on £400,000 – the amount of the specific gift less the nil rate band for 2008/2009 – £160,000.

Specific gift to non-exempt beneficiary free of tax, residue to exempt beneficiary

13.18   It may be that the specific gift is expressed to be free of tax, or if nothing is said, then it will be treated as being free of tax. In this situation, the specific gift must be grossed up to find the amount which after deducting the tax will leave the amount of the gift.

Thus if a will contains a legacy of £300,000 to a child, and that gift is expressed to be free of tax, or nothing is said, and the residue is given to an exempt beneficiary, assuming that the nil rate band has been absorbed by lifetime gifts, the legacy will have to be grossed up:

$$£300 \times \frac{100}{100-40} = £500,000$$

The beneficiary will receive the £300,000 legacy in full, but the residuary beneficiary will have to bear the burden of the inheritance tax.

Specific gift to exempt beneficiary, part of residue to exempt beneficiary

13.19   If there is a specific gift to an exempt beneficiary, the spouse, and a gift of part of the residue to a charity, the share of the residue passing to the non-exempt beneficiary is taxed on the actual amount.

Specific gift to non-exempt beneficiary subject to tax, part of residue to exempt beneficiary

13.20   In order to calculate the inheritance tax, the specific gift should be deducted from the residue, and the part of the residue going to the non-exempt beneficiary calculated. The specific gift should then be added to the non-exempt residue, and the inheritance tax calculated.

Specific gifts to non-exempt beneficiaries, some subject to tax, some not, residue to exempt beneficiary; specific gifts to non-exempt beneficiaries, some subject to tax, some not, residue to exempt and non-exempt beneficiaries; specific gifts to non-exempt beneficiaries free of tax, residue to exempt and non-exempt beneficiaries

13.21   These wills all involve complicated calculations in order to determine the rate of inheritance tax. As they are met infrequently in practice, they are not considered in this book.

Chapter 14

Capital gains tax

OVERVIEW

14.1   After death, the personal representatives will need to settle any liability for CGT incurred by the deceased when he was alive. The personal representatives will of course be able to offset the deceased's annual exemption against the liability, and it may be that other exemptions and reliefs will be available.

Any losses incurred by the deceased can be offset against any gains made by the deceased in the tax year of death, but they cannot be carried forward and set off against any losses incurred by the personal representatives. However, s 62(2) of the Taxation of Chargeable Gains Act 1992 permits allowable losses sustained by an individual in the year of assessment in which he dies to be deducted from chargeable gains accruing to the deceased in the three years of assessment preceding the year of assessment in which the death occurs, taking chargeable gains accruing in a later year before those accruing in an earlier year.

The personal representatives are deemed to acquire the assets at market value at the date of death (s 62(1)). Normally the value for IHT purposes will be accepted as being the market value for both IHT and CGT. Frequently the personal representatives will vest the property in the legatees, in which event s 62(4) provides that no chargeable gain shall accrue to the personal representatives, but instead the legatees are treated as acquiring the asset at the market value at the date of death. 'Legatee' is widely defined in s 64(2) as including any person taking under a testamentary disposition or on an intestacy or partial intestacy, whether he takes beneficially or as trustee, and a person taking under a *donatio mortis causa* shall be treated (except for the purposes of s 62) as a legatee and his acquisition as made at the time of the donor's death.

Section 64(1) permits the legatee to deduct:

(a)   any expenditure within s 38(2) incurred by him in relation to the transfer of the asset to him by the personal representatives or trustees; and

(b)   any such expenditure incurred in relation to the transfer of the asset by the personal representatives or trustees.

Sections , 72(1) and 73(1) provide that on the death of the life tenant there is a deemed disposal by the trustees, but no chargeable gain accrues. However, s 74(2) provides that if hold-over relief has been claimed, these provisions do not apply, but any chargeable gain accruing to the trustees is restricted to the amount of the held-over gain. Thus if a settlement was created *inter vivos*, and any gain made by the settlor was held over, the held-over gain becomes chargeable on the death of the life tenant, but not the gain accruing from the date of transfer to the date of death. These rules apply to settlements created before 22 March 2006; after that date the rules only apply to immediate post death interests, transitional serial interests and disabled persons interests where the disabled person has a life interest as defined in the Inheritance Tax Act 1984.

It may be necessary for the personal representatives to sell assets in order to complete the administration of the estate. Any gain will be computed in accordance with normal principles, and the personal representatives are entitled to the annual exemption for the year of death, and the two subsequent tax years; the remaining gain will be subject to tax at 18 per cent. Note that s 64(1) does not apply in this situation, but the Revenue has issued Statements of Practice, SP 2/04, which contain a scale of permitted deductions. In addition, in *IRC v Richards Executors [1971] 1 WLR 571*, executors paid fees to solicitors for investigations, valuations, the obtaining of a confirmation in Scotland and the resealing of the confirmation in England. It was held that the proportion of fees applicable to some stocks and shares was deductible in calculating the capital gains of the executors.

Personal representatives are not allowed to claim the private residence exemption, but by Statutory Concession D5 they can still claim it if the house is occupied by the beneficiary entitled to the house under the will or intestacy as his only or main residence, and was so occupied before the death of the deceased. This concession has now been incorporated into the Taxation of Chargeable Gains Act 1992 by the Finance Act 2004. The 2004 Act has inserted a new section after s 225 of the Taxation of Chargeable Gains Act 1992, which provides that personal representatives can claim the private residence exemption if the following conditions are satisfied:

(a) immediately before and immediately after the death of the deceased person the dwelling house or part of the dwelling house was the only or main residence of one or more individuals;

(b) that individual or one of those individuals has a relevant entitlement, two or more of those individuals have relevant entitlements, and the relevant entitlements account for, or the relevant entitlements together account for, 75 per cent of the net proceeds of disposal.

'Relevant entitlement' means an entitlement as legatee of the deceased person to, or to an interest in possession in, the whole or any part of the net proceeds of disposal.

'Net proceeds of sale' is defined as:

(a) the proceeds of the disposal of the asset realised by the personal representatives; less

(b) any incidental costs allowable as a deduction in accordance with s 38(1)(C) in computing the gain accruing to the personal representatives on that disposal.

It is to be assumed that none of the proceeds is required to meet liabilities of the deceased person's estate (including any liability for inheritance tax).

Sections 178 and 179 of the Inheritance Tax Act 1984 (ITA) provide that if quoted shares are sold at a loss within 12 months of death, the lower value can be substituted for IHT purposes. Where this is done, the lower value also becomes the acquisition value of the personal representatives for CGT purposes, so that they cannot claim loss relief as well. If several shareholdings are sold, the gains and losses must be aggregated. There is a similar provision with regard to the sale of land within four years of death, but it is unclear whether the sale price also becomes the acquisition value for CGT purposes as well. Section 187 of the ITA 1984 provides that the market value for the purposes of CGT of shares for which the relief is claimed shall be their sale value; there is no similar provision with regard to land, and so it could be argued that the lower value did not have to be substituted for CGT purposes. However, s 274 of the Taxation of Chargeable Gains Act 1992 provides that where on the death of any person inheritance tax is chargeable on the value of his estate immediately before his death and the value of an asset has been ascertained (whether in any proceedings or otherwise) for the purposes of that tax, the value so ascertained shall be taken for the purposes of this Act to be the market value of that asset at the date of death. Thus it is probable that personal representatives cannot claim a loss for both CGT and IHT as far as land is concerned. (See Barlow, King & King, *Wills Administration and Taxation* (7th edition, Sweet & Maxwell) page 229.)

It should be noted that losses incurred by personal representatives cannot be transferred to beneficiaries.

Chapter 15

Income tax

INCOME ARISING BEFORE DEATH

15.1   It is the duty of personal representatives to ensure that any income tax due to the date of death is paid or, if a repayment is due, that it is claimed (s 74(1), Taxes Management Act 1970). Payment or repayment may affect the amount of IHT due on death.

The personal representatives should report the death to the Inspector of Taxes, and submit a return for the period from 6 April to the date of death. The Revenue can assess personal representatives within three tax years from the end of the tax year in which death occurred; assessments can go back six years from date of assessment.

PERSONAL ALLOWANCES

15.2   The deceased is entitled to full personal allowances for the year of death.

How do you distinguish between income of the deceased and income of the estate?

15.3   The crucial date is the date when it is received or credited. For succession purposes it may have to be apportioned, but for income tax purposes the crucial date is the date when the payment should be received or credited.

Shares may be valued on a *cum div* basis with the result that the dividend may be subject to IHT. When the dividend is paid, it will be subject to income tax. This can result in an element of double taxation. Section 669 of the Income Tax (Trading and Other Income) Act 2005 (ITTOIA) affords some relief, but only to a residuary beneficiary who is absolutely entitled.

THE ADMINISTRATION PERIOD

15.4   This runs from the date of death to the date when the administration of the estate is complete, or in other words, when the residue is ascertained. The personal representatives are liable only for basic rate tax, but they cannot claim any personal allowances. However, they may be able to offset interest on money borrowed to pay IHT.

The personal representatives are responsible for completing any income tax return. If basic rate tax has been deducted at source, it need not be included in any tax return by the personal representatives. However, if the personal representatives are in receipt of untaxed income, for example rents, they must notify the appropriate tax district, and complete a return.

Note that the rule in *Re Earl of Chesterfield's Trusts* does not affect liability for income tax.

If the personal representatives have had to borrow money in order to pay the inheritance tax due on personalty, the interest is deductible in computing the income tax liability of the personal representatives. Note that it is only the interest paid in respect of a period ending within one year of the making of the loan (ss 403–405, Income Tax Act 2007).

If inheritance tax is payable on realty, use should be made of the right to pay by instalments so that there is no need to borrow.

TAXATION OF BENEFICIARIES

General legacies

15.5   General legacies usually do not carry interest or income. However, if interest is payable, it is assessable under s 369, ITTOIA. Normally the interest should be paid gross.

Specific legatees

15.6   Specific legatees are entitled to the income from the date of death, but they are not liable for income tax until the asset is vested in them. The income will then be taxed as part of the specific legatee's income in the year in which it arises.

Annuities

15.7   The personal representatives should deduct tax at basic rates when paying.

Annuities may be expressed in different ways. For example:

(a)   the annuitant is to have such sum as after deduction of basic rate income tax will leave £750;

(b)   the annuitant is to have £750 free of income tax.

Residuary beneficiaries with a limited interest

15.8   The personal representatives must deduct income tax at basic rate before paying any income to a beneficiary, and the beneficiary includes the grossed up amount in his return. All the income paid to a beneficiary in a year of assessment is taxed in that year. Personal representatives should therefore be wary of saving up income, and paying it all in one tax year. It could mean that the beneficiary will have to pay higher rate tax, which he would not have had to pay if the income had been paid regularly.

Residuary beneficiaries with an absolute interest

15.9   Income tax is payable only on the income, not on distributions of capital. Under s 652 *et seq*, ITTOIA, personal representatives must calculate the assumed income entitlement, which is in effect the undistributed income accruing from the residuary estate.

If there is any distribution to the residuary beneficiary, whether it is capital or income, the first part of that distribution is deemed to be income.

For example, A and B are the personal representatives of T. They receive the following income:

(a)   tax year of death: £800;

(b)   second year: £1,200.

A and B do not distribute any of the assets or income in the tax year of death. In the second year, they vest T's house in the residuary beneficiaries. The residuary beneficiaries will be deemed to have been paid the income of £2,000.

Personal representatives should be wary about retaining capital and income. If it is paid to a beneficiary at the end of the administration period, it could mean that the beneficiary will have to pay higher rate tax. On the other hand, delay may be desirable if, for example, it is known that the beneficiary is about to retire and will suffer a drop in income.

TAX DEDUCTION CERTIFICATES

15.10   Personal representatives can be required to supply beneficiaries with Form R185 showing the amount of income paid and the tax deducted.

Chapter 16

Tax consequences of different gifts, variations and disclaimers

SPOUSE OR CIVIL PARTNER – ABSOLUTE OR LIFE INTEREST?

Inheritance tax

16.1 It makes no difference initially, as far as IHT is concerned, whether the spouse or civil partner has an absolute interest or an immediate post death interest under the will of a deceased spouse or civil partner. No IHT will be payable because of the spouse or civil partner exemption. However, if the spouse or civil partner has an absolute interest, the spouse or civil partner can make use of the *inter vivos* exemptions from IHT and, in addition, can make PETs. A spouse or civil partner with an immediate post death interest, as opposed to an absolute interest, will not be able to do so out of the capital – the subject of the immediate post death interest – unless the trustees have the power to advance capital to the life tenant and do so.

Note that the spouse or civil partner exemption is limited to £55,000 if the spouse or civil partner is not domiciled in the UK.

Capital gains tax

16.2 Where a spouse or civil partner has an absolute interest, any gain belongs to the spouse or civil partner.

Where a spouse or civil partner has an immediate post death interest, any gain belongs to the trustees. The trustees will be entitled to half the annual exemption available to private individuals, but the rate of tax on the gains will be 18 per cent.

The spouse or civil partner will also be entitled to the annual exemption in his or her own right.

Income tax

16.3 It makes no difference, as far as income tax is concerned, whether the spouse or civil partner has an absolute interest or only an immediate post death interest. The spouse or civil partner will be liable to income tax on all income received.

NIL RATE BAND GIFT

16.4   A very effective method of saving IHT prior to the introduction of the transferable nil rate band was for the will to contain a legacy up to the nil rate band to the children, with the residue to the spouse or civil partner.

Note the following points:

(a)   PETs and *inter vivos* chargeable transfers made in the seven years before death will reduce the nil rate band;

(b)   be careful not to exceed the nil rate band – grossing up may apply if there is a gift free of tax to children or grandchildren with the residue going to the spouse or civil partner;

(c)   consider imposing a limit on the legacy in case the nil rate band is substantially increased;

(d)   be careful also to ensure that a nil rate band legacy does not include agricultural property and business property qualifying for 100 per cent relief as it is a waste of the relief.

Whilst this idea has lost much of its usefulness as a means of saving IHT, it still has its uses if there are personal concerns, for example, children from previous marriages. A NRB legacy to them from a parent's estate remainder to a second or third spouse will ensure that the children do get something from the parent's estate.

NIL RATE BAND DISCRETIONARY TRUST

16.5   This is where an amount not exceeding the nil rate band is settled on a discretionary trust for the benefit of the spouse or civil partner and children. Usually the trustees are given power to accept an IOU from the surviving spouse or civil partner or a charge on the matrimonial home for the amount of the nil rate band legacy. On the death of the surviving spouse or civil partner, the amount due under the IOU or charge is deductible from the estate of the surviving spouse or civil partner.

Inheritance tax

16.6   No inheritance tax falls due on creation, but there is a possibility of a charge on distributions and on each tenth anniversary. However, the amount of IHT payable should be small.

When a beneficiary dies, the trust property will not form part of the beneficiary's estate for IHT purposes.

Capital gains tax

16.7   The trustees will be entitled to half of the annual exemption available to an individual.

If the trustees dispose of any assets, and become liable to CGT, the rate of tax is 18 per cent.

Death normally wipes out any capital gain, so that a beneficiary acquires the assets at market value as at the date of death. This will not happen with discretionary trusts.

Income tax

16.8 The trustees will pay income tax at 40 per cent (dividends 32.5 per cent), but if the income is paid to a beneficiary who is not a basic rate taxpayer, the beneficiary will be able to recover the tax paid, although the 10 per cent paid on dividends is not recoverable.

Again this type of will has lost much of its popularity since the introduction of the transferable nil rate band, but is is still useful if there are personal issues, and if the surviving spouse remarries. These issues are explored in more detail in *Estate Planning for the Middle Income Client* by this author and published by Tottel Publishing.

TWO-YEAR DISCRETIONARY TRUST

Inheritance tax

16.9 Section 144 of the Inheritance Tax Act 1984 (ITA) provides that any termination of a discretionary trust within two years of death is not a transfer of value for IHT purposes. Any termination is read back into the will.

IHT may have to be paid on the death of the testator. If there is an appointment in favour of the spouse or civil partner, the spouse or civil partner exemption will apply.

Appointments should not be made within three months of death. The reason for this is that s 65(4) provides that there is no charge when property leaves the settlement if the event in question occurs within a quarter beginning with the day on which the settlement commenced. Section 144(2) provides that the section does not apply in that situation.

Capital gains tax

16.10 There is no special treatment for CGT purposes. If the administration of the estate has been completed, the trustees will be deemed to acquire the assets at market value as at the date of death. If there is an appointment, the trustees will be deemed to dispose of the assets at market value on the date of the appointment. If the administration of the estate has not been completed, the position is unclear. It is arguable that the trustees are disposing of a chose in action, which has a nil base cost for CGT purposes as it is a new type of property coming into existence on death, but the market value of which is near the value of the assets the trustees will ultimately receive if the estate is solvent. It is believed that HMRC do not take this point.

ABSOLUTE GIFTS TO CHILDREN AND GRANDCHILDREN

16.11   As the children or grandchildren will not be able to give a valid receipt for capital until they are 18, the personal representatives will usually become trustees of the gift.

Inheritance tax

16.12   If the beneficiary dies under the age of 18, the property will still form part of the beneficiary's estate for IHT purposes. However, there will be no charge when the beneficiary attains 18, or if the trustees exercise their power of advancement.

Capital gains tax

16.13   Any gain made by the trustees will belong to the beneficiary. There will not be a deemed disposal when the beneficiary attains 18.

Income tax

16.14   Trustees pay income tax at basic rate; depending on his or her income, the beneficiary will be able to recover the tax paid, or may be liable to higher rate tax.

CONTINGENT GIFTS TO CHILDREN AND GRANDCHILDREN

Inheritance tax

16.15   Contingent gifts to children in wills may be a bereaved minor's trust.

In order for a trust to be treated as being for bereaved minors, the following conditions must be satisfied:

(a)   the property must be held on a statutory trust for the benefit of a bereaved minor under ss 46 and 47(1) of the Administration of Estates Act 1925; or

(b)   held on trust for the benefit of a bereaved minor, and the following conditions are satisfied:

   (i)   the trust must be established under the will of the deceased parent of the bereaved minor;

   (ii)   the trust must provide that the bereaved minor, if he has not done so before attaining the age of 18, will on attaining that age become absolutely entitled to the settled property, any income arising from it, and any income that has arisen from the property held in the trust for his benefit which has been accumulated before that time;

(iii) the trust must also provide that so long as the bereaved minor is living and under the age of 18, if any of the settled property is applied for the benefit of a beneficiary, it is applied for the benefit of the bereaved minor; and

(iv) the trust must also provide that so long as the bereaved minor is living and under the age of 18, either the bereaved minor is entitled to all of the income (if there is any) arising from any of the settled property or no such income may be applied for the benefit of any other person.

A 'bereaved minor' is defined as a person who has not yet attained the age of 18 and at least one of whose parents has died. A step-parent and someone with parental responsibility for a child can also create such a settlement.

The IHT consequences of a bereaved minor's trust are that IHT may be payable on the death of the parent, but after that, there is no further charge to IHT.

It is possible to have a trust for a bereaved minor contingent on him attaining the age of 25, but there will be a charge to IHT when the child attains that age.

Other gifts in wills to minors will be subject to the relevant property regime, which means that IHT may be payable on the death of the testator, and in addition, it will be payable on every tenth anniversary of the death of the testator, and also whenever the minor satisfies the contingency.

Capital gains tax

16.16   The trustees are entitled to a maximum of half the annual exemption available to an individual; the rate of tax is 18 per cent.

When a beneficiary satisfies the contingency and becomes absolutely entitled, there is a deemed disposal by the trustees at market value. Hold-over relief will be available if the trust assets are business assets; it will apply to all assets if the settlement is a bereaved minors trust.

Income tax

16.17   Trustees will pay income tax at 40 per cent or 32.5 per cent. The beneficiary may be able to recover this tax; alternatively, the beneficiary may be liable for more if his income is large enough.

A bereaved minors trust where the age contingency is 18 will constitute a trust for a vulnerable person, which can receive special treatment as far as income tax and capital gains tax are concerned. The trustees and the parent or guardian of the minor must elect for these provisions to apply, and if the election is made, it is assumed that any income or capital gains are taxed as if they were the income of the bereaved minor. This should substantially reduce the income tax charge.

FREE OF TAX LEGACIES

16.18   The basic rule is that any gift in a will of property in the UK is free of IHT. However, if a legacy is tax free, and the residue goes to an exempt beneficiary, the legacy will have to be grossed up (see **para 13.18**).

VARIATIONS AND DISCLAIMERS

Inheritance tax

16.19   Section 142(1) of the ITA 1984 provides that:

'Where within the period of two years after a person's death –

(a)   any of the dispositions (whether effected by will, under the law relating to intestacy or otherwise) of the property comprised in his estate immediately before his death are varied, or

(b)   the benefit conferred by any of those dispositions is disclaimed,

by an instrument in writing made by the persons or any of the persons who benefit or would benefit under the dispositions, the Act shall apply as if the variation had been effected by the deceased or, as the case may be, the disclaimed benefit had never been conferred.'

Variations

16.20   The following points should be noted with regard to variations:

(a)   s 142(1) of the ITA 1984 applies to both intestacies and wills;

(b)   a surviving joint tenant can use s 142(1), although it may be that a survivng joint tenant cannot use the severed share to create an immediate post death interest or bereaved minors' trust;

(c)   the variation must be made within two years of the date of death;

(d)   there must be an instrument in writing;

(e)   the section does not apply to a settlement where the deceased was the life tenant;

(f)   the section does not permit the variation of a gift where the deceased reserved a benefit;

(g)   the section does not apply if consideration was given for the variation. An indemnity as regards IHT or income tax might infringe this provision;

(h)   the parties to a variation must be of full age and capacity. If not, the court may be prepared to sanction a variation under the Variation of Trusts Act 1958. To be effective, any order must be made within two years of death;

(i)   if extra IHT is payable, the personal representatives must join in the election;

(j)   the election must be in the deed of variation. Since 1 August 2002, there is no need for notice to be given to the Revenue unless the variation means that more IHT is payable;

(k)   once property has been varied, it cannot be varied again; however, there can be several variations as long as the property is different.

Disclaimers

16.21   Any beneficiary can refuse to accept a gift, unless he has expressly or impliedly accepted the gift, or fails to disclaim within a reasonable time. As long as gifts are unconnected, a beneficiary can accept one gift and refuse another. If a non-residuary gift is disclaimed, the gift becomes part of the residue; if a residuary gift is disclaimed, the property passes to those persons entitled under the intestacy rules.

Section 142 of the ITA 1984 applies to disclaimers as well as variations.

Capital gains tax

16.22   Section 62(6) of the Taxation of Chargeable Gains Act 1992 provides that:

'Where within the period of two years after a person's death any of the dispositions (whether effected by will, under the law relating to intestacy or otherwise) of the property of which he was competent to dispose are varied, or the benefit conferred by any of those dispositions is disclaimed, by an instrument in writing made by the persons or any of the persons who benefit under the dispositions:

(a)   the variation or disclaimer shall not constitute a disposal for the purposes of this Act; and

(b)   this section shall apply as if the variation had been effected by the deceased or, as the case may be, the disclaimed benefit had never been conferred.'

Note that the section applies to property held by the deceased as a joint tenant.

Income tax

Variations

16.23   Income arising between the date of death and the variation belongs to the original beneficiary.

A variation may be deemed to be a settlement, and the anti-avoidance provisions in the ICTA 1988 may apply.

Disclaimers

16.24   The income belongs to the beneficiary who takes as a result of the disclaimer.

Chapter 17

Taxation of settlements

IMMEDIATE POST DEATH INTERESTS

Inheritance tax

Inheritance tax on the creation of an immediate post death interest

17.1   In order for a settlement to qualify as an immediate post death interest, the following conditions must be satisfied:

(a)   the settlement must be effected by will or under the law relating to intestacy;

(b)   the life tenant must have become beneficially entitled to the interest in possession on the death of the testator or intestate;

(c)   s 71A Inheritance Tax Act 1984 (ITA) does not apply to the property in which the interest subsists or the interest is not a disabled person's interest;

(d)   condition (c) has been satisfied at all times since the life tenant became beneficially entitled to the interest in possession.

If an immediate post death interest is created on death, the usual charging rules apply, so that if the spouse or civil partner is the life tenant, no IHT will be payable because of the spouse or civil partner exemption, provided the spouse or civil partner is domiciled in the UK.

Position of the life tenant

17.2   For IHT purposes, the life tenant is deemed to own the trust assets (s 49(1) ITA). As a consequence, the remainderman owns nothing – a reversionary interest is normally excluded property for IHT purposes (s 48, ITA 1984). If a person is entitled to the income for a period less than life, he will still be deemed to own the trust assets. If there is more than one life tenant, they will be deemed to own the appropriate share of the trust fund (s 50(1) and (2), ITA 1984).

Death of the life tenant

17.3 On the death of the life tenant, for IHT purposes, he is treated as being the owner of all the underlying trust assets (ss 5 and 49, ITA 1984). The trustees are liable for the proportion of IHT due in respect of the trust property, if any.

Exemptions and reliefs

17.4 It may be possible to claim the following exemptions and reliefs:

(a) Section 52(1) of the ITA 1984 provides that where at any time during the lifetime of a person beneficially entitled to an interest in possession his interest comes to an end, IHT is payable as if at that time he had made a transfer of value. Section 53(2) provides that tax shall not be chargeable under s 52 if the person whose interest in the property comes to an end becomes on the same occasion beneficially entitled to the property or to another interest in possession in the property. So if the life tenant becomes absolutely entitled to the trust assets, there will be no charge to IHT.

(b) The spouse or civil partner exemption. If the spouse or civil partner of the life tenant becomes absolutely entitled to the assets in the trust, the spouse exemption will apply. Section 18(1) of the ITA 1984 provides that a transfer of value is an exempt transfer to the extent that the value transferred is attributable to property which becomes comprised in the estate of the transferor's spouse or civil partner, or, so far as the value transferred is not so attributable, to the extent that the estate is increased.

Note that the spouse or civil partner must be domiciled in the UK.

(c) Gifts of excluded property. No IHT is payable in respect of gifts of excluded property. Excluded property comprises the following:

    (i) property situated outside the UK if the person beneficially entitled to it is an individual domiciled outside the UK (s 6(1));

    (ii) a reversionary interest unless:

        — it has at any time been acquired (whether by the person entitled to it or by a person previously entitled to it) for a consideration in money or money's worth; or

        — it is one to which the settlor or his spouse is or has been beneficially entitled (s 48(1));

    (iii) s 48(3) of the ITA 1984 provides that where property comprised in a settlement is situated outside the UK:

        — the property (but not a reversionary interest in the property) is excluded property unless the settlor was domiciled in the UK at the time when the settlement was made; and

        — s 6(1) applies to a reversionary interest in the property, but does not otherwise apply in relation to that property.

Thus normally there is no charge to IHT on any transfers of reversionary interests. The life tenant is deemed to own the underlying assets for IHT purposes, and therefore it would be wrong to charge dealings with reversionary interests.

(d)   Charities. Gifts to charities are exempt.

(e)   Variations and disclaimers. It is only settlements created on death which can be varied. Settlements in which the deceased had been a beneficiary cannot be varied. Disclaimers apply to both.

(f)   Business property relief and agricultural property relief. Property qualifying for 100 per cent relief can be transferred to a settlement without incurring any charge to IHT. However, in order to claim the relief on death within seven years of a lifetime transfer, the trustees must still own the property or replacement property, and the trustees will have to satisfy the qualifying conditions themselves before they can claim the reliefs.

What happens if the taxpayer is the life tenant under a settlement and uses the settled property in his business? For IHT purposes, a life tenant under an immediate post death interest is deemed to be beneficially entitled to the property in which the life interest subsists. In *Fetherstonaugh v IRC [1984] STC 261, CA*, a life tenant used 1,845 acres of settled property for his farming business. It was held that the settled property was 'property consisting of a business or an interest in a business'.

Section 105(1)(e) provides that any land or building, machinery or plant which, immediately before the transfer, was used wholly or mainly for the purposes of a business carried on by the transferor and was settled property in which he was then beneficially entitled to an interest in possession qualifies for business property relief at 50 per cent.

What is the relationship between the *Fetherstonaugh* decision and s 105(1)(e)? It seems that where the settled property and the rest of the life tenant's business are transferred together at the same time, 100 per cent business property relief is available. Thus if the life tenant of a settlement comprising a factory carries on business there as a sole trader, 100 per cent relief will be available if the business and factory are transferred together. However, if the factory is transferred separately, only 50 per cent relief will be available. On the other hand, if the life tenant dies owning the business, 100 per cent relief will apply to both the factory and the business. It may be that 100% relief in this situation will only be available if the transfer is on death.

HMRC take the view that the person with the interest in possession is the owner of the property for the purposes of claiming agricultural property relief. Thus if the life tenant farms the settled property for at least two years before death, 100 per cent agricultural property relief will be available on his death. 100 per cent relief is still available if the property is tenanted, and the tenancy was granted after 1 September 1995. On the other hand, if the tenancy was granted before 1 September 1995, only

50 per cent agricultural property relief will be available if there is no right to obtain vacant possession within 24 months. In addition, the life tenant must have been entitled to the property for seven years.

For more information, readers are referred to *Inheritance Tax 2008/09* (Core Tax Annual: Tottel Publishing).

(g) Section 90 of the ITA 1984 provides that where under the terms of a settlement a person is entitled by way of remuneration for his services as trustee to an interest in possession in property comprised in the settlement, then except to the extent that the interest in possession represents more than a reasonable amount of remuneration:

    (i) the interest shall be left out of account in determining for the purpose of the ITA 1984 the value of his estate immediately before his death; and

    (ii) tax shall not be charged under s 52 when the interest comes to an end.

(h) Section 146(6) of the ITA 1984 provides that anything which is done in compliance with an order under the Inheritance (Provision for Family and Dependants) Act 1975 or occurs on the coming into force of such an order, and which would (apart from this subsection) constitute an occasion on which tax is chargeable under any provision, other than s 79, shall not constitute such an occasion; and where an order under the 1975 Act provides for property to be settled or for the variation of a settlement, and (apart from this subsection) tax would be charged under s 52(1) on the coming into force of the order, s 52(1) shall not apply.

(i) Pre 22 March 2006 life interest trusts. The tax treatment is basically the same as for immediate post death interests.

CAPITAL GAINS TAX

The creation of the settlement

17.5 If a settlement is created by will or arises on an intestacy, then the normal rule applies – no capital gains tax is payable on death. The personal representatives will be deemed to acquire the assets at market value as at the date of death, and when they become trustees, they will be deemed to acquire the trust assets at market value as at the date of death.

Death of the life tenant

17.6 There is a deemed disposal and reacquisition by the trustees on the death of a life tenant, but no chargeable gain or allowable loss accrues (s 72(1), TCGA 1992). If more than one beneficiary is entitled to the settled property, there will be a deemed disposal and reacquisition of the appropriate part of the fund.

Section 38(4) provides that any provision introducing the assumption that assets are sold and immediately reacquired shall not imply that any expenditure is incurred as incidental to the sale or reacquisition.

Termination of a life interest on death when the settlement continues

17.7   Where a life interest terminates on death and settlement continues there is a deemed disposal and reacquisition by the trustees, but no chargeable gain accrues.

TAXATION OF SETTLEMENTS OTHER THAN IMMEDIATE POST DEATH INTERESTS, DISABLED PERSONS TRUSTS AND BEREAVED MINORS TRUSTS

Inheritance tax

Inheritance tax on the creation of the trust

17.8   If the settlement is created by will, the settled assets will be part of the testator's estate, and will be subject to IHT in accordance with the normal principles; these are discussed in **chapter 13.**

The ten-yearly charge

17.9   Section 64 of the ITA 1984 imposes a charge on relevant property, which is defined by s 58(1) as settled property in which no qualifying interest in possession subsists. The value charged is the value of the relevant property comprised in the settlement, less agricultural property relief and business property relief.

The settlement has its own cumulative total, which is defined in s 66(5) as the aggregate of:

(a)   the values transferred by any chargeable transfers made by the settlor in the period of seven years ending with the day on which the settlement commenced; and

(b)   the amounts on which any charges to tax were imposed under s 65 in respect of the settlement in the ten years before the anniversary concerned.

Section 65 imposes a charge to IHT *inter alia* when property leaves a settlement. This is examined in more detail in the next section.

The rate of tax is 30 per cent of the rate which would be charged on a lifetime chargeable transfer (6 per cent).

Exit charges

17.10   These arise in two situations:

(a)   where property comprised in a settlement ceases to be relevant property; and

(b)   if (a) does not apply, where the trustees of the settlement make a disposition as a result of which the value of relevant property comprised in the settlement is less than it would be but for the disposition (s 65(1), ITA 1984).

A termination of the settlement, or the distribution of some of the property to the beneficiaries, both fall within (a).

When (a) does not apply, (b) will catch any disposition by the trustees of the settlement which reduces the value of the relevant property comprised in the settlement.

Section 65(4) of the ITA 1984 provides that there is no charge if the event in question occurs within a quarter, beginning with the day on which the settlement commenced or with a ten-year anniversary. Thus there will be no charge if the event giving rise to the charge occurs within three months of the establishment of the settlement, or an anniversary charge.

Section 65(5) provides that tax will not be charged in respect of a payment of costs and expenses so far as fairly attributable to relevant property. Neither is tax payable if the payment is income of any person for the purposes of income tax.

The amount chargeable is the amount by which the value of the relevant property in the settlement is less immediately after the event in question than it would be but for the event (s 65(2)(a)).

The rate of tax is a proportion of the rate charged on the last ten-year anniversary. The proportion is so many fortieths as there are complete successive quarters in the period beginning with the most recent anniversary and ending with the day before the occasion of the charge (s 69(4)). Thus, if four years have elapsed since the last ten-yearly charge, the rate of tax will be 16/40 of the rate charged on the last ten-year anniversary, 16 quarters having elapsed since the last ten-yearly charge.

Special rules apply to the calculation of the exit charge before the tenth anniversary.

Capital gains tax

17.11   The rules applicable to trusts with an interest in possession apply to trusts without an interest in possession. However, hold-over relief may apply to all assets, it is not limited to business assets.

Appendices

Appendix 1 Non-Contentious Probate Rules

Appendix 2 Statutory provisions

Wills Act 1837, ss 9, 18, 18A, 24, 33
Administration of Estates Act 1925, ss 35, 36, 41
Trustee Act 1925, ss 19, 31, 32
Trustee Act 2000, ss 3–9

Appendix 3 HMRC Form IHT 4 and Guidance Notes

Appendix 4 IHTM43001 Transferable Nil Rate Band

Appendix 5 District probate registries and sub-registries

Non-Contentious Probate Rules 1987

SI 1987/2024

Made 24 November 1987

Authority: Supreme Court Act 1981, s 127; Colonial Probates Act 1892, s 2(5)

1 Citation and commencement

These Rules may be cited as the Non-Contentious Probate Rules 1987 and shall come into force on 1st January 1988.

ANNOTATIONS

Initial commencement

Specified date
Specified date: 1 January 1988: see above.

2 Interpretation

(1) In these Rules, unless the context otherwise requires–

'the Act' means the *Supreme Court Act 1981* [Senior Courts Act 1981];

'authorised officer' means any officer of a registry who is for the time being authorised by the President to administer any oath or to take any affidavit required for any purpose connected with his duties;

'the Crown' includes the Crown in right of the Duchy of Lancaster and the Duke of Cornwall for the time being;

['district judge' means a district judge of the Principal Registry;]

'grant' means a grant of probate or administration and includes, where the context so admits, the resealing of such a grant under the Colonial Probates Acts 1892 and 1927;

'gross value' in relation to any estate means the value of the estate without deduction for debts, incumbrances, funeral expenses or inheritance tax (or other capital tax payable out of the estate);

['judge' means a judge of the High Court;]

'oath' means the oath required by rule 8 to be sworn by every applicant for a grant;

'personal applicant' means a person other than a trust corporation who seeks to obtain a grant without employing a solicitor [or probate practitioner], and 'personal application' has a corresponding meaning;

['probate practitioner' means a person to whom section 23(1) of the Solicitors Act 1974 does not apply by virtue of section 23(2) of that Act [or section 55 of the Courts and Legal Services Act 1990;]]

['registrar' means the district probate registrar of the district probate registry–

   (i)   to which an application for a grant is made or is proposed to be made,

   (ii)   in rules 26,40,41 and 61(2), from which the grant issued, and

   (iii)   in rules 46,47 and 48, from which the citation has issued or is proposed to be issued;]

'registry' means the Principal Registry or a district probate registry;

['the senior district judge' means the Senior District Judge of the Family Division or, in his absence, the senior of the district judges in attendance at the Principal Registry;]

...

...

'the Treasury Solicitor' means the solicitor for the affairs of Her Majesty's Treasury and includes the solicitor for the affairs of the Duchy of Lancaster and the solicitor of the Duchy of Cornwall;

'trust corporation' means a corporation within the meaning of section 128 of the Act as extended by section 3 of the Law of Property (Amendment) Act 1926.

(2) A form referred to by number means the form so numbered in the First Schedule; and such forms shall be used wherever applicable, with such variation as a [district judge or] registrar may in any particular case direct or approve.

ANNOTATIONS

Initial commencement

Specified date
Specified date: 1 January 1988: see r 1.

Amendment
Para (1): in definition 'the Act' words 'Supreme Court Act 1981' in italics revoked and subsequent words in square brackets substituted by the Constitutional Reform Act 2005, s 59(5), Sch 11, Pt 1, para 1(2).
   Date in force: to be appointed: see the Constitutional Reform Act 2005, s 148(1).
   Para (1): definition 'district judge' inserted by SI 1991/1876, r 6(a).
   Para (1): definition 'judge' inserted by SI 1991/1876, r 6(b).
   Para (1): in definition 'personal applicant' words 'or probate practitioner' in square brackets inserted by SI 1998/1903, r 3(a).
   Date in force: 14 September 1998: see SI 1998/1903, r 1(1).
   Para (1): definition 'probate practitioner' inserted by SI 1998/1903, r 3(b).
   Date in force: 14 September 1998: see SI 1998/1903, r 1(1).

Para (1): in definition 'probate practitioner' words 'or section 55 of the Courts and Legal Services Act 1990;' in square brackets inserted by SI 2004/2985, r 2.
Date in force: 7 December 2004: see SI 2004/2985, r 1.
Para (1): definition 'registrar' substituted by SI 1991/1876, r 6(c).
Para (1): definition 'the senior district judge' substituted, for definition 'the Senior Registrar' as originally enacted, by SI 1991/1876, r 6(d).
Para (1): definition 'statutory guardian' omitted revoked by SI 1991/1876, r 2.
Para (1): definition 'testamentary guardian' omitted revoked by SI 1991/1876, r 2.
Para (2): words in square brackets substituted by SI 1991/1876, r 7(1).

Modification
References to solicitors etc modified to include references to bodies recognised under the Administration of Justice Act 1985, s 9, by the Solicitors' Incorporated Practices Order 1991, SI 1991/2684, arts 4, 5, Sch 1.

[3   Application of other rules]

[(1) Subject to the provisions of these rules and to any enactment, the Rules of the Supreme Court 1965 as they were in force immediately before 26th April 1999 shall apply, with any necessary modifications to non-contentious probate matters, and any reference in these rules to those rules shall be construed accordingly.

(2) Nothing in Order 3 of the Rules of the Supreme Court shall prevent time from running in the Long Vacation.]

ANNOTATIONS

Amendment
Substituted by SI 1999/1015, r 2.
Date in force: 26 April 1999: see SI 1999/1015, r 1.

4   Applications for grants through solicitors [or probate practitioners]

(1) A person applying for a grant through a solicitor [or probate practitioner] may apply at any registry or sub-registry.

(2) Every solicitor [or probate practitioner] through whom an application for a grant is made shall give the address of his place of business within England and Wales.

ANNOTATIONS

Initial commencement

Specified date
Specified date: 1 January 1988: see r 1.

Amendment
Provision heading: words 'or probate practitioners' in square brackets inserted by SI 1998/1903, r 4(a).
Date in force: 14 September 1998: see SI 1998/1903, r 1(1).
Para (1): words 'or probate practitioner' in square brackets inserted by SI 1998/1903, r 4(b).
Date in force: 14 September 1998: see SI 1998/1903, r 1(1).

Para (2): words 'or probate practitioner' in square brackets inserted by SI 1998/1903, r 4(b).

Date in force: 14 September 1998: see SI 1998/1903, r 1(1).

Modification

References to solicitors etc modified to include references to bodies recognised under the Administration of Justice Act 1985, s 9, by the Solicitors' Incorporated Practices Order 1991, SI 1991/2684, arts 4, 5, Sch 1.

5 Personal applications

(1) A personal applicant may apply for a grant at any registry or sub-registry.

(2) Save as provided for by rule 39 a personal applicant may not apply through an agent, whether paid or unpaid, and may not be attended by any person acting or appearing to act as his adviser.

(3) No personal application shall be proceeded with if–

(a)   it becomes necessary to bring the matter before the court by action or summons[, unless a judge, district judge or registrar so permits];

(b)   an application has already been made by a solicitor [or probate practitioner] on behalf of the applicant and has not been withdrawn; or

(c)   the [district judge or] registrar so directs.

(4) After a will has been deposited in a registry by a personal applicant, it may not be delivered to the applicant or to any other person unless in special circumstances the [district judge or] registrar so directs.

(5) A personal applicant shall produce a certificate of the death of the deceased or such other evidence of the death as the [district judge or] registrar may approve.

(6) A personal applicant shall supply all information necessary to enable the papers leading to the grant to be prepared in the registry.

(7) Unless the [district judge or] registrar otherwise directs, every oath or affidavit required on a personal application shall be sworn or executed by all the deponents before an authorised officer.

(8) No legal advice shall be given to a personal applicant by an officer of a registry and every such officer shall be responsible only for embodying in proper form the applicant's instructions for the grant.

ANNOTATIONS

Initial commencement

Specified date
Specified date: 1 January 1988: see r 1.

Amendment
Para (3): in sub-para (a) words ', unless a judge, district judge or registrar so permits' in square brackets inserted by SI 1998/1903, r 5.

Date in force: 14 September 1998: see SI 1998/1903, r 1(1).

Para (3): in sub-para (b) words 'or probate practitioner' in square brackets inserted by SI 1998/1903, r 6.

Date in force: 14 September 1998: see SI 1998/1903, r 1(1).

Para (3): in sub-para (c) words 'district judge or' in square brackets inserted by SI 1991/1876, r 7(1).

Para (4): words 'district judge or' in square brackets inserted by SI 1991/1876, r 7(1).

Para (5): words 'district judge or' in square brackets inserted by SI 1991/1876, r 7(1).

Para (7): words 'district judge or' in square brackets inserted by SI 1991/1876, r 7(1).

Modification

References to solicitors etc modified to include references to bodies recognised under the Administration of Justice Act 1985, s 9, by the Solicitors' Incorporated Practices Order 1991, SI 1991/2684, arts 4, 5, Sch 1.

6 Duty of [district judge or] registrar on receiving application for grant

(1) A [district judge or] registrar shall not allow any grant to issue until all inquiries which he may see fit to make have been answered to his satisfaction.

(2) Except with the leave of a [district judge or] registrar, no grant of probate or of administration with the will annexed shall issue within seven days of the death of the deceased and no grant of administration shall issue within fourteen days thereof.

ANNOTATIONS

Initial commencement

Specified date
Specified date: 1 January 1988: see r 1.

Amendment

Provision heading: words in square brackets inserted by SI 1991/1876, r 7(1).
Paras (1), (2): words in square brackets inserted by SI 1991/1876, r 7(1).

7 Grants by district probate registrars

(1) No grant shall be made by a ... registrar–

(a) in any case in which there is contention, until the contention is disposed of; or

(b) in any case in which it appears to him that a grant ought not to be made without the directions of a judge or a [district judge].

(2) In any case in which paragraph (1)(b) applies, the ... registrar shall send a statement of the matter in question to the Principal Registry for directions.

(3) A [district judge] may either confirm that the matter be referred to a judge and give directions accordingly or may direct the ... registrar to proceed with the matter in accordance with such instructions as are deemed necessary, which may include a direction to take no further action in relation to the matter.

ANNOTATIONS

Initial commencement

Specified date
Specified date: 1 January 1988: see r 1.

Amendment
Paras (1), (3): words omitted revoked, and words in square brackets substituted, by SI 1991/1876, r 7(2), (3).
    Para (2): words omitted revoked by SI 1991/1876, r 7(2).

8   Oath in support of grant

(1) Every application for a grant other than one to which rule 39 applies shall be supported by an oath by the applicant in the form applicable to the circumstances of the case, and by such other papers as the [district judge or] registrar may require.

(2) Unless otherwise directed by a [district judge or] registrar, the oath shall state where the deceased died domiciled.

(3) Where the deceased died on or after 1st January 1926, the oath shall state whether or not, to the best of the applicant's knowledge, information and belief, there was land vested in the deceased which was settled previously to his death and not by his will and which remained settled land notwithstanding his death.

(4) On an application for a grant of administration the oath shall state in what manner all persons having a prior right to a grant have been cleared off and whether any minority or life interest arises under the will or intestacy.

ANNOTATIONS

Initial commencement

Specified date
Specified date: 1 January 1988: see r 1.

Amendment
Paras (1), (2): words in square brackets inserted by SI 1991/1876, r 7(1).

9   Grant in additional name

Where it is sought to describe the deceased in a grant by some name in addition to his true name, the applicant shall depose to the true name of the deceased and shall specify some part of the estate which was held in the other name, or give any other reason for the inclusion of the other name in the grant.

ANNOTATIONS

Initial commencement

Specified date
Specified date: 1 January 1988: see r 1.

10   Marking of wills

(1) Subject to paragraph (2) below, every will in respect of which an application for a grant is made–

  (a)   shall be marked by the signatures of the applicant and the person before whom the oath is sworn; and

  (b)   shall be exhibited to any affidavit which may be required under these Rules as to the validity, terms, condition or date of execution of the will.

(2) The [district judge or] registrar may allow a facsimile copy of a will to be marked or exhibited in lieu of the original document.

ANNOTATIONS

Initial commencement

Specified date
Specified date: 1 January 1988: see r 1.

Amendment
Para (2): words in square brackets inserted by SI 1991/1876, r 7(1).

11   Engrossments for purposes of record

(1) Where the [district judge or] registrar considers that in any particular case a facsimile copy of the original will would not be satisfactory for purposes of record, he may require an engrossment suitable for facsimile reproduction to be lodged.

(2) Where a will–

  (a)   contains alterations which are not to be admitted to proof; or

  (b)   has been ordered to be rectified by virtue of section 20(1) of the Administration of Justice Act 1982,

there shall be lodged an engrossment of the will in the form in which it is to be proved.

(3) Any engrossment lodged under this rule shall reproduce the punctuation, spacing and division into paragraphs of the will and shall follow continuously from page to page on both sides of the paper.

ANNOTATIONS

Initial commencement

Specified date
Specified date: 1 January 1988: see r 1.

Amendment
Para (1): words in square brackets inserted by SI 1991/1876, r 7(1).

12   Evidence as to due execution of will

(1) Subject to paragraphs (2) and (3) below, where a will contains no attestation clause or the attestation clause is insufficient, or where it appears to the [district judge or] registrar that there is doubt about the due execution of the will, he shall before admitting it to proof require an affidavit as to due execution from one or more of the attesting witnesses or, if no attesting witness is conveniently available, from any other person who was present when the will was executed; and if the [district judge or] registrar, after considering the evidence, is satisfied the will was not duly executed, he shall refuse probate and mark the will accordingly.

(2) If no affidavit can be obtained in accordance with paragraph (1) above, the [district judge or] registrar may accept evidence on affidavit from any person he may think fit to show that the signature on the will is in the handwriting of the deceased, or of any other matter which may raise a presumption in favour of due execution of the will, and may if he thinks fit require that notice of the application be given to any person who may be prejudiced by the will.

(3) A [district judge or] registrar may accept a will for proof without evidence as aforesaid if he is satisfied that the distribution of the estate is not thereby affected.

ANNOTATIONS

Initial commencement

Specified date
Specified date: 1 January 1988: see r 1.

Amendment
Para (3): words in square brackets inserted by SI 1991/1876, r 7(1).

13   Execution of will of blind or illiterate testator

Before admitting to proof a will which appears to have been signed by a blind or illiterate testator or by another person by direction of the testator, or which for any other reason raises doubt as to the testator having had knowledge of the contents of the will at the time of its execution, the [district judge or] registrar shall satisfy himself that the testator had such knowledge.

ANNOTATIONS

Initial commencement

Specified date
Specified date: 1 January 1988: see r 1.

Amendment
Words in square brackets inserted by SI 1991/1876, r 7(1).

14   Evidence as to terms, condition and date of execution of will

(1) Subject to paragraph (2) below, where there appears in a will any obliteration, interlineation, or other alteration which is not authenticated in the

manner prescribed by section 21 of the Wills Act 1837, or by the re-execution of the will or by the execution of a codicil, the [district judge or] registrar shall require evidence to show whether the alteration was present at the time the will was executed and shall give directions as to the form in which the will is to be proved.

(2) The provisions of paragraph (1) above shall not apply to any alteration which appears to the [district judge or] registrar to be of no practical importance.

(3) If a will contains any reference to another document in such terms as to suggest that it ought to be incorporated in the will, the [district judge or] registrar shall require the document to be produced and may call for such evidence in regard to the incorporation of the document as he may think fit.

(4) Where there is a doubt as to the date on which a will was executed, the [district judge or] registrar may require such evidence as he thinks necessary to establish the date.

ANNOTATIONS

Initial commencement

Specified date
Specified date: 1 January 1988: see r 1.

Amendment
Paras (1), (4): words in square brackets inserted by SI 1991/1876, r 7(1).

15 Attempted revocation of will

Any appearance of attempted revocation of a will by burning, tearing, or otherwise destroying and every other circumstance leading to a presumption of revocation by the testator, shall be accounted for to the [district judge's or] registrar's satisfaction.

ANNOTATIONS

Initial commencement

Specified date
Specified date: 1 January 1988: see r 1.

Amendment
Words in square brackets inserted by SI 1991/1876, r 7(5).

16 Affidavit as to due execution, terms etc, of will

A [district judge or] registrar may require an affidavit from any person he may think fit for the purpose of satisfying himself as to any of the matters referred to in rules 13, 14 and 15, and in any such affidavit sworn by an attesting witness or other person present at the time of the execution of a will the deponent shall depose to the manner in which the will was executed.

Appendix 1

ANNOTATIONS

Initial commencement

Specified date
Specified date: 1 January 1988: see r 1.

Amendment
Words in square brackets inserted by SI 1991/1876, r 7(1).

17 Wills proved otherwise than under section 9 of the Wills Act 1837

(1) Rules 12 to 15 shall apply only to a will that is to be established by reference to section 9 of the Wills Act 1837 (signing and attestation of wills).

(2) A will that is to be established otherwise than as described in paragraph (1) of this rule may be so established upon the [district judge or] registrar being satisfied as to its terms and validity, and includes (without prejudice to the generality of the foregoing)–

(a) any will to which rule 18 applies; and

(b) any will which, by virtue of the Wills Act 1963, is to be treated as properly executed if executed according to the internal law of the territory or state referred to in section 1 of that Act.

ANNOTATIONS

Initial commencement

Specified date
Specified date: 1 January 1988: see r 1.

Amendment
Para (2): words in square brackets inserted by SI 1991/1876, r 7(1).

18 Wills of persons on military service and seamen

Where the deceased died domiciled in England and Wales and it appears to the [district judge or] registrar that there is prima facie evidence that a will is one to which section 11 of the Wills Act 1837 applies, the will may be admitted to proof if the registrar is satisfied that it was signed by the testator or, if unsigned, that it is in the testator's handwriting.

ANNOTATIONS

Initial commencement

Specified date
Specified date: 1 January 1988: see r 1.

Amendment
Words in square brackets inserted by SI 1991/1876, r 7(1).

19   Evidence of foreign law

Where evidence as to the law of any country or territory outside England and Wales is required on any application for a grant, the [district judge or] registrar may accept–

   (a)   an affidavit from any person whom, having regard to the particulars of his knowledge or experience given in the affidavit, he regards as suitably qualified to give expert evidence of the law in question; or

   (b)   a certificate by, or an act before, a notary practising in the country or territory concerned.

ANNOTATIONS

Initial commencement

Specified date
Specified date: 1 January 1988: see r 1.

Amendment
Words in square brackets inserted by SI 1991/1876, r 7(1).

20   Order of priority for grant where deceased left a will

Where the deceased died on or after 1 January 1926 the person or persons entitled to a grant in respect of a will shall be determined in accordance with the following order of priority, namely–

   (a)   the executor (but subject to rule 36(4)(d) below);

   (b)   any residuary legatee or devisee holding in trust for any other person;

   (c)   any other residuary legatee or devisee (including one for life) or where the residue is not wholly disposed of by the will, any person entitled to share in the undisposed of residue (including the Treasury Solicitor when claiming bona vacantia on behalf of the Crown), provided that–

      (i)   unless a [district judge or] registrar otherwise directs, a residuary legatee or devisee whose legacy or devise is vested in interest shall be preferred to one entitled on the happening of a contingency, and

      (ii)   where the residue is not in terms wholly disposed of, the [district judge or] registrar may, if he is satisfied that the testator has nevertheless disposed of the whole or substantially the whole of the known estate, allow a grant to be made to any legatee or devisee entitled to, or to share in, the estate so disposed of, without regard to the persons entitled to share in any residue not disposed of by the will;

   (d)   the personal representative of any residuary legatee or devisee (but not one for life, or one holding in trust for any other person), or of any person entitled to share in any residue not disposed of by the will;

   (e)   any other legatee or devisee (including one for life or one holding in

201

trust for any other person) or any creditor of the deceased, provided that, unless a [district judge or] registrar otherwise directs, a legatee or devisee whose legacy or devise is vested in interest shall be preferred to one entitled on the happening of a contingency;

(f) the personal representative of any other legatee or devisee (but not one for life or one holding in trust for any other person) or of any creditor of the deceased.

ANNOTATIONS

Initial commencement

Specified date
Specified date: 1 January 1988: see r 1.

Amendment
Paras (c), (e): words in square brackets inserted by SI 1991/1876, r 7(1).

21 Grants to attesting witnesses, etc

Where a gift to any person fails by reason of section 15 of the Wills Act 1837, such person shall not have any right to a grant as a beneficiary named in the will, without prejudice to his right to a grant in any other capacity.

ANNOTATIONS

Initial commencement

Specified date
Specified date: 1 January 1988: see r 1.

22 Order of priority for grant in case of intestacy

(1) Where the deceased died on or after 1 January 1926, wholly intestate, the person or persons having a beneficial interest in the estate shall be entitled to a grant of administration in the following classes in order of priority, namely–

(a) the surviving [spouse or civil partner];

(b) the children of the deceased and the issue of any deceased child who died before the deceased;

(c) the father and mother of the deceased;

(d) brothers and sisters of the whole blood and the issue of any deceased brother or sister of the whole blood who died before the deceased;

(e) brothers and sisters of the half blood and the issue of any deceased brother or sister of the half blood who died before the deceased;

(f) grandparents;

(g) uncles and aunts of the whole blood and the issue of any deceased uncle or aunt of the whole blood who died before the deceased;

(h) uncles and aunts of the half blood and the issue of any deceased uncle or aunt of the half blood who died before the deceased.

(2) In default of any person having a beneficial interest in the estate, the Treasury Solicitor shall be entitled to a grant if he claims bona vacantia on behalf of the Crown.

(3) If all persons entitled to a grant under the foregoing provisions of this rule have been cleared off, a grant may be made to a creditor of the deceased or to any person who, notwithstanding that he has no immediate beneficial interest in the estate, may have a beneficial interest in the event of an accretion thereto.

(4) Subject to paragraph (5) of rule 27, the personal representative of a person in any of the classes mentioned in paragraph (1) of this rule or the personal representative of a creditor of the deceased shall have the same right to a grant as the person whom he represents provided that the persons mentioned in sub-paragraphs (b) to (h) of paragraph (1) above shall be preferred to the personal representative of a spouse [or a civil partner] who has died without taking a beneficial interest in the whole estate of the deceased as ascertained at the time of the application for the grant.

ANNOTATIONS

Initial commencement

Specified date
Specified date: 1 January 1988: see r 1.

Amendment
Para (1): in sub-para (a) words 'spouse or civil partner' in square brackets substituted by SI 2005/2114, art 2(6), Sch 6, para 2(1), (2).
    Date in force: 5 December 2005: see SI 2005/2114, art 1.
    Para (4): words 'or a civil partner' in square brackets inserted by SI 2005/2114, art 2(6), Sch 6, para 2(1), (3).
    Date in force: 5 December 2005: see SI 2005/2114, art 1.

23   Order of priority for grant in pre-1926 cases

Where the deceased died before 1st January 1926, the person or persons entitled to a grant shall, subject to the provisions of any enactment, be determined in accordance with the principles and rules under which the court would have acted at the date of death.

ANNOTATIONS

Initial commencement

Specified date
Specified date: 1 January 1988: see r 1.

24   Right of assignee to a grant

(1) Where all the persons entitled to the estate of the deceased (whether under a will or on intestacy) have assigned their whole interest in the estate to one or more persons, the assignee or assignees shall replace, in the order of priority for a grant of administration, the assignor or, if there are two or more assignors, the assignor with the highest priority.

(2) Where there are two or more assignees, administration may be granted with the consent of the others to any one or more (not exceeding four) of them.

(3) In any case where administration is applied for by an assignee the original instrument of assignment shall be produced and a copy of the same lodged in the registry.

ANNOTATIONS

Initial commencement

Specified date
Specified date: 1 January 1988: see r 1.

25 Joinder of administrator

(1) A person entitled in priority to a grant of administration may, without leave, apply for a grant with a person entitled in a lower degree, provided that there is no other person entitled in a higher degree to the person to be joined, unless every other such person has renounced.

(2) Subject to paragraph (3) below, an application for leave to join with a person entitled in priority to a grant of administration a person having no right or no immediate right thereto shall be made to a [district judge or] registrar, and shall be supported by an affidavit by the person entitled in priority, the consent of the person proposed to be joined as administrator and such other evidence as the [district judge or] registrar may direct.

(3) Unless a [district judge or] registrar otherwise directs, there may without any such application be joined with a person entitled in priority to administration–

    (a)   any person who is nominated under paragraph (3) of rule 32 or paragraph (3) of rule 35;

    (b)   a trust corporation.

ANNOTATIONS

Initial commencement

Specified date
Specified date: 1 January 1988: see r 1.

Amendment
Paras (2), (3): words in square brackets inserted by SI 1991/1876, r 7(1).

26 Additional personal representatives

(1) An application under section 114(4) of the Act to add a personal representative shall be made to a [district judge or] registrar and shall be supported by an affidavit by the applicant, the consent of the person proposed to be added as personal representative and such other evidence as the [district judge or] registrar may require.

(2) On any such application the [district judge or] registrar may direct that a note shall be made on the original grant of the addition of a further personal

representative, or he may impound or revoke the grant or make such other order as the circumstances of the case may require.

ANNOTATIONS

Initial commencement

Specified date
Specified date: 1 January 1988: see r 1.

Amendment
Words in square brackets inserted by SI 1991/1876, r 7(1).

27 Grants where two or more persons entitled in same degree

[(1) Subject to paragraphs (1A), (2) and (3) below, where, on an application for probate, power to apply for a like grant is to be reserved to such other of the executors as have not renounced probate, notice of the application shall be given to the executor or executors to whom power is to be reserved; and, unless the district judge or registrar otherwise directs, the oath shall state that such notice has been given.

(1A) Where power is to be reserved to executors who are ... partners in a firm, ... notice need not be given to them under paragraph (1) above if probate is applied for by another partner in that firm.]

(2) Where power is to be reserved to partners of a firm, notice for the purposes of paragraph (1) above may be given to the partners by sending it to the firm at its principal or last known place of business.

(3) A [district judge or] registrar may dispense with the giving of notice under paragraph (1) above if he is satisfied that the giving of such a notice is impracticable or would result in unreasonable delay or expense.

(4) A grant of administration may be made to any person entitled thereto without notice to other persons entitled in the same degree.

(5) Unless a [district judge or] registrar otherwise directs, administration shall be granted to a person of full age entitled thereto in preference to a guardian of a minor, and to a living person entitled thereto in preference to the personal representative of a deceased person.

(6) A dispute between persons entitled to a grant in the same degree shall be brought by summons before a [district judge or] registrar.

[(7) The issue of a summons under this rule in a registry shall be noted forthwith in the index of pending grant applications.]

(8) If the issue of a summons under this rule is known to the [district judge or] registrar, he shall not allow any grant to be sealed until such summons is finally disposed of.

ANNOTATIONS

Initial commencement

Specified date
Specified date: 1 January 1988: see r 1.

Amendment
Paras (1), (1A): substituted for original para (1) by SI 1991/1876, r 8(1).
  Para (1A): words omitted revoked by SI 1998/1903, r 7(1).
  Date in force: 14 September 1998: see SI 1998/1903, r 1(1).
  Paras (3), (5), (6), (8): words in square brackets inserted by SI 1991/1876, r 7(1).
  Para (7): substituted by SI 1998/1903, r 7(2).
  Date in force: 14 September 1998: see SI 1998/1903, r 1(1).

28   Exceptions to rules as to priority

(1) Any person to whom a grant may or is required to be made under any enactment shall not be prevented from obtaining such a grant notwithstanding the operation of rules 20, 22, 25 or 27.

(2) Where the deceased died domiciled outside England and Wales rules 20, 22, 25 or 27 shall not apply except in a case to which paragraph (3) of rule 30 applies.

ANNOTATIONS

Initial commencement

Specified date
Specified date: 1 January 1988: see r 1.

[29   Grants in respect of settled land]

[(1) In this rule 'settled land' means land vested in the deceased which was settled prior to his death and not by his will, and which remained settled land notwithstanding his death.

(2) The person or persons entitled to a grant of administration limited to settled land shall be determined in accordance with the following order of priority:

  (i)   the special executors in regard to settled land constituted by section 22 of the Administration of Estates Act 1925;

  (ii) the trustees of the settlement at the time of the application for the grant; and

  (iii) the personal representatives of the deceased.

(3) Where there is settled land and a grant is made in respect of the free estate only, the grant shall expressly exclude the settled land.]

ANNOTATIONS

Amendment
Substituted by SI 1991/1876, r 9.

30   Grants where deceased died domiciled outside England and Wales

(1) Subject to paragraph (3) below, where the deceased died domiciled outside England and Wales, [a district judge or registrar may order that a grant, limited in such way as the district judge or registrar may direct,] do issue to any of the following persons–

> (a)   to the person entrusted with the administration of the estate by the court having jurisdiction at the place where the deceased died domiciled; or
>
> (b)   where there is no person so entrusted, to the person beneficially entitled to the estate by the law of the place where the deceased died domiciled or, if there is more than one person so entitled, to such of them as the [district judge or] registrar may direct; or
>
> (c)   if in the opinion of the [district judge or] registrar the circumstances so require, to such person as the [district judge or] registrar may direct.

(2) A grant made under paragraph (1)(a) or (b) above may be issued jointly with such person as the [district judge or] registrar may direct if the grant is required to be made to not less than two administrators.

(3) Without any order made under paragraph (1) above–

> (a)   probate of any will which is admissible to proof may be granted–
>
> > (i)   if the will is in the English or Welsh language, to the executor named therein; or
> >
> > (ii)   if the will describes the duties of a named person in terms sufficient to constitute him executor according to the tenor of the will, to that person; or
>
> (b)   where the whole or substantially the whole of the estate in England and Wales consists of immovable property, a grant in respect of the whole estate may be made in accordance with the law which would have been applicable if the deceased had died domiciled in England and Wales.

ANNOTATIONS

Initial commencement

Specified date
Specified date: 1 January 1988: see r 1.

Amendment
Para (1): first words in square brackets substituted and other words in square brackets inserted by SI 1991/1876, rr 7(1), 10.
   Para (2): words in square brackets inserted by SI 1991/1876, r 7(1).

31   Grants to attorneys

(1) Subject to paragraphs (2) and (3) below, the lawfully constituted attorney of a person entitled to a grant may apply for administration for the use and benefit

of the donor, and such grant shall be limited until further representation be granted, or in such other way as the [district judge or] registrar may direct.

(2) Where the donor referred to in paragraph (1) above is an executor, notice of the application shall be given to any other executor unless such notice is dispensed with by the [district judge or] registrar.

[(3) Where the donor referred to in paragraph (1) above lacks capacity within the meaning of the Mental Capacity Act 2005 (c 9) and the attorney is acting under an enduring power of attorney or lasting power of attorney, the application shall be made in accordance with rule 35.]

ANNOTATIONS

Initial commencement

Specified date
Specified date: 1 January 1988: see r 1.

Amendment
Paras (1), (2): words in square brackets inserted by SI 1991/1876, r 7(1).
   Para (3): substituted by SI 2007/1898, art 6, Sch 1, para 13(1), (2).
   Date in force: 1 October 2007: see SI 2007/1898, art 1.

32   Grants on behalf of minors

(1) Where a person to whom a grant would otherwise be made is a minor, administration for his use and benefit, limited until he attains the age of eighteen years, shall, unless otherwise directed, and subject to paragraph (2) of this rule, be granted to

[(a)   a parent of the minor who has, or is deemed to have, parental responsibility for him in accordance with–

   (i)   section 2(1), 2(2) or 4 of the Children Act 1989,

   (ii)   paragraph 4 or 6 of Schedule 14 to that Act, or

   (iii)   an adoption order within the meaning of section 12(1) of the Adoption Act 1976 [or section 46(1) of the Adoption and Children Act 2002], or

[(aa)   a person who has, or is deemed to have, parental responsibility for the minor by virtue of section 12(2) of the Children Act 1989(a) where the court has made a residence order under section 8 of that Act in respect of the minor in favour of that person; or]

[(ab)   a step-parent of the minor who has parental responsibility for him in accordance with section 4A of the Children Act 1989; or]

(b)   a guardian of the minor who is appointed, or deemed to have been appointed, in accordance with section 5 of the Children Act 1989 or in accordance with paragraph 12, 13 or 14 of Schedule 14 to that Act]; [or]

[(ba)   a special guardian of the minor who is appointed in accordance with section 14A of the Children Act 1989; or] (bb) an adoption agency which has parental responsibility for the minor by virtue of section 25(2) of the Adoption and Children Act 2002; or]

[(c) a local authority which has, or is deemed to have, parental responsibility for the minor by virtue of section 33(3) of the Children Act 1989 where the court has made a care order under section 31(1)(a) of that Act in respect of the minor and that local authority is designated in that order;]

provided that where the minor is sole executor and has no interest in the residuary estate of the deceased, administration for the use and benefit of the minor limited as aforesaid, shall, unless a [district judge or] registrar otherwise directs, be granted to the person entitled to the residuary estate.

[(2) A district judge or registrar may by order appoint a person to obtain administration for the use and benefit of the minor, limited as aforesaid, in default of, or jointly with, or to the exclusion of, any person mentioned in paragraph (1) of this rule; and the person intended shall file an affidavit in support of his application to be appointed.]

(3) Where there is only one person competent and willing to take a grant under the foregoing provisions of this rule, such person may, unless a [district judge or] registrar otherwise directs, nominate any fit and proper person to act jointly with him in taking the grant.

ANNOTATIONS

Initial commencement

Specified date
Specified date: 1 January 1988: see r 1.

Amendment
Para (1): sub-paras (a), (b) substituted by SI 1991/1876, r 3.
   Para (1): in sub-para (a)(iii) words 'or section 46(1) of the Adoption and Children Act 2002' in square brackets inserted by SI 2005/3504, art 4(a).
   Date in force: 30 December 2005: see SI 2005/3504, art 1.
   Para (1): sub-para (aa) inserted by SI 1998/1903, r 8(1).
   Date in force: 14 September 1998: see SI 1998/1903, r 1(1).
   Para (1): sub-para (ab) inserted by SI 2005/3504, art 4(b).
   Date in force: 30 December 2005: see SI 2005/3504, art 1.
   Para (1): in sub-para (b) word 'or' in square brackets inserted by SI 1998/1903, r 8(2).
   Date in force: 14 September 1998: see SI 1998/1903, r 1(1).
   Para (1): sub-paras (ba), (bb) inserted by SI 2005/3504, art 4(c).
   Date in force: 30 December 2005: see SI 2005/3504, art 1.
   Para (1): sub-para (c) inserted by SI 1998/1903, r 8(3).
   Date in force: 14 September 1998: see SI 1998/1903, r 1(1).
   Para (1): words 'district judge or' in square brackets inserted by SI 1991/1876, r 7(1).
   Para (2): substituted by SI 1991/1876, r 4.
   Para (3): words in square brackets inserted by SI 1991/1876, r 7(1).

33 Grants where a minor is a co-executor

(1) Where a minor is appointed executor jointly with one or more other executors, probate may be granted to the executor or executors not under

disability with power reserved to the minor executor, and the minor executor shall be entitled to apply for probate on attaining the age of eighteen years.

(2) Administration for the use and benefit of a minor executor until he attains the age of eighteen years may be granted under rule 32 if, and only if, the executors who are not under disability renounce or, on being cited to accept or refuse a grant, fail to make an effective application therefor.

ANNOTATIONS

Initial commencement

Specified date
Specified date: 1 January 1988: see r 1.

34 Renunciation of the right of a minor to a grant

(1) The right of a minor executor to probate on attaining the age of eighteen years may not be renounced by any person on his behalf.

(2) The right of a minor to administration may be renounced only by a person [appointed] under paragraph (2) of rule 32, and authorised by the [district judge or] registrar to renounce on behalf of the minor.

ANNOTATIONS

Initial commencement

Specified date
Specified date: 1 January 1988: see r 1.

Amendment
Para (2): first word in square brackets substituted and second words in square brackets inserted by SI 1991/1876, rr 5, 7(1).

35 Grants in case of [lack of mental capacity]

(1) Unless a [district judge or] registrar otherwise directs, no grant shall be made under this rule unless all persons entitled in the same degree as the [person who lacks capacity within the meaning of the Mental Capacity Act 2005] referred to in paragraph (2) below have been cleared off.

(2) Where a [district judge or] registrar is satisfied that a person entitled to a grant [lacks capacity within the meaning of the Mental Capacity Act 2005 to manage] his affairs, administration for his use and benefit, limited until further representation be granted or in such other way as the [district judge or] registrar may direct, may be granted in the following order of priority–

    (a)   to the person authorised by the Court of Protection to apply for a grant;

    (b)   where there is no person so authorised, to the lawful attorney of the [person who lacks capacity within the meaning of the Mental Capacity Act 2005] acting under a registered enduring power of attorney [or lasting power of attorney];

    (c)   where there is no such attorney entitled to act, or if the attorney shall renounce administration for the use and benefit of the [person who lacks capacity within the meaning of the Mental Capacity Act 2005], to the person entitled to the residuary estate of the deceased.

(3) Where a grant is required to be made to not less than two administrators, and there is only one person competent and willing to take a grant under the foregoing provisions of this rule, administration may, unless a [district judge or] registrar otherwise directs, be granted to such person jointly with any other person nominated by him.

(4) Notwithstanding the foregoing provisions of this rule, administration for the use and benefit of the [person who lacks capacity within the meaning of the Mental Capacity Act 2005] may be granted to such [other person] as the [district judge or] registrar may by order direct.

(5) [Unless the applicant is the person authorised in paragraph (2)(a) above,] Notice of an intended application under this rule shall be given to the Court of Protection.

ANNOTATIONS

Initial commencement

Specified date
Specified date: 1 January 1988: see r 1.

Amendment
Provision heading: words 'lack of mental capacity' in square brackets substituted by SI 2007/1898, art 6, Sch 1, para 13(1), (3).
 Date in force: 1 October 2007: see SI 2007/1898, art 1.
 Para (1): words 'district judge or' in square brackets inserted by SI 1991/1876, r 7(1).
 Para (1): words 'person who lacks capacity within the meaning of the Mental Capacity Act 2005' in square brackets substituted by SI 2007/1898, art 6, Sch 1, para 13(1), (4).
 Date in force: 1 October 2007: see SI 2007/1898, art 1.
 Para (2): words 'district judge or' in square brackets in both places they occur inserted by SI 1991/1876, r 7(1).
 Para (2): words 'lacks capacity within the meaning of the Mental Capacity Act 2005 to manage' in square brackets substituted by SI 2007/1898, art 6, Sch 1, para 13(1), (5)(a).
 Date in force: 1 October 2007: see SI 2007/1898, art 1.
 Para (2): in sub-paras (b), (c) words 'person who lacks capacity within the meaning of the Mental Capacity Act 2005' in square brackets substituted by virtue of SI 2007/1898, art 6, Sch 1, para 13(1), (5)(b).
 Date in force: 1 October 2007: see SI 2007/1898, art 1.
 Para (2): in sub-para (b) words 'or lasting power of attorney' in square brackets inserted by SI 2007/1898, art 6, Sch 1, para 13(1), (5)(c).
 Date in force: 1 October 2007: see SI 2007/1898, art 1.
 Para (3): words 'district judge or' in square brackets inserted by SI 1991/1876, r 7(1).
 Para (4): words 'person who lacks capacity within the meaning of the Mental Capacity Act 2005' in square brackets substituted by SI 2007/1898, art 6, Sch 1, para 13(1), (6).
 Date in force: 1 October 2007: see SI 2007/1898, art 1.
 Para (4): words 'other person' in square brackets substituted by SI 1998/1903, r 9(1).
 Date in force: 14 September 1998: see SI 1998/1903, r 1(1).
 Para (4): words 'district judge or' in square brackets inserted by SI 1991/1876, r 7(1).

Para (5): words from 'Unless' to 'paragraph (2)(a) above,' in square brackets inserted by SI 1998/1903, r 9(2).

Date in force: 14 September 1998: see SI 1998/1903, r 1(1).

36 Grants to trust corporations and other corporate bodies

(1) An application for a grant to a trust corporation shall be made through one of its officers, and such officer shall depose in the oath that the corporation is a trust corporation as defined by these Rules and that it has power to accept a grant.

(2)

(a) Where the trust corporation is the holder of an official position, any officer whose name is included on a list filed with the [senior district judge] of persons authorised to make affidavits and sign documents on behalf of the office holder may act as the officer through whom the holder of that official position applies for the grant.

(b) In all other cases a certified copy of the resolution of the trust corporation authorising the officer to make the application shall be lodged, or it shall be deposed in the oath that such certified copy has been filed with the [senior district judge], that the officer is therein identified by the position he holds, and that such resolution is still in force.

(3) A trust corporation may apply for administration otherwise than as a beneficiary or the attorney of some person, and on any such application there shall be lodged the consents of all persons entitled to a grant and of all persons interested in the residuary estate of the deceased save that the [district judge or] registrar may dispense with any such consents as aforesaid on such terms, if any, as he may think fit.

(4)

(a) Subject to sub-paragraph (d) below, where a corporate body would, if an individual, be entitled to a grant but is not a trust corporation as defined by these Rules, administration for its use and benefit, limited until further representation be granted, may be made to its nominee or to its lawfully constituted attorney.

(b) A copy of the resolution appointing the nominee or the power of attorney (whichever is appropriate) shall be lodged, and such resolution or power of attorney shall be sealed by the corporate body, or be otherwise authenticated to the [district judge's or] registrar's satisfaction.

(c) The nominee or attorney shall depose in the oath that the corporate body is not a trust corporation as defined by these Rules.

(d) The provisions of paragraph (4)(a) above shall not apply where a corporate body is appointed executor jointly with an individual unless the right of the individual has been cleared off.

37   Renunciation of probate and administration

(1) Renunciation of probate by an executor shall not operate as renunciation of any right which he may have to a grant of administration in some other capacity unless he expressly renounces such right.

(2) Unless a [district judge or] registrar otherwise directs, no person who has renounced administration in one capacity may obtain a grant thereof in some other capacity.

[(2A) Renunciation of probate or administration by members of a partnership–

   (a)   may be effected, or

   (b)   subject to paragraph (3) below, may be retracted by any two of them with the authority of the others and any such renunciation or retraction shall recite such authority.]

(3) A renunciation of probate or administration may be retracted at any time with the leave of a [district judge or] registrar; provided that only in exceptional circumstances may leave be given to an executor to retract a renunciation of probate after a grant has been made to some other person entitled in a lower degree.

(4) A direction or order giving leave under this rule may be made either by the registrar of a district probate registry where the renunciation is filed or by a [district judge].

38   Notice to Crown of intended application for grant

In any case in which it appears that the Crown is or may be beneficially interested in the estate of a deceased person, notice of intended application for a grant shall be given by the applicant to the Treasury Solicitor, and the [district judge or] registrar may direct that no grant shall issue within 28 days after the notice has been given.

ANNOTATIONS

Initial commencement

Specified date
Specified date: 1 January 1988: see r 1.

Amendment
Words in square brackets inserted by SI 1991/1876, r 7(1).

39   Resealing under Colonial Probates Acts 1892 and 1927

(1) An application under the Colonial Probates Acts 1892 and 1927 for the resealing of probate or administration granted by the court of a country to which those Acts apply may be made by the person to whom the grant was made or by any person authorised in writing to apply on his behalf.

(2) On any such application an Inland Revenue affidavit or account shall be lodged.

(3) Except by leave of a [district judge or] registrar, no grant shall be resealed unless it was made to such a person as is mentioned in sub-paragraph (a) or (b) of paragraph (1) of rule 30 or to a person to whom a grant could be made under sub-paragraph (a) of paragraph (3) of that rule.

(4) No limited or temporary grant shall be resealed except by leave of a [district judge or] registrar.

(5) Every grant lodged for resealing shall include a copy of any will to which the grant relates or shall be accompanied by a copy thereof certified as correct by or under the authority of the court by which the grant was made, and where the copy of the grant required to be deposited under subsection (1) of section 2 of the Colonial Probates Act 1892 does not include a copy of the will, a copy thereof shall be deposited in the registry before the grant is resealed.

(6) The [district judge or] registrar shall send notice of the resealing to the court which made the grant.

(7) Where notice is received in the Principal Registry of the resealing of a grant issued in England and Wales, notice of any amendment or revocation of the grant shall be sent to the court by which it was resealed.

ANNOTATIONS

Initial commencement

Specified date
Specified date: 1 January 1988: see r 1.

Amendment
Paras (3), (4), (6): words in square brackets inserted by SI 1991/1876, r 7(1).

40   Application for leave to sue on guarantee

An application for leave under section 120(3) of the Act or under section 11(5) of the Administration of Estates Act 1971 to sue a surety on a guarantee given for the purposes of either of those sections shall, unless the [district judge or] registrar otherwise directs under rule 61, be made by summons to a [district judge or] registrar and notice of the application shall be served on the administrator, the surety and any co-surety.

ANNOTATIONS

Initial commencement

Specified date
Specified date: 1 January 1988: see r 1.

Amendment
Words in square brackets inserted by SI 1991/1876, r 7(1).

41   Amendment and revocation of grant

(1) Subject to paragraph (2) below, if a [district judge or] registrar is satisfied that a grant should be amended or revoked he may make an order accordingly.

(2) Except on the application or with the consent of the person to whom the grant was made, the power conferred in paragraph (1) above shall be exercised only in exceptional circumstances.

ANNOTATIONS

Initial commencement

Specified date
Specified date: 1 January 1988: see r 1.

Amendment
Para (1): words in square brackets inserted by SI 1991/1876, r 7(1).

42   Certificate of delivery of Inland Revenue affidavit

Where the deceased died before 13th March 1975 the certificate of delivery of an Inland Revenue affidavit required by section 30 of the Customs and Inland Revenue Act 1881 to be borne by every grant shall be in Form 1.

ANNOTATIONS

Initial commencement

Specified date
Specified date: 1 January 1988: see r 1.

43   Standing searches

[(1) Any person who wishes to be notified of the issue of a grant may enter a standing search for the grant by lodging at, or sending by post to any registry or sub-registry, a notice in Form 2.]

(2) A person who has entered a standing search will be sent an office copy of any grant which corresponds with the particulars given on the completed Form 2 and which–

(a)   issued not more than twelve months before the entry of the standing search; or

(b)   issues within a period of six months after the entry of the standing search.

(3)

(a)   Where an applicant wishes to extend the said period of six months, he or his solicitor [or probate practitioner] may lodge at, or send by post to, [the registry or sub-registry at which the standing search was entered] written application for extension.

(b)   An application for extension as aforesaid must be lodged, or received by post, within the last month of the said period of six months, and the standing search shall thereupon be effective for an additional period of six months from the date on which it was due to expire.

(c)   A standing search which has been extended as above may be further extended by the filing of a further application for extension subject to the same conditions as set out in sub-paragraph (b) above.

ANNOTATIONS

Initial commencement

Specified date
Specified date: 1 January 1988: see r 1.

Amendment
Para (1): substituted by SI 1991/1876, r 11(1).
   Para (3): in sub-para (a) words 'or probate practitioner' in square brackets inserted by SI 1998/1903, r 6.
   Date in force: 14 September 1998: see SI 1998/1903, r 1(1).
   Para (3): in sub-para (a) words from 'the registry' to 'search was entered' in square brackets substituted by SI 1991/1876, r 11(2).

Modification
References to solicitors etc modified to include references to bodies recognised under the Administration of Justice Act 1985, s 9, by the Solicitors' Incorporated Practices Order 1991, SI 1991/2684, arts 4, 5, Sch 1.

44   Caveats

(1) Any person who wishes to show cause against the sealing of a grant may enter a caveat in any registry or sub-registry, and the [district judge or] registrar shall not allow any grant to be sealed (other than a grant ad colligenda bona or a grant under section 117 of the Act) if he has knowledge of an effective caveat; provided that no caveat shall prevent the sealing of a grant on the day on which the caveat is entered.

(2) Any person wishing to enter a caveat (in these Rules called 'the caveator'), or a solicitor [or probate practitioner] on his behalf, may effect entry of a caveat–

- (a) by completing Form 3 in the appropriate book at any registry or sub-registry; or

- (b) by sending by post at his own risk a notice in Form 3 to any registry or sub-registry and the proper officer shall provide an acknowledgement of the entry of the caveat.

(3)

- (a) Except as otherwise provided by this rule or by rules 45 or 46, a caveat shall be effective for a period of six months from the date of entry thereof, and where a caveator wishes to extend the said period of six months, he or his solicitor [or probate practitioner] may lodge at, or send by post to, the registry or sub-registry at which the caveat was entered a written application for extension.

- (b) An application for extension as aforesaid must be lodged, or received by post, within the last month of the said period of six months, and the caveat shall thereupon (save as otherwise provided by this rule) be effective for an additional period of six months from the date on which it was due to expire.

- (c) A caveat which has been extended as above may be further extended by the filing of a further application for extension subject to the same conditions as set out in sub-paragraph (b) above.

[(4) An index of caveats entered in any registry or sub-registry shall be maintained and upon receipt of an application for a grant, the registry or sub-registry at which the application is made shall cause a search of the index to be made and the appropriate district judge or registrar shall be notified of the entry of a caveat against the sealing of a grant for which the application has been made.]

(5) Any person claiming to have an interest in the estate may cause to be issued from the [nominated registry] a warning in Form 4 against the caveat, and the person warning shall state his interest in the estate of the deceased and shall require the caveator to give particulars of any contrary interest in the estate; and the warning or a copy thereof shall be served on the caveator forthwith.

(6) A caveator who has no interest contrary to that of the person warning, but who wishes to show cause against the sealing of a grant to that person, may within eight days of service of the warning upon him (inclusive of the day of such service), or at any time thereafter if no affidavit has been filed under paragraph (12) below, issue and serve a summons for directions.

(7) On the hearing of any summons for directions under paragraph (6) above the [district judge or] registrar may give a direction for the caveat to cease to have effect.

(8) Any caveat in force when a summons for directions is issued shall remain in force until the summons has been disposed of unless a direction has been given under paragraph (7) above [or until it is withdrawn under paragraph (11) below].

(9) The issue of a summons under this rule shall be notified forthwith to the [nominated registry].

(10) A caveator having an interest contrary to that of the person warning may within eight days of service of the warning upon him (inclusive of the day of such service) or at any time thereafter if no affidavit has been filed under paragraph (12) below, enter an appearance in the [nominated registry] by filing Form 5 ... ; and he shall serve forthwith on the person warning a copy of Form 5 sealed with the seal of the court.

(11) A caveator who has not entered an appearance to a warning may at any time withdraw his caveat by giving notice at the registry or sub-registry at which it was entered, and the caveat shall thereupon cease to have effect; and, where the caveat has been so withdrawn, the caveator shall forthwith give notice of withdrawal to the person warning.

(12) If no appearance has been entered by the caveator or no summons has been issued by him under paragraph (6) of this rule, the person warning may at any time after eight days of service of the warning upon the caveator (inclusive of the day of such service) file an affidavit in the [nominated registry] as to such service and the caveat shall thereupon cease to have effect provided that there is no pending summons under paragraph (6) of this rule.

(13) Unless a [district judge or, where application to discontinue a caveat is made by consent, a registrar] by order made on summons otherwise directs, any caveat in respect of which an appearance to a warning has been entered shall remain in force until the commencement of a probate action.

(14) Except with the leave of a [district judge], no further caveat may be entered by or on behalf of any caveator whose caveat is either in force or has ceased to have effect under paragraphs (7) or (12) of this rule or under rule 45(4) or rule 46(3).

[(15) In this rule, 'nominated registry' means the registry nominated for the purpose of this rule by the senior district judge or in the absence of any such nomination the Leeds District Probate Registry.]

ANNOTATIONS

Initial commencement

Specified date
Specified date: 1 January 1988: see r 1.

Amendment
Para (1): words 'district judge or' in square brackets inserted by SI 1991/1876, r 7(1).
  Para (2): words 'or probate practitioner' in square brackets inserted by SI 1998/1903, r 6.
  Date in force: 14 September 1998: see SI 1998/1903, r 1(1).

Para (3): in sub-para (a) words 'or probate practitioner' in square brackets inserted by SI 1998/1903, r 6.
Date in force: 14 September 1998: see SI 1998/1903, r 1(1).
Para (4): substituted by SI 1998/1903, r 11(1).
Date in force: 14 September 1998: see SI 1998/1903, r 1(1).
Para (5): words 'nominated registry' in square brackets substituted by SI 1998/1903, r 11(2).
Date in force: 14 September 1998: see SI 1998/1903, r 1(1).
Para (7): words 'district judge or' in square brackets inserted by SI 1991/1876, r 7(1).
Para (8): words in square brackets inserted by SI 1991/1876, r 12(1).
Para (9): words 'nominated registry' in square brackets substituted by SI 1998/1903, r 11(2).
Date in force: 14 September 1998: see SI 1998/1903, r 1(1).
Para (10): words 'nominated registry' in square brackets substituted by SI 1998/1903, r 11(2).
Date in force: 14 September 1998: see SI 1998/1903, r 1(1).
Para (10): words omitted revoked by SI 1991/1876, r 12(2).
Para (12): words 'nominated registry' in square brackets substituted by SI 1998/1903, r 11(2).
Date in force: 14 September 1998: see SI 1998/1903, r 1(1).
Para (13): words in square brackets substituted by SI 1991/1876, rr 7(3), 12(3).
Para (14): words in square brackets substituted by SI 1991/1876, r 7(3).
Para (15): inserted by SI 1998/1903, r 11(3).
Date in force: 14 September 1998: see SI 1998/1903, r 1(1).

Modification
References to solicitors etc modified to include references to bodies recognised under the Administration of Justice Act 1985, s 9, by the Solicitors' Incorporated Practices Order 1991, SI 1991/2684, arts 4, 5, Sch 1.

45   Probate actions

(1) Upon being advised by the court concerned of the commencement of a probate action the [senior district judge] shall give notice of the action to every caveator other than the plaintiff in the action in respect of each caveat that is in force.

(2) In respect of any caveat entered subsequent to the commencement of a probate action the [senior district judge] shall give notice to that caveator of the existence of the action.

(3) Unless a [district judge] by order made on summons otherwise directs, the commencement of a probate action shall operate to prevent the sealing of a grant (other than a grant under section 117 of the Act) until application for a grant is made by the person shown to be entitled thereto by the decision of the court in such action.

(4) Upon such application for a grant, any caveat entered by the plaintiff in the action, and any caveat in respect of which notice of the action has been given, shall cease to have effect.

Appendix 1

ANNOTATIONS

Initial commencement

Specified date
Specified date: 1 January 1988: see r 1.

Amendment
Paras (1), (2): words in square brackets substituted by SI 1991/1876, r 7(4).
  Para (3): words in square brackets substituted by SI 1991/1876, r 7(3).

46 Citations

(1) Any citation may issue from the Principal Registry or a district probate registry and shall be settled by a [district judge or] registrar before being issued.

(2) Every averment in a citation, and such other information as the registrar may require, shall be verified by an affidavit sworn by the person issuing the citation (in these Rules called the 'citor'), provided that the [district judge or] registrar may in special circumstances accept an affidavit sworn by the citor's solicitor [or probate practitioner].

(3) The citor shall enter a caveat before issuing a citation and, unless a [district judge] by order made on summons otherwise directs, any caveat in force at the commencement of the citation proceedings shall, unless withdrawn pursuant to paragraph (11) of rule 44, remain in force until application for a grant is made by the person shown to be entitled thereto by the decision of the court in such proceedings, and upon such application any caveat entered by a party who had notice of the proceedings shall cease to have effect.

(4) Every citation shall be served personally on the person cited unless the [district judge or] registrar, on cause shown by affidavit, directs some other mode of service, which may include notice by advertisement.

(5) Every will referred to in a citation shall be lodged in a registry before the citation is issued, except where the will is not in the citor's possession and the [district judge or] registrar is satisfied that it is impracticable to require it to be lodged.

(6) A person who has been cited to appear may, within eight days of service of the citation upon him (inclusive of the day of such service), or at any time thereafter if no application has been made by the citor under paragraph (5) of rule 47 or paragraph (2) of rule 48, enter an appearance in the registry from which the citation issued by filing Form 5 and shall forthwith thereafter serve on the citor a copy of Form 5 sealed with the seal of the registry.

ANNOTATIONS

Initial commencement

Specified date
Specified date: 1 January 1988: see r 1.

Amendment
Para (1): words 'district judge or' in square brackets inserted by SI 1991/1876, r 7(1).
  Para (2): words 'district judge or' in square brackets inserted by SI 1991/1876, r 7(1).

Para (2): words 'or probate practitioner' in square brackets inserted by SI 1998/1903, r 6.

Date in force: 14 September 1998: see SI 1998/1903, r 1(1).

Para (3): words in square brackets substituted by SI 1991/1876, r 7(3).

Para (4): words 'district judge or' in square brackets inserted by SI 1991/1876, r 7(1).

Para (5): words 'district judge or' in square brackets inserted by SI 1991/1876, r 7(1).

47   Citation to accept or refuse or to take a grant

(1) A citation to accept or refuse a grant may be issued at the instance of any person who would himself be entitled to a grant in the event of the person cited renouncing his right thereto.

(2) Where power to make a grant to an executor has been reserved, a citation calling on him to accept or refuse a grant may be issued at the instance of the executors who have proved the will or the survivor of them or of the executors of the last survivor of deceased executors who have proved.

(3) A citation calling on an executor who has intermeddled in the estate of the deceased to show cause why he should not be ordered to take a grant may be issued at the instance of any person interested in the estate at any time after the expiration of six months from the death of the deceased, provided that no citation to take a grant shall issue while proceedings as to the validity of the will are pending.

(4) A person cited who is willing to accept or take a grant may, after entering an appearance, apply ex parte by affidavit to a [district judge or] registrar for an order for a grant to himself.

(5) If the time limited for appearance has expired and the person cited has not entered an appearance, the citor may–

(a)   in the case of a citation under paragraph (1) of this rule, apply to a [district judge or] registrar for an order for a grant to himself;

(b)   in the case of a citation under paragraph (2) of this rule, apply to a [district judge or] registrar for an order that a note be made on the grant that the executor in respect of whom power was reserved has been duly cited and has not appeared and that all his rights in respect of the executorship have wholly ceased; or

(c)   in the case of a citation under paragraph (3) of this rule, apply to a [district judge or] registrar by summons (which shall be served on the person cited) for an order requiring such person to take a grant within a specified time or for a grant to himself or to some other person specified in the summons.

(6) An application under the last foregoing paragraph shall be supported by an affidavit showing that the citation was duly served.

(7) If the person cited has entered an appearance but has not applied for a grant under paragraph (4) of this rule, or has failed to prosecute his application with reasonable diligence, the citor may–

(a) in the case of a citation under paragraph (1) of this rule, apply by summons to a [district judge or] registrar for an order for a grant to himself;

(b) in the case of a citation under paragraph (2) of this rule, apply by summons to a [district judge or] registrar for an order striking out the appearance and for the endorsement on the grant of such a note as is mentioned in sub-paragraph (b) of paragraph (5) of this rule; or

(c) in the case of a citation under paragraph (3) of this rule, apply by summons to a [district judge or] registrar for an order requiring the person cited to take a grant within a specified time or for a grant to himself or to some other person specified in the summons;

and the summons shall be served on the person cited.

ANNOTATIONS

Initial commencement

Specified date
Specified date: 1 January 1988: see r 1.

Amendment
Paras (4), (5), (7): words in square brackets inserted by SI 1991/1876, r 7(1).

48   Citation to propound a will

(1) A citation to propound a will shall be directed to the executors named in the will and to all persons interested thereunder, and may be issued at the instance of any citor having an interest contrary to that of the executors or such other persons.

(2) If the time limited for appearance has expired, the citor may–

(a) in the case where no person has entered an appearance, apply to a [district judge or] registrar for an order for a grant as if the will were invalid and such application shall be supported by an affidavit showing that the citation was duly served; or

(b) in the case where no person who has entered an appearance proceeds with reasonable diligence to propound the will, apply to a [district judge or] registrar by summons, which shall be served on every person cited who has entered an appearance, for such an order as is mentioned in paragraph (a) above.

ANNOTATIONS

Initial commencement

Specified date
Specified date: 1 January 1988: see r 1.

Amendment
Para (2): words in square brackets inserted by SI 1991/1876, r 7(1).

49   Address for service

All caveats, citations, warnings and appearances shall contain an address for service in England and Wales.

ANNOTATIONS

Initial commencement

Specified date
Specified date: 1 January 1988: see r 1.

50   Application for order to attend for examination or for subpoena to bring in a will

(1) An application under section 122 of the Act for an order requiring a person to attend for examination may, unless a probate action has been commenced, be made to a [district judge or] registrar by summons which shall be served on every such person as aforesaid.

(2) An application under section 123 of the Act for the issue by a [district judge or] registrar of a subpoena to bring in a will shall be supported by an affidavit setting out the grounds of the application, and if any person served with the subpoena denies that the will is in his possession or control he may file an affidavit to that effect in the registry from which the subpoena issued.

ANNOTATIONS

Initial commencement

Specified date
Specified date: 1 January 1988: see r 1.

Amendment
Words in square brackets inserted by SI 1991/1876, r 7(1).

51   Grants to part of an estate under section 113 of the Act

An application for an order for a grant under section 113 of the Act to part of an estate may be made to a [district judge or] registrar, and shall be supported by an affidavit setting out the grounds of the application, and

    (a)   stating whether the estate of the deceased is known to be insolvent; and

    (b)   showing how any person entitled to a grant in respect of the whole estate in priority to the applicant has been cleared off.

ANNOTATIONS

Initial commencement

Specified date
Specified date: 1 January 1988: see r 1.

Amendment
Words in square brackets inserted by SI 1991/1876, r 7(1).

52 Grants of administration under discretionary powers of court, and grants ad colligenda bona

An application for an order for–

(a)   a grant of administration under section 116 of the Act; or

(b)   a grant of administration ad colligenda bona,

may be made to a [district judge or] registrar and shall be supported by an affidavit setting out the grounds of the application.

ANNOTATIONS

Initial commencement

Specified date
Specified date: 1 January 1988: see r 1.

Amendment
Words in square brackets inserted by SI 1991/1876, r 7(1).

53 Applications for leave to swear to death

An application for leave to swear to the death of a person in whose estate a grant is sought may be made to a [district judge or] registrar, and shall be supported by an affidavit setting out the grounds of the application and containing particulars of any policies of insurance effected on the life of the presumed deceased together with such further evidence as the [district judge or] registrar may require.

ANNOTATIONS

Initial commencement

Specified date
Specified date: 1 January 1988: see r 1.

Amendment
Words in square brackets inserted by SI 1991/1876, r 7(1).

54 Grants in respect of nuncupative wills and copies of wills

(1) Subject to paragraph (2) below, an application for an order admitting to proof a nuncupative will, or a will contained in a copy or reconstruction thereof where the original is not available, shall be made to a [district judge or] registrar.

(2) In any case where a will is not available owing to its being retained in the custody of a foreign court or official, a duly authenticated copy of the will may be admitted to proof without the order referred to in paragraph (1) above.

(3) An application under paragraph (1) above shall be supported by an affidavit setting out the grounds of the application, and by such evidence on affidavit as the applicant can adduce as to–

(a)   the will's existence after the death of the testator or, where there is no such evidence, the facts on which the applicant relies to rebut the presumption that the will has been revoked by destruction;

(b)   in respect of a nuncupative will, the contents of that will; and

(c)   in respect of a reconstruction of a will, the accuracy of that reconstruction.

(4) The [district judge or] registrar may require additional evidence in the circumstances of a particular case as to due execution of the will or as to the accuracy of the copy will, and may direct that notice be given to persons who would be prejudiced by the application.

ANNOTATIONS

Initial commencement

Specified date
Specified date: 1 January 1988: see r 1.

Amendment
Paras (1), (4): words in square brackets inserted by SI 1991/1876, r 7(1).

55   Application for rectification of a will

(1) An application for an order that a will be rectified by virtue of section 20(1) of the Administration of Justice Act 1982 may be made to a [district judge or] registrar, unless a probate action has been commenced.

(2) The application shall be supported by an affidavit, setting out the grounds of the application, together with such evidence as can be adduced as to the testator's intentions and as to whichever of the following matters as are in issue:–

(a)   in what respects the testator's intentions were not understood; or

(b)   the nature of any alleged clerical error.

(3) Unless otherwise directed, notice of the application shall be given to every person having an interest under the will whose interest might be prejudiced[, or such other person who might be prejudiced,] by the rectification applied for and any comments in writing by any such person shall be exhibited to the affidavit in support of the application.

(4) If the [district judge or] registrar is satisfied that, subject to any direction to the contrary, notice has been given to every person mentioned in paragraph (3) above, and that the application is unopposed, he may order that the will be rectified accordingly.

ANNOTATIONS

Initial commencement

Specified date
Specified date: 1 January 1988: see r 1.

Amendment
Paras (1), (4): words in square brackets inserted by SI 1991/1876, r 7(1).
   Para (3): words ', or such other person who might be prejudiced,' in square brackets inserted by SI 1998/1903, r 12.
   Date in force: 14 September 1998: see SI 1998/1903, r 1(1).

56   Notice of election by surviving spouse [or civil partner] to redeem life interest

(1) Where a surviving spouse [or civil partner] who is the sole or sole surviving personal representative of the deceased is entitled to a life interest in part of the residuary estate and elects under section 47A of the Administration of Estates Act 1925 to have the life interest redeemed, he may give written notice of the election to the [senior district judge] in pursuance of subsection (7) of that section by filing a notice in Form 6 in the Principal Registry or in the district probate registry from which the grant issued.

(2) Where the grant issued from a district probate registry, the notice shall be filed in duplicate.

(3) A notice filed under this rule shall be noted on the grant and the record and shall be open to inspection.

ANNOTATIONS

Initial commencement

Specified date
Specified date: 1 January 1988: see r 1.

Amendment
Provision heading: words 'or civil partner' in square brackets inserted by SI 2005/2114, art 2(6), Sch 6, para 2(1), (4).
   Date in force: 5 December 2005: see SI 2005/2114, art 1.
   Para (1): words 'or civil partner' in square brackets inserted by SI 2005/2114, art 2(6), Sch 6, para 2(1), (4).
   Date in force: 5 December 2005: see SI 2005/2114, art 1.
   Para (1): words 'senior district judge' in square brackets substituted by SI 1991/1876, r 7(4).

[57   Index of grant applications]

[(1) The senior district judge shall maintain an index of every pending application for a grant made in any registry or sub-registry.

(2) Every registry or sub-registry in which an application is made shall cause the index to be searched and shall record the result of the search.]

ANNOTATIONS

Amendment
Substituted by SI 1998/1903, r 13.
   Date in force: 14 September 1998: see SI 1998/1903, r 1(1).

58 Inspection of copies of original wills and other documents

An original will or other document referred to in section 124 of the Act shall not be open to inspection if, in the opinion of a [district judge or] registrar, such inspection would be undesirable or otherwise inappropriate.

ANNOTATIONS

Initial commencement

Specified date
Specified date: 1 January 1988: see r 1.

Amendment
Words in square brackets inserted by SI 1991/1876, r 7(1).

59 Issue of copies of original wills and other documents

Where copies are required of original wills or other documents deposited under section 124 of the Act, such copies may be facsimile copies sealed with the seal of the court and issued either as office copies or certified under the hand of a [district judge or] registrar to be true copies.

ANNOTATIONS

Initial commencement

Specified date
Specified date: 1 January 1988: see r 1.

Amendment
Words in square brackets inserted by SI 1991/1876, r 7(1).

[60 Costs]

[(1) Order 62 of the Rules of the Supreme Court 1965 shall not apply to costs in non-contentious probate matters, and Parts 43, 44 (except rules 44.9 to 44.12), 47 and 48 of the Civil Procedure Rules 1998 ('the 1998 Rules') shall apply to costs in those matters, with the modifications contained in paragraphs (3) to (7) of this rule.

(2) Where detailed assessment of a bill of costs is ordered, it shall be referred–

(a)   where the order was made by a district judge, to a district judge, a costs judge or an authorised court officer within rule 43.2(1)(d)(iii) or (iv) of the 1998 Rules;

(b)   where the order was made by a registrar, to that registrar or, where this is not possible, in accordance with sub-paragraph (a) above.

(3) Every reference in Parts 43, 44, 47 and 48 of the 1998 Rules to a district judge shall be construed as referring only to a district judge of the Principal Registry.

(4) The definition of 'costs officer' in rule 43.2(1)(c) of the 1998 Rules shall have effect as if it included a paragraph reading–

'(iv)   a district probate registrar.'

(5) The definition of 'authorised court officer' in rule 43.2(1)(d) of the 1998 Rules shall have effect as if paragraphs (i) and (ii) were omitted.

(6) Rule 44.3(2) of the 1998 Rules (costs follow the event) shall not apply.

(7) Rule 47.4(2) of the 1998 Rules shall apply as if after the words 'Supreme Court Costs Office' there were inserted ', the Principal Registry of the Family Division or such district probate registry as the court may specify'.

(8) Except in the case of an appeal against a decision of an authorised court officer (to which rules 47.20 to 47.23 of the 1998 Rules apply), an appeal against a decision in assessment proceedings relating to costs in non-contentious probate matters shall be dealt with in accordance with the following paragraphs of this rule.

(9) An appeal within paragraph (8) above against a decision made by a district judge, a costs judge (as defined by rule 43.2(1)(b) of the 1998 Rules) or a registrar, shall lie to a judge of the High Court.

(10) Part 52 of the 1998 Rules applies to every appeal within paragraph (8) above, and any reference in Part 52 to a judge or a district judge shall be taken to include a district judge of the Principal Registry of the Family Division.

(11) The 1998 Rules shall apply to an appeal to which Part 52 or rules 47.20 to 47.23 of those Rules apply in accordance with paragraph (8) above in the same way as they apply to any other appeal within Part 52 or rules 47.20 to 47.23 of those Rules as the case may be; accordingly the Rules of the Supreme Court 1965 and the County Court Rules 1981 shall not apply to any such appeal.]

ANNOTATIONS

Amendment
Substituted by SI 2003/185, rr 4, 5.
    Date in force: 24 February 2003: see SI 2003/185, r 1; for transitional provisions see r 3 thereof.

61 Power to require applications to be made by summons

(1) [Subject to rule 7(2),] a [district judge or] registrar may require any application to be made by summons to a [district judge or] registrar in chambers or a judge in chambers or open court.

(2) An application for an inventory and account shall be made by summons to a [district judge or] registrar.

(3) A summons for hearing by a [district judge or] registrar shall be issued out of the registry in which it is to be heard.

(4) A summons to be heard by a judge shall be issued out of the Principal Registry.

ANNOTATIONS

Initial commencement

Specified date
Specified date: 1 January 1988: see r 1.

Amendment
Paras (1)–(3): words in square brackets inserted by SI 1991/1876, rr 7(1), 14.

62 Transfer of applications

A registrar to whom any application is made under these Rules may order the transfer of the application to another [district judge or] registrar having jurisdiction.

ANNOTATIONS

Initial commencement

Specified date
Specified date: 1 January 1988: see r 1.

Amendment
Words in square brackets inserted by SI 1991/1876, r 7(1).

[62A Exercise of a registrar's jurisdiction by another registrar]

[A registrar may hear and dispose of an application under these Rules on behalf of any other registrar by whom the application would otherwise have been heard, if that other registrar so requests or an application in that behalf is made by a party making an application under these Rules; and where the circumstances require it, the registrar shall, without the need for any such request or application, hear and dispose of the application.]

ANNOTATIONS

Amendment
Inserted by SI 1998/1903, r 14.
  Date in force: 14 September 1998: see SI 1998/1903, r 1(1).

63 Power to make orders for costs

On any application dealt with by him on summons, the … registrar shall have full power to determine by whom and to what extent the costs are to be paid.

ANNOTATIONS

Initial commencement

Specified date
Specified date: 1 January 1988: see r 1.

Amendment
Words omitted revoked by SI 1991/1876, r 7(2).

64 Exercise of powers of judge during Long Vacation

All powers exercisable under these Rules by a judge in chambers may be exercised during the Long Vacation by a [district judge].

ANNOTATIONS

Initial commencement

Specified date
Specified date: 1 January 1988: see r 1.

Amendment
Words in square brackets substituted by SI 1991/1876, r 7(3).

65 Appeals from [district judges or] registrars

(1) An appeal against a decision or requirement of a [district judge or] registrar shall be made by summons to a judge.

(2) If, in the case of an appeal under the last foregoing paragraph, any person besides the appellant appeared or was represented before the [district judge or] registrar from whose decision or requirement the appeal is brought, the summons shall be issued within seven days thereof for hearing on the first available day and shall be served on every such person as aforesaid.

[(3) This rule does not apply to an appeal against a decision in proceedings for the assessment of costs.]

ANNOTATIONS

Initial commencement

Specified date
Specified date: 1 January 1988: see r 1.

Amendment
Para (1): words 'district judge or' in square brackets inserted by SI 1991/1876, r 7(1), (6).
  Para (2): words 'district judge or' in square brackets inserted by SI 1991/1876, r 7(1), (6).
  Para (3): inserted by SI 2003/185, r 6.
  Date in force: 24 February 2003: see SI 2003/185, r 1; for transitional provisions see r 3 thereof.

66 Service of summons

(1) A judge or [district judge] or, where the application is to be made to a district probate registrar, that registrar, may direct that a summons for the service of which no other provision is made by these Rules shall be served on such person or persons as the [judge, district judge or registrar] [may direct].

(2) Where by these Rules or by any direction given under the last foregoing paragraph a summons is required to be served on any person, it shall be served not less than two clear days before the day appointed for the hearing, unless a judge or [district judge or] registrar at or before the hearing dispenses with service on such terms, if any, as he may think fit.

ANNOTATIONS

Initial commencement

Specified date
Specified date: 1 January 1988: see r 1.

Amendment
Para (1): words 'district judge' in square brackets substituted by SI 1991/1876, r 7(3).
Para (1): words 'judge, district judge or registrar' in square brackets substituted by SI 1998/1903, r 15.
Date in force: 14 September 1998: see SI 1998/1903, r 1(1).
Para (1): words 'may direct' in square brackets substituted by SI 1991/1876, r 7(7).
Para (2): words 'district judge or' in square brackets inserted by SI 1991/1876, r 7(1).

67 Notices, etc

Unless a [district judge or] registrar otherwise directs or these Rules otherwise provide, any notice or other document required to be given to or served on any person may be given or served in the manner prescribed by Order 65 Rule 5 of the Rules of the Supreme Court 1965.

ANNOTATIONS

Initial commencement

Specified date
Specified date: 1 January 1988: see r 1.

Amendment
Words in square brackets inserted by SI 1991/1876, r 7(1).

68 Application to pending proceedings

Subject in any particular case to any direction given by a judge or [district judge or] registrar, these Rules shall apply to any proceedings which are pending on the date on which they come into force as well as to any proceedings commenced on or after that date.

ANNOTATIONS

Initial commencement

Specified date
Specified date: 1 January 1988: see r 1.

Amendment
Words in square brackets inserted by SI 1991/1876, r 7(1).

69 Revocation of previous rules

(1) Subject to paragraph (2) below, the rules set out in the Second Schedule are hereby revoked.

(2) The rules set out in the Second Schedule shall continue to apply to such extent as may be necessary for giving effect to a direction under rule 68.

SCHEDULE 1
FORMS

Rule 2(2)

Form 1

Certificate of Delivery of Inland Revenue Affidavit

Rule 42

And it is hereby certified that an Inland Revenue affidavit has been delivered wherein it is shown that the gross value of the said estate in the United Kingdom (exclusive of what the said deceased may have been possessed of or entitled to as a trustee and not beneficially) amounts to £ ... ... and that the net value of the estate amounts to £ ... ..

And it is further certified that it appears by a receipt signed by an Inland Revenue officer on the said affidavit that £ ... ... on account of estate duty and interest on such day has been paid.

Form 2

Standing Search

Rule 43(1)

In the High Court of Justice Family Division

[The Principal (or...District Probate) Registry]

I/We apply for the entry of a standing search so that there shall be sent to me/us an office copy of every grant of representation in England and Wales in the estate of–

Full name of deceased: ....

Full address: ....

Alternative or alias names: ....

Exact date of death: ....

which either has issued not more than 12 months before the entry of this application or issues within 6 months thereafter.

Signed ....

Name in block letters ....

Full address ....

Reference No. (if any)..

ANNOTATIONS

Initial commencement

Specified date
Specified date: 1 January 1988: see r 1.

Amendment
Words in square brackets substituted by SI 1991/1876, r 11(3).

Form 3

Caveat

Rule 44(2)

In the High Court of Justice Family Division

The Principal (*or*.. District Probate) Registry.

Let not grant be sealed in the estate of (*full name and address*) deceased, who died on the .... day of 19 .... without notice to (*name of party by whom or on whose behalf the caveat is entered*).

Dated this .... day of .... 19 ....

(*Signed*) .... (*to be signed by the caveator's solicitor* [*or probate practitioner*] *or by the caveator if acting in person*)

whose address for service is: ....

Solicitor[/probate practitioner] for the said .... (*If the caveator is acting in person, substitute 'In person'.*)

ANNOTATIONS

Initial commencement

Specified date
Specified date: 1 January 1988: see r 1.

Amendment
Words 'or probate practitioner' in square brackets inserted by SI 1998/1903, r 16(a).
    Date in force: 14 September 1998: see SI 1998/1903, r 1(1).
    Words '/probate practitioner' in square brackets inserted by SI 1998/1903, r 16(b).
    Date in force: 14 September 1998: see SI 1998/1903, r 1(1).

Form 4

Warning to Caveator

Rule 44(5)

In the High Court of Justice Family Division

[(The nominated registry as defined by rule 44(15))]

To .... of .... a party who has entered a caveat in the estate of .... deceased.

You have eight days (starting with the day on which this warning was served on you):

(i) to enter an appearance either in person or by your solicitor [or probate practitioner], at the [(name and address of the nominated registry)] setting out what interest you have in the estate of the above-named .... of .... deceased contrary to that of the party at whose instance this warning is issued; or

(ii)if you have no contrary interest but wish to show cause against the sealing of a grant to such party, to issue and serve a summons for [directions by a district judge of the Principal Registry or a registrar of] a district probate registry.

If you fail to do either of these, the court may proceed to issue a grant of probate or administration in the said estate notwithstanding your caveat.

Dated the .... day of .... 19 ....

Issued at the instance of ....

(Here set out the name and interest (including the date of the will, if any, under which the interest arises) of the party warning, the name of his solicitor [or probate practitioner] and the address for service. If the party warning is acting in person, this must be stated.) .... Registrar

ANNOTATIONS

Initial commencement

Specified date
Specified date: 1 January 1988: see r 1.

Amendment
Words '(The nominated registry as defined by rule 44(15))' in square brackets substituted by SI 1998/1903, r 17(b).
   Date in force: 14 September 1998: see SI 1998/1903, r 1(1).
   Words 'or probate practitioner' in square brackets in both places they occur inserted by SI 1998/1903, r 17(a).
   Date in force: 14 September 1998: see SI 1998/1903, r 1(1).
   Words '(name and address of the nominated registry)' in square brackets substituted by SI 1998/1903, r 17(c).
   Date in force: 14 September 1998: see SI 1998/1903, r 1(1).
   Words from 'directions by' to 'a registrar of' in square brackets substituted by SI 1991/1876, r 7(8).

Form 5

Appearance to Warning or Citation

Rules 44(10), 46(6)

In the High Court of Justice Family Division

The Principal (*or* .... District Probate) Registry Caveat No .... dated the .... day of .... 19 .... (Citation dated the .... day of .... 19 ....)

Full name and address of deceased: ....

Full name and address of person warning (*or* citor): ....

(*Here set out the interest of the person warning, or citor, as shown in warning or citation.*)

Full name and address of caveator (or person cited).

(*Here set out the interest of the caveator or person cited, stating the date of the will (if any) under which such interest arises.*)

Enter an appearance for the above-named caveator (*or* person cited) in this matter.

Dated the .... day of .... 19 ....

(*Signed*) ....

whose address for service is: ....

.... Solicitor[/probate practitioner] (*or* In person).

ANNOTATIONS

Initial commencement

Specified date
Specified date: 1 January 1988: see r 1.

Amendment
Words '/probate practitioner' in square brackets inserted by SI 1998/1903, r 18.
    Date in force: 14 September 1998: see SI 1998/1903, r 1(1).

Form 6

Notice of Election to Redeem Life Interest

Rule 56

In the High Court of Justice Family Division

The Principal (*or* .... District Probate) Registry

In the estate of .... deceased.

Whereas .... of .... died on the
.... day of .... 19 ....
wholly/partially intestate leaving his/her/lawful wife/husband[/civil partner]
and .... lawful issue of the said deceased;

And whereas Probate/Letters of Administration of the estate of the said ....
.... were granted to me, the said ....
(and to .... of ....) at the Probate
Registry on the .... day of .... 19 .... ;

And whereas (the said .... has ceased to be a personal
representative because ....) and I am (now) the sole
personal representative;

Now I, the said .... hereby given notice in
accordance with section 47A of the Administration of Estates Act 1925 that I
elect to redeem the life interest to which I am entitled in the estate of the late
.... by retaining £ .... its capital value, and
£ .... the costs of the transaction.

Dated the .... day of .... 19 ....

(Signed) ....

To the [senior district judge] of the Family Division.

ANNOTATIONS

Initial commencement

Specified date
Specified date: 1 January 1988: see r 1.

Amendment

Words '/civil partner' in square brackets inserted by SI 2005/2114, art 2(6), Sch 6, para 2(1), (5).
   Date in force: 5 December 2005: see SI 2005/2114, art 1.
   Words 'senior district judge' in square brackets substituted by SI 1991/1876, r 7(4).

SCHEDULE 2
REVOCATIONS

Rule 69

Rules revoked	References
The Non-Contentious Probate Rules 1954	SI 1954/796
The Non-Contentious Probate (Amendment) Rules 1961	SI 1961/72
The Non-Contentious Probate (Amendment) Rules 1962	SI 1962/2653
The Non-Contentious Probate (Amendment) Rules 1967	SI 1967/748
The Non-Contentious Probate (Amendment) Rules 1968	SI 1968/1675
The Non-Contentious Probate (Amendment) Rules 1969	SI 1969/1689
The Non-Contentious Probate (Amendment) Rules 1971	SI 1971/1977

The Non-Contentious Probate (Amendment) Rules 1974	SI 1974/597
The Non-Contentious Probate (Amendment) Rules 1976	SI 1976/1362
The Non-Contentious Probate (Amendment) Rules 1982	SI 1982/446
The Non-Contentious Probate (Amendment) Rules 1983	SI 1983/623
The Non-Contentious Probate (Amendment) Rules 1985	SI 1985/1232

ANNOTATIONS

Initial commencement

Specified date
Specified date: 1 January 1988: see r 1.

Appendix 2

Statutory provisions

Wills Act 1837

1837 CHAPTER 26

An Act for the amendment of the Laws with respect to Wills

[3rd July 1837]

[9   Signing and attestation of wills]

[No will shall be valid unless—

(*a*)   *it is in writing, and signed by the testator, or by some other person in his presence and by his direction; and*

(*b*)   *it appears that the testator intended by his signature to give effect to the will; and*

(*c*)   *the signature is made or acknowledged by the testator in the presence of two or more witnesses present at the same time; and*

(*d*)   *each witness either—*

(*i*)   *attests and signs the will; or*

(*ii*)   *acknowledges his signature,*

in the presence of the testator (but not necessarily in the presence of any other witness),

but no form of attestation shall be necessary.]

ANNOTATIONS

Extent
This Act does not extend to Scotland: see s 35.

Amendment
Substituted, in relation to England and Wales, by the Administration of Justice Act 1982, s 17.
   Repealed, in relation to Northern Ireland, by the Wills and Administration Proceedings (NI) Order 1994, SI 1994/1899, art 38, Sch 3.

[18   Will to be revoked by marriage]

[(1) Subject to subsections (2) to (4) below, a will shall be revoked by the testator's marriage.

(2) A disposition in a will in exercise of a power of appointment shall take effect notwithstanding the testator's subsequent marriage unless the property so appointed would in default of appointment pass to his personal representatives.

(3) Where it appears from a will that at the time it was made the testator was expecting to be married to a particular person and that he intended that the will should not be revoked by the marriage, the will shall not be revoked by his marriage to that person.

(4) Where it appears from a will that at the time it was made the testator was expecting to be married to a particular person and that he intended that a disposition in the will should not be revoked by his marriage to that person,—

> *(a)   that disposition shall take effect notwithstanding the marriage; and*

> *(b)   any other disposition in the will shall take effect also, unless it appears from the will that the testator intended the disposition to be revoked by the marriage.]*

ANNOTATIONS

Extent
This Act does not extend to Scotland: see s 35.

Amendment
Substituted, in relation to England and Wales, by the Administration of Justice Act 1982, s 18(1).

Repealed, in relation to Northern Ireland, by the Wills and Administration Proceedings (NI) Order 1994, SI 1994/1899, art 38, Sch 3.

[18A   Effect of dissolution or annulment of marriage on wills]

[(1) Where, after a testator has made a will, *a decree* [an order or decree] of a court [of civil jurisdiction in England and Wales] dissolves or annuls his marriages [or his marriage is dissolved or annulled and the divorce or annulment is entitled to recognition in England and Wales by virtue of Part II of the Family Law Act 1986],—

> [(a)   provisions of the will appointing executors or trustees or conferring a power of appointment, if they appoint or confer the power on the former spouse, shall take effect as if the former spouse had died on the date on which the marriage is dissolved or annulled, and

> (b)   any property which, or an interest in which, is devised or bequeathed to the former spouse shall pass as if the former spouse had died on that date,]

except in so far as a contrary intention appears by the will.

(2) Subsection (1)(b) above is without prejudice to any right of the former spouse to apply for financial provision under the Inheritance (Provision for Family and Dependants) Act 1975.

(3) ...]

ANNOTATIONS

Extent
This Act does not extend to Scotland: see s 35.

Amendment
Inserted, in relation to England and Wales, by the Administration of Justice Act 1982, s 18(2).

Sub-s (1): first words in italics prospectively repealed with savings and subsequent words in square brackets prospectively substituted with savings by the Family Law Act 1996, s 66(1), Sch 8, para 1, as from a day to be appointed, for savings see s 66(2), Sch 9, para 5 thereof; second words in square brackets inserted, and third words in square brackets substituted, by the Family Law Act 1986, s 53; paras (a), (b) substituted by the Law Reform (Succession) Act 1995, s 3.

Sub-s (3): repealed by the Law Reform (Succession) Act 1995, s 5, Schedule.

24 Wills shall be construed, as to the estate comprised, to speak from the death of the testator

... every will shall be construed, with reference to the real estate and personal estate comprised in it, to speak and take effect as if it had been executed immediately before the death of the testator, unless a contrary intention shall appear by the will.

ANNOTATIONS

Initial commencement

Specified date
Specified date: 1 January 1838 (with effect in relation to wills made after that date): see s 34.

Extent
This Act does not extend to Scotland: see s 35.

Amendment
Repealed, in relation to Northern Ireland, by the Wills and Administration Proceedings (NI) Order 1994, 1994/1899, art 38, Sch 3.

Words omitted repealed by the Statute Law Revision (No 2) Act 1888.

[33 Gifts to children or other issue who leave issue living at the testator's death shall not lapse]

[(1) Where—

(*a*)   *a will contains a devise or bequest to a child or remoter descendant of the testator; and*

(*b*)   *the intended beneficiary dies before the testator, leaving issue; and*

(*c*)   *issue of the intended beneficiary are living at the testator's death,*

then, unless a contrary intention appears by the will, the devise or bequest shall take effect as a devise or bequest to the issue living at the testator's death.

(2) Where—

(*a*)   *a will contains a devise or bequest to a class of person consisting of children or remoter descendants of the testator; and*

(*b*)   *a member of the class dies before the testator, leaving issue, and*

(*c*)   *issue of that member are living at the testator's death, then, unless a contrary intention appears by the will, the devise or bequest shall take effect as if the class included the issue of its deceased member living at the testator's death.*

(3) Issue shall take under this section through all degrees, according to their stock, in equal shares if more than one, any gift or share which their parent would have taken and so that no issue shall take whose parent is living at the testator's death and so capable of taking.

(4) For the purposes of this section—

> *(a) the illegitimacy of any person is to be disregarded; and*

> *(b) a person conceived before the testator's death and born living thereafter is to be taken to have been living at the testator's death.]*

ANNOTATIONS

Extent
This Act does not extend to Scotland: see s 35.

Amendment
Substituted, in relation to England and Wales, by the Administration of Justice Act 1982, s 19.
   Repealed, in relation to Northern Ireland, by the Wills and Administration Proceedings (NI) Order 1994, SI 1994/1899, art 38, Sch 3.

Administration of Estates Act 1925

1925 CHAPTER 23

An Act to consolidate Enactments relating to the Administration of the Estates of Deceased Persons

[9th April 1925]

35 Charges on property of deceased to be paid primarily out of the property charged

(1) Where a person dies possessed of, or entitled to, or, under a general power of appointment (including the statutory power to dispose of entailed interests) by his will disposes of, an interest in property, which at the time of his death is charged with the payment of money, whether by way of legal mortgage, equitable charge or otherwise (including a lien for unpaid purchase money), and the deceased has not by will deed or other document signified a contrary or other intention, the interest so charged, shall as between the different persons claiming through the deceased, be primarily liable for the payment of the charge; and every part of the said interest, according to its value, shall bear a proportionate part of the charge on the whole thereof.

(2) Such contrary or other intention shall not be deemed to be signified—

> (a) by a general direction for the payment of debts or of all the debts of

the testator out of his personal estate, or his residuary real and personal estate, or his residuary real estate; or

(b)   by a charge of debts upon any such estate;

unless such intention is further signified by words expressly or by necessary implication referring to all or some part of the charge.

(3) Nothing in this section affects the right of a person entitled to the charge to obtain payment or satisfaction thereof either out of the other assets of the deceased or otherwise.

ANNOTATIONS

Initial commencement

Specified date
Specified date: 1 January 1926.

Extent
This Act does not extend to Scotland: see s 58(3).

36   Effect of assent or conveyance by personal representative

(1) A personal representative may assent to the vesting, in any person who (whether by devise, bequest, devolution, appropriation or otherwise) may be entitled thereto, either beneficially or as a trustee or personal representative, of any estate or interest in real estate to which the testator or intestate was entitled or over which he exercised a general power of appointment by his will, including the statutory power to dispose of entailed interests, and which devolved upon the personal representative.

(2) The assent shall operate to vest in that person the estate or interest to which the assent relates, and, unless a contrary intention appears, the assent shall relate back to the death of the deceased.

(3) ...

(4) An assent to the vesting of a legal estate shall be in writing, signed by the personal representative, and shall name the person in whose favour it is given and shall operate to vest in that person the legal estate to which it relates; and an assent not in writing or not in favour of a named person shall not be effectual to pass a legal estate.

(5) Any person in whose favour an assent or conveyance of a legal estate is made by a personal representative may require that notice of the assent or conveyance be written or endorsed on or permanently annexed to the probate or letters of administration, at the cost of the estate of the deceased, and that the probate or letters of administration be produced, at the like cost, to prove that the notice has been placed thereon or annexed thereto.

(6) A statement in writing by a personal representative that he has not given or made an assent or conveyance in respect of a legal estate, shall, in favour of a purchaser, but without prejudice to any previous disposition made in favour of another purchaser deriving title mediately or immediately under the personal representative, be sufficient evidence that an assent or conveyance has not been

given or made in respect of the legal estate to which the statement relates, unless notice of a previous assent or conveyance affecting that estate has been placed on or annexed to the probate or administration.

A conveyance by a personal representative of a legal estate to a purchaser accepted on the faith of such a statement shall (without prejudice as aforesaid and unless notice of a previous assent or conveyance affecting that estate has been placed on or annexed to the probate or administration) operate to transfer or create the legal estate expressed to be conveyed in like manner as if no previous assent or conveyance had been made by the personal representative.

A personal representative making a false statement, in regard to any such matter, shall be liable in like manner as if the statement had been contained in a statutory declaration.

(7) An assent or conveyance by a personal representative in respect of a legal estate shall, in favour of a purchaser, unless notice of a previous assent or conveyance affecting that legal estate has been placed on or annexed to the probate or administration, be taken as sufficient evidence that the person in whose favour the assent or conveyance is given or made is the person entitled to have the legal estate conveyed to him, and upon the proper trusts, if any, but shall not otherwise prejudicially affect the claim of any person rightfully entitled to the estate vested or conveyed or any charge thereon.

(8) A conveyance of a legal estate by a personal representative to a purchaser shall not be invalidated by reason only that the purchaser may have notice that all the debts, liabilities, funeral, and testamentary or administration expenses, duties, and legacies of the deceased have been discharged or provided for.

(9) An assent or conveyance given or made by a personal representative shall not, except in favour of a purchaser of a legal estate, prejudice the right of the personal representative or any other person to recover the estate or interest to which the assent or conveyance relates, or to be indemnified out of such estate or interest against any duties, debts, or liability to which such estate or interest would have been subject if there had not been any assent or conveyance.

(10) A personal representative may, as a condition of giving an assent or making a conveyance, require security for the discharge of any such duties, debt, or liability, but shall not be entitled to postpone the giving of an assent merely by reason of the subsistence of any such duties, debt or liability if reasonable arrangements have been made for discharging the same; and an assent may be given subject to any legal estate or charge by way of legal mortgage.

(11) This section shall not operate to impose any stamp duty in respect of an assent, and in this section 'purchaser' means a purchaser for money or money's worth.

(12) This section applies to assents and conveyances made after the commencement of this Act, whether the testator or intestate died before of after such commencement.

ANNOTATIONS

Initial commencement

Specified date
Specified date: 1 January 1926.

Extent
This Act does not extend to Scotland: see s 58(3).

Amendment
Sub-s (3): repealed by the Law of Property (Miscellaneous Provisions) Act 1994, s 21(2), Sch 2.

41 Powers of personal representative as to appropriation

(1) The personal representative may appropriate any part of the real or personal estate, including things in action, of the deceased in the actual condition or state of investment thereof at the time of appropriation in or towards satisfaction of any legacy bequeathed by the deceased, or of any other interest or share in his property, whether settled or not, as to the personal representative may seem just and reasonable, according to the respective rights of the persons interested in the property of the deceased:

Provided that—

> (i) an appropriation shall not be made under this section so as to affect prejudicially any specific devise or bequest;
>
> (ii) an appropriation of property, whether or not being an investment authorised by law or by the will, if any, of the deceased for the investment of money subject to the trust, shall not (save as hereinafter mentioned) be made under this section except with the following consents:—
>
>> (a) when made for the benefit of a person absolutely and beneficially entitled in possession, the consent of that person;
>>
>> (b) when made in respect of any settled legacy share or interest, the consent of either the trustee thereof, if any (not being also the personal representative), or the person who may for the time being be entitled to the income:
>>
>> If the person whose consent is so required as aforesaid is an infant or [lacks capacity (within the meaning of the Mental Capacity Act 2005) to give the consent, it] shall be given on his behalf by his parents or parent, testamentary or other guardian < ... > [or a person appointed as deputy for him by the Court of Protection], or if, in the case of an infant, there is no such parent or guardian, by the court on the application of his next friend;

(iii) no consent (save of such trustee as aforesaid) shall be required on behalf of a person who may come into existence after the time of appropriation, or who cannot be found or ascertained at that time;

(iv) if [no deputy is appointed for a person who lacks capacity to consent] then, if the appropriation is of an investment authorised by law or by the will, if any, of the deceased for the investment of money subject to the trust, no consent shall be required on behalf of the [said person];

(v) if, independently of the personal representative, there is no trustee of a settled legacy share or interest, and no person of full age and capacity entitled to the income thereof, no consent shall be required to an appropriation in respect of such legacy share or interest, provided that the appropriation is of an investment authorised as aforesaid.

[(1A) The county court has jurisdiction under proviso (ii) to subsection (1) of this section where the estate in respect of which the application is made does not exceed in amount or value the county court limit.]

(2) Any property duly appropriated under the powers conferred by this section shall thereafter be treated as an authorised investment, and may be retained or dealt with accordingly.

(3) For the purposes of such appropriation, the personal representative may ascertain and fix the value of the respective parts of the real and personal estate and the liabilities of the deceased as he may think fit, and shall for that purpose employ a duly qualified valuer in any case where such employment may be necessary; and may make any conveyance (including an assent) which may be requisite for giving effect to the appropriation.

(4) An appropriation made pursuant to this section shall bind all persons interested in the property of the deceased whose consent is not hereby made requisite.

(5) The personal representative shall, in making the appropriation, have regard to the rights of any person who may thereafter come into existence, or who cannot be found or ascertained at the time of appropriation, and of any other person whose consent is not required by this section.

(6) This section does not prejudice any other power of appropriation conferred by law or by the will (if any) of the deceased, and takes effect with any extended powers conferred by the will (if any) of the deceased, and where an appropriation is made under this section, in respect of a settled legacy, share or interest, the property appropriated shall remain subject to all [trusts] and powers of leasing, disposition, and management or varying investments which would have been applicable thereto or to the legacy, share or interest in respect of which the appropriation is made, if no such appropriation had been made.

(7) If after any real estate has been appropriated in purported exercise of the powers conferred by this section, the person to whom it was conveyed disposes of it or any interest therein, then, in favour of a purchaser, the appropriation

shall be deemed to have been made in accordance with the requirements of this section and after all requisite consents, if any, had been given.

(8) In this section, a settled legacy, share or interest includes any legacy, share or interest to which a person is not absolutely entitled in possession at the date of the appropriation, also an annuity, and 'purchaser' means a purchaser for money or money's worth.

(9) This section applies whether the deceased died intestate or not, and whether before or after the commencement of this Act, and extends to property over which a testator exercises a general power of appointment, including the statutory power to dispose of entailed interests, and authorises the setting apart of a fund to answer an annuity by means of the income of that fund or otherwise.

ANNOTATIONS

Initial commencement

Specified date
Specified date: 1 January 1926.

Extent
This Act does not extend to Scotland: see s 58(3).

Amendment
Sub-s (1): in para (ii) words 'lacks capacity (within the meaning of the Mental Capacity Act 2005) to give the consent, it' in square brackets substituted by the Mental Capacity Act 2005, s 67(1), Sch 6, para 5(1), (2)(a)(i).
    Date in force: 1 October 2007: see SI 2007/1897, art 2(1)(d).
    Sub-s (1): in para (ii) words omitted repealed by the the Mental Health Act 1959, s 149(1), Sch 7, Pt I.
    Sub-s (1): in para (ii) words 'or a person appointed as deputy for him by the Court of Protection' in square brackets substituted by the Mental Capacity Act 2005, s 67(1), Sch 6, para 5(1), (2)(a)(ii).
    Date in force: 1 October 2007: see SI 2007/1897, art 2(1)(d).
    Sub-s (1): in para (iv) words 'no deputy is appointed for a person who lacks capacity to consent' in square brackets substituted by the Mental Capacity Act 2005, s 67(1), Sch 6, para 5(1), (2)(b).
    Date in force: 1 October 2007: see SI 2007/1897, art 2(1)(d).
    Sub-s (1): in para (iv) words 'said person' in square brackets substituted by the Mental Health Act 1959, s 149(1), Sch 7, Pt I.
    Sub-s (1A): inserted by the County Courts Act 1984, s 148(1), Sch 2, Part III, para 13.
    Sub-s (6): word 'trusts' in square brackets substituted by the Trusts of Land and Appointment of Trustees Act 1996, s 25(1), Sch 3, para 6(1), (3); for savings in relation to entailed interests created before the commencement of that Act, and savings consequential upon the abolition of the doctrine of conversion, see s 25(4), (5) thereof.
    Date in force: 1 January 1997: see SI 1996/2974, art 2.

Trustee Act 1925

1925 CHAPTER 19

An Act to consolidate certain enactments relating to trustees in England and Wales

[9th April 1925]

[19   Power to insure]

[(1) A trustee may—

- (a)   insure any property which is subject to the trust against risks of loss or damage due to any event, and

- (b)   pay the premiums out of the trust funds.

(2) In the case of property held on a bare trust, the power to insure is subject to any direction given by the beneficiary or each of the beneficiaries—

- (a)   that any property specified in the direction is not to be insured;

- (b)   that any property specified in the direction is not to be insured except on such conditions as may be so specified.

(3) Property is held on a bare trust if it is held on trust for—

- (a)   a beneficiary who is of full age and capacity and absolutely entitled to the property subject to the trust, or

- (b)   beneficiaries each of whom is of full age and capacity and who (taken together) are absolutely entitled to the property subject to the trust.

(4) If a direction under subsection (2) of this section is given, the power to insure, so far as it is subject to the direction, ceases to be a delegable function for the purposes of section 11 of the Trustee Act 2000 (power to employ agents).

(5) In this section 'trust funds' means any income or capital funds of the trust.]

ANNOTATIONS

Amendment
Substituted by the Trustee Act 2000, s 34(1).
   Date in force: 1 February 2001 (in relation to trusts created before or after that date): see the Trustee Act 2000, s 34(3) and SI 2001/49, art 2.
Maintenance Advancement and Protective Trusts

31   Power to apply income for maintenance and to accumulate surplus income during a minority

(1) Where any property is held by trustees in trust for any person for any interest whatsoever, whether vested or contingent, then, subject to any prior interests or charges affecting that property—

(i)   during the infancy of any such person, if his interest so long continues, the trustees may, at their sole discretion, pay to his parent or guardian, if any, or otherwise apply for or towards his maintenance, education, or benefit, the whole or such part, if any, of the income of that property as may, in all the circumstances, be reasonable, whether or not there is—

(a)   any other fund applicable to the same purpose; or

(b)   any person bound by law to provide for his maintenance or education; and

(ii) if such person on attaining the age of [eighteen years] has not a vested interest in such income, the trustees shall thenceforth pay the income of that property and of any accretion thereto under subsection (2) of this section to him, until he either attains a vested interest therein or dies, or until failure of his interest:

Provided that, in deciding whether the whole or any part of the income of the property is during a minority to be paid or applied for the purposes aforesaid, the trustees shall have regard to the age of the infant and his requirements and generally to the circumstances of the case, and in particular to what other income, if any, is applicable for the same purposes; and where trustees have notice that the income of more than one fund is applicable for those purposes, then, so far as practicable, unless the entire income of the funds is paid or applied as aforesaid or the court otherwise directs, a proportionate part only of the income of each fund shall be so paid or applied.

(2) During the infancy of any such person, if his interest so long continues, the trustees shall accumulate all the residue of that income [by investing it, and any profits from so investing it] from time to time in authorised investments, and shall hold those accumulations as follows:—

(i)   If any such person—

(a)   attains the age of [eighteen years], or marries under that age [or forms a civil partnership under that age], and his interest in such income during his infancy[, or until his marriage or his formation of a civil partnership,] is a vested interest; or

(b)   on attaining the age of [eighteen years] or on marriage[, or formation of a civil partnership,] under that age becomes entitled to the property from which such income arose in fee simple, absolute or determinable, or absolutely, or for an entailed interest;

the trustees shall hold the accumulations in trust for such person absolutely, but without prejudice to any provision with respect thereto contained in any settlement by him made under any statutory powers during his infancy, and so that the receipt of such person after marriage [or formation of a civil partnership], and though still an infant, shall be a good discharge; and

249

(ii)   In any other case the trustees shall, notwithstanding that such person had a vested interest in such income, hold the accumulations as an accretion to the capital of the property from which such accumulations arose, and as one fund with such capital for all purposes, and so that, if such property is settled land, such accumulations shall be held upon the same trusts as if the same were capital money arising therefrom;

but the trustees may, at any time during the infancy of such person if his interest so long continues, apply those accumulations, or any part thereof, as if they were income arising in the then current year.

(3) This section applies in the case of a contingent interest only if the limitation or trust carries the intermediate income of the property, but it applies to a future or contingent legacy by the parent of, or a person standing in loco parentis to, the legatee, if and for such period as, under the general law, the legacy carries interest for the maintenance of the legatee, and in any such case as last aforesaid the rate of interest shall (if the income available is sufficient, and subject to any rules of court to the contrary) be five pounds per centum per annum.

(4) This section applies to a vested annuity in like manner as if the annuity were the income of property held by trustees in trust to pay the income thereof to the annuitant for the same period for which the annuity is payable, save that in any case accumulations made during the infancy of the annuitant shall be held in trust for the annuitant or his personal representatives absolutely.

(5) This section does not apply where the instrument, if any, under which the interest arises came into operation before the commencement of this Act.

ANNOTATIONS

Initial commencement

Specified date
Specified date: 1 January 1926.

Extent
This section does not extend to Scotland: see s 71(3).

Amendment
Sub-s (1): words in square brackets substituted by the Family Law Reform Act 1969, s 1(3), Sch 1, Part I.

Sub-s (2): words 'by investing it, and any profits from so investing it' in square brackets substituted by the Trustee Act 2000, s 40(1), Sch 2, Pt II, para 25.

Date in force: 1 February 2001: see SI 2001/49, art 2.

Sub-s (2): in para (i)(a) words 'eighteen years' in square brackets substituted by the Family Law Reform Act 1969, s 1(3), Sch 1, Part I.

Sub-s (2): in para (i)(a) words 'or forms a civil partnership under that age' in square brackets inserted by the Civil Partnership Act 2004, s 261(1), Sch 27, para 5(1), (2)(a).

Date in force: 5 December 2005: see SI 2005/3175, art 2(2).

Sub-s (2): in para (i)(a) words ', or until his marriage or his formation of a civil partnership,' in square brackets substituted by the Civil Partnership Act 2004, s 261(1), Sch 27, para 5(1), (2)(b).

Date in force: 5 December 2005: see SI 2005/3175, art 2(2).

Sub-s (2): in para (i)(b) words 'eighteen years' in square brackets substituted by the Family Law Reform Act 1969, s 1(3), Sch 1, Part I.

Sub-s (2): in para (i)(b) words ', or formation of a civil partnership,' in square brackets inserted by the Civil Partnership Act 2004, s 261(1), Sch 27, para 5(1), (3).

Date in force: 5 December 2005: see SI 2005/3175, art 2(2).

Sub-s (2): in para (i) words 'or formation of a civil partnership' in square brackets inserted by the Civil Partnership Act 2004, s 261(1), Sch 27, para 5(1), (4).

Date in force: 5 December 2005: see SI 2005/3175, art 2(2).

32 Power of advancement

(1) Trustees may at any time or times pay or apply any capital money subject to a trust, for the advancement or benefit, in such manner as they may, in their absolute discretion, think fit, of any person entitled to the capital of the trust property or of any share thereof, whether absolutely or contingently on his attaining any specified age or on the occurrence of any other event, or subject to a gift over on his death under any specified age or on the occurrence of any other event, and whether in possession or in remainder or reversion, and such payment or application may be made notwithstanding that the interest of such person is liable to be defeated by the exercise of a power of appointment or revocation, or to be diminished by the increase of the class to which he belongs:

Provided that—

(a) the money so paid or applied for the advancement or benefit of any person shall not exceed altogether in amount one-half of the presumptive or vested share or interest of that person in the trust property; and

(b) if that person is or becomes absolutely and indefeasibly entitled to a share in the trust property the money so paid or applied shall be brought into account as part of such share; and

(c) no such payment or application shall be made so as to prejudice any person entitled to any prior life or other interest, whether vested or contingent, in the money paid or applied unless such person is in existence and of full age and consents in writing to such payment or application.

[(2) This section does not apply to capital money arising under the Settled Land Act 1925.]

(3) This section does not apply to trusts constituted or created before the commencement of this Act.

ANNOTATIONS

Initial commencement

Specified date
Specified date: 1 January 1926.

Extent
This section does not extend to Scotland: see s 71(3).

Amendment
Sub-s (2): substituted by the Trusts of Land and Appointment of Trustees Act 1996, s 25(1), Sch 3, para 3(8); for savings in relation to entailed interests created before the commencement of that Act, and savings consequential upon the abolition of the doctrine of conversion, see s 25(4), (5) thereof.

Trustee Act 2000

2000 CHAPTER 29

An Act to amend the law relating to trustees and persons having the investment powers of trustees; and for connected purposes.

[23rd November 2000]

PART II
INVESTMENT

3 General power of investment

(1) Subject to the provisions of this Part, a trustee may make any kind of investment that he could make if he were absolutely entitled to the assets of the trust.

(2) In this Act the power under subsection (1) is called 'the general power of investment'.

(3) The general power of investment does not permit a trustee to make investments in land other than in loans secured on land (but see also section 8).

(4) A person invests in a loan secured on land if he has rights under any contract under which—

    (a)   one person provides another with credit, and

    (b)   the obligation of the borrower to repay is secured on land.

(5) 'Credit' includes any cash loan or other financial accommodation.

(6) 'Cash' includes money in any form.

ANNOTATIONS

Initial commencement

To be appointed
To be appointed: see s 42(2).

Appointment
Appointment: 1 February 2001: see SI 2001/49, art 2.

Extent
This section does not extend to Scotland: see s 42(4).

4 Standard investment criteria

(1) In exercising any power of investment, whether arising under this Part or otherwise, a trustee must have regard to the standard investment criteria.

(2) A trustee must from time to time review the investments of the trust and consider whether, having regard to the standard investment criteria, they should be varied.

(3) The standard investment criteria, in relation to a trust, are—

    (a)   the suitability to the trust of investments of the same kind as any particular investment proposed to be made or retained and of that particular investment as an investment of that kind, and

    (b)   the need for diversification of investments of the trust, in so far as is appropriate to the circumstances of the trust.

ANNOTATIONS

To be appointed
To be appointed: see s 42(2).

Appointment
Appointment: 1 February 2001: see SI 2001/49, art 2.

Extent
This section does not extend to Scotland: see s 42(4).

5 Advice

(1) Before exercising any power of investment, whether arising under this Part or otherwise, a trustee must (unless the exception applies) obtain and consider proper advice about the way in which, having regard to the standard investment criteria, the power should be exercised.

(2) When reviewing the investments of the trust, a trustee must (unless the exception applies) obtain and consider proper advice about whether, having regard to the standard investment criteria, the investments should be varied.

(3) The exception is that a trustee need not obtain such advice if he reasonably concludes that in all the circumstances it is unnecessary or inappropriate to do so.

(4) Proper advice is the advice of a person who is reasonably believed by the trustee to be qualified to give it by his ability in and practical experience of financial and other matters relating to the proposed investment.

ANNOTATIONS

Initial commencement

To be appointed
To be appointed: see s 42(2).

Appointment
Appointment: 1 February 2001: see SI 2001/49, art 2.

Extent
This section does not extend to Scotland: see s 42(4).

6 Restriction or exclusion of this Part etc

(1) The general power of investment is—

    (a)   in addition to powers conferred on trustees otherwise than by this Act, but

    (b)   subject to any restriction or exclusion imposed by the trust instrument or by any enactment or any provision of subordinate legislation.

(2) For the purposes of this Act, an enactment or a provision of subordinate legislation is not to be regarded as being, or as being part of, a trust instrument.

(3) In this Act 'subordinate legislation' has the same meaning as in the Interpretation Act 1978.

ANNOTATIONS

Initial commencement

To be appointed
To be appointed: see s 42(2).

Appointment
Appointment: 1 February 2001: see SI 2001/49, art 2.

Extent
This section does not extend to Scotland: see s 42(4).

7 Existing trusts

(1) This Part applies in relation to trusts whether created before or after its commencement.

(2) No provision relating to the powers of a trustee contained in a trust instrument made before 3rd August 1961 is to be treated (for the purposes of section 6(1)(b)) as restricting or excluding the general power of investment.

(3) A provision contained in a trust instrument made before the commencement of this Part which—

    (a)   has effect under section 3(2) of the Trustee Investments Act 1961 as a power to invest under that Act, or

    (b)   confers power to invest under that Act,

is to be treated as conferring the general power of investment on a trustee.

ANNOTATIONS

Initial commencement

To be appointed
To be appointed: see s 42(2).

Appointment
Appointment: 1 February 2001: see SI 2001/49, art 2.

Extent
This section does not extend to Scotland: see s 42(4).

PART III
ACQUISITION OF LAND

8 Power to acquire freehold and leasehold land

(1) A trustee may acquire freehold or leasehold land in the United Kingdom—

    (a)   as an investment,

    (b)   for occupation by a beneficiary, or

    (c)   for any other reason.

(2) 'Freehold or leasehold land' means—

    (a)   in relation to England and Wales, a legal estate in land,

    (b)   in relation to Scotland—

        (i)   the estate or interest of the proprietor of the dominium utile or, in the case of land not held on feudal tenure, the estate or interest of the owner, or

        (ii)   a tenancy, and

    (c) in relation to Northern Ireland, a legal estate in land, including land held under a fee farm grant.

(3) For the purpose of exercising his functions as a trustee, a trustee who acquires land under this section has all the powers of an absolute owner in relation to the land.

ANNOTATIONS

Initial commencement

To be appointed
To be appointed: see s 42(2).

Appointment
Appointment: 1 February 2001: see SI 2001/49, art 2.

Extent
This section does not extend to Scotland: see s 42(4).

9 Restriction or exclusion of this Part etc

The powers conferred by this Part are—

    (a)   in addition to powers conferred on trustees otherwise than by this Part, but

(b) subject to any restriction or exclusion imposed by the trust instrument or by any enactment or any provision of subordinate legislation.

ANNOTATIONS

Initial commencement

To be appointed
To be appointed: see s 42(2).

Appointment
Appointment: 1 February 2001: see SI 2001/49, art 2.

Extent
This section does not extend to Scotland: see s 42(4).

Appendix 3

HMRC Form IHT 4 and Guidance Notes

 **HM Revenue & Customs**

Inheritance Tax account

IHT400

When to use this form

Fill in this form if:
- the deceased died on or after 18 March 1986, and
- there is Inheritance Tax to pay, or
- there is no Inheritance Tax to pay, but the estate does not qualify as an excepted estate.

The IHT400 letter, page 4, gives details about excepted estates.

Deadline

You must send this form to us within 12 months of the date of death. Interest will be payable after six months.

The Inheritance Tax (IHT) account

The account is made up of this form and separate Schedules. You will have to fill in some of the Schedules.

To help you get started
- Gather the deceased's papers and the information you have about the deceased's estate. Make a list of the deceased's assets, liabilities, investments and other financial interests and any gifts made.
- Fill in boxes 1 to 28 then work through pages 4 and 5 of this form to identify which Schedules you will need. If you do not have them all:
  – download them from **www.hmrc.gov.uk/inheritancetax/** or
  – phone the Helpline to request them.
- Fill in the Schedules before moving on to complete this form.

IHT reference

If there is any tax to pay, you will need to apply for an IHT reference and payslip before you send this form to us. You can apply online at **www.hmrc.gov.uk/inheritancetax/** or fill in form IHT422 and send it to us. Apply for a reference at least two weeks before you plan to send us this form.

Filling in this form

- Use the IHT400 Notes to help you fill in this form.
- Fill in the form in ink.
- Make full enquiries so you can show that the figures you give and the statements you make are correct.
- If an instrument of variation has been signed before applying for a grant, fill in the form to show the effect of the Will/intestacy and instrument together. *See IHT400 Notes.*

Answer all the questions and fill in the boxes to help us process your form.

Help

For more information or help or another copy of this form:
- go to **www.hmrc.gov.uk/inheritancetax/**
- phone our Helpline on **0845 30 20 900**
  – if calling from outside the UK, phone **+44 115 974 3009**.

Deceased's details

1 Deceased's name	**4** Was the deceased male or female?
Title - enter MR, MRS, MISS, MS or other title	Male ☐ Female ☐
Surname	**5** Deceased's date of birth *DD MM YYYY*
First name(s)	**6** Where was the deceased domiciled at the date of death?
	• England & Wales ☐
	• Scotland ☐
2 Date of death *DD MM YYYY*	• Northern Ireland ☐
	• other country ☐ *specify country in box below.*
3 Inheritance Tax reference number (if known)	
See note at the top of this form	See IHT400 Notes for information about domicile.
	If the deceased was not domiciled in the UK, fill in **IHT401** now, and then the rest of the form.

Please turn over

IHT400   Page 1   HMRC 09/08

Appendix 3

If the deceased was domiciled in Scotland at the date of death

| 7 | Has the legitim fund been discharged in **full** *following the death? See IHT400 Notes* |

Yes ☐ *Go to box 8*

No ☐ *Please provide a full explanation in the 'Additional information' boxes, pages 15 and 16*

Deceased's details

| 8 | Was the deceased:

- married or in a civil partnership ☐
- single ☐
- widowed or a surviving civil partner ☐
- divorced or a former civil partner? ☐

| 9 | If the deceased was married or in a civil partnership at the time of their death, on what date did the marriage or registration of the civil partnership take place?
DD MM YYYY

☐☐ ☐☐ ☐☐☐☐

| 10 | Who survived the deceased? *Tick all that apply*

- a spouse or civil partner ☐
- brothers or sisters ☐
- parents ☐
- children ☐ number ☐☐
- grandchildren ☐ number ☐☐

| 11 | Deceased's last known permanent address
Postcode

☐☐☐☐ ☐☐☐☐

House number

☐☐☐☐

Rest of address, including house name or flat number

| 12 | Was the property in box 11 owned or part-owned by the deceased or did the deceased have a right to live in the property?

Yes ☐ *Go to box 13*

No ☐ *Give details below. For example, 'deceased lived with daughter' or 'address was a nursing home'*

| 13 | Deceased's occupation, or former occupation if retired, for example, 'retired doctor'.

| 14 | Deceased's National Insurance number (if known)

☐☐ ☐☐ ☐☐ ☐☐ ☐

| 15 | Deceased's Income Tax or Unique Taxpayer Reference (if known)

☐☐☐☐☐ ☐☐☐☐☐

| 16 | Did anyone act under a power of attorney granted by the deceased during their lifetime? This may have been a general, enduring or lasting power of attorney.

No ☐

Yes ☐ *Please enclose a copy of the power of attorney*

Contact details of the person dealing with the estate

For example, a solicitor or executor.

17 Name and address of the firm or person dealing with the estate

Name

Postcode

House or building number

Rest of address, including house name or flat number

18 Contact name *if different from box 17*

19 Phone number

20 DX number and town (if used)

21 Contact's reference

22 Fax number

23 If we have to repay any overpaid Inheritance Tax, we need to know who to make the cheque out to.

Do you want any cheque we send to be made out to the firm or person shown at box 17?

Yes ☐ *Go to box 24*

No ☐ *Give the name(s) here, as you would like them to appear on the cheque.*

Deceased's Will

24 Did the deceased leave a Will?

No ☐ *Go to box 29*

Yes ☐ *Go to box 25. Please enclose a copy of the Will and any codicils when sending us your account. If an instrument of variation alters the amount of Inheritance Tax payable on this estate, please also send a copy.*

25 Is the address of the deceased as shown in the Will the same as the deceased's last known permanent address (at box 11)?

No ☐ *Go to box 26*

Yes ☐ *Go to box 27*

26 What happened to the property given as the deceased's residence in the Will?

If the deceased sold the property but used all the sale proceeds to buy another main residence for themselves and this happened more than once, there is no need to give details of all the events. Simply say that the 'residence was replaced by the current property'. In all other cases give details of exactly what happened to the property, and give the date of the event(s).

Items referred to in the Will but not included in the estate

Only fill in boxes 27 and 28 if the deceased left a Will. If not go to box 29.

| 27 | Are you including on this form all assets specifically referred to in the Will? (For example, land, buildings, personal possessions, works of art or shares.) |

No ☐ *Go to box 28*

Yes ☐ *Go to box 29*

28 Items referred to in the Will and not included on this form (any gifts should be shown on form IHT403)

Items given away as gifts, sold or disposed of before the deceased's death	Who was the item given or sold to, or what happened to it?	Date of gift, sale or disposal	Value of the item at the date of gift, sale or disposal £	If the item was sold, what did the deceased do with the sale proceeds?

What makes up your Inheritance Tax account – Schedules

To make a complete account of the estate you may need to complete some separate Schedules.
Answer the following questions by ticking the No or Yes box.

29 Transfer of unused nil rate band

Do you want to transfer any unused nil rate band from the deceased's spouse or civil partner who died before them?

No ☐ Yes ☐ Use Schedule **IHT402**

30 Gifts and other transfers of value

Did the deceased make any lifetime gifts or other transfers of value on or after 18 March 1986? *See IHT400 Notes*

No ☐ Yes ☐ Use Schedule **IHT403**

31 Jointly owned assets

Did the deceased jointly own any assets (other than business or partnership assets) with any other person(s)?

No ☐ Yes ☐ Use Schedule **IHT404**

32 Houses, land, buildings and interests in land

Did the deceased own any house, land or buildings or rights over land in the UK in their sole name?

No ☐ Yes ☐ Use Schedule **IHT405**

33 Bank and building society accounts

Did the deceased hold any bank or building society accounts in their sole name, including National Savings and Premium Bonds?

No ☐ Yes ☐ Use Schedule **IHT406**

34 Household and personal goods

Did the deceased own any household goods or personal possessions?

No ☐ Yes ☐ Use Schedule **IHT407**

If the deceased did **not** own any household goods or personal possessions or they do not have any value, please explain the circumstances in the 'Additional information' boxes on pages 15 and 16.

35 Household and personal goods donated to charity

Do the people who inherit the deceased's household goods and personal possessions want to donate some or all of them to a UK registered charity and deduct charity exemption from the value of the estate?
For example, they may wish to donate the deceased's furniture to a charity shop.

No ☐ Yes ☐ Use Schedule **IHT408**

What makes up your Inheritance Tax account – **Schedules** continued

36 **Pensions**

Did the deceased have any provision for retirement other than the State pension? *For example, a pension from an employer, a personal pension policy (or an alternatively secured pension)*

No ☐ Yes ☐ Use Schedule **IHT409**

37 **Life assurance and annuities**

Did the deceased pay premiums on any life assurance policies, annuities or other products which are payable either to their estate, to another person or which continue after death?

No ☐ Yes ☐ Use Schedule **IHT410**

38 **Listed stocks and shares**

Did the deceased own any listed stocks and shares (excluding control holdings)?

No ☐ Yes ☐ Use Schedule **IHT411**

39 **Unlisted stocks and shares and control holdings**

Did the deceased own any unlisted stocks and shares (including AIM and OFEX), or any control holdings of any listed shares?

No ☐ Yes ☐ Use Schedule **IHT412**

40 **Business relief, business and partnership interests and assets**

Do you want to deduct business relief from any business interests and assets owned by the deceased or a partnership in which they were a partner?

No ☐ Yes ☐ Use Schedule **IHT413**

41 **Farms, farmhouses and farmland**

Do you want to deduct agricultural relief from any farmhouses, farms or farmland owned by the deceased?

No ☐ Yes ☐ Use Schedule **IHT414**

42 **Interest in another estate**

Was the deceased entitled to receive any legacy or assets from the estate of someone who died before them and that they had not received before they died?

No ☐ Yes ☐ Use Schedule **IHT415**

43 **Debts due to the estate**

Was the deceased owed any money by way of personal loans or mortgage at the date of death?

No ☐ Yes ☐ Use Schedule **IHT416**

44 **Foreign assets**

Did the deceased own any assets outside the UK either in their sole name or jointly with others?

No ☐ Yes ☐ Use Schedule **IHT417**

45 **Assets held in trust**

Did the deceased have any right to benefit from any assets held in trust (including the right to receive assets held in a trust at some future date)?

No ☐ Yes ☐ Use Schedule **IHT418**

46 **Debts owed by the deceased**

Do you wish to include a deduction from the estate for debts and liabilities of the following types:
- money that was spent on behalf of the deceased and which was not repaid
- loans
- liabilities related to a life assurance policy where the sum assured will not be fully reflected in the estate
- debts that the deceased guaranteed on behalf of another person?

No ☐ Yes ☐ Use Schedule **IHT419**

47 **National Heritage assets**

Is any asset already exempt or is exemption now being claimed, on the grounds of national, scientific, historic, artistic, scenic or architectural interest? Or does any such asset benefit from an Approved Maintenance Fund for the upkeep and preservation of national heritage assets?

No ☐ Yes ☐ Use Schedule **IHT420**

If you answered Yes to any of questions 29 to 47, please fill in the Schedule for that asset. The Schedule number is shown at the end of each question.

48 Do you have all of the Schedules you need?

No ☐
- download the Schedules from **www.hmrc.gov.uk/inheritancetax/** or
- phone us on **0845 30 20 900** (**+44 115 974 3009** from outside the UK), or
- ask for them by email **hmrc.ihtorderline@btconnect.com**

When you have got all the Schedules you need, fill them in before you go to box 49.

Yes ☐ *Fill in the Schedules **now** before going to box 49*

Appendix 3

Estate in the UK

Use this section to tell us about assets owned by the deceased in the UK. You should include all assets owned outright by the deceased and the **deceased's share** of **jointly owned** assets. You will need to copy figures from the Schedules you have filled in. Any assets the deceased had outside the UK should be shown on form IHT417 and **not** in boxes 49 to 96.

Jointly owned assets

Enter '0' in the box if the deceased did not own any of the assets described.

		Column A	Column B
49	Jointly owned assets (form IHT404, box 5)		£
50	Jointly owned assets (form IHT404, box 10)	£	

Assets owned outright by the deceased

Enter the value of the assets owned outright by the deceased in the amount boxes attached to each question. Enter '0' in the box if the deceased did not own any of the assets described.

		Column A	Column B
51	Deceased's residence (except farmhouses and jointly owned houses) (form IHT405, box 7). Include the value of jointly owned houses at box 49 and farmhouses at box 68 instead		£
52	Bank and building society accounts in the deceased's sole name (form IHT406, box 1)	£	
53	Cash (in coins or notes) and uncashed traveller's cheques	£	
54	Premium Bonds and National Savings & Investments products (form IHT406, box 5)	£	
55	Household and personal goods (form IHT407, box 6)	£	
56	Pensions (form IHT409, boxes 7 and 15). Include the value of any pensions arrears due at the date of death	£	
57	Life assurance and mortgage protection policies (form IHT410, box 6)	£	
58	Add up all the figures in **Column A** (boxes 50 to 57)	£	
59	Add up all the figures in **Column B** (boxes 49 + 51)		£

Estate in the **UK** continued

		Column A	Column B
60	Copy the figure from box 58	£	
61	Copy the figure from box 59		£
62	UK Government and municipal securities (form IHT411, box 1), but include dividends and interest at box 64	£	
63	Listed stocks, shares and investments that did not give the deceased control of the company (form IHT411, box 2)	£	
64	Dividends or interest on stocks, shares and securities	£	
65	Traded unlisted and unlisted shares except control holdings (form IHT412 box 1 + box 2)	£	
66	Traded unlisted and unlisted shares except control holdings (see IHT412 Notes)		£
67	Control holdings of unlisted, traded unlisted and listed shares (form IHT412 box 3 + box 4 + box 5)		£
68	Farms, farmhouses and farmland (give details on IHT414 and IHT405)		£
69	Businesses including farm businesses, business assets and timber		£
70	Other land, buildings and rights over land (form IHT405, box 8)		£
71	Interest in another estate (form IHT415, box 7)		£
72	Interest in another estate (form IHT415, box 9)	£	
73	Debts due to the estate (form IHT416, box 3 total)	£	
74	Income Tax or Capital Gains Tax repayment	£	
75	Trust income due to the deceased – *see IHT400 Notes*	£	
76	Other assets and income due to the deceased (enter details in the 'Additional information' boxes on pages 15 and 16 of this form if not given elsewhere)	£	
77	Add up all the figures in **Column A** (boxes 60 to 76)	£	
78	Add up all the figures in **Column B** (boxes 61 to 71)		£
79	Gross total of the estate in the UK (box 77 + box 78)	£	

263

Deductions from the estate in the UK incurred up to the date of death

80 Mortgages, secured loans and other debts payable out of property or assets owned outright by the deceased and shown in **column B** on pages 6 and 7. For example, a mortgage secured on the deceased's house or a loan secured on a business. Enter the name of the creditor and say which property or asset the deduction relates to and describe the liability.

Name of creditor	Property or asset and description of liability	Amount £
	Total mortgages and secured loans	£

81 Funeral expenses

Funeral costs	£
Headstone	£
Other costs (please specify)	
Total cost of funeral	£

82 Other liabilities

Enter any other liabilities that have not been shown in boxes 80 or 81. (For example, outstanding gas and electricity bills, credit card balances or nursing home fees.)

Creditor's name and description of the liability	Amount £
Total other liabilities	

Deductions from the estate in the UK continued

Deductions summary

		Column A	Column B
83	Box 80 figure		£
84	Box 81 + box 82	£	
85	Box 77 *minus* box 84. If the result is a minus figure enter '0' in the box and enter the deficit in box 88	£	
86	Box 78 *minus* box 83. If the result is a minus figure enter '0' in the box and enter the deficit in box 87		£
87	Enter the deficit figure from box 86 (if there is one)	£	
88	Enter the deficit figure from box 85 (if there is one)		£
89	Box 85 *minus* box 87	£	
90	Box 86 *minus* box 88		£
91	Total estate in the UK (box 89 + box 90)	£	

Exemptions and reliefs

92 Exemptions and reliefs deducted from the assets in the deceased's sole name shown in **column A** on pages 6 and 7 - *see IHT400 Notes*. If you are deducting spouse or civil partner exemption, enter the spouse or civil partner's full name, date and country of birth and their domicile.

Do not include exemptions or reliefs on jointly owned assets, these should be deducted on form IHT404, at box 9.

Describe the exemptions and reliefs you are deducting. For example 'cash gift to charity in the Will' and show how the amount has been calculated - please use the 'Additional information' boxes on pages 15 and 16 of this form if you need more space.	Amount deducted £
Total exemptions and reliefs from assets in **column A** £	

Exemptions and reliefs continued

93	Exemptions and reliefs deducted from the assets in the deceased's sole name shown in **column B** on pages 6 and 7 - *see IHT400 Notes*. If you are deducting spouse or civil partner exemption enter the spouse or civil partner's full name, date and country of birth and their domicile (unless already given at box 92). **Do not include exemptions or reliefs on jointly owned assets, these should be deducted on form IHT404, at box 4.**

Describe the exemptions and reliefs you are deducting, for example, 'agricultural relief on farm' and show how the amount has been calculated - please use the 'Additional information' boxes on pages 15 and 16 if you need more space	Amount £
Total exemptions and reliefs from assets in **column B**	£

94	Box 89 *minus* box 92	£
95	Box 90 *minus* box 93	£
96	Total net estate in the UK, after exemptions and reliefs (box 94 + box 95)	£

Other assets taken into account to calculate the tax

		Column A	Column B
97	Foreign houses, land, businesses and control holdings (form IHT417, box 5)		£
98	Other foreign assets (form IHT417, box 10)	£	
99	Assets held in trust on which the trustees would like to pay the tax now (form IHT418, box 12)		£
100	Assets held in trust on which the trustees would like to pay the tax now (form IHT418, box 17)	£	
101	Nominated assets. Include details of the nominated assets in the 'Additional information' boxes on pages 15 and 16 - *see IHT400 Notes*	£	
102	Box 98 + box 100 + box 101	£	
103	Box 97 + box 99		£
104	Gifts with reservation and pre-owned assets (IHT403, box 17)	£	
105	Assets held in trust on which the trustees are not paying the tax now (IHT418, box 18)	£	
106	Alternatively secured pension fund(s) (form IHT409, boxes 32 or 42 - only where the date of death is between 06/04/06 and 05/04/07 inclusive)	£	
107	Total other assets taken into account to calculate the tax (box 102 + box 103 + box 104 + box 105 + box 106)	£	
108	Total chargeable estate (box 96 + box 107)	£	

Working out the Inheritance Tax

ℹ If there is no Inheritance Tax to pay, you do not need to fill in this page and should go to box 119 on page 12.

If you are filling in this form yourself without the help of a solicitor or other adviser, you do not have to work out the tax yourself; we can do it for you – but first read the following note about paying Inheritance Tax by instalments.

Paying Inheritance Tax by instalments
Instead of paying all of the Inheritance Tax at once, you may pay some of it in 10 annual instalments (that is, one instalment each year for 10 years). You can pay by instalments on any assets shown in **column B** on pages 6 and 7 that have not been sold.

Interest will be payable on the instalments.
The total value of the assets on which you may pay the tax by instalments is box 95 + box 97 + box 99 (if any).

109 Are you filling in the form without the help of a solicitor or other adviser and you wish us to work out the tax for you?

No ☐ *Go to 'Simple Inheritance Tax calculation'*

Yes ☐ *Go to box 110*

110 Do you wish to pay the tax on the amount shown in box 95 + box 97 + box 99 by instalments?

No ☐ *Go to box 118*

Yes ☐ *If any of the assets in **column B** have been **sold**, write the total value of those assets here*

£ _____

Now go to box 118

Simple Inheritance Tax calculation

You can use the simple calculation in boxes 111 to 117 to work out the Inheritance Tax on the estate as long as the following apply:
- you are paying the tax on or before the last day of the sixth month after the death occurred so no interest is payable
- you want to pay all of the tax now and not pay by instalments on property in column B (see note above about paying Inheritance Tax by instalments)
- the total of any lifetime gifts is below the Inheritance Tax nil rate band
- you are not deducting double taxation relief on any foreign assets *(see note on IHT400 Calculation)*
- you are not deducting successive charges relief on assets inherited by the deceased in the last five years from another estate on which Inheritance Tax was paid *(see note on IHT400 Calculation)*.

If the simple calculation does not apply to you, you will need to use the form IHT400 calculation to work out the Inheritance Tax due then continue to fill in this form at box 118.

111 Total chargeable value of of gifts made by the deceased within the seven years before their death (form IHT403 box 7) — £ _____

112 Aggregate chargeable transfer (box 108 + box 111) — £ _____

113 Inheritance Tax nil rate band at the date of death
See IHT400 Rates and Tables — £ _____

114 Transferable nil rate band (form IHT402, box 20) — £ _____

115 Total nil rate band (box 113 + box 114) — £ _____

116 Value chargeable to tax (box 112 *minus* box 115) — £ _____

117 Inheritance Tax (box 116 x 40%) — £ _____ · ☐☐

Direct Payment Scheme

This is a scheme under which participating banks and building societies will release funds from the deceased's accounts directly to HM Revenue & Customs to pay Inheritance Tax. For National Savings & Investments, see the note on page 14.

| 118 | Do you wish to use the Direct Payment Scheme? |

No ☐

Yes ☐   *Fill in form IHT423 (you will need a separate form for each bank and building society account concerned)*

Declaration

| 119 | I/We wish to apply for the following type of grant (see note 'Grant of representation' in IHT400 Notes to decide on the type of grant) |

- Probate ☐

- Confirmation ☐

- Letters of Administration ☐

- Letters of Administration with Will annexed ☐

- Other (please specify)

[   ]

To the best of my/our knowledge and belief, the information I/we have given and the statements I/we have made in this account and the Schedules attached (together called 'this account') are correct and complete.
Please tick the Schedules you have filled in.

IHT401 ☐	IHT408 ☐	IHT415 ☐
IHT402 ☐	IHT409 ☐	IHT416 ☐
IHT403 ☐	IHT410 ☐	IHT417 ☐
IHT404 ☐	IHT411 ☐	IHT418 ☐
IHT405 ☐	IHT412 ☐	IHT419 ☐
IHT406 ☐	IHT413 ☐	IHT420 ☐
IHT407 ☐	IHT414 ☐	

I/We have made the fullest enquiries that are reasonably practicable in the circumstances to find out the open market value of all the items shown in this account. The value of items in the box(es) listed below are provisional estimates which are based on all the information available to me/us at this time.

I/We will tell HM Revenue & Customs Inheritance Tax the exact value(s) as soon as I/we know it and I/we will pay any additional tax and interest that may be due.

List the boxes in the account that are provisional here.

[   ]

Where Schedule IHT 402 has been filled in I/we declare that to the best of my/our knowledge and belief:
- the deceased and their spouse or civil partner were married or in a civil partnership at the date the spouse or civil partner died
- where a Deed of Variation has not been provided there has been no change to the people who inherited the estate of the spouse or civil partner.

I/We understand that I/we may be liable to prosecution if I/we deliberately conceal any information that affects the liability to Inheritance Tax arising on the deceased's death, or if I/we deliberately include information in this account which I/we know to be false.

I/We understand that I/we may have to pay financial penalties if this account is delivered late or is incorrect by reason of my/our negligence or fraud, or if I/we fail to remedy anything in this account which is incorrect in any material respect within a reasonable time of it coming to my/our notice.

I/We understand that the issue of the grant does not mean that:
- I/we have paid all the Inheritance Tax and interest that may be due on the estate, or
- the statements made and the values included in this account are accepted by HM Revenue & Customs Inheritance Tax.

I/We understand that HM Revenue & Customs Inheritance Tax:
- will only look at this account in detail after the grant has been issued
- may need to ask further questions and discuss the value of items shown in this account
- may make further calculations of tax and interest payable to help the persons liable for the tax to make provision to meet the tax liability.

I/We understand that I/we may have to pay interest on any unpaid tax according to the law where:
- I/we have elected to pay tax by instalments
- additional tax becomes payable for any reason.

Each person delivering this account, whether as executor, intending administrator or otherwise must sign on page 13 to indicate that they have read and agreed the statements above.

Declaration continued

Surname

First name(s)

Postcode

House number

Rest of address, including house name or flat number

Signature

Date *DD MM YYYY*

Surname

First name(s)

Postcode

House number

Rest of address, including house name or flat number

Signature

Date *DD MM YYYY*

Surname

First name(s)

Postcode

House number

Rest of address, including house name or flat number

Signature

Date *DD MM YYYY*

Surname

First name(s)

Postcode

House number

Rest of address, including house name or flat number

Signature

Date *DD MM YYYY*

269

Appendix 3

Checklist

For more information look at the relevant page in the IHT400 Notes.
Use the checklist to remind you of:

- the actions you should take, and
- the additional information you should include when sending the Inheritance Tax forms
  to HM Revenue & Customs Inheritance Tax.

- If the deceased died leaving a Will, provide a copy of the Will, and any codicils.

  No ☐   Yes ☐

- If the estate has been varied in any way and the variation results in either an increase or decrease in the amount of tax, provide a copy of the instrument of variation.

  No ☐   Yes ☐

- Any professional valuation of stocks and shares.

  No ☐   Yes ☐

- Any professional valuation of household effects or personal possessions.

  No ☐   Yes ☐

- Any professional valuation of houses, land and buildings.

  No ☐   Yes ☐

- A copy of any insurance policy (and annuity, if appropriate) where the deceased was paying the premiums for the benefit of someone else and any trust documents if the policy has been written in trust.

  No ☐   Yes ☐

- A copy of any trust deed(s), if the trustees are paying tax at the same time as you apply for the grant.

  No ☐   Yes ☐

- Any evidence of money owed to the deceased, including loan agreements and related trusts or policies and any evidence of the debts being released.

  No ☐   Yes ☐

- A copy of any joint life assurance policy or policy on the life of another person.

  No ☐   Yes ☐

- A copy of any structural survey and/or correspondence with the loss adjuster about any structurally damaged property.

  No ☐   Yes ☐

- If you are deducting agricultural relief, a plan of the property and a copy of the lease or agreement for letting (where appropriate).

  No ☐   Yes ☐

- If you are deducting business relief, a copy of the partnership agreement (where appropriate) and the last two years' accounts.

  No ☐   Yes ☐

- If you are deducting double taxation relief or unilateral relief, provide evidence of the foreign tax, in the form of an assessment of the foreign tax, a certificate of the foreign tax paid and (if available) the official receipt.

  No ☐   Yes ☐

- Any written evidence of debts to close friends or family.

  No ☐   Yes ☐

- Have all executors signed page 13 of this form?

  No ☐   Yes ☐

- If you have calculated your own tax, have you enclosed the calculation and your payment with this form?

  No ☐   Yes ☐

- If you are applying for a grant, have you enclosed form IHT421 *Probate summary*?

  No ☐   Yes ☐

Direct Payment Scheme (if used)

- If you are using the Direct Payment Scheme, have you sent a form IHT423 to each organisation from which funds will be provided? *See IHT423*

  No ☐   Yes ☐

- If you want HM Revenue & Customs Inheritance Tax to call for payment from National Savings & Investments, provide a letter detailing the investments to be used and confirmation of how much of the tax is to be paid by National Savings & Investments and official letters from the relevant National Savings & Investments office stating the value of those investments - *see IHT11*.

  No ☐   Yes ☐

- If you want HM Revenue & Customs Inheritance Tax to call for payment from British Government stock, provide a letter detailing the investments to be used and confirmation of how much of the tax is to be paid by Government stock - *see IHT11*. Please phone the Helpline for a copy of the IHT11 or go to:
  www.hmrc.gov.uk/inheritancetax/

Return addresses and contact details

- If you are applying for a grant in England, Wales or Northern Ireland you should send the forms to our Nottingham office (the DX addresses are for solicitors, practitioners and banks)

HM Revenue & Customs
Inheritance Tax
Ferrers House
PO Box 38
Castle Meadow Road
Nottingham
NG2 1BB
DX 701201 NOTTINGHAM 4

Phone **0845 30 20 900**

- If you are applying for Confirmation in Scotland you should send the forms to our Edinburgh office (the DX addresses are for solicitors, practitioners and banks)

HM Revenue & Customs
Inheritance Tax
Meldrum House
15 Drumsheugh Gardens
Edinburgh
EH3 7UG
DX ED 542001 EDINBURGH 14

Phone **0845 30 20 900**

- If you want to know more about any particular aspect of Inheritance Tax or have specific questions about completing the forms go to **www.hmrc.gov.uk/inheritancetax/**

Or phone the Probate and Inheritance Tax Helpline on **0845 30 20 900. (+44 115 974 3009** from outside the UK)

- If you need a copy of any of our forms or leaflets you can download them from our website, phone the Probate and Inheritance Tax Helpline to order them, or email our orderline at **hmrc.ihtorderline@btconnect.com**

Additional information

Use this space:
- to explain the circumstances where the deceased did not own any household effects or personal possessions or they do not have any value (box 34)
- to give us any additional information we ask for, including details of:
  - any claim for discharge of legal rights (box 7)
  - other assets and income due to the deceased (box 76)
  - nominated assets (box 101)
  - successive charges relief (IHT400 Calculation, box 10).

Additional information continued

IHT400   Page 15

271

Appendix 3

Additional information continued

ⓘ If you need more space, please continue on a separate sheet.

IHT400   Page 16

272

HM Revenue & Customs

Guide to completing your Inheritance Tax account

This guide will help you:

- fill in the forms you need to complete your Inheritance Tax account
- follow the correct procedure to apply for a grant of probate, and
- pay the correct amount of Inheritance Tax, if there is any to pay.

Website: www.hmrc.gov.uk/inheritancetax/
Helpline: 0845 30 20 900

IHT400 Notes **Version 0.14 Final**

Contents

Contents

We have a range of services for people with disabilities, including guidance in braille, audio and large print. For details please phone our Helpline on **0845 30 20 900**.

Ffoniwch 0845 302 1489 i dderbyn fersiynau Cymraeg o ffurflenni a chanllawiau.

Index of help for filling in the boxes on form IHT400 by box number

Filling in form IHT400

This guide will help you fill in form IHT400 and also includes help for the Schedules we sent you, some of which you may need to fill in

Introduction

What is in this guide?

As well as form IHT400, you may need to fill in some of the Schedules that go with it. The notes in this guide follow the box numbers in form IHT400. Notes to help you fill in the Schedules are also included in this guide.

In this guide and in form IHT400 we refer to the person who has died as 'the deceased'.

We hope this guide will answer most of your questions. If you need more help:

- go to **www.hmrc.gov.uk/inheritancetax/** or
- phone our Probate and Inheritance Tax Helpline on **0845 30 20 900**.

These notes apply where a person died on or after 18 April 1986. If a person died before this date, please phone our Helpline.

What we have sent you

If you are applying for a grant without the help of a solicitor or other agent, you should have received form IHT400, this guide and some of the Schedules that we think apply to most estates (see page 4 for information about grants). But it is your responsibility to make sure you fill in the correct Schedules. You do not need to fill in any that do not apply, even if we have included them with the pack.

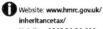
Website: **www.hmrc.gov.uk/inheritancetax/**

Helpline: **0845 30 20 900**

If you need any of the other Schedules, download them from our website or phone our IHT Helpline.

When you may not need to fill in form IHT400

Excepted estates

An excepted estate is an estate where no Inheritance Tax (IHT) is due and a full Inheritance Tax account on form IHT400 is not required.

If the estate is an excepted estate, use form **IHT205** *Return of estate information* instead. If you know that Inheritance Tax is due, you do not need to read pages 2 and 3 of this guide.

There are three types of excepted estate:

- low value estates
- exempt estates
- foreign domiciliaries.

The rules that apply to deaths on or after 1 September 2006 start on page 2.

1

Appendix 3

For deaths before 1 September 2006 phone our Helpline or go to our website.

Do not fill in form IHT400 if the estate is an excepted estate. In some estates you may only need to fill in part of the form. You will need to fill in a different form of account for some special types of grant. There is more information about different types of grant on page 4. If any of these apply, phone our Helpline to find out what form to use.

Gross value of the estate
The total value of all the assets that make up the deceased's estate before any of their debts are taken off.

Low value estates
These are estates where there can be no liability to Inheritance Tax (IHT) because the gross value of the estate does not exceed the IHT nil rate band. The conditions for these estates are that:
- the deceased died domiciled in the United Kingdom (UK)
- the gross value of the estate does not exceed the Inheritance Tax nil rate band (see note on page 3)
- if the estate includes any assets in trust, they are held in a single trust and the gross value does not exceed £150,000
- if the estate includes foreign assets, their gross value does not exceed £100,000
- if there are any specified transfers, their chargeable value does not exceed £150,000
- the deceased had not made a gift with reservation of benefit
- no charge arises on the individual's death under any of the provisions relating to Alternatively Secured Pensions.

Specified transfers
Gifts of cash, household and personal goods, listed shares or securities or outright gifts of land or buildings to individuals, not gifts into trust. For an estate to qualify as an excepted estate, specified transfers made within 7 years of death cannot exceed £150,000.

Exempt estates
These are estates where there can be no liability to IHT because the gross value of the estate does not exceed £1 million and there is no tax to pay because one or both of the following exemptions apply:
- spouse or civil partner exemption
- charity exemption.

No other exemption or relief can be taken into account. Spouse or civil partner exemption can only be deducted if both spouses or civil partners have always been domiciled in the UK. Charity exemption can only be deducted if the gift is an absolute gift to the organisation concerned.

Gift with reservation of benefit
A gift which is not fully given away so that the person getting the gift does so with conditions attached or the person making the gift keeps back some benefit for themselves.

The conditions for these estates are that:
- the deceased died domiciled in the UK
- the gross value of the estate does not exceed £1 million and the net chargeable value of the estate after deduction of liabilities and spouse or civil partner exemption and/or charity exemption only does not exceed the IHT threshold
- if the estate includes any assets in trust, they are held in a single trust and the gross value does not exceed £150,000 (unless the settled property passes to a spouse or civil partner, or to a charity, in which case the limit is waived)
- if the estate includes foreign assets, their gross value does not exceed £100,000

Domicile
Generally, a person's domicile is where they have their fixed and permanent home and to which, when they are absent, they always have the intention of returning.

2

278

- if there are any specified transfers, their chargeable value does not exceed £150,000, and the deceased had not made a gift with reservation of benefit
- no charge arises on the individual's death under any of the provisions relating to Alternatively Secured Pensions.

In Scotland, the spouse or civil partner exemption and/or charity exemption must be calculated on the basis that any entitlement to legitim against the estate will be claimed in full. In other words, only the minimum amount of spouse or civil partner exemption and/or charity exemption available after accounting for legitim can be deducted to establish whether the IHT nil rate band is exceeded.

 Legitim

Under Scottish law certain family members may have legal rights to some of the assets in a person's estate. Broadly, 'Legitim' is a Scottish legal term for the rights a child may have to some assets in a parent's estate.

Foreign domiciliaries

These are the estates where there can be no liability to IHT because the gross value of the estate in the UK does not exceed £150,000.

The conditions for these estates are that:
- the deceased died domiciled outside the UK
- the deceased was never domiciled in the UK or treated as domiciled in the UK for IHT purposes
- the deceased's UK estate consisted only of cash or listed shares and securities passing under a Will or intestacy or by survivorship.

Inheritance Tax (IHT) nil rate band

When you are deciding if the value of the estate is below the IHT nil rate band (for excepted estates only) the correct nil rate band to use depends on the date of death and the date you apply for the grant.

If the death was between 6 August and 5 April (inclusive) in any one tax year, you should use the nil rate band that applied at the date of death.

If the death was after 5 April but before 6 August in any one tax year, and you are applying for a grant before 6 August of that year, the nil rate band that applies is the one from the tax year before that in which the deceased died.

You can find a list of nil rate bands on form IHT400 *Rates and tables*.

3

279

Appendix 3

Grants of representation

You need a grant of representation to get access to most assets in the deceased's estate. There are a number of different types of grant. In England, Wales and Northern Ireland, the two most common types are:

- a grant of probate, where the deceased has left a Will, and
- a grant of letters of administration, where the deceased has not left a Will.

In Scotland, the grant is a grant of Confirmation. Throughout this guide, we refer to all types of grant of representation as the 'grant'.

Special types of grant

There are a number of special types of grant that may apply in certain circumstances. For example:

- a grant for a limited period of time, perhaps while there is a legal dispute about the validity of a Will
- a grant that is limited to certain assets, perhaps where the estate consists of perishable goods that need to be preserved, or where the deceased has appointed an executor for certain assets.
  For example, an author might appoint a literary executor.

Your local Probate Registry can tell you more about these special types of grant and whether they might be of use in dealing with the deceased's estate. They will also tell you the type of grant concerned. Make sure you tick the correct box or enter this in box 119 on page 12 of form IHT400.

You will still need to fill in form IHT400 in full where the grant is for a limited period of time. Where the grant is limited to certain assets, we tell you how to fill in form IHT400 below. There is information about applying for a grant on pages 58 to 62 of this guide.

When form IHT400 need NOT be filled in completely

There are certain types of grant where you do not have to fill in form IHT400 completely.

- When the proposed grant is to be limited to certain assets. In this case you should include the assets to be covered by the grant in pages 6 to 10 of form IHT400. All the other assets that are part of the deceased's estate, but are to be excluded from the grant, should be included in box 76 on form IHT400. You should also fill in pages 1 to 5 and boxes 83 to 108 of form IHT400 and answer the questions on pages 4 and 5. You will also need to complete and sign the declaration on pages 12 and 13. You should only fill in (at this stage) any Schedules that apply to the assets for which the grant is required.
- If you need to apply for a Settled Land Grant because land continues to be settled land after the death of the life tenant, then Schedule IHT418 should not be filled in. Instead form IHT400 and Schedule IHT405 should be used to provide details of the settled land. You should add the following words in a blank space in the declaration on page 12 'limited to the settled land of which true particulars and value are given'. All the other property that is in the deceased's estate should be entered in box 105 on form IHT400. You should fill in pages 1 to 5 of form IHT400 as if they related to the settled land only.

4

- When the deceased left no estate and the grant is required only for assets (not settled land) of which the deceased was a trustee, you only need to fill in boxes 1 to 22 and the declaration on pages 12 and 13 of form IHT400. You do not need to include the assets in the account, or fill in boxes 23 to 118 of form IHT400.

Delivering a reduced account when there is no tax to pay

If there is no tax to pay because most or all of the estate is exempt from Inheritance Tax, you may able to fill in a reduced form IHT400. You should first check to see if the estate is an excepted estate by reading pages 1 to 3 of this guide. If it is an excepted estate you should use form IHT205 *Return of estate information* and not read any more of this guide.

To be able to fill in a reduced form IHT400 the deceased must have been domiciled in the UK at the date of death and there must be assets or legacies passing under the Will or intestacy to one of the following exempt beneficiaries:
- the deceased's surviving spouse or civil partner - either directly or to a trust the spouse or civil partner has the right to benefit from
- a UK charity - either directly or to a UK trust set up for charitable purposes
- a UK national body such as the British Museum or the National Trust.

If you need to know whether a particular national body or charity qualifies for the exemption you should call the Probate and Inheritance Tax Helpline on **0845 30 20 900** for advice.

You will then need to add together the gross value (the value before taking off liabilities, reliefs or exemptions) of any assets passing to anyone other than the exempt beneficiaries listed above and any of the following which are not passing to exempt beneficiaries:
- the deceased's share of any jointly owned assets
- any assets the deceased gave away in the seven years before death
- any assets the deceased gave away, but in which they reserved a benefit
- assets outside the UK that do not pass under the UK Will or intestacy.

If the total is less than or equal to the Inheritance Tax nil rate band then you may fill in a reduced form IHT400. If you are claiming a transfer of unused nil rate band, you may add that to the nil rate band at the date of death. If the total is less than the nil rate band and transfer of unused nil rate band, you may fill in a reduced form IHT400.

Death on active service

If the deceased was a member of the armed forces or certain associated services whose death was caused by injury or disease on active service there is a complete exemption from Inheritance Tax on the estate passing on death. A reduced form IHT400 can be delivered if this applies. The exemption does not cover lifetime gifts.

What do I need to fill in if I can send a reduced form IHT400?

If you are able to fill in a reduced form IHT400, you only need to fill in the following parts of the form:
- boxes 1 to 28 - complete in full
- boxes 29 to 48 - you must answer all the questions, but you may not need to fill in all of the schedules.

5

281

If you answer 'yes' to any of the following questions you must fill in
the schedule:

- 29 – fill in Schedule IHT402
- 30 – fill in Schedule IHT403
- 31 – fill in Schedule IHT404
- 35 – fill in Schedule IHT408
- 36 – fill in Schedule IHT409
- 44 – fill in Schedule IHT417
- 45 – fill in Schedule IHT418
- 47 – fill in Schedule IHT420.

Where an asset included in any of the above schedules passes to an exempt
beneficiary, you may include your own estimate of the 'open market value'
but you must not include a nominal value.

If you answer 'yes' to any other questions you do not need to fill in the
relevant schedule if all of the assets concerned pass to exempt
beneficiaries. Instead you should write the value of those assets directly on
the form IHT400 in the boxes on pages 6 and 7.

This means that if the residue of the estate is left in shares to a number of
beneficiaries, for example, 'a half share to my wife and the remaining
half share to my children equally' you must fill in a full form IHT400.

You should fill in the boxes on pages 6 to 10 for the various assets and
liabilities. Where the asset passes to an exempt beneficiary, you may
include your own estimate of the 'open market value' but you must not
include a nominal value.

List all the assets passing to exempt beneficiaries in boxes 92 and 93
as appropriate.

Leave out boxes 109 and 110 as there should not be any tax to pay, but fill
in boxes 111 to 117 to make sure.

Leave out box 118, but complete the declaration at box 119. You do
not need to list any estimated values where the assets pass to
exempt beneficiaries.

Use the checklist on page 14 to make sure you remember to enclose all the
documents we need to see, but do not enclose supporting valuations if the
assets concerned pass to exempt beneficiaries.

6

Changes to the administration of an estate

Where there are to be changes in the administration of an estate, you can apply for a grant to allow the administration to continue, provided the assets concerned were included in an earlier grant.

England, Wales and Northern Ireland

You **must** use form Cap A5C (available from our Helpline) (or form Cap A5N in Northern Ireland) if you are applying for a:

- Grant of Double Probate   – Where an executor (perhaps due to ill health) was not party to the initial grant, but on regaining health the executor wishes to take up office.
- Grant de bonis non administratis – When the only or last surviving executor dies without fully dealing with estate.

When you have filled in the form, send it to the Probate Registry. **Please do not send it to us first.**

Scotland

If you need an 'Eik to Confirmation' for additional assets or to amend an estate, you should fill in form C4 *Corrective Inventory* and send it to us. After we have checked it, we will stamp and return the form to you so you can send it to the Sheriff or Commissary Clerk. If you need an 'Eik to Confirmation ad non executa' (where the estate has not been fully administered and none of the original executors, or substitutes, remain in office) you should get form X-1 from the Sheriff or Commissary Clerk.

Inheritance Tax and the grant

You must pay any Inheritance Tax and interest that is due before you can get a grant. Tax on certain assets may be paid by 10 annual instalments. The law says that we must charge interest from the first day of the seventh month after the month in which the person died.

For example, if a person dies on 7 January, we charge interest from 1 August. It does not matter why you have not paid the tax by then. Interest will still be due.

There is more information about instalments later in this guide on page 53.

Wartime compensation payments

If the deceased received a compensation payment during their lifetime for personal harm suffered at the hands of the Japanese or Nazi Governments, you should reduce the amount of tax charged on the estate by the smaller of:
- 40% of the payments received, or
- the amount of tax payable before allowing the deduction.

For example, the deceased received a payment of £10,000, which would give a deduction of £10,000 x 40% = £4,000. The Inheritance Tax on the estate before the deduction was £5,000. The tax can be reduced by £4,000. To apply the reduction you should include the figure for the reduction in tax at box 17 on form IHT400 *Calculation*. Applying the reduction can only reduce the tax liability to nil, it cannot result in a repayment of tax.

If the deceased died having made a claim but before they received the payment, you should include the amount claimed in box 76 on form IHT400 and then reduce the tax as above. You should send copies of

7

Appendix 3

any correspondence showing details of the deceased's claim with form IHT400. If no correspondence exists give details in the 'Additional information' boxes on pages 15 and 16 of form IHT400.

When must I send in the form?

Form IHT400 must be sent to us within 12 months of the end of the month of death. If the form is sent in after that time without reasonable excuse you may be liable to a penalty not exceeding £200. Additionally, should the delay extend another 12 months, that is, two years after death, you may be liable to an additional penalty up to £3,000. There is more about penalties in the customer guide to Inheritance Tax on our website or alternatively in our factsheet IHT13 (available from our Helpline).

ⓘ Website: **www.hmrc.gov.uk/ inheritancetax/**
Helpline: **0845 30 20 900**

Who to contact and why

When you have looked through all the deceased's papers and made a rough list of all their assets and debts, you will have to write to each organisation concerned to get the date of death value of the assets and debts and to ask if the deceased held any other assets or accounts with that organisation.

For example, you may know that the deceased had an account at a particular bank, but only have a copy of an old bank statement. You should write to that bank asking for the balance of the account at the date of death and also ask if the deceased held any other accounts, investments or safety deposit boxes with them.

You may need to contact some other organisations as well. These could include:

- Personal or occupational pension schemes to see if any pension payments will continue after death, or if a lump sum is payable. You should also ask if the deceased had an 'alternatively secured pension' or had made any changes to their pension arrangements shortly before they died. This information will help you to answer the questions on the form.
- Insurance companies to find out if the deceased had any insurance policies which paid out to the estate or someone else or whether the deceased had any policies written in trust.
- Energy or phone suppliers to see if the deceased owed them any money or if any overpaid money is due to be refunded to the estate.
- The local council for details of any outstanding or overpaid council tax.
- National Savings & Investments (NS&I) to find out the value of any National Savings Certificates or whether the deceased had any unclaimed Premium Bond prizes.
- Any solicitors, accountants or financial advisors who dealt with the deceased's affairs.
- The deceased's close family and friends (especially to find out if the deceased made any gifts).
- Anyone named in the Will who might know about the deceased's affairs.

You will need to make detailed enquiries so that you find out everything you can about the deceased's estate and what assets and debts you should include on the form.

8

What values to include	The law says that for Inheritance Tax, you have to value all assets as if each item had been sold on the date the deceased died. We call this the 'open market value'. There is more information about valuing assets later in this guide. Round the value of assets down to the nearest pound and liabilities up to the nearest pound.

Estimated values

You should make full enquiries to find out the exact value for each item in the estate. However, if you are having difficulty with one or two items, such as an Income Tax repayment or household bill, or perhaps details of foreign tax or income due from a trust, the law says that you may include a provisional estimate. You should make the best estimate that you can. You will need to list the boxes that contain provisional estimates in box 119 of form IHT400.

It is your responsibility to tell us the correct figure as soon as you know it.

Documents you must keep	You do not need to send us copies of documents, for example, a letter from a bank with the balance in an account or evidence of household bills, unless we specifically ask you to provide a copy in this guide. However, you must keep safe all documents that you have used to fill in form IHT400 and the Schedules because we may ask you for some or all of them after you have obtained the grant.

Original documents

If you have to return an original document, such as a life assurance or trust or a loan agreement, you should keep a copy in case we ask you to provide it.

Getting started – how to fill in your Inheritance Tax account	The flowchart on pages 2 and 3 of the *Quick start guide* included with these forms, takes you through the step-by-step process of how to deal with your Inheritance Tax account. You can obtain a copy of the *Quick start guide* from our Helpline.
Instruments of variation	An instrument of variation is a legal document which allows the beneficiaries of an estate to change the terms of the Will or intestacy after the death. The IHT400 should be filled in to show any effect the variation has on the Inheritance Tax due. For example, if the deceased's children inherit part of the estate and redirect assets to the surviving spouse, increasing spouse or civil partner exemption, the IHT400 should show the increased exemption at boxes 92 and 93. If the variation affects a matter of general law, such as severing a joint tenancy, the IHT400 should show the legal position at the date of death, before the effect of the instrument of variation.

9

285

Filling in form IHT400 (pages 1 to 5) — fill in all the boxes that apply by giving the information we ask for fully and comprehensively. Tick the 'Yes' or 'No' boxes, as appropriate

Follow the instructions on the form.
Failure to answer the questions fully may result in delay.

Further guidance is given below where necessary.

If you need to mark a particular box to indicate an answer, you can use a 'tick' or a 'cross'.

> ☐ 3 **Inheritance Tax reference number**
> If there is any IHT to pay, you will need an IHT reference number and a payslip before you can make the payment.
>
> Fill in form IHT422 *Application for an Inheritance Tax reference* and send it to the address shown on that form or apply online at:
> **www.hmrc.gov.uk/inheritancetax/**

Deceased's details, pages 1 and 2

☐ 6 **Domicile**

A person's domicile is usually the country where their main home is. The UK is not a 'country' when establishing a person's domicile. So a person will have a domicile in England and Wales, or Scotland or Northern Ireland; in these notes we refer to all of these as the 'UK'. The Channel Islands and the Isle of Man are foreign countries when considering domicile. You only need to read the rest of this note if you think the deceased was not domiciled in the UK.

Even though the deceased may have been domiciled abroad, there are some special rules that mean we can treat the deceased as if they were domiciled in the UK. The rules are that:

- if a person has lived in the UK for a long time, so that they were resident for Income Tax purposes for at least 17 out of the 20 years ending with the tax year in which they died, or
- if a person was domiciled in the UK under English law at any time in the three years before they died

the law says that we can treat the deceased as if they were domiciled in the UK when they died. This means that we can charge Inheritance Tax on the deceased's worldwide estate even though they were not domiciled in the UK when they died.

Also, if the terms of a Double Taxation Convention or Agreement apply a person may be treated as having more than one domicile. The terms of the convention or agreement will say which domicile is to be used.

10

286

If any of these special rules apply and the deceased is treated for Inheritance Tax purposes as being domiciled in the UK, you should still enter the name of the foreign country in the box, but fill in the rest of the form as if the deceased was domiciled in the UK.

If the special rules do not apply and the deceased was domiciled outside the UK, you should fill in Schedule IHT401 *Domicile outside the United Kingdom* to give us details.

If the deceased was domiciled in Scotland at the date of death, page 2

| 7 | This only applies if the deceased died domiciled in Scotland. See page 3 for an explanation of 'legitim'. Please use the 'Additional information' boxes on the IHT400 pages 15 and 16 if you need to provide any other information about a claim for legal rights. |

| 14 | **National Insurance number** |

Enter the deceased's National Insurance number. If the state pension was paid directly to a bank or building society, the reference shown in the bank or building society statements is the National Insurance number. If the deceased was still working, you can find the National Insurance number on their payslip, or form P60 or on letters from HM Revenue & Customs, such as a notice of coding.

| 15 | **Income Tax or Unique Taxpayer Reference** |

The Income Tax or Unique Taxpayer Reference (UTR) can be found on correspondence from HM Revenue & Customs if the deceased was a self assessment taxpayer.

| 16 | **Power of attorney** |

You should answer 'Yes' to this question if the deceased had signed a general, enduring or lasting power of attorney and that power was used by the Attorney during the deceased's lifetime. A copy of the power of attorney should be enclosed with the form.

Contact details of the person dealing with the estate, page 3

| 17 to 22 | If you are applying for a grant without the help of a solicitor or accountant to act for you and it is difficult for us to contact you by phone during the day, we cannot discuss the estate with another person without your written authority. You may want us to write to you, but for someone else – perhaps a husband, wife, civil partner or other relative – to be able to deal with phone calls. If so, enter their name and details in boxes 18 and 19. |

Authority for repayment of Inheritance Tax, page 3

| 23 | If we need to repay any Inheritance Tax, the cheque will be made out in the names of all the people who have signed the form. If you do not have a bank account in those names, it may be difficult for you to cash the cheque. |

11

287

To avoid this difficulty, you can say in the box on page 3 how you would like the cheque made out. If there are three or four executors and you want the cheque made out to just one or maybe two of them, enter the name(s) of the people here. If a solicitor or other agent is acting on your behalf and the cheque is to be made out to their firm, tick 'yes' here.

What makes up your Inheritance Tax account – Schedules, pages 4 and 5

Website: **www.hmrc.gov.uk/ inheritancetax/**
Helpline: **0845 30 20 900**

In some circumstances we need additional information about the deceased's circumstances or particular assets. You must provide this information on the Schedules that accompany form IHT400. Answer the questions on pages 4 and 5 of the IHT400 to find out which Schedules you need. You may need more than one copy of a particular Schedule.

You will have received a selection of the more frequently used Schedules. If you need others you can download them from our website or phone our Helpline and ask for the ones you need. If you received Schedules you do not need, do not use them.

Where necessary, the following additional notes will help you to decide which Schedules you need to fill in.

29 **Transfer of unused nil rate band**
Fill in Schedule IHT402 Transfer of unused nil rate band if the deceased died on or after 9 October 2007, they had a spouse or civil partner who died before them and you wish to claim a transfer of unused nil rate band to add to the nil rate band on the deceased's estate.

This will apply if the estate of the spouse or civil partner who died first did not use up all of the nil rate band available, usually because most of the estate passed to the surviving spouse or civil partner or the estate was smaller than the nil rate band at the time of the first death.

30 **Gifts and other transfers of value**
You can enter 'No' and do not need to provide any details if the only gifts made by the deceased were:
• to their husband, wife or civil partner and spouse or civil partner exemption applies
• outright gifts to any individual which do not exceed £250 in any one year. (These will be covered by the small gifts exemption.)
• outright gifts to any individual of money or listed stocks and shares that are wholly covered by the annual and/or gifts out of income exemptions
• outright gifts made regularly from income that did not exceed £3,000 in total each year.

These exemptions are detailed on page 72 of this guide.

If the deceased had made any other gifts or 'transfers of value' since 18 March 1986, including transfers into trust, payment of insurance premiums for the benefit of another person, advances out of a trust fund or any assets that were taken out of a trust before death, you must fill in Schedule IHT403 *Gifts and other transfers of value*. In general, a 'transfer of value' is any transaction where the deceased did not receive full value in exchange.

12

288

31   **Jointly owned assets**

Bank and building society accounts, stocks and shares, household goods, freehold and leasehold property are the assets most usually owned in joint names. We call all the assets that are owned jointly 'joint assets'. Fill in Schedule IHT404 *Jointly owned assets* if the deceased owned any UK assets in joint names with one or more people.

32   **Houses, land, buildings and interests in land**

As well as owning land and buildings, the deceased may have had interests in land or rights over land which should be shown on Schedule IHT405. Examples of these interests and rights include:

- mineral rights
- fishing rights
- rights of way.

36   **Pensions**

Fill in Schedule IHT409 *Pensions* if:

- the deceased was being paid a pension from an employer or a personal pension scheme or a retirement annuity contract
- a lump sum became payable from such a source as a result of the deceased's death
- the deceased had made any changes to their pension provision in the two years before they died
- the deceased had the benefit of an alternatively secured pension fund under a registered pension scheme
- the deceased had the benefit of an unsecured pension fund under a registered pension scheme and the following applied
  - they became entitled to the benefit on the death of the original scheme member who was aged 75 or more
  - the original scheme member had an alternatively secured pension when they died
  - the deceased was a relevant dependant of the original scheme member.

Unsecured pension

An unsecured pension fund is a fund of money in a registered pension scheme that has been earmarked for the benefit of a member or a dependant, but has not been used to secure a pension by buying a pension through the scheme or an annuity (other than a short term annuity payable for no more than five years ending before the beneficiary reaches the age of 75).

13

289

Appendix 3

Alternatively Secured Pension

An Alternatively Secured Pension is an unsecured pension fund for the benefit of someone who is aged 75 or over. A 'dependant' of a member of a registered pension scheme is a person who, at the date of the scheme member's death, was:

- the spouse or civil partner of the member
- a child of the member who was under the age of 23
- a child of the member who was on or over the age of 23 and in the opinion of the scheme administrator was dependent on the scheme member because of physical or mental impairment.

A 'relevant dependant' is a dependant who, at the date of the scheme member's death, was:

- the spouse or civil partner of the scheme member, or
- financially dependent on the member at that time.

37 Life assurance and annuities

Fill in form IHT410 *Life assurance and annuities* if the deceased paid either regular, monthly, or lump sum premiums for:

- insurance policies which are payable to the estate
- a mortgage protection policy
- unit-linked investment bonds with insurance companies or other financial service providers that pay out 100% of the value of the units to the estate
- investment or re-investment plans, bonds or contracts with financial service providers that pay out to the estate on death
- insurance policies and unit-linked investment bonds, etc., that are payable to beneficiaries under a trust and do not form part of the estate
- joint life assurance policies under which the deceased was one of the lives assured but that remain in force after the death
- insurance policies on the life of another person but under which the deceased was to benefit, or
- if the deceased received any payments under an annuity that continued after death, or under which a lump sum was payable as a result of their death.

38 Listed stocks and shares

Fill in Schedule IHT411 *listed stocks and shares* if the deceased owned any stocks and shares which were listed on a recognised Stock Exchange or any UK Government or municipal securities. Shares in Public Limited Companies (PLCs) will be listed. If the deceased had a control holding of shares in a listed company (and this will be very rare) you should not put them on this schedule, but use Schedule IHT412 *unlisted stocks and shares, and control holdings* instead.

14

290

39   **Unlisted stocks and shares, and control holdings**

Fill in Schedule IHT412 *unlisted stocks and shares, and control holdings* if the deceased owned any shares in a private limited company that were not listed on the Stock Exchange. You should also fill in this schedule if the deceased owned any shares that are:

- listed on the Alternative Investment Market (AIM), Unlisted Securities Market or traded on OFEX
- held in a Business Expansion Scheme (BES) or Business Start-up Scheme (BSS)
- listed on a recognised Stock Exchange and the deceased had control of the company.

44   **Foreign assets**

Fill in Schedule IHT417 *Foreign assets* to give details of any overseas assets owned by the deceased, including any jointly owned overseas assets. Do not include here details of foreign shares that are listed on the London Stock Exchange. We call all the assets that the deceased owned overseas 'foreign assets'. The Channel Islands and the Isle of Man are foreign countries so assets held there are foreign assets.

45   **Assets held in trust**

We call assets that are held in trust 'settled property'. We say that the deceased had an 'interest in possession' where they had the right to:

- the income from assets (for example, dividends from shares, interest from a bank account, or rent from let property), or
- payments of a fixed amount each year, often in regular instalments, or
- live in a house or use the contents without paying any rent.

In some circumstances where a person has an interest in possession in settled property they are treated for Inheritance Tax purposes as if they owned those assets personally. You should fill in form IHT418 *Assets held in trust* if the deceased's interest in possession was in:

- a trust set up before 22 March 2006, or
- a trust that was set up on or after 22 March 2006 **and was**
  - an immediate post death interest
  - a disabled person's interest
  - a transitional serial interest.

What is an immediate post death interest?

An immediate post death interest is one where the beneficiary is entitled to a benefit from a trust, and:

- the trust was set up under a Will or under the rules of intestacy
- the beneficiary became entitled to their benefit on the death of the person who set up the trust (the settlor)
- the trust is not for a disabled person or a bereaved minor.

Appendix 3

What is a disabled person's interest?

A disabled person's interest arises where:

- more than half of the assets in a trust in which nobody has a right to benefit that are applied for the benefit of a disabled person, or
- an individual (the settlor) who is suffering from a condition likely to lead to them becoming disabled as described below sets up a trust using their own assets and the following conditions apply
  - there is no interest in possession during the settlor's life
  - any trust property that applies during the settlor's life is applied for their benefit
  - if the trust is brought to an end during the settlor's life the assets must become the property of the settlor or part of a disabled person's trust
  - a disabled person became entitled to an interest in possession in a trust
  - that came into existence on or after 22 March 2006
- the beneficiary is a disabled person and the trust was set up on or after 22 March 2006.

Definition of a disabled person

For this purpose a disabled person is a person who:

- is not able to administer their own property or manage their own affairs, because of a mental disorder, within the meaning of the Mental Health Act 1983, or
- receives an Attendance Allowance under Section 64 of the Social Security Contributions & Benefits Act 1992 or of the Social Security Contributions & Benefits (Northern Ireland) Act 1992, or would receive an Attendance Allowance if they were not prevented from doing so because they were undergoing treatment for renal failure in hospital, or
- receives a Disability Living Allowance under Section 71 of those Acts because they are entitled to the care component at the highest or middle rate, or would be entitled to it if they had not been provided with certain accommodation, or
- satisfies the Commissioners of HMRC that they would have been in receipt of either benefit had they met the residence conditions.

Transitional serial interest

There are two types of transitional serial interest. The first type is where an interest in possession trust arises on or after 22 March 2006 and before 6 April 2008, but it follows a previous interest in possession that already existed before 22 March 2006.

The second type is where the interest in possession trust arises on the death, on or after 22 March 2006, of the holder of a previous interest in possession and either:

- the new holder is the spouse or civil partner of the previous holder, or
- the settled property consists of a contract of life insurance.

If you would like more information on transitional serial interests, go to the customer guide at **www.hmrc.gov.uk/inheritancetax/**

46 **Debts owed by the deceased**

Fill in Schedule IHT419 *Debts owed by the deceased* to give details of any:

- money that the deceased had borrowed from close friends or relatives
- money that close friends or relatives had spent on behalf of the deceased and is to be repaid from the estate
- other loans, or
- guarantee debts that you are deducting from the estate.

You do not need to fill in Schedule IHT419 if the debt is a mortgage secured against a property shown in Schedule IHT405 *Houses, land, buildings and interest in land.* Instead the mortgage should be shown in box 80 on form IHT400.

47 **National Heritage assets**

Conditional exemption from Inheritance Tax may be allowed on certain assets that are of national interest. The assets are pictures, prints, books, manuscripts, works of art and scientific objects. They can include antiques and other objects that do not produce income.

To qualify for exemption they must be pre-eminent for their natural, scientific, historic, or artistic interest, or be historically associated with a building that qualifies for conditional exemption.

Buildings can qualify if they should be preserved because of their outstanding historic or architectural interest. Land can also qualify if it is needed for the preservation of buildings that are of outstanding historic or architectural interest, or if it is of outstanding scenic, historic or scientific interest.

The exemption applies as long as certain conditions are met. The conditions broadly are that the asset must:

- be kept in the UK
- be preserved
- remain in the ownership of the person giving the undertaking
- be accessible to the public.

You can also offer to pay some or all of the tax by transferring these types of items to the Crown.

Fill in Schedule IHT420 *National Heritage assets. Conditional exemption and offers in lieu of tax* if either of these apply.

Approved maintenance fund

An approved maintenance fund is a trust fund that has been approved by HMRC for the maintenance of property that it has designated as land of outstanding scenic, scientific or historic interest, a building of outstanding historic or architectural interest, land essential to protect that building's character and amenities or contents historically associated with that building.

48 When you have identified which Schedules you need you should fill them in before going on to page 6 of form IHT400.

17

Filling in the Schedules — additional notes

Introduction

Wherever possible we have included the notes on the Schedule. The following Schedules have additional notes you can find here:

Schedule IHT403
Gifts and other transfers of value

What is a gift?

The law says that there will be a gift whenever there is 'a loss to the donor' (the 'donor' is the person making the gift).

It is not just outright gifts, such as giving a cheque for £10,000 to someone on a special occasion, that are relevant for Inheritance Tax. This can happen in different ways.

> **Example**
> - A parent sells a house to their son for less than they could sell the property on the open market. For Inheritance Tax purposes, this would result in a loss to the donor.
> - A person holds shares in a company that give them control of that company. They sell a few shares to a relative but this means losing control of the company and reduces the value of their other shares. For Inheritance Tax purposes, this would result in a loss to the donor.

Please tell us about any assets given away (gifts) or transferred by the deceased where there was a 'loss to the donor' on or after 18 March 1986.

Time limits

When we consider the value of a person's estate we generally look at the seven year period before their date of death. However, rarely, gifts made before that seven year period need to be taken into account. See page 22.

18

294

Value of gifts

It is important that you supply the value of any gifts made by the deceased in case the value needs to be deducted from the nil rate band, so we can work out how much tax is payable.

Include full details of all gifts that are not wholly covered by spouse or civil partner exemption, small gifts exemption or annual exemption. Full details of these exemptions can be found on page 72 of this guide.

Who pays the Inheritance Tax on a gift?

If the total value of the gifts is below the Inheritance Tax nil rate band, the gifts use up the nil rate band first. The tax payable on the estate takes into account the gifts, but the recipients do not have to pay any of the tax themselves. The tax will be paid by the personal representatives.

Example	
A makes a gift of £100,000 on 3 May 2005 and dies on 18 July 2006.	
A's estate on death is £300,000.	
Inheritance Tax is calculated:	
IHT nil rate band on 18 July 2006	£285,000
Less gift	£100,000
Nil rate band available	£185,000
A's estate on death	£300,000
Less available nil rate band	£185,000
Chargeable	£115,000
Tax on estate at 40% = £115,000 x 40%	
Tax due	= £46,000

If the gifts total more than the nil rate band for Inheritance Tax, then the tax is due on the gifts themselves and is payable by the recipients of the gifts.

Example	
B makes a gift of £300,000 on 10 May 2005 and dies on 27 August 2006.	
B's estate on death is £500,000. Inheritance Tax due on the gift is calculated:	
Gift	£300,000
Less IHT nil rate band on 27 August 2006	£285,000
Chargeable	£15,000
Tax on gift at 40% = £15,000 x 40%	
Tax due	= £6,000
The Inheritance Tax on the estate, payable by the personal representatives, is £500,000 x 40% = £200,000.	

Appendix 3

Gifts made within seven years before death

| 1 | **Gifts or assets transferred** |

This includes gifts of cash or other assets and any other arrangements that have given rise to a 'loss to the donor'. This may include:

- granting a lease at less than a full market rent
- re-arranging the shares in a private company, or altering the rights attached to the shares
- agreeing to act as a guarantor for someone else's debts.

If you are not sure whether to include details of a particular transaction, please phone our Helpline.

2	**Trusts and settlements created by the deceased during their lifetime**
and	
3	

This includes gifts of cash or other assets as well as any other arrangements with the trustees that have given rise to a 'loss to the donor'. If the gift was made on or after 22 March 2006 we will calculate tax using the rate of tax appropriate to the date the gift was made, unless one of the following conditions apply:

- the trust was set up for the benefit of a person who was disabled at the time the assets were transferred into trust, or
- the trust was set up by a person who is suffering from a condition which can be expected to lead to them becoming disabled, and
  - the gift was from their own assets
  - the trust is for their own benefit.

See page 16 of this guide for a definition of a disabled person.

| 4 | **Premiums paid on a life assurance policy** |

You should answer 'yes' to this question if the deceased has made a gift by paying the premium(s) on a life assurance policy for the benefit of someone else. Please ignore policies where the only person to benefit would be the deceased's spouse or civil partner. You should provide a copy of:

- the life assurance policy, and
- any related documents such as trust deeds and loan agreements.

If there is more than one insurance policy and they are all identical, you only need to send a copy of one policy. You must include details of all premiums paid and provide copies of the policy documents, even if you are deducting exemption as gifts made out of income. (See page 21.)

In some circumstances, the deceased may have purchased an annuity as well as paying the premiums on a life assurance policy for the benefit of someone else. There are rules that might apply in such circumstances and the exemption as gifts made out of income may not be available against the premiums.

Please provide a copy of the annuity documents and life assurance policy if the deceased had:

- purchased an annuity (at any time), and
- paid the premiums on a life assurance policy for the benefit of someone else, and
- the life assurance policy was taken out after 27 March 1974.

| 5 | **The deceased ceased to have a right to benefit from assets** |

The deceased may have been entitled to benefit from the assets held in a trust or settlement, but during their lifetime that entitlement came to an end. This may be in whole or in part.

Their entitlement to benefit from the asset may have come to an end because of the terms of a trust or because the deceased asked the trustees to alter or terminate their entitlement.

| 6 | **Gifts treated as exempt because they are gifts out of income** |

If you are claiming that gifts made by the deceased are exempt as gifts made as part of normal expenditure out of income, please fill in the table on page 6 of this Schedule, as well as giving details of the gifts on page 2 of the Schedule.

Further information about the 'normal expenditure out of income' exemption can be found at page 72 of this guide.

Gifts with reservation of benefit

A gift with reservation is one where the recipient does not fully own it or where the donor either reserves or takes some benefit from it.

Where this happens the law says that we can include the assets as part of the deceased's estate at death. This rule only applies to gifts made on or after 18 March 1986 and there is no seven year limit as there is for outright gifts.

The most common examples of gifts with reservation include:
- A parent (now deceased) gave their house to their son, but continued to live there without paying rent.
- A parent put a building society account into their daughter's name but the interest the money earned continued to be paid to the parent.

If the parent in the first example made an arrangement to pay rent at the market rate, then the parent (the donor) would not have reserved benefit.

Details about the gift should be entered on page 2 of form IHT403, 'Gifts made within the seven years before death' instead.

There may be times when a gift is originally given with reservation of benefit and the reservation ceases at a later date. For example, a parent gives their house to their son and continues to live there without paying rent. Two years later the parent starts to pay rent at the market rate. This means that the reservation has ceased.

Once the reservation has ceased, the gift becomes an outright gift. We will consider the gift to have been made on the date the reservation ceased. In this example this will be on the first date the rent (at market rate) is paid.

When we calculate the tax due, the seven year period would begin on the date the reservation ceased.

If the deceased died within the seven year period, do not enter details here. Give details on page 2, 'Gifts made within the seven years before death' instead and include the value of the property at the time the reservation ceased.

Appendix 3

Please note, the law says that where a gift with reservation becomes an outright gift, you cannot deduct any of the exemptions from the value of the gift.

If you need help or more information, please phone our Helpline.

Pre-owned assets

In some situations, where a person benefits from assets they owned previously, a charge to Inheritance Tax may arise under the rules relating to gifts with reservation.

An Income Tax charge on pre-owned assets (POA) was introduced in the 2005–06 tax year. This charge applies to assets that a person disposed of, but continued to obtain benefit from. It can also apply when a person contributed to the purchase of an asset for another person that they subsequently obtain benefit from.

The legislation gives you the option to elect to have the asset treated as part of your estate for Inheritance Tax purposes, under the reservation of benefit rules. So long as the election remains in place, you will not have to pay the Income Tax.

To make this election you must have submitted a form IHT500 *Election for Inheritance Tax to apply to asset previously owned* before 31 January after the year in which you became liable to the charge, or exceptionally, if you can show a reasonable excuse for failure to submit the form by the deadline, at a later date. It is not possible for an election to be made on the deceased's behalf after death.

Earlier transfers

This part of the form is about any gifts made by the deceased (the donor) in the period before the gifts shown on pages 2 to 4 of the form. To work out whether tax is payable on any gift, the law says that we must add it to any chargeable gifts made in the seven years before the gift concerned. For example, if the deceased made a gift six years before they died, we will add that gift to any chargeable gifts made in the seven years before the gift was made.

A chargeable gift is any gift that is not wholly covered by exemptions and:
- was made before 18 March 1986, or
- was made between 18 March 1986 and 21 March 2006 and was given to a company or the trustees of a discretionary trust
- was made on or after 22 March 2006 unless it was a gift
  – to another individual
  – to a disabled trust
  – into a bereaved minor's trust on the coming to an end of an immediate post-death interest.

Gifts from one individual to another are not chargeable gifts and should not be included in this section of the form.

You should not include these earlier gifts with the estate on death because they are only relevant in working out tax payable on gifts. We will take any earlier gifts into account when looking at the gifts after you have taken out the grant.

22

298

Gifts made as part of normal expenditure out of income	The table on page 6 is a guide to the information you must provide if you want to show that the regular gifts made by the deceased formed part of their normal expenditure out of income and were therefore exempt.
	Full details are required of the deceased's income and expenditure for each year for which the exemption is being deducted, so that you show that the gifts were made out of the deceased's income rather than out of capital.
	You do not have to provide copies of bank statements or bills at this stage, but you should be prepared to provide documentary evidence of the deceased's income and expenditure if we ask you for it after you have sent us the form.

Schedule IHT404
Jointly owned assets

Establishing the deceased's share	The deceased's share of the asset for Inheritance Tax purposes may be different from the legal position and you will need to establish the deceased's share.
	Where land and buildings are owned in joint names, the deeds to the property will usually set out the share of each owner. But, with other assets, each owner's share will usually correspond to their contribution to the asset. Where the deceased's share does not correspond to their contribution to the asset you will need to explain why the deceased's share is different on Schedule IHT404 *Jointly owned assets.*
Businesses	You must not include any business assets owned jointly by a partnership on the Schedule IHT404. Such assets should be included on Schedule IHT413 *Business and partnership interests and assets* and in box 69 on page 7 of form IHT400.
Foreign property	The way in which assets may be owned jointly in the UK does not usually apply in other countries. You must not include any jointly owned foreign property on Schedule IHT404. Complete Schedule IHT417 *Foreign assets* giving details of the foreign property and, in the 'Additional information' boxes on pages 15 and 16 of the IHT400, enter the details of the other joint owners. You should use the questions on page 2 of Schedule IHT404 as a guide to the information we need.

23

Appendix 3

Houses and land

If the deceased owned any houses or land jointly give details of the properties here.

Household goods

If the deceased was a joint owner of household goods and effects, they should be included here as joint property. Group the items together in the same categories and list them in the same order as shown on Schedule IHT407 *Household and personal goods*.

Insurance policies and bonds

If you have deducted any money owed under a joint mortgage in box 2 on Schedule IHT404 and a policy was assigned to repay the mortgage, include the value of the deceased's share of the policy proceeds as an asset on Schedule IHT404 at box 6.

If the deceased was entitled to benefit from a 'joint life and survivor' policy (see Schedule IHT410 *Life assurance and annuities*), give the name of the insurance company, the policy number and the value of the deceased's interest in the policy on the Schedule IHT404 at box 6. This is a complex area. You can find out more on the subject of life assurance policies in the customer guide at **www.hmrc.gov.uk/inheritancetax/**

How to value joint property

The rules for valuing joint property are the same as the rules for valuing assets owned by the deceased alone. For more information about valuing assets see pages 65 to 71 of this guide. In the case of bank and building society accounts, stocks and shares find out the whole value and then include the value of the deceased's share.

Example
The deceased owned a joint account with two other people that was worth £9,000 at the date of death. They had all contributed equally to the money in the account. The value of the deceased's share would be an exact one third of the whole (that is, £3,000).

24

300

However, in the case of a house or land, the open market value of a share is likely to be less than a share calculated in this way, as a discount may be appropriate. The amount of the discount will vary depending on the circumstances of each property and whether English or Scots law applies.

English law – To give us a starting point, you may reduce the arithmetical share of the value of the whole of the property by 10%. This will give us an indication of the value of the share of the property. This figure of 10% is only to give us a starting point. The amount of the discount, as well as the value estimated for the whole of the property, may need to be changed after the grant has been issued.

Example
The deceased owned a house worth £120,000 jointly with one other person. The arithmetical value of the deceased's share is £60,000 and this may be reduced by 10% (or £6,000). The value to include is £54,000.

Scots law – Under Scots law a joint owner has a right to raise an action for division and sale. A discount for joint ownership will reflect the cost and possible delay of raising such an action. The cost is not related to the value of the property, so cannot be calculated in percentage terms. As a starting point you may deduct £4,000 from the value of the whole property before calculating the arithmetical value of the deceased's share as the value to be included in the account. **This is only a starting point. The value estimated may need to be changed after Confirmation has been obtained.**

The other joint owner is a spouse or civil partner

Whether English or Scots law applies you must not apply any discount if the other joint owner is the deceased's spouse or civil partner. Special rules prevent this discount from applying, so you should include the deceased's arithmetical share of the whole value of the house or land.

We will usually ask the Valuation Office to give us their opinion of the value of the deceased's property. They will take into account the circumstances of any jointly owned property and amount of discount to be allowed. If the Valuation Office cannot accept the figures you have used, they will try to agree a value with you. If the agreed value is more than the figure that you have suggested, you may have to pay some more tax (and interest).

25

301

Schedule IHT407
Household and personal goods

Valuing household and personal goods

Information on how to value household and personal goods can be found on page 68 of this guide.

We only want individual values for the assets described in boxes 1 to 3 on Schedule IHT407. All other household goods can be added together and the total value entered in box 4.

Schedule IHT408
Household and personal goods donated to charity

Charity exemption

Sometimes the people inheriting the deceased's household and personal goods want to give some or all of the items to charity. For example, by donating them to a charity shop. If they decide to do that they will only be able to deduct charity exemption from the value of the goods if they sign an instrument of variation (IOV). For more information on IOVs go to the customer guide at **www.hmrc.gov.uk/inheritancetax/**

Schedule IHT408 is a standard form that allows the beneficiaries to make such a donation and benefit from charity exemption without having to sign an IOV.

All the beneficiaries who have inherited the goods should complete and sign the Declaration to show whether all or some of the goods are being given to charity and which charity or charities are going to benefit.

Schedule of items

If some, but not all, of the goods are being given to charity, the beneficiaries making the gift should complete the Schedule of items to show which items are being gifted and the value of those items.

All the items donated to charity in this way should also be included in Schedule IHT407.

The amount of charity exemption claimed should be shown in box 92 on form IHT400.

26

Schedule IHT409
Pensions

Personal pension policies replaced annuity contracts from 1 July 1988. Where we refer to personal pension policies this also applies to *retirement annuity* contracts.

If the deceased owned a *retirement annuity* contract, complete Schedule IHT409 *Pensions* as if it were a personal pension policy.

Approved or unapproved schemes

For Income Tax purposes, pension schemes and personal pension policies are registered as approved or unapproved. The scheme papers or policy documents should indicate the status of the scheme. If they do not, the Scheme Administrator will be able to tell you. If the benefits are payable under an unapproved scheme, please give details (on the 'Additional information' box on form IHT400) of benefits payable under the scheme and those taken by the deceased as well as answering the questions on Schedule IHT409 *Pensions*.

If you want to discuss a particular situation with us, please phone **0131 777 4296**. (Please note this phone number is for Inheritance Tax pension enquiries only.)

Continuing pension payments

In most cases, the payment of a pension or other benefit will cease when the person entitled to it dies. In some cases, the pension may be guaranteed for a fixed period and the person entitled to it dies before the end of that period. The payments may then continue to be paid to the estate. The value of the right to receive the remainder of the payments should be included on this Schedule and on form IHT400.

Lump sum benefit

Examples of changes to benefits
Some pension schemes or personal pension policies pay out a lump sum benefit when the person dies. This is often referred to as the death benefit. The lump sum is an asset of the deceased's estate and should be included on form IHT400 if:
- it is payable to the deceased's personal representative, either by right or because there is no one else who qualifies for the payment, or
- the deceased could, right up until their death, have signed a 'nomination' (either for the first time or after having revoked an existing 'nomination') that bound the trustees of the pension scheme to make the payment to the person named by the deceased.

27

Appendix 3

Letter of wishes

A binding nomination is different from a 'letter of wishes'. A letter of wishes records what the deceased would like to happen with the death benefit and does not bind the trustees of the pension scheme to follow the deceased's wishes.

It is important to find out whether or not the deceased could bind the trustees with a nomination. Many pension schemes and policies provide a form that is called a nomination, but which usually goes on to say that the trustees are not bound to follow the deceased's wishes. If the deceased signed such a form, they have signed a letter of wishes and not a binding nomination.

Changes to pension benefits

Most pension schemes and personal pension policies allow the member to dispose of the death benefits and to make changes to the benefits that they are entitled to under the scheme or policy. Usually, the member can:
- nominate or appoint the death benefits to someone else
- assign the death benefits into a trust
- make changes to the pension benefits they intend to take and when they intend to take them (some examples of the sort of changes that might be made are in the next section).

If the deceased made a nomination, appointment or assignment or made any changes to the pension benefits in the two years before they died there may be a liability to Inheritance Tax. If this applies, please complete the section headed 'Changes to pension benefits'.

Examples of changes to benefits
Some examples of changes in benefit that might be made are:
- where the deceased reached pension age and decided not to take the payment of their pension at that time or chose to take 'income drawdown', or
- where the deceased, having got to pension age and chosen to take 'income drawdown' decided at a later date (and whilst in ill health) to reduce the level of income taken, or
- where the deceased, having got to pension age and chosen to take 'phased retirement,' decides at a later date (and whilst in ill health) to reduce the number of segments taken.

'**Income drawdown**' is a particular situation where the deceased has reached pension age but has chosen not to buy an annuity that will provide their pension. Instead, they decide to 'draw' a certain level of income from the retirement fund with a view to buying an annuity at a later date.

'**Phased retirement**' is where the deceased has divided their pension entitlement into a series of segments and has agreed with their pension provider a plan on retirement to take so many segments each year.

Where the deceased has given away any benefits, or has made some changes to the benefits they were entitled to, it is possible that they may have made a transfer of value. Enter the details we ask for above on form IHT409 *Pensions* and we will look at what you have said after the grant has been issued. If we think there has been a transfer of value, we will discuss the value with you.

If you wish to include your own value for the benefits given away, enter a figure on Schedule IHT403 *Gifts and other transfers of value*. Use the 'Additional information' boxes on pages 15 and 16 on form IHT400 to show how you have arrived at your value.

Valuing the benefits given away

The value of the benefits given away or the impact of the changes made will depend to a large extent on the deceased's health at the date of the nomination, appointment or change. Please provide some evidence of the deceased's state of health and life expectancy at that time so we can establish the value. A letter from the deceased's doctor is the best sort of evidence.

If obtaining a letter from the deceased's doctor will delay your application for a grant, you do not have to have it before you send form IHT400 to us. However, we will need to see the letter as soon as you receive it after the grant has been issued.

Contributions to a pension scheme within two years of death

Contributions to a pension scheme by the scheme member or their employer may be a transfer of value (gift) if the contributions are made when the scheme member is in ill health.

Alternatively Secured Pension funds

An Alternatively Secured Pension fund (ASP) is a fund of money in a registered pension scheme that has been earmarked for the benefit of a member or a dependant (who is aged 75 or more) but has not been used to secure a pension by buying a pension through the scheme or an annuity (other than a short term annuity payable for no more than five years).

A 'dependant' of a member of a registered pension scheme is a person who, at the date of the scheme member's death, was:
- the spouse or civil partner of the member
- a child of the member who was under the age of 23
- a child of the member who was on or over the age of 23 and in the opinion of the Scheme Administrator was dependent on the scheme member because of physical or mental impairment.

A 'relevant dependant' is a dependant who, at the date of the scheme member's death, was:
- the spouse or civil partner of the scheme member, or
- financially dependent on the member at that time.

29

305

Appendix 3

Tax charge on alternatively secured pension funds

If the deceased had an alternatively secured pension fund as the original scheme member, the value of the fund which is left at the date of death is aggregated with the deceased's estate for Inheritance Tax purposes. The total Inheritance Tax payable is then apportioned between the personal representatives of the estate and the administrators of the pension scheme. Any part of the fund which is going to be used to provide benefits for the deceased's relevant dependants is ignored, because the Inheritance Tax charge is deferred until the death of the relevant dependant.

Any part of the fund that is passing to a UK charity is exempt.

If you are not sure whether the deceased's pension was an Alternatively Secured Pension you should contact the pension provider.

Dependant's pension fund

If the deceased benefited from a dependant's unsecured or a dependant's Alternatively Secured Pension (ASP) fund as a dependant of a member of a registered pension scheme, there may also be an Inheritance Tax charge.

This charge will arise in the following two situations:

- the deceased benefited from a dependant's unsecured or a dependant's ASP fund as the 'relevant dependant' of a scheme member who died with an ASP

- the deceased benefited from a dependant's ASP fund derived from the pension lump sum death benefit of a scheme member who died before the age of 75.

In the first situation the Inheritance Tax would be calculated by reference to the estate of the original scheme member and not the estate of the relevant dependant. The tax would be paid by the administrators of the pension scheme, who would complete forms IHT100 *Inheritance Tax Account, chargeable event* and IHT100g *Alternatively Secured Pension chargeable event* to tell us about it.

In the second situation the value of the dependant's ASP fund will be aggregated with the value of the estate of the dependant and the tax payable will be apportioned between the personal representatives of the estate and the administrators of the pension scheme.

Schedule IHT411
Listed stocks and shares

Dividends and interest

Include in boxes 1 and 2 any dividends and interest on the assets that were due at the date of death, but have not yet been paid. More information on the different types of dividends payable and what to include can be found in 'How to value the assets' in this guide.

Unit trusts

When you are filling in Schedule IHT411, please enter the full name of the unit trust, for example, 'AXA Equity & Law Unit Trust Managers, Pacific Basin Trust Accumulation Units'.

Newspapers do not show dividends due on unit trusts. You will need to ask the fund managers what you should include as the declared dividend.

Personal Equity Plans (PEPs)

If the deceased owned a PEP you should obtain a valuation from the PEP managers. Enclose it with the Schedule and enter 'see attached valuation' on the appropriate part. Copy the value of the shares in the PEP to the appropriate column, but do not include any deductions for managers' fees. If you cannot obtain a valuation, list the shares held in the PEP on the form and value them in the same way as other shares. You must include a figure for any uninvested cash held in the PEP with the value for the shares.

Individual Savings Accounts (ISAs)

Only shares listed on a recognised stock exchange may be held in an ISA. If the deceased held any shares in an ISA, you should include those shares in box 2 on Schedule IHT411. List the shares on the Schedule and value them in the same way as other shares. You must include a figure for any uninvested cash held in the ISA, but do not include any other cash or insurance policies held in an ISA with the value for the shares.

Put cash held in an ISA in box 1 on Schedule IHT406 *Bank and building society accounts and National Savings & Investments.* Shares listed on a foreign stock exchange may also be held in an ISA. You should include foreign shares (other than those listed on the London Stock Exchange) on Schedule IHT417 *Foreign assets.*

Shares listed on these markets should be entered as follows:
- AIM, the Alternative Investment Market, include any shares on form IHT412 *Unlisted stocks and shares and control holdings.*
- NASDAQ, the National Association of Securities Dealers Automated quotations, include any shares on Schedule IHT417 *Foreign assets.*
- EASDAQ, the European Association of Securities Dealers Automated Quotations, include on Schedule IHT417 *Foreign assets.*
- OFEX, an unregulated trading facility for dealing in unquoted shares, include any shares in box 1 on Schedule IHT412 *Unlisted stocks and shares, and control holdings.*
- USM, the Unlisted Securities Market. This is only relevant if the deceased died before December 1996. Include any shares on Schedule IHT412 *Unlisted stocks and shares, and control holdings.*

31

| **UK Government and municipal securities** | 1 | This box should be used to list all UK Government and municipal securities, including: |

• Treasury Stock, Exchequer Stock, Convertible Stock, Consolidated Stock and Loan, Funding stock, Savings Bonds, Victory Bonds, War Loans
• Government Stock held on the Bank of England Register (previously held on the National Savings Register)
• cities or towns, dock, harbour and water boards, Port of London Authority, Agricultural Mortgage Corporation, Northern Ireland municipal stock.

All UK municipal securities, mortgages, debentures and stock in counties, cities or towns, dock, harbour and water boards, Port of London authority, Agricultural Mortgage Corporation and Northern Ireland municipal stock.

Listed stocks, shares and investments [2] All stocks, shares, debentures and other securities listed on the Stock Exchange Daily Official List should be listed in these boxes. These include:

• unit trusts
• investment trusts
• Open-Ended Investment Companies
• Personal Equity Plans
• shares held in an Individual Savings Account
• foreign shares listed on the London Stock Exchange.

Box 2 should be used for holdings of listed shares that did **not** give the deceased control of the company.

If the deceased held shares that gave them control of the company they should be shown on Schedule IHT412 *Unlisted stocks and shares and control holdings* and not here.

Schedule IHT412
Unlisted stocks and shares, and control holdings

Valuing unlisted shares

Information on how to value unlisted shares is given in 'How to value the assets' on page 66 of this guide.

We will usually ask HM Revenue & Customs, Shares and Assets Valuation to consider the value of unlisted shares; their Helpline phone number is **0115 974 2222**.

Traded unlisted stocks and shares [1] *and* [4] You should include the following shares in these boxes:

• shares listed on the Alternative Investment Market (AIM)
• shares traded on OFEX (an unregulated trading facility for dealing in unlisted shares).

Shares which **did not** give the deceased control of the company should be listed in box 1.

Shares which **did** give the deceased control of the company should be listed in box 4.

Unlisted stock, shares and investments   `2` *and* `3`

You should include the following shares in these boxes:
- unlisted shares and securities in private limited companies
- shares held in a Business Expansion Scheme (BES) or in a Business Start-up Scheme (BSS).

Shares which **did not** give the deceased control of the company should be listed in box 2.

Shares which **did** give the deceased control of the company should be listed in box 3.

Listed stocks, shares and investments that gave the deceased control of the company   `5`

You should include the following in this box. All stocks, shares, debentures and other securities listed on the Stock Exchange Daily Official List which gave the deceased control of the company.

Business relief

If you want to deduct business relief from unlisted stocks and shares, and control holdings of listed stocks and shares you should read the notes in this guide for Schedule IHT413 *Business and partnership interests and assets.*

Business relief and gifts of unlisted stocks and shares, and control holdings

For business relief to apply to a gift of unlisted stocks and shares, and control holdings the following additional special rules apply:
- the shares must have been owned by the person receiving the gift from the date of gift to the date the transferor died
- the share must not have been subject to a binding contract for sale at the date of death
- the shares would have qualified for business relief if the person receiving the gift had made a transfer of the shares at the date of death.

The last rule does not apply to control holdings of listed shares or unlisted shares which were unlisted at the date of gift and remained unlisted throughout the period between the gift and the death of the deceased (or death of the person who received the gift, if they died first).

Schedule IHT413
Business and partnership interests and assets

You must fill in Schedule 413 *Business and partnership interests and assets* if the deceased owned:
• a business or part of a business, or
• an asset used in a business and you are deducting business relief.

If necessary, complete a separate form for each business partnership or asset used in a business. For more information on business relief visit our website at **www.hmrc.gov.uk/inheritancetax/** or phone our Helpline on **0845 30 20 900**.

For business relief on shares use Schedule IHT412 *Unlisted stocks and shares, and control holdings* instead of Schedule IHT413.

When is business relief available

The relief is available for transfers of certain types of business, business assets and shares. The deceased must have owned the assets for a minimum period, generally two years, and the assets must also qualify under a number of other rules.

What is the rate of relief?

If the asset qualifies for relief, the rate at which relief is allowed is shown in the table on page 35. The relief is given by deducting the relevant percentage of the capital value of the asset.

If the asset qualifies for 100% relief, you should include the value of the asset in box 69 on form IHT400. You should deduct the relief using the same figure in box 93 on form IHT400.

34

Rate of relief table

Type of interest in the business	Date of death on or after 6 April 1996	Date of death between 10 March 1992 and 5 April 1996 inclusive	Date of death between 17 March 1987 and 9 March 1992 inclusive
Business or interest in a business	100%	100%	50%
Control holdings of shares in in an 'unlisted' company	100%	100%	50%
Substantial holdings of shares in an 'unlisted' company	100%	100%	50%
Other shares in an 'unlisted' company	100%	50%	30%
Control holding of shares in a 'listed' company	50%	50%	50%
Land, buildings or plant and machinery used in a business	50%	50%	30%
Land, buildings or plant and machinery held in a trust	50%	50%	30%

Definitions

Listed company
A company that is listed on a recognised stock exchange. This includes shares traded on the American NASDAQ and European EASDAQ for deaths after 9 March 1992.

Unlisted company
A company that is not listed on a recognised stock exchange. Some companies, although they are listed in the Stock Exchange Daily Official List, are still regarded as 'unlisted' when considering business relief. These include:
• shares listed on the Alternative Investment Market (AIM)
• shares listed on the Unlisted Securities Market (USM).
For shares listed on the USM, there are rules that apply to deaths before 10 March 1992. Please phone our Helpline if the deceased owned shares listed on the USM and the date of death, or date of gift, is before 10 March 1992.

Control holding
A holding of stocks and shares that gives a person control of a company. For Inheritance Tax a person controls a company if they can control the majority (more than 50%) of the voting powers on all questions affecting the company as a whole.

Substantial holding
A holding of stocks and shares that gives the owner more than 25% of the voting powers on all questions affecting the company as a whole.

35

311

Appendix 3

IHT400 Notes   *Guide to completing your Inheritance Tax account*

Used in a business
Land, buildings or plant and machinery will only qualify for business relief if it is used in a business in which the deceased was a partner at the date of death or if it was used by a company that was controlled by the deceased.

Held in trust
Land, buildings or plant and machinery held in trust will only qualify for business relief if the deceased had the right to benefit from the trust and the asset was used in a business carried on by the deceased.

Valuing a business

Information on how to value the businesses is given on page 70 of this guide.

Ownership, contract for sale and business interests details

`1` Ownership

If you have answered 'No' to this question, the deceased has not owned the assets for long enough to qualify for business relief. However, there are rules where business relief may still be available. These rules apply where:
• the deceased inherited the asset on death, or
• the asset has replaced other assets that qualified for business relief.
You can find more information about this in the customer guide at **www.hmrc.uk/inheritancetax/** or by phoning our Helpline.

`3` Contract for sale

If the business or business interest was subject to a binding contract for sale at the date of death, business relief will not normally be due unless either of the two conditions given at box 6 applies.

Business relief on lifetime gifts of business and partnership interests and assets

Complete this section if you are deducting business relief in connection with a lifetime gift as at the date of gift. You must answer each of the questions so we can decide if the relief is due.

On the form we refer to the period between the date of gift and the date the deceased died as the 'relevant period'.

You must consider whether, if the person who received the gift had made a transfer of the property at the date of death, the transfer would have qualified for business relief, known as a 'notional transfer'.

> **Note**
> If the conditions for both agricultural relief and business relief are met, agricultural relief is allowed in preference to business relief. Business relief is not allowed instead of, or in addition to, agricultural relief.

36

312

Schedule IHT414
Agricultural relief

When is agricultural relief available?

Agricultural relief is available for transfers of agricultural property and certain shareholdings in farming companies. There are three basic rules:

1 the property must be agricultural property
2 the deceased must have owned the property for a minimum number of years, and
3 the property must have been used for agricultural purposes.

What is agricultural relief?

For the purposes of agricultural relief, agricultural property is agricultural land or pasture in the UK, Channel Islands or the Isle of Man used in the growing of crops or intensive rearing of animals for food consumption. Buildings used for the intensive rearing of livestock or fish and woodlands are treated as agricultural property if their occupation is ancillary to the occupation of agricultural land or pasture.

It also includes any farmhouses, cottages or buildings that are of a 'character appropriate' to the property. This means that they must be proportionate in size and nature to the requirements of the farming activities conducted on the agricultural land or pasture in question.

What is the rate of relief?

The relief is calculated by deducting the relevant percentage of the capital value of the asset. So, if the property qualifies for 100% relief, you should include the value of the assets in box 68 on form IHT400. You should deduct the relief using the same figure in box 93.

	Date of death on or after 10 March 1992
Land with vacant possession	100%
Land that is let	50%
Land that was let after 31 August 1995	100%

There are some circumstances where the higher rate of relief can apply to land that is let.

It is possible that the relief may be available at the higher rate if the land was subject to a tenancy that began before 10 March 1981. There are three other conditions that apply. They are that:

- the deceased has owned the land since 10 March 1981
- the land would have qualified for full agricultural relief under the law at that date, and
- the deceased did not have and could not have had the right to vacant possession between 10 March 1981 and the date of death.

Give full details of the reasons why you think this applies in this case in the 'Any other information' box on page 4.

37

313

Appendix 3

> **Note**
> If the conditions for both agricultural relief and business relief are met, agricultural relief is allowed in preference to business relief. Business relief is not allowed instead of, or in addition to, agricultural relief.

The rules on agricultural relief are complicated and you can find more information in our customer guide at **www.hmrc.gov.uk/inheritancetax/**

Binding contract for sale   `3`   If, before the deceased died, all or part of the property was subject to a binding contract for sale where contracts have been exchanged (or in Scotland, when missives have been concluded) but the sale had not been completed, agricultural relief will not be due. You should give details of the sale, and clearly identify the part of the property that was sold on the plan you supply.

Use of agricultural land   `5`   Describe the agricultural activities carried out by each occupier. State whether it was:
- an arable, pastoral or mixed farm
- the type of crops usually grown, and
- the type of livestock that grazed the land.

If a variety of livestock grazed the land, give us some idea about the number of animals and acreage used by each type.

Tell us if the agricultural activity stopped at any time. State when this happened and why. Agricultural relief may still be due if the property was managed under an agro-environmental or habitat scheme arrangement.

`6`   Describe the agricultural activities carried out by the deceased. State whether it was:
- an arable, pastoral or mixed farm
- the type of crops usually grown, and
- the type of livestock that grazed the land.

If a variety of livestock grazed the land, give us some idea about the number of animals and acreage used by each type.

If the deceased granted a grazing licence or grasskeep (conacre in Northern Ireland), provide a copy of the licence if there is one, or give full details of the grazing licence in box 5.

You should also tell us if the deceased left the property or stopped the agricultural activity. State when this happened and why. Agricultural relief may still be due if the property was managed under an agro-environmental or habitat scheme arrangement.

Farmhouses and cottages   `12` *to* `15`   We need full details of all the houses and cottages from which you are deducting agricultural relief. If you need more space, please download or photocopy extra copies of page 3 of Schedule IHT414.

Agricultural relief and lifetime transfers [17 to 20]

If you are claiming agricultural relief on a gift you must answer questions 17 to 20 to help us decide if the relief is due.

Schedule IHT418
Assets held in trust

Deceased's interest in possession

You must complete Schedule IHT418 if the deceased had an interest in possession and the trust is one of the following.

- A trust that was set up before 22 March 2006 from which the deceased was entitled to benefit.
- An immediate post-death interest.
- A disabled person's interest.
- A transitional serial interest.

All these interests are explained at pages 15 and 16 of these notes.

Foreign trusts

If the deceased had a right to benefit from settled property where the assets are overseas, and the person who set up the trust was domiciled outside the UK when the trust was created, please answer questions 2 to 5 only.

Who should tell us about a trust?

The trustees of the trust must give us full details of assets and liabilities that make up the trust and who must pay any Inheritance Tax that is due.

However, we need to know the total net value of settled property to be included in the estate so that we can work out the total tax that is due. In certain circumstances the trustees will pay the tax at the same time as you apply for a grant. This may happen where the trustees and the personal representatives are the same people.

If this applies here, please supply full details of all the assets and liabilities on the form and send us a copy of the deed of trust. If the trustees and the personal representatives are the same people and you give us details of the settled property, we may ask for a formal account to be completed and signed by the trustees. We will only do this in exceptional circumstances.

If the trustees and the personal representatives are different people or if you have only been able to give brief details on the form, we will ask the trustees to complete a separate account.

Assets in the trust

If you have full details of the assets held in trust you can give us those details at boxes 8 and 13. If you need more space to list the assets, you can use the 'Any other information' box on page 4 of Schedule IHT418. Liabilities that relate to the assets can be shown in boxes 9 and 14. See page 72 of this guide for information about exemptions and reliefs.

39

315

How to value assets held in trust

The rules for valuing settled property are the same as the rules for valuing assets owned by the deceased. For more information on valuing assets see pages 65 to 71 of this guide.

Insurance policies held on trust

You should make sure that under the terms of the policy the deceased's interest is one of the interests where the value of the trust should be included as part of their estate for Inheritance Tax purposes. If this is the case, tell us:

• the names and addresses of the trustees, and
• the value of the deceased's interest in the policy.

Please attach a copy of the policy.

Future right to assets in a trust

19 to 23

The deceased may have been entitled to some assets in a trust but someone else is receiving the benefit from them during that person's life. The deceased's estate will not receive the assets until after the other person has died. This is also known as a 'reversionary interest' or an 'interest in expectancy'. Tax will only be due on this future right in rare circumstances and you should answer question 20 to see if the value should be included in form IHT400 or not.

Schedule IHT420
National Heritage assets

Heritage exemption

Please complete Schedule IHT420 *National Heritage assets* if:
• you are aware that the trustees intend to claim heritage exemption, or
• any asset of the trust has at any previous time benefited from either
  – heritage exemption, or
  – an approved maintenance fund.

Transfers of assets that form part of the country's national heritage may be conditionally exempt from Inheritance Tax.

Inheritance Tax is not paid when the asset passes to a new owner on death or by way of a gift. To qualify for the exemption the new owner must agree to look after the item, allow public access to it and, if it is moveable, keep it in the UK. But it is only a conditional exemption. If the new owner does not keep to the agreement, the exemption is withdrawn and tax is payable. Tax is also payable if the item is sold.

What items qualify for conditional exemption?

A wide range of heritage assets may qualify for the exemption.

- Outstanding historical buildings, estates and parklands and works of art, furnishings, sculptures, for example, linked to these or to other historical buildings.
- Buildings of outstanding architectural interest.
- Land of outstanding historical interest or of outstanding natural beauty or with spectacular views including woodlands, heathland etc.
- Land of outstanding scientific interest including special areas for the conservation of wildlife, plants and trees.
- Paintings, portraits, drawings, watercolours, furniture, sculptures, books, manuscripts, ceramics etc., of artistic, historic or scientific interest in their own right.

Who decides what items qualify?

HM Revenue & Customs decides if an item qualifies for conditional exemption with assistance and advice from the Government's heritage advisory agencies.

- English Heritage (for historic land, buildings and their contents in England).
- Natural England (scenic land in England).
- English Nature (land of special scientific interest in England).
- Historic Scotland (for historic buildings and land in Scotland).
- Scottish Natural Heritage (for scenic land and land of special scientific interest in Scotland).
- Cadw: Welsh Historic Monuments (for buildings in Wales).
- Countryside Council for Wales (for land in Wales).
- Environment and Heritage Service (for land and buildings in Northern Ireland).
- Forestry Commission (for woodland areas).
- Museums, Libraries and Archives Council (MLA) for paintings, portraits, drawings, watercolours, furniture, sculptures, books, manuscripts of artistic, historic or scientific interest in their own right.

Offers in lieu of Inheritance Tax

You can offer to pay some or all of the tax and interest for which you are liable by transferring national heritage assets to the Crown. The rules are complicated. In particular, we cannot accept assets from you before you have taken out a grant of representation. If we do accept a transfer of assets as payment of tax we will repay any overpaid tax to you.

1.   You should use Schedule IHT420 *National heritage assets*, to give details of the assets on which you wish to claim conditional exemption. After you have submitted form IHT400 our Heritage Team will ask you for further information about your claim.

2.   Some assets will already be benefiting from conditional exemption when the transfer on death or gift occurs. Please provide as much information as possible about the earlier claim so that we can trace our files.

Appendix 3

| 3 | Provide details of the assets you wish to transfer in lieu of tax. The value of these assets must also be included in the IHT400 and the Inheritance Tax paid on delivery of the IHT400. If we accept your offer of assets in lieu of tax and, as a result, you have overpaid the tax, we will repay any overpaid tax to you.
Our Heritage team will contact you for further details of the assets when you have submitted form IHT400. |

Where can I get more information?

If you want more information on heritage assets, conditional exemption or offers in lieu you can look at our website **www.hmrc.gov.uk/inheritancetax/** or speak to someone in our Heritage Team by phoning the Probate and Inheritance Tax Helpline on **0845 30 20 900** and asking to be put through to the Heritage Team.

42

318

Filling in form IHT400 (pages 6 to 16) — estate in the UK

Assets on which tax may or may not be paid by instalments

You must fill in pages 6 to 10 with details of all the deceased's assets and liabilities. These pages are divided into two columns labelled column A and column B. The Inheritance Tax on all assets shown in column A must be paid before you can get a grant of representation (or Confirmation in Scotland). The Inheritance Tax on assets in column B may be paid in 10 annual instalments (that is, one instalment each year for 10 years) provided that the assets concerned have not been sold. You will have to pay interest on the instalments.

After you have filled in pages 6 to 10 you will be able to decide, at box 110, if you wish to pay the tax on the assets in column B by instalments.

Jointly owned assets, page 6

 49 *and* **50**

You must include the value of the deceased's share of all jointly owned assets in boxes 49 and 50. You will also need to give full details of these on Schedule IHT404. There is more information about jointly owned assets on page 23 of this guide.

You must include the value of all the assets described in questions 51 to 76 that were owned in the UK by the deceased in their own name when they died.

Assets owned outright by the deceased, pages 6 and 7

51   **Deceased's residence (except farmhouses and jointly owned houses)**
Include the value of the deceased's home.

If the deceased's home is a farmhouse on which you are deducting agricultural relief, do not include it here. Include it at box 68 instead. If the deceased had moved to a nursing or other residential home before they died and their home was vacant, include the value of the house here and not box 70. If the deceased's residence was let at the date of death, include it at box 70 and not at box 51.

You must also fill in Schedule IHT405 *Houses, land, buildings and interests in land* giving full details of the deceased's home if it was let, or a farmhouse. If the deceased's residence was jointly owned include it in box 49 and fill in IHT404 *Jointly owned assets.*

43

319

Appendix 3

52 **Bank and building society accounts**

List each account or investment on Schedule IHT406 *Bank and building society accounts and National Savings & Investments* (or form C1 *Inventory* in Scotland) and include in this box the total for:

- current, deposit, high interest, fixed interest, term, bond and money market accounts with a bank, building society, mutual, friendly or co-operative society
- accounts with supermarkets or insurance companies
- National Savings Bank accounts
- TESSA accounts
- cash in an Individual Savings Account (ISA).

How to value bank and building society accounts

The bank or building society will be able to tell you how much was in each account when the deceased died and how much interest was due, but not paid, up to the date of death. If you have separate figures for capital and interest, please add them together on Schedule IHT406. Business bank accounts should not be entered on Schedule IHT406 *Bank and building society accounts*, they should be included on page 7 of the IHT400 and Schedule IHT413 *Business and partnership interests and assets*.

53 **Cash**

Include in this box:

- any cash held by the deceased or kept at home or elsewhere such as safe deposit boxes
- cash held for the deceased by someone else, for example, a stockbroker
- traveller's cheques
- any uncashed cheques made out to the deceased.

Sterling traveller's cheques should be included at face value. If the traveller's cheques are in one of the major foreign currencies, convert them to sterling using the closing mid-price at the date of death. You can find currency conversions in the financial pages of a daily newspaper or you may also find this information on the Internet.

54 **Premium Bonds and National Savings & Investments products**

List each investment separately on Schedule IHT406 *Bank and building society accounts and National Savings & Investments* (or form C1 *Inventory* in Scotland) and include in this box the total for items such as:

- Premium Bonds, including any unclaimed or uncashed prizes
- National Savings Certificates
- National Savings Capital or Deposit bonds
- National Savings Income bonds
- Pensioners Guaranteed Income bonds
- Children's Bonus bonds
- First Option bonds
- Save As You Earn contracts
- Year Plans.

44

320

You can find out the value of all National Savings investments by sending off form NSA 904. You can get this form from the Post Office. If the reply gives separate figures for capital and for interest owed, but not paid, up to the date of death, please add them together on form IHT406.

| 55 | **Household and personal goods** |

Enter in box 55 the total value of all household goods and personal possessions which have been listed on Schedule IHT407 *Household and personal goods* and copy the figure from box 6 on that Schedule into box 55 on form IHT400.

| 56 | **Pensions** |

Enter in box 56 the total of the figures in boxes 7 and 15 of Schedule IHT409 *Pensions*, plus the value of any pension arrears due to the deceased from the last monthly payments to the date of death.

| 57 | **Life assurance and mortgage protection policies** |

Enter in box 57 the total amount payable:

- from life assurance policies, including bonuses
- under mortgage protection policies (you can find out more about joint mortgage protection policies on page 24 of this guide)
- under unit-linked investment schemes that pay 101% of the unit value on death
- under investment or re-investment plans, bonds or contracts with a financial services provider that pay out on death
- for the value of the deceased's interest in joint life insurance policies under which the deceased was one of the lives insured, but that remain in force after the death
- for the value of insurance policies on the life of another person but under which the deceased was to benefit
- from insurance policies that are part of an Individual Savings Account
- under private medical insurance to cover hospital or other health charges incurred before death.

Fill in Schedule IHT410 *Life assurance and annuities* to give details of each insurance policy.

| 62 | **UK Government and municipal securities** |

Enter in box 62 the total value for:

- Treasury Stock, Exchequer Stock, Convertible Stock, Consolidated Stock and Loan, Funding stock, Savings Bonds, Victory Bonds, War Loans
- Government Stock held on the Bank of England Register (previously held on the National Savings Register)
- cities or towns, dock, harbour and water boards, Port of London Authority, Agricultural Mortgage Corporation, Northern Ireland municipal stock.

Fill in Schedule IHT411 to give details of each investment. Copy the figure from box 1 of that schedule to box 62, IHT400.

45

321

Appendix 3

63 **Listed stocks, shares and investments**

Enter in box 63 the total value for:

- all stocks, shares, debentures and other securities listed in the Stock Exchange Daily Official List
- unit trusts
- investment trusts
- Open-ended Investment Companies
- Personal Equity Plans (PEPs)
- shares that are part of an Individual Savings Account (ISA)
- foreign shares that are listed on the London Stock Exchange.

Do not include listed shares that gave the deceased control of the company. Include those at box 67 instead.

There is guidance about how to value stocks and shares on page 65 of this guide.

You will also need to fill in Schedule IHT411 *Listed stocks and shares* listing all the deceased's stocks, shares and investments. Copy the figure from box 2 of that Schedule to box 63 on form IHT400.

64 **Dividends or interest on stocks, shares and securities**

Enter in box 64 the total value of dividends and interest on assets in boxes 62, 63, 65, 66 and 67 due at the date of death but which had not yet been paid.

65 **Traded unlisted and unlisted shares except control holdings**

Where a company is not listed on the UK Stock Exchange, any foreign recognised Stock Exchange or alternative market, its shares and securities are classified as unlisted.

Enter in box 65 the total value of:

- unlisted stocks and shares in private limited companies
- shares held in a Business Expansion Scheme (BES) or in a Business Start-up Scheme (BSS)

on which the deceased did not have control of the company.

Include the stocks and shares on IHT412 *Unlisted stocks and shares, and control holdings.*

66 You may pay the tax on some traded unlisted and unlisted shares by instalments but this will be very rare. See the notes on form IHT412 about paying tax by instalments.

67 **Control holdings of unlisted, traded unlisted and listed shares**

Include in this box the total value for:

- shares listed on the Alternative Investment Market (AIM)
- shares traded on OFEX

on which the deceased had control of the company.

Include the stocks and shares on IHT412 *Unlisted stocks and shares, and control holdings.*

46

322

68 **Farms, farmhouses and farmland**

Include in this box the total value of farms, farmhouses and farmland on which you are deducting agricultural relief.

You must also fill in Schedule IHT405 *Houses, land, buildings and interests in land* giving full details of the farms, farmhouses and farmland and Schedule IHT414 *Agricultural relief* to deduct agricultural relief.

69 **Businesses including farm businesses, business assets and timber**

Include the net value of the deceased's interest in box 69. If the deceased took part in more than one business, you may need to fill in a separate Schedule IHT413 *Business and partnership interests and assets* for each business or partnership. Enter the total value of all the businesses in the appropriate box.

Farm business

Include in this box any assets that the deceased owned and were still used by the deceased for farming business activities.

Business property

Include the value of any property owned by the deceased from which they ran a business, either alone or in partnership, (for example, a hotel, a shop, or a factory). If it was a farming business, include the value of the property in box 68.

Interest in a business

Include the net value of the deceased's interest in a business or a farming business. If the deceased was in partnership, enter the value in box 69.

If the deceased took part in more than one business, you may need to fill in a separate Schedule IHT413 *Business and partnership interests and assets* for each business interest.

Interest in the partnership

Include the net value of the deceased's interest in a partnership. If the deceased took part in more than one partnership, you may need to fill in a separate Schedule IHT413 *Business and partnership interests and assets* for each partnership interest.

Business assets

Include here the value of any assets that the deceased owned and were used by the deceased for business activities.

Timber and woodland

Include the value of any timber and woodland owned by the deceased that is not part of a farm. Most farms will include coppices, small woods and belts of trees that shelter the land. Include these with the value for the farm in box 68.

70 **Other land, buildings and rights over land**

Include in this box the value of any other land, buildings or rights over land not included in boxes elsewhere.

These may include:
- rental properties
- lock-up garages

Appendix 3

- redundant land
- derelict property
- quarries
- airfields
- fishing or other rights attached to land.

Fill in Schedule IHT405 *Houses, land, buildings and interests in land* with details of the land or property.

71 and 72 **Interest in another estate**

The deceased may have had the right to a legacy or share of an estate of someone who died before them. If the deceased died before receiving the full legacy or share from that estate, include a value in this box for the assets that they still have to receive. You will need to fill in Schedule IHT415 *Interest in another estate* to give details of this interest.

73 **Debts due to the estate**

Enter the total value of:
- money that the deceased had lent personally to someone and which had not been repaid at the date of death
- money which the deceased had lent to trustees linked to a life assurance policy held in trust
- money for which the deceased held a promissory note
- money for which the deceased held an 'IOU'
- money owing to the deceased from a director's loan account or current account with a company.

You will need to fill in Schedule IHT416 *Debts due to the estate* to give details of each sum owed to the deceased.

Debts due to deceased and secured by mortgage

Enter the total amount of money the deceased had lent to someone that was secured by a mortgage and had not been repaid at the date of death. You will need to fill in Schedule IHT416 *Debts due to the estate* giving details of each mortgage.

74 **Income Tax or Capital Gains Tax repayment**

Enter in box 74 the total amount any Income Tax or Capital Gains Tax actually repaid to the estate or a reasonable estimate of any sum that might be repayable to the deceased. An Income Tax repayment may be due if the deceased died early in the tax year and received a pension and other income where tax was deducted at source.

75 **Trust income due to the deceased**

Enter in this box income due to the deceased from a trust. This could be income that the trustees had received but not paid to the deceased or income that had accrued, but not been paid to the trustees.

For the purposes of answering this question it does not matter whether or not the value of the trust property is to be treated as part of the deceased's estate for Inheritance Tax purposes. The trustees of the trust should be able to tell you the figure to include in box 75.

76 **Other assets and income due to the deceased**

Enter in box 76 the total value of any other assets not listed in boxes 49 to 75 or income due to the deceased not paid at the date of death. Include here the gross amount of any rent from let property that was due to the deceased. Include the property itself separately on Schedule IHT405 *Houses, land, buildings and interests in land.*

Other assets and income

Enter the total amount of:

- money owed in salary, wages or director's fees
- benefits (other than arrears of pension) due but unclaimed from the Department for Work and Pensions. (Include arrears of pension in box 56.)
- any refunds from gas, electricity or water suppliers
- any insurance premium or licence refunds
- lump sums payable to the estate from an annuity, pension scheme or policy
- money due to the deceased from the sale of real and leasehold property where the contract for sale had been exchanged before the death but the sale had not been completed by the time the deceased died
- any other assets not included elsewhere.

Deductions from the estate incurred up to the date of death, pages 8 and 9

80 **Mortgages and secured loans**

Include in this box any money that was secured by a mortgage on the buildings or land shown on pages 6 and 7. If the same mortgage was secured on property in two or more of boxes 49 to 71, and at the same time an exemption or relief is due, that mortgage will have to be apportioned between the properties. Also, in the rare instance where there is only one property within the categories described by boxes 49 to 71, but part of that property is used wholly or mainly for business purposes and part is not, then the mortgage should normally be apportioned between the part of the property used for the business and the part that is not.

If the deceased had a mortgage protection policy, include the mortgage in box 80 and include the money due to the estate from the policy in box 57.

81 **Funeral expenses**

You may deduct funeral costs and reasonable mourning expenses. You may also deduct the cost of a headstone or tombstone marking the site of the deceased's grave.

These expenses may also include a reasonable amount to cover the cost of:

- flowers
- refreshments provided for the mourners after the service
- necessary expenses incurred by the executor or administrator in arranging the funeral.

Use the space provided to give details of other costs that are being deducted.

49

82 **Other liabilities**

Only include debts that the deceased actually owed at the date they died. You must not include fees for professional services carried out after death unless the fees were incurred in obtaining a refund of Income Tax or Capital Gains Tax and the refund is shown as an asset of the estate in box 74. This means that probate fees, any solicitor's or estate agent's fees and any valuation fees incurred in dealing with the deceased's estate cannot be deducted.

List all the debts owed by the deceased at the date they died. Fill in the name of the person or organisation that is owed the money and say briefly why the money is owed. If you include a deduction for solicitor's or accountant's fees, give the dates for the period during which the work was done. Add up the liabilities and enter the total in this box.

Loans

Fill in Schedule IHT419 *Debts owed by the deceased* to give details of any loans made to the deceased.

Uncleared cheques

If you include cheques written by the deceased, but which had not cleared before they died, please say who the cheques were written out to and for what goods or services. Uncleared cheques that were written by the deceased as gifts cannot be deducted as liabilities of the estate.

Money being repaid

Fill in Schedule IHT419 *Debts owed by the deceased* to give details about money being repaid to relatives.

Guarantee debts

Fill in Schedule IHT419 *Debts owed by the deceased* to give details about any guarantee debts.

Dealing with a deficit, page 9

85
and
86

If the figure in box 85 or box 86 is a minus figure (because the liabilities on the assets in column A or column B were greater than the value of the assets) you can deal with the deficit as follows:

- if the figure in box 85 is a minus, write '0' in box 85 and deduct the deficit at box 88
- if the figure in box 86 is a minus, write '0' in box 86 and deduct the deficit at box 87
- if the figure at box 89 or box 90 is a minus, write '0' in box 89 or 90 and deduct the deficit from the foreign property (if there is any) by adding the deficit to the liabilities in box 2 on Schedule IHT417 *Foreign Assets*
- if the foreign property is also a deficit, write '0' in box 3 on Schedule IHT417.

Exemptions and reliefs, page 9

92 **Exemptions and reliefs deducted from assets in column A**

You can find more information about exemptions and reliefs on page 72 of this guide. Most exemptions and reliefs apply to particular assets. So the amount of the exemption or relief is limited to the value of the asset after any liabilities have been taken away. Enter here the exemption or relief to be deducted from the assets included in column A of pages 6 and 7.

50

326

Some exemptions, for example, charity exemption, may apply to the estate as a whole. Where this applies, apportion the relief between the assets concerned, irrespective of how the legacy will be funded, so a proportion of the relief may apply to the assets in column A and the other part to the assets in column B.

Estate Duty paid on death of spouse

If the deceased had the right to benefit from a trust set up by the Will or intestacy of a spouse or former spouse who died before 13 November 1974, the capital value is left out of the account if Estate Duty was paid or was treated as paid on the earlier death in respect of those assets and the deceased was 'not competent to dispose' of the assets. For example, if the deceased was given the power to say how the settled property should be dealt with either during their lifetime or on their death, they would be competent to dispose of the assets and the exclusion would not apply.

Excluded property

If the deceased was domiciled outside the UK and was not resident or ordinarily resident in the UK when they died, foreign currency bank accounts held with certain banks in the UK are 'excluded property'. A foreign currency account with any 'High Street' bank, such as Barclays or Royal Bank of Scotland will qualify. Foreign currency accounts with other banks such as:

- ANZ Grindlays Bank Plc
- Banque Nationale de Paris Plc
- Italian International Bank Plc
- Wesleyan Savings Bank Plc

will also qualify. Phone our Helpline if you need to check whether or not a foreign currency account qualifies as 'excluded property'. Include the bank accounts in box 52 of form IHT400, but deduct the value in box 92.

If the deceased was not ordinarily resident in the UK when they died, all UK Government securities issued after 29 April 1996, for example, 9% Conversion Stock 2011 or 6$^1/_4$% Treasury Stock 2010, are excluded property. Include the securities in box 62 of form IHT400, but deduct the value in box 92.

If you are making a deduction for excluded property from the assets in a trust, any apportioned income included in box 74 is also exempt. However, the exemption does not apply to any accrued income that had not been paid to the deceased and is included in box 74.

Exemptions and reliefs, page 10

93 **Exemptions and reliefs deducted from the assets in column B**
Most exemptions and reliefs apply to particular assets. So the amount of the exemption or relief is limited to the value of the asset after any liabilities have been taken away. Enter here the exemption or relief to be deducted from the assets included in column B of pages 6 and 7.

51

327

Some exemptions, for example, charity exemption, may apply to the estate as a whole. Where this applies, apportion the relief between the assets concerned, irrespective of how the legacy will be funded, so a proportion of the relief may apply to the assets in column A and the other part to the assets in column B.

If you are deducting business or agricultural relief from an asset, you also need to fill in Schedule IHT413 *Business or partnership interests and assets* or Schedule IHT414 *Agricultural relief* as appropriate.

Other assets taken into account to calculate the tax, page 10

Include in the boxes on page 10 all the other assets which need to be taken into account in order to calculate the Inheritance Tax.

99 and 100

Assets held in trust on which the trustees would like to pay the tax now
The trustees of a trust in which the deceased was entitled to a benefit may choose to pay the tax on that trust at the same time as the tax is paid on the deceased's estate. If that is the case, enter in boxes 99 or 100 the value of the assets held in the trust on which the tax is being paid now. See page 15 of this guide for more information on trusts.

101

Nominated assets
If the deceased, during their lifetime, gave written instructions (usually called a 'nomination') that an asset was to pass to a particular person, we call that a nominated asset. This does not include legacies in a Will or a 'letter of wishes' found with the Will. Enter here the value of any assets that pass in this way.

Use the 'Additional information' pages on form IHT400 to give a description of the nominated assets and the name of the person who is to receive the assets.

105

Assets held in trust on which the trustees are not paying the tax now
If the trustees are going to pay the tax due on the trust separately, enter here the value of the assets in trust. The value of the trust assets have to be added to the total value of the estate in order to work out the total Inheritance Tax due, but the trustees will be sent a separate calculation of the tax due on the trust.

Working out the Inheritance Tax, page 11

If there is no Inheritance Tax to pay, you do not need to fill in page 11.

If you are filling in form IHT400 without the help of a solicitor or other adviser you do not need to work out the tax due yourself, we can do it for you. But you do need to decide if you wish to pay some of the tax by instalments, if there are any assets in the estate shown in column B on pages 6 and 7.

Read the following information about paying Inheritance Tax by instalments and then answer question 110.

52

Paying Inheritance Tax by instalments

What are payments of Inheritance Tax by instalments?

Inheritance Tax due on certain assets may be paid by 10 annual instalments, that is, one instalment per year for 10 years.

Interest will normally be payable on each instalment.

On what type of assets can I pay by instalments?
You may pay by instalments on unsold:

- land and buildings
- certain shares and securities
- the net value of a business or an interest in a business (after any business relief has been deducted)
- timber.

The most common asset on which you may pay the tax by instalments is the deceased's house.

The IHT400 lists the assets on which tax may **not** be paid by instalments in **column A** on pages 6 and 7 and assets on which tax may be paid by instalments in **column B** on pages 6 and 7.

Do I have to pay by instalments on assets on which instalments are available?

No. You can choose to pay all of the tax on delivery of form IHT400, if you wish.

We will ask you whether or not you wish to pay by instalments at box 110.

Some of the Schedules are divided into assets on which tax may **not** be paid by instalments and assets on which tax may be paid by instalments. You will then have copied the figures from the Schedules on to the form IHT400 into the correct columns.

On what type of shares can I pay the tax by instalments?
You may pay Inheritance Tax by instalments on shares or securities in a company if:

- they gave the deceased control of the company at the time of the transfer
- they are unlisted, and
  - you can show that the Inheritance Tax on their value could not be paid in one sum without undue hardship, or
  - at least 20% of the tax for which the same person is liable, in the same capacity, is on assets (including the shares in question) that qualify for payment by instalments
- they are unlisted shares and their value is more than £20,000 and the shares represent at least 10% of the nominal value of the company's shares.

These shares are shown in boxes 66 and 67 of the IHT400, not boxes 62, 63 or 65.

Appendix 3

Interest-free instalments

Interest is usually payable on instalments of Inheritance Tax, but there are a few assets which qualify for interest relief. They are:

- agricultural property that qualifies for agricultural relief
- shares, securities, businesses or interests in businesses
- woodlands, where there is an Inheritance Tax charge on disposal.

Each instalment of Inheritance Tax on these assets is interest free if it is paid before the due date. If it is paid after the due date, interest will be charged from the due date to the date of payment.

`110` If you do not want to work out the tax yourself, indicate in box 110 the total value of the assets shown in column B on pages 6 and 7 which are unsold and on which you wish to pay the tax by instalments. If there are no assets on which you wish to pay the tax by instalments, enter '0' in box 110 next to the '£' sign. If you are working out the tax yourself you will be asked on form IHT400 *Calculation* on which assets you are paying the tax by instalments.

Simple Inheritance Tax calculation

`111`
to
`117`

If the estate is straightforward and you want to pay all of the tax now, you may be able to use page 11 to work out the tax. Read the paragraph above box 111 to see if the simple calculation will work for you. If the simple calculation does not work for you, go to the form IHT400 *Calculation* to work out the tax now, then continue with this form from box 118.

Direct Payment Scheme

`118` There is a Direct Payment Scheme for bank and building society accounts. Under the Direct Payment Scheme participating banks and building societies will release funds from the deceased's accounts direct to HM Revenue & Customs to pay Inheritance Tax. The accounts in question must be in the deceased's sole name, so you cannot use joint accounts for this method of payment.

Many banks and building societies are part of this scheme, but you should check with the deceased's bank or building society before going any further.

If you wish to use this scheme you should identify yourself to the banks or building societies to which you expect to give instructions to transfer money and prove that you are an appropriate personal representative. Contact each organisation to find out what their requirements are for you to do this. We recommend that you do this well before you intend to apply for a grant of representation to avoid unnecessary delays later on.

You should fill in a form IHT423 *Direct Payment Scheme bank or building society account* for each bank or building society that will be making the transfer of funds. Then you should send form(s) IHT423 to the banks or building societies that will be making the transfers at the same time that you send the forms IHT400 and IHT421 *Probate summary* to our Nottingham office if you are taking out a grant in England, Wales or Northern Ireland, or our Edinburgh office if you are taking out a grant in Scotland.

The banks or building societies will transfer the money to us. They will be able to tell you how long it will normally take them to make the transfer. Once we receive notification of the payment, we will link the payment to your IHT400 and provided all is in order, we will stamp and issue form IHT421 *Probate summary*.

Declaration,
page 12

[119] All the people who will be named on the grant as executors or administrators must now carefully read the declarations and warnings on page 12.

Tick the boxes to say which type of grant you are applying for and which Schedules you are including.

Provisional estimates

List any values you have included in the form which are provisional. If you have included provisional estimates in form IHT400 or on any of the Schedules, it is your responsibility to tell us what the final figures are as soon as you know them.

Signatures

Each person should give their full name and address, sign and date the form in the spaces provided on page 13.

In signing the form, each person confirms that they have read the declaration and warnings and that they agree that the information given in form IHT400, the Schedules and any other supporting papers is correct.

Changes to the estate

If the value of any asset or debt changes, you must tell us; give our reference if you can, otherwise tell us the full name and date of death of the deceased. It is only necessary to tell us of changes which affect the tax payable. If the estate is exempt because it passes to the deceased's spouse or civil partner, it is only necessary to tell us about changes which result in Inheritance Tax being payable.

What to do after you have filled in form IHT400

Form IHT421
Probate summary
— England, Wales and
Northern Ireland

If you are applying for a grant in England, Wales or Northern Ireland, fill in form IHT421 *Probate summary*. It tells the Probate Registry what values you have included on form IHT400. The Probate Registry needs this information before it can issue a grant. Fill in form IHT421 after you have filled in and signed form IHT400.

Form C1 *Inventory*
— Scotland

If you are applying for a grant of Confirmation in Scotland, fill in form C1 *Inventory*. The Sheriff Court needs the form before it can issue a grant.

55

331

Appendix 3

When you have filled in and signed all the forms

When you have filled in and signed form IHT400 and filled in any Schedules, including form IHT421 or form C1, use the checklist on page 14 of the IHT400 to make sure that you have got all the papers that you need to send to us. Then follow the notes on the following pages that apply to you.

When you must send us form IHT400 before doing anything else

There are two situations when form IHT400, all the completed Schedules and any other supporting documents must be sent to HMRC Inheritance Tax before you go any further. These are if:

- you have answered question 6 on page 1 of the form to say that the deceased died domiciled outside the UK, or if the deceased was only treated as domiciled in the UK (if there is any tax to pay and you have calculated the tax yourself, please include your payment as well)
- the grant is needed for land that was settled property before the deceased's death and that remains settled property after the death.

Which office to use?

Our addresses are given at the back of this guide. We tell you which office to contact below. When we have checked the papers, we will tell you what to do next.

Which procedure should I follow?

When you have applied for a grant, or if you need to send the forms to us before you can apply for the grant, you should send the papers to our:

- **Nottingham office**, if you applying for a grant in England, Wales or Northern Ireland.
- **Edinburgh office**, if you are applying for Confirmation in Scotland.

Where do I get information about Probate?

Phone the Probate and Inheritance Tax Helpline on **0845 30 20 900** for forms and advice on probate.

What if I want you to work out the tax for me?

There are different procedures to follow depending on whether you are applying for a grant in England and Wales, Northern Ireland, or Scotland. Please follow the steps on the flowchart, on pages 60, 61 or 62, that applies to you .

What happens when I get a grant?

When you have got the grant, it does not mean that you have paid all the Inheritance Tax and interest on the estate. If you sent us the form before the grant, we look at the details you have given and if there are no obvious errors, we will accept the tax that you have shown us is due.

The Inheritance Tax on the estate may change

Once we have returned form IHT421 *Probate summary* or form C1 *Inventory* we will look at form IHT400 in more detail. We may ask you questions to help us understand what you have said on the form and any Schedules. We may discuss the value of any assets in the estate and question whether any debts are properly deducted. We will look carefully at any deduction for exemptions, reliefs and exclusions you have made.

We may also send you statements that show you the tax and interest you must pay, particularly if you have said that you wish to pay some of the tax by instalments.

Provisional estimates

If you have included provisional estimates in form IHT400 or on any of the Schedules, it is your responsibility to tell us what the final figures are as soon as you know them.

You must tell us about other changes to the estate

If the value of any assets or debt changes and as a result the amount of Inheritance Tax due changes you must tell us. You can help us by giving us our reference if you can. Otherwise tell us the full name and date of death of the deceased.

IHT400 Notes   *Guide to completing your Inheritance Tax account*

Applying for a grant in England and Wales – if you are a taxpayer or solicitor working out the tax

You will need an Inheritance Tax reference number (see page 10). If you wish to use the IHT Direct Payment Scheme (DPS), find out whether the deceased's bank and/or building society is part of the scheme and if so make sure you have complied with their requirements.

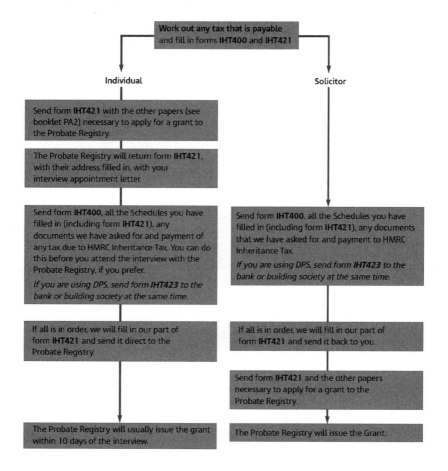

Applying for a grant in Scotland – if you are a taxpayer or solicitor working out the tax

You will need an Inheritance Tax reference number (see page 10). If you wish to use the IHT Direct Payment Scheme (DPS), find out whether the deceased's bank and/or building society is part of the scheme and if so make sure you have complied with their requirements.

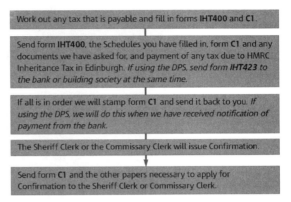

Work out any tax that is payable and fill in forms **IHT400** and **C1**.

Send form **IHT400**, the Schedules you have filled in, form **C1** and any documents we have asked for, and payment of any tax due to HMRC Inheritance Tax in Edinburgh. *If using the DPS, send form IHT423 to the bank or building society at the same time.*

If all is in order we will stamp form **C1** and send it back to you. *If using the DPS, we will do this when we have received notification of payment from the bank.*

The Sheriff Clerk or the Commissary Clerk will issue Confirmation.

Send form **C1** and the other papers necessary to apply for Confirmation to the Sheriff Clerk or Commissary Clerk.

Applying for a grant in Northern Ireland – if you are a taxpayer or solicitor working out the tax

You will need an Inheritance Tax reference number (see page 10). If you wish to use the IHT Direct Payment Scheme (DPS), find out whether the deceased's bank and/or building society is part of the scheme and if so make sure you have complied with their requirements.

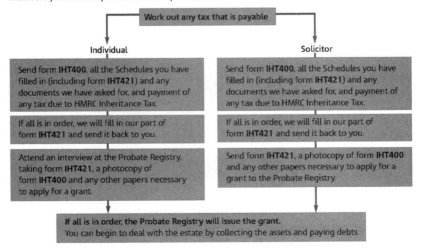

Work out any tax that is payable

Individual

Send form **IHT400**, all the Schedules you have filled in (including form **IHT421**) and any documents we have asked for, and payment of any tax due to HMRC Inheritance Tax.

If all is in order, we will fill in our part of form **IHT421** and send it back to you.

Attend an interview at the Probate Registry, taking form **IHT421**, a photocopy of form **IHT400** and any other papers necessary to apply for a grant.

Solicitor

Send form **IHT400**, all the Schedules you have filled in (including form **IHT421**) and any documents we have asked for, and payment of any tax due to HMRC Inheritance Tax.

If all is in order, we will fill in our part of form **IHT421** and send it back to you.

Send form **IHT421**, a photocopy of form **IHT400** and any other papers necessary to apply for a grant to the Probate Registry.

If all is in order, the Probate Registry will issue the grant.
You can begin to deal with the estate by collecting the assets and paying debts.

59

IHT400 Notes   *Guide to completing your Inheritance Tax account*

Applying for a grant in England and Wales – without the help of a solicitor and you want us to work out the tax for you

If using the **IHT Direct Payment Scheme (DPS)** find out whether the deceased's bank and/or building society are part of the scheme and if so make sure you have complied with their requirements.

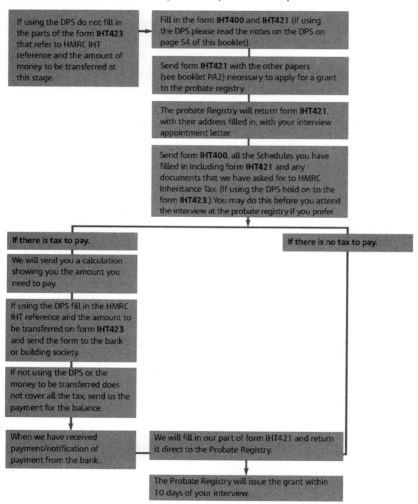

If using the DPS do not fill in the parts of the form **IHT423** that refer to HMRC IHT reference and the amount of money to be transferred at this stage.

Fill in the form **IHT400** and **IHT421** (if using the DPS please read the notes on the DPS on page 54 of this booklet).

Send form **IHT421** with the other papers (see booklet PA2) necessary to apply for a grant to the probate registry.

The probate Registry will return form **IHT421**, with their address filled in, with your interview appointment letter.

Send form **IHT400**, all the Schedules you have filled in including form **IHT421** and any documents that we have asked for to HMRC Inheritance Tax. (If using the DPS hold on to the form **IHT423**.) You may do this before you attend the interview at the probate registry if you prefer.

If there is tax to pay.

If there is no tax to pay.

We will send you a calculation showing you the amount you need to pay.

If using the DPS fill in the HMRC IHT reference and the amount to be transferred on form **IHT423** and send the form to the bank or building society.

If not using the DPS or the money to be transferred does not cover all the tax, send us the payment for the balance.

When we have received payment/notification of payment from the bank...

We will fill in our part of form IHT421 and return it direct to the Probate Registry.

The Probate Registry will issue the grant within 10 days of your interview.

IHT400 Notes   *Guide to completing your Inheritance Tax account*

Applying for a grant in Scotland – without the help of a solicitor and you want us to work out the tax for you

If using the **IHT Direct Payment Scheme (DPS)** find out whether the deceased's bank and/or building society are part of the scheme and if so make sure you have complied with their requirements.

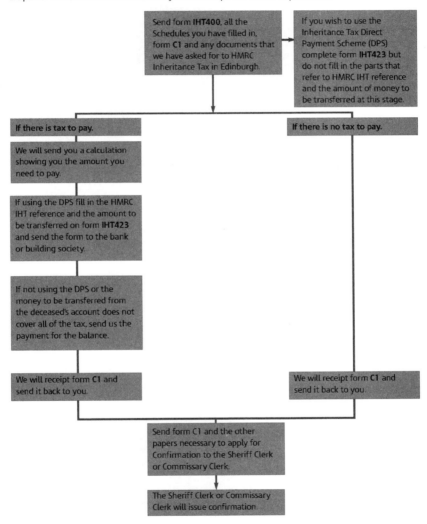

Send form **IHT400**, all the Schedules you have filled in, form **C1** and any documents that we have asked for to HMRC Inheritance Tax in Edinburgh.

If you wish to use the Inheritance Tax Direct Payment Scheme (DPS) complete form **IHT423** but do not fill in the parts that refer to HMRC IHT reference and the amount of money to be transferred at this stage.

If there is tax to pay.

We will send you a calculation showing you the amount you need to pay.

If using the DPS fill in the HMRC IHT reference and the amount to be transferred on form **IHT423** and send the form to the bank or building society.

If not using the DPS or the money to be transferred from the deceased's account does not cover all of the tax, send us the payment for the balance.

We will receipt form **C1** and send it back to you.

If there is no tax to pay.

We will receipt form **C1** and send it back to you.

Send form C1 and the other papers necessary to apply for Confirmation to the Sheriff Clerk or Commissary Clerk.

The Sheriff Clerk or Commissary Clerk will issue confirmation.

61

IHT400 Notes   *Guide to completing your Inheritance Tax account*

Applying for a grant in Northern Ireland – without the help of a solicitor and you want us to work out the tax for you

If using the **IHT Direct Payment Scheme (DPS)** find out whether the deceased's bank and/or building society are part of the scheme and if so make sure you have complied with their requirements.

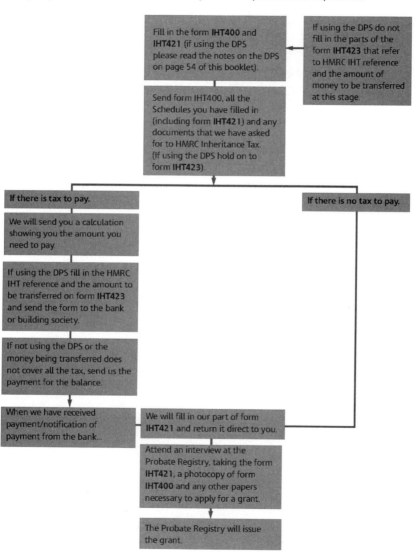

Fill in the form **IHT400** and **IHT421** (if using the DPS please read the notes on the DPS on page 54 of this booklet).

If using the DPS do not fill in the parts of the form **IHT423** that refer to HMRC IHT reference and the amount of money to be transferred at this stage.

Send form IHT400, all the Schedules you have filled in (including form **IHT421**) and any documents that we have asked for to HMRC Inheritance Tax. (If using the DPS hold on to form **IHT423**).

If there is tax to pay.

We will send you a calculation showing you the amount you need to pay.

If using the DPS fill in the HMRC IHT reference and the amount to be transferred on form **IHT423** and send the form to the bank or building society.

If not using the DPS or the money being transferred does not cover all the tax, send us the payment for the balance.

If there is no tax to pay.

When we have received payment/notification of payment from the bank...

We will fill in our part of form **IHT421** and return it direct to you.

Attend an interview at the Probate Registry, taking the form **IHT421**, a photocopy of form **IHT400** and any other papers necessary to apply for a grant.

The Probate Registry will issue the grant.

62

338

Paying Inheritance Tax

Payment in advance

You can pay the tax that is due either by electronic transfer, cheque, Bank Giro credit or by using National Savings & Investments owned by the deceased.

If you think more tax will be payable, you can make a payment on account. If you do we will not charge you interest on the amount you have paid from the date we receive it. You must give the IHT reference when you make a payment. See form IHT400, page 1 for information on IHT references. If you pay too much on account, we will pay you interest when we return the money to you.

Electronic transfer (CHAPS/BACS)

Contact your bank to find out how to make payment by electronic transfer. You will need to give your bank details of our bank account. This is as follows:

Bank	Sort code	Account number
Bank of England	10-53-92	23430303

Give the full name of the deceased, the date of death and the IHT reference number.

Payment by cheque

Make your cheque payable to 'HM Revenue & Customs' and:

- put a line through any space left on the pay line
- cross your cheque 'Account payee'
- write the full name of the deceased and the date of death on the back of the cheque.

Place the cheque and payslip in the envelope we have provided and send it to us.

Do not send the IHT400 and the Schedules in the same envelope as your cheque. They should be sent to our offices in:

- Nottingham, if you are applying for a grant of representation in England, Wales or Northern Ireland
- Edinburgh, if you are applying for a grant of Confirmation in Scotland.

Our addresses can be found at the back of this guide.

63

Appendix 3

Bank Giro Credit

If you wish to pay by Bank Giro, please take your cheque and payslip to your bank.

National Savings & Investments products

You may pay some or all of the tax and interest that needs to be paid before you can apply for a grant by using National Savings & Investments products owned by the deceased. However, it can take up to four weeks to process a payment. Please see leaflet IHT11 for full details on how to make a payment in this way.

Paying tax by offering assets to the Crown

You can offer to pay some or all of the tax and interest for which you are liable by transferring national heritage property to the Crown. We cannot accept property from you before you have taken out a grant of representation. If we do accept a transfer of property as payment of tax, we will repay the money to you up to the value of the property we accept.

For further information, please go to **www.hmrc.gov.uk/heritage** or speak to someone in our Heritage Team by phoning the Probate and Inheritance Tax Helpline on **0845 30 20 900.**

What happens if listed shares or land and buildings are sold for less than their value?

If:
- shares listed on the Stock Exchange are sold within one year of the date of death, or
- land and buildings are sold within four years of the date of death for less than the value included on form IHT400, we may be able to reduce the Inheritance Tax. Phone our Helpline if this applies to you and we will tell you what you have to do.

How to make sure there is no more tax to pay

If you have worked out that there is no tax to pay we will check the form IHT400 and, if we agree, we will send you a letter confirming that there is no tax to pay.

If there is some tax to pay on the estate, then when we think that the value of all the assets and debts in the estate is settled and you have paid all the tax and interest, we will send you a letter confirming this.

64

340

How to value the assets — for Inheritance Tax (IHT) purposes use the 'open market' value of an asset.

Estimating a value

The open market value is the price the asset might reasonably fetch if it was sold on the open market at the time of the transfer. This represents the realistic selling price of an asset, not an insurance value or replacement value.

You should be able to value some of the estate assets quite easily, for example, money in bank accounts or stocks and shares. In other instances, you may need the help of a professional valuer. If you do decide to employ a valuer, make sure you ask them to give you the 'open market value' of the asset.

What value to use

If you do not know the exact amount or value of any item, such as an Income Tax refund or household bill, do not put off applying for a grant just because you do not know the exact figures. You may use an estimated figure.

Do not guess at a value, but try to work out an estimate based on the information you have.

If you are including an estimate, enter details of the estimated values in the declaration on page 12 of form IHT400.

Stocks and shares

How to value stocks and shares

You do not have to get a professional valuation for quoted stocks and shares. You can value shares quoted on the London Stock Exchange by finding the price of the shares in the financial pages of a newspaper.

First of all, make a list of all the shares, including the name, nominal value and types of shares – for example, 'A N Other Plc 10p ordinary shares'. Then, if you are using a newspaper, find the shareholding and enter the price given for each shareholding. To find out the value of the shares, multiply the number of shares by the price given. So, if the deceased held 1,250 shares and the price was 1093.5p, the value for the holding is £13,668.75.

Sometimes, for unit trusts, the newspaper may show two prices, take the lower one.

Take the value of the shares on the day the person died – remember that a newspaper printed on the day the deceased died will have share prices for the day before.

65

341

Appendix 3

The 'quarter-up' price

If you use a share valuing service, they will tell you what the end of day quotation was for each of the shares. The price will appear as a range such as 1091–1101p. To work out the value of the shares, you need to work out the 'quarter-up' price. This is the lower price, plus one quarter of the difference between the two prices. So, in this example, the price would be 1091p plus one quarter of 10p, or 2.5p. The price for the shares would be 1093.5p.

What 'xd' means

If a dividend was due when the deceased died, the shares will be marked 'xd'. Such a marking indicates that the dividend will be paid to the deceased's estate and you will need to include a value in the estate.

To work out the value of the dividend, multiply the number of shares by the dividend per share. Sometimes the dividend may be given as a percentage, say 2.6%. Where this is the case, you can work out the dividend by finding out the percentage of the nominal value of the stock. So if the deceased had owned £400 of loan stock, the dividend would be 2.6% of £400 or £10.40.

The deceased died on a day the stock exchange was closed

If the deceased died on a day the Stock Exchange was closed, take the price for either the next or last day when the Stock Exchange was open, whichever is the lower. For example, if the person died on a Sunday you can take the price for either the Monday after or the Friday before. You can choose whether to use the price for Monday or Friday for each separate shareholding.

Shares in a private company that are not listed on the Stock Exchange

For private company shares, enter the open market value of the shares. You may need to contact the company's secretary or accountant to get this value. Do not include just the nominal value of such shares - for example, the nominal value for one thousand £1 ordinary shares is £1,000 - unless that genuinely reflects the open market value of the shares.

UK Government Stock

You can find out the value of UK Government Stock from your bank or stockbroker or from the UK Debt Management Office website at **www.dmo.gov.uk/**

Stock Exchange markings	The Stock Exchange Daily Official List includes a number of markings that may affect the value of the stocks and shares. Some of the markings increase the value of the shares. Include any increase in the value in box 63 on form IHT400. Some markings decrease the value and you will need to deduct the adjustment from the value you include for the shares. Others show that the deceased was entitled to some new shares at the date of death. Explanations of the markings are as follows:

- '**xd' (ex-dividend)** – the dividend that is due remains payable to the deceased. Include the net value of the dividend on Schedule IHT411.
- '**IK' ('gilts' plus interest)** – the interest that has accrued is part of the value at the date of death. Include the net* interest that has accrued from the date interest was last paid up to date of death on Schedule IHT411.
- '**IM' (fixed interest securities, loan and debenture stock plus interest)** – this is the same as 'IK', but applies to a different type of security. Include the net* interest that has accrued from the date interest was last paid up to date of death on Schedule IHT411.

Carry the total for all dividends to box 64 on form IHT400.

- '**IK ... X' ('gilts' minus interest)** – interest due from the date of death to the date of payment of interest is deducted from the value at the date of death. Take the net* interest that has accrued from the date of death to the date interest was paid away from the value of the stock. If a separate interest payment has been received, include the net amount of the interest payment on Schedule IHT411.
- '**IM ... X' (fixed interest securities, loan and debenture stock minus interest)** – this is the same as 'IK ... X', but applies to a different type of security. Take the net* interest that has accrued from the date of death to the date interest was paid away from the value of the stock. If a separate interest payment has been received, include the net amount of the interest payment on Schedule IHT411.

* net of Income Tax at basic rate

- '**XC' (ex-capitalisation)** – include the new shares.
- '**XR' (ex-rights)** – account for the value of the new shares or rights.
- '**XE' (ex-entitlement)** – include the new shares or warrants, if any.

If you do not know how many new shares, rights or warrants to include, the company's registrar should be able to tell you. Include the new shares, rights or warrants with the original holding in boxes 63, 65, 66 and 67 on form IHT400.

National Savings & Investments	**Finding the value of National Savings & Investments**

- Write to National Savings & Investments and ask for a letter giving:
  - the value of the deceased's investments at the date of death
  - the National Savings reference.

67

343

IHT400 Notes   *Guide to completing your Inheritance Tax account*

- For most National Savings Bank Accounts, National Savings Capital Bonds and Children's Bonds or FIRST Option Bonds:

  National Savings & Investments
  Glasgow
  G58 1SB

- For National Savings Certificates, Save as you Earn contracts and Year Plans, Cash Mini ISA or TESSA ISA:

  National Savings & Investments
  Durham
  DH99 1NS

- For Premium Bonds, National Savings Income Bonds, Guaranteed Equity Bonds and Pensioners Guaranteed Income Bonds

  National Savings & Investments
  Blackpool
  FY3 9YP

You can phone the National Savings general enquiry line on **0845 964 5000** (the office is open 7:00 am to midnight seven days a week) or email **customerenquiries@nsandi.com**

Household and personal goods

The term 'household and personal goods' means things such as furniture, pictures, paintings, china, TV, audio and video equipment, cameras, jewellery, cars, caravans, boats, antiques, stamp collections and so on. You do not have to get a professional valuation, although it might be worth doing so if you think any items may be worth more than £500, or for items specifically mentioned in the Will.

If you estimate the value, remember to use the open market value, not an insurance or replacement value. A valuation 'for insurance', although a good place to start, may be the cost to replace the items and not necessarily a realistic price for which the items might be sold. The insurance value is often higher than the price you might reasonably expect to get for an item if you sold it on the open market.

A realistic price is likely to be the value the item might fetch if sold at auction or through the local paper.

Land and buildings

Do I have to get a professional valuation for land and buildings?
You do not have to get the property professionally valued, but you must take all reasonable steps to put a value on the property. Advertisements in the local estate agents, newspapers and the Internet for properties that are very similar to the deceased's property may help you to make a realistic estimate of the value.

Condition of the property
Take account of the state of repair of the property (which may decrease its value). But you must also take account of any features that might make it attractive to a builder or developer, such as large gardens, or access to other land that is suitable for development (which may increase its value).

68

If there is a range of values for the property

If you come to a range of values for the property, it is probably best to adopt a value that is somewhere in between the highest and lowest values that you have got.

If I find the property is worth more than my initial estimate

If, having arrived at your figure and before you apply for a grant, you find out about other information that casts doubts on your estimate, you must reconsider it. For example, if you have estimated that the property was worth £150,000, but when you try to sell the property you market it at £170,000 and receive some offers at that figure or more, it suggests that the open market value for the property may be more like £170,000. We recommend that you do reconsider your figure, taking into account such things as the length of time since the death and movements in the property market and, if necessary, change your figure.

Land and buildings apart from the deceased's home

Include the open market value for any other land and buildings that were owned by the deceased, for example:

- farms
- business property, for example, a hotel, shop, factory
- timber and woodlands
- other land and buildings such as lock up garages, redundant or derelict land, quarries, airfields, and
- other rights that attach to land such as fishing or shooting rights.

Value the property as we explained above, although it is more likely you may need professional advice if the estate contains this sort of land. Write the address or location of the property in the space provided.

Valuing the right to live in the house

It is very common for a married couple or civil partners to own their house jointly. Usually, they own their house as joint tenants and, on death of the first to die, their share passes automatically to the survivor, so that when the survivor dies the whole property is part of their estate.

If, however, a married couple or civil partners own their house as tenants-in-common, where each owns a distinct share of the property, the first to die can say what is to happen to their share of the property in their Will. The Will might say something along the lines that:

'... while my husband/wife/civil partner remains alive and desires to reside in the property and keeps the same in good repair and insured to its full value with insurers approved by my trustees and pays all rates, outgoings etc my trustees shall not make any objection to such residence and shall not disturb or restrict it in any way and shall not take any steps to enforce the trust for sale or to realise (sell) any share therein or to obtain any rent or profit from the property ...'

On the survivor's death, the property passes on to someone else, usually a child. So the surviving spouse or civil partner continues to live in the house, owning half of it in their own name and occupying the other half under the protection of the Will.

69

Appendix 3

Although the Will does not talk in terms of leaving the property in trust for the husband/wife/civil partner for life, the wording is such that, for Inheritance Tax, it has the same effect.

If you are dealing with the survivor's estate and they occupied their matrimonial or civil partnership home (or a property that replaced it) under such terms, you will need to treat the survivor's estate as if they were entitled to benefit from a trust.

The same rules about trusts apply. So you need to include an interest in the house as a 'trust' asset and the open market value of the house (or share of the house) is the value of the trust asset.

If, within seven years of their death, the survivor ceases to occupy the property, or the property is sold and not all the proceeds are reinvested in a replacement property, the survivor will be treated as making a transfer of the trust capital in which they ceased to benefit. Include that value as a gift.

Valuing a business

If you are deducting business relief at 100% from the value of the deceased's business or interest in a business, there is no need to adjust the value taken from the accounts. Write this value in box 7 of Schedule IHT413. Copy this figure to the appropriate box on page 7 of form IHT400.

Remember to deduct the relief using the same figure on form IHT400 at box 93.

If you are not deducting business relief at 100% from the value of the deceased's business or interest in a business, you will need to adjust the value taken from the accounts. You will need to adjust the value where the assets are included in the accounts at 'book value' or where the assets are included separately in form IHT400.

Book value

Book value is a company's value as it appears on a balance sheet, equal to total assets and intangible assets such as goodwill, minus liabilities. The value of assets as they appear on a balance sheet will be equal to the cost of the assets less accumulated depreciation. Book value therefore often differs substantially from the open market value.

Open market value

For Inheritance Tax, the open market value of an asset is the price it might reasonably fetch if it was sold on the open market at the time of the transfer of that asset.

Other than land, the assets most commonly included in business accounts at book value are business stock and goodwill. You may be including the land separately in form IHT400. If so, you will need to take that value, or the deceased's share of it, away from the value of the deceased's interest in the business.

If not, you will need to obtain open market values for land and any other assets included at book value such as stock and goodwill. If the open market value is more that the book value, add the increase in value, or the deceased's share of that increase, to the value of the deceased's interest in the business. If the open market value is less than the book value, deduct the decrease in value, or the deceased's share of that decrease, from the value of the deceased's interest in the business.

Explain how you have arrived at your value for the business or interest in a business in box 9 on Schedule IHT413. If you need more space, please use the 'Additional information' box 25 on form IHT400.

Lloyd's Underwriters

If the deceased was an Underwriter at Lloyd's, include a value for the deceased's business as an Underwriter as an interest in a business.

Valuing money

You should include as assets of the deceased's estate all kinds of money and debts owed to the deceased at the date of death.

Examples are:
- money that the deceased had lent to someone else and which had not been repaid at the date of death
- money that the deceased had lent to trustees linked to a life assurance policy held in trust
- money for which the deceased held a promissory note or 'IOU'
- money that the deceased had lent to someone and that is secured by a mortgage over property
- money owing to the deceased from a director's loan account or current account with a company.

What value to use?
Include the face value of the loan, after taking off any repayments that have been made.

71

Exemptions and reliefs — this section gives more detailed information about exemptions and reliefs.

Exemptions that only apply to lifetime gifts

Small gifts up to £250 in any tax year to any one person. Such small gifts can be given to any number of different people.

Annual exemption of £3,000 in any one tax year. You can carry forward all or part of the £3,000 exemption that has not been used to the next tax year but no further.

Lifetime gifts that represent normal expenditure out of the transferor's income. These are exempt provided that the transferor's established standard of living is not reduced by the gifts, that the gifts came out of income and not capital and there is an established pattern of giving.

These gifts can include:
• monthly or regular payments to someone, including gifts for Christmas or other festivals, birthdays or other anniversaries
• regular premiums on a life assurance policy.

Fill in pages 2 and 6 of Schedule IHT403 if you want to deduct this exemption.

Gifts in consideration of marriage or civil partnership up to the following amounts:
• £5,000 if the gift is made by a parent or step-parent of either party to the marriage or civil partnership
• £2,500 if the gift is made by a grandparent of one of the parties
• £1,000 in any other case.

Exemptions that apply to lifetime gifts and transfers on death

Spouse and civil partner exemption

All transfers between legally married spouses and legally registered civil partners are exempt with one exception. If the person making the transfer is domiciled in the UK and the recipient is not, the spouse or civil partner exemption is limited to £55,000.

There is a special rule if the deceased benefited from a trust set up by the Will or intestacy of a spouse or former spouse who died before 13 November 1974. The value of the trust is not taken into account if:
• Estate Duty was paid or treated as paid in the earlier death in the assets in the trust, and
• the deceased was not able to dispose of the assets.

If the deceased was given the power to say how the assets should be dealt with during their lifetime or on their death, the exemption would not apply. If you are deducting this exemption from the assets in a trust, any apportioned income due in box 75 form IHT400 is also exempt. But the exemption does not apply to accrued income that had not been paid to the deceased and included in box 75.

 Website:**www.hmrc.gov.uk/ inheritancetax/**
Helpline: **0845 30 20 900**

Gifts and bequests to UK charities

All lifetime gifts and bequests on death to UK registered charities are exempt provided the gift was made to the charity outright.

Gifts to national bodies

Gifts and bequests to registered housing associations, political parties, national museums, the National Trust and certain other bodies concerned with the preservation of the National Heritage or of a public nature are exempt. The exemption may be limited if the gift was not made to the organisation outright.

If you are not sure whether one of these exemptions applies because the money did not pass direct to the organisation or if the Will restricts how the money should be used, phone our Helpline and explain the circumstances.

National Heritage exemptions

There are a number of exemptions available for gifts of heritage and other historic property. If you are claiming these exemptions, complete Schedule IHT420 *National heritage assets*.

Reliefs that may apply to lifetime gifts and transfers on death

Agricultural relief and business relief may apply to transfers of agricultural or business assets. These reliefs are covered in the sections on Schedule IHT414 *Agricultural relief* and Schedule IHT413 *Business and partnership interests and assets*.

Other reliefs

There are two other exemptions that apply to gifts. These only apply if the total of gifts made during the deceased's lifetime is more than the tax threshold when the deceased died so that there is some tax to pay on the gifts themselves.

Taper relief

If there is any tax to pay on a gift, the tax is reduced by a sliding scale for gifts made more than three but less than seven years before the death, so long as the total of the gifts made by the deceased exceeds the nil rate band.

The tax must be paid by the person who received the gift so the relief would not normally be relevant in working out the tax that must be paid before you can apply for a grant.

However, if the person who received the gift would like to pay their tax when you apply for a grant, you can send the payments together. You must still follow all the steps on form IHT400 to work out the tax that you must pay on the deceased's estate. The example here helps you to work out the tax that is payable on a lifetime transfer. Please enter the calculations you have made on the 'Additional information' pages of the IHT400 and say how the payment you are sending should be used.

73

349

Appendix 3

The amount of taper relief depends on the length of time by which the deceased survived the transfer. The tax charged is reduced by charging the following percentages of the full rate.

Years between transfer and death	Taper relief %
Three to four	20%
Four to five	40%
Five to six	60%
Six to seven	80%

Example

C made a gift of £300,000 on 1 February 2002. C died on 20 June 2005. The nil rate band at the date of death was £275,000.

The gift exceeds the nil rate band by £25,000.

Full rate of tax on the gift: 40% x £25,000 = £10,000.

The gift is within three to four years of the death, so taper relief at 20% is due. Taper relief: £10,000 x 20% = £2,000.

Revised tax charge: £10,000 less £2,000 = £8,000.

Fall in value relief

If the value of the assets given away has fallen between the date of gift and the date of death, tax may be charged on the lower value at death.

The relief only applies if the value of the gifts exceeds the nil rate band. There are other rules so phone our Helpline if you think this relief may apply. If you wish to deduct this relief, include the date of death value in the 'description of assets' column on Schedule IHT403, but do not alter the value at the date of death. We will look at the claim after the grant.

Where to include items in the estate

To help you fill in the form IHT400 correctly we have produced this list of assets and debts commonly included in a person's estate, together with the Schedule number, box number on the form IHT400 where you need to include it, and where any information about completing that box that can be found in this guide.

Item	Schedule(s)	Included in box on IHT400	IHT400 notes page
Agricultural land	IHT405, IHT414	68	37, 47
Antiques	IHT407	55	26, 45, 68
Bank accounts	IHT406	52	44
Boats	IHT407	55	26, 68
Building society accounts	IHT406	52	44
Business	IHT413	69	34, 47, 70
Business property	IHT405, IHT413	69	34, 47
Business assets	IHT413	69	34, 47
Capital Gains Tax liability	–	82	–
Capital Gains Tax repayment	–	74	48
Caravans	IHT407	55	26, 68
Cars	IHT407	55	26, 68
Cash (coins and notes)	–	53	44
Credit card bills	–	82	–
Debts owed to friends or family	IHT419	82	17, 50
Debts owed to the deceased	IHT416	73	48
Dividends on listed stocks and shares	IHT411	64	31, 46, 67
Dividends on unlisted stocks and shares	IHT412	64	46, 67
Farm business assets	IHT414	69	34, 37, 47, 70
Farms	IHT405, IHT414	68	37, 47
Farmhouses	IHT405, IHT414	68	37, 47
Farmland	IHT405, IHT414	68	37, 47
Foreign bank accounts	IHT417	98	15
Foreign houses land and buildings	IHT417	97	15
Foreign shares	IHT417	98	15
Furniture	IHT407	55	26, 45, 68
Gifts made by the deceased	IHT403	111	12, 18
Gilts (UK Government Securities)	IHT411	62	45, 66
Guarantee debts	IHT419	82	50
House or flat (deceased's residence)	IHT405	51	43, 68
Houses and flats (rented to others)	IHT405	70	47, 68
Household bills	–	82	–
Income tax liability	–	82	–
Income tax repayment	–	74	48
Interest in another estate	IHT415	71, 72	48
Interest on bank accounts	IHT406	52	44
Interest on building society accounts	IHT406	52	44
Interest on stocks and shares	IHT411	64	46, 67

75

351

Appendix 3

	Schedule(s)	Included in box on IHT400	IHT400 notes page
Jewellery	IHT407	55	26, 68
Joint bank and building society accounts	IHT404	50	13, 23
Joint household bills	IHT404	50	13, 23
Joint life assurance policy	IHT404	50	13, 23
Jointly owned houses, flats and land	IHT404	49	13, 23
Jointly owned household goods	IHT404	50	13, 23
Joint mortgage	IHT404	49	13, 23
Joint mortgage protection policy	IHT404	50	24
Land (other than farmland)	IHT405	70	47, 68, 69
Life assurance policies	IHT410	57	14, 45
Mortgage	-	80	49
Mortgage protection policies	-	57	-
National Savings & Investment products	IHT406	54	44, 67
Nominated assets	-	101	52
Paintings and works of art	IHT407	55	26, 45, 68
Pension arrears	-	56	45
Pension funds	IHT409	56	13, 27, 45
Premium Bonds	IHT406	54	44
Reversionary interest	IHT418	76	40
Secured loans	IHT419	80	49
Stocks and shares listed on the Stock Exchange	IHT411	63	14, 31, 46, 65, 66, 67
Stocks and shares traded on AIM	IHT412	65	32
Timber	IHT405	69	47
Trust assets	IHT418	99, 100, 105	15, 39, 52
Trust income	-	75	48
UK Government securities	IHT411	62	45, 66
Unit Trust	IHT411	63	65
Unlisted stocks and shares	IHT412	65	15, 32
Unsecured loans	IHT419	82	-
Woodlands	IHT405, IHT413	69	47

76

IHT400 feedback form

How much of this guide did you read?

All of it ☐

Most of it ☐

Some of it ☐

Hardly any of it ☐

How easy was it to understand this guide?

I understood it easily ☐

I understood most of it
but some of it could
be clearer * ☐

It was hard to understand ☐

I did not understand it ☐

* If you ticked this box, please say which parts
could be clearer

```
[                              ]
[                              ]
[                              ]
[                              ]
[                              ]
```

3 **How easy was it to complete form IHT400?**

The form was easy to follow and
I knew what to do ☐

Most of the form was easy to follow but
some parts could be clearer * ☐

It was hard to follow and I was not
always sure what I had to do * ☐

I could not complete it without help ☐

* If you ticked either of these boxes, please say which parts
could be easier to understand

```
[                              ]
[                              ]
[                              ]
[                              ]
[                              ]
[                              ]
```

If you have any other comments about form IHT400,
this guide or any of the Schedules you had to complete,
please enter them over the page.

If you need more space, continue on a separate sheet
of paper.

77

353

Appendix 3

Additional information

If you need to please continue on a separate sheet of paper.

354

Contacts

If you need a copy of any of our forms you can:

- download them from our website **www.hmrc.gov.uk/inheritancetax/** or
- contact the Inheritance Tax orderline
  - email **hmrc.ihtorderline@btconnect.gov.uk**
  - phone **0845 30 20 900**
  - fax **0845 234 1010.**

If you want to know more about any particular aspect of Inheritance Tax, please visit our website or phone the Probate and Inheritance Tax Helpline.

DX addresses have been included for use by solicitors and banks

Nottingham Office
HM Revenue & Customs Inheritance Tax
Ferrers House
PO Box 38
Castle Meadow Road
Nottingham NG2 1BB

DX 701201 NOTTINGHAM 4.

Edinburgh office
HM Revenue & Customs Inheritance Tax
Meldrum House
15 Drumsheugh Gardens
Edinburgh EH3 7UG

DX ED 542001 EDINBURGH 14.

Belfast office
HM Revenue & Customs Inheritance Tax
Level 3
Dorchester House
52-58 Great Victoria Street
Belfast BT2 7QL

DX 2001 NR BELFAST 2.

Our website and Helpline

Website: **www.hmrc.gov.uk/inheritancetax/**

Helpline: **0845 30 20 900.**

This booklet has no legal power. It reflects the tax law at the time of writing. We may need to take into account special circumstances for a particular estate. More information about Inheritance Tax can be found in the Customer Guide to Inheritance Tax on our website at **www.hmrc.gov.uk/inheritancetax** or, if you do not have access to the Internet, by phoning our Helpline.

79

Appendix 3

Further information

**Service
Commitment**

For more information about our service commitment go to
www.hmrc.gov/about/sc.htm

**If you have
a complaint**

For more information about our complaints procedures go to
www.hmrc.gov.uk and look for *Complaints* within the *Search* facility.

**How we use your
information**

Data Protection Act

HM Revenue & Customs is a Data Controller under the Data Protection
Act 1998. We hold information for the purposes specified in our
notification to the Information Commissioner, including the assessment and
collection of tax and duties, the payment of benefits and the prevention
and detection of crime, and may use this information for any of them.

We may get information about you from others, or we may give information
to them. If we do, it will only be as the law permits to:

- check the accuracy of information
- prevent or detect crime
- protect public funds.

We may check information we receive about you with what is already in
our records. This can include information provided by you, as well as by
others, such as other government departments or agencies and overseas
tax and customs authorities. We will not give information to anyone
outside HM Revenue & Customs unless the law permits us to do so. For
more information go to **www.hmrc.gov.uk** and look for *Data Protection Act*
within the *Search* facility.

Confidentiality

You have a right to the same high degree of confidentiality that all
taxpayers have. We have a legal duty to keep your affairs completely
confidential and cannot give information to others about an estate, trust or
transfer even if they have an interest in it, unless the law permits us to do
so. This means we may only discuss a taxpayer's affairs with that person, or
with someone else that the taxpayer has appointed to act for them. In the
case of someone who has died, this means that we can only discuss an
estate with the people (or person) who have signed and delivered form
IHT400, that is the executors or administrators, or another person
appointed to act for them; usually a solicitor or an accountant.

80

356

IHTM43001 Transferable Nil Rate Band

IHTM43001 Transferable Nil Rate Band: introduction

The ability to transfer nil rate band (TNRB) between the estates of husband and wife or civil partners was introduced in the FA08. The legislation relating to the transfer of unused nil rate band is contained within IHTA84/S8A-C.

The effect of TNRB is that when a surviving spouse or civil partner dies, the nil rate band available at their death will be increased by the proportion of the nil rate band that was not used on the death of their spouse or civil partner.

TNRB is available where the death of the surviving spouse or civil partner occurs on or after 9th October 2007. For spouses, the first death can have occurred at any time before or after that date and the relief therefore applies where the first death occurred under IHT, Capital Transfer Tax or Estate Duty and there was unused nil rate band.

For civil partnerships the first death must have occurred on or after 5 December 2005, the date the Civil Partnership Act became law in the United Kingdom. While it was possible to enter into a civil partnership in other countries prior to this date, the Act states that where a relationship was recognised under overseas law before the UK Act came into force, the parties to the relationship are to be treated as having formed a civil partnership recognised in the UK on the date the Act came into force.

While the benefit of the unused nil rate band accrues to the estate of the surviving spouse or civil partner, there is no requirement for assets to have passed to the spouse or civil partner on the first death. The legislation refers to unused nil rate band rather than property passing to the surviving spouse or civil partner. So property that passed as an exempt or relievable transfer (for example, a transfer to charity or for national purposes or property that attracted business or agricultural relief) will not use up the nil rate band. And where the value of an estate is below the IHT nil rate band at the date of the first death, the full amount of the nil rate band that is not used is available for transfer.

Example

On the first death the entire estate valued at £150,000 was left to the deceased's son. If the nil rate band was £300,000, this would result in 50% of the nil rate band being available to transfer to the surviving spouse or civil partner.

Because it is the unused nil rate band that is transferred, there can be no TNRB at the second estate if IHT was paid on any part of the estate on the death of first spouse or civil partner. Estate here has the normal meaning for IHT and includes assets held in trust, gifts with reservation and joint property passing by survivorship. Gifts that cumulate with the death estate will also use up the available nil rate band at the first death.

IHTM43002 Transferable Nil Rate Band: what constitutes a valid marriage?

The case of Holland (Executor of Holland deceased) v IRC SPC 350 confirmed that, for IHT purposes, the term spouse refers only to the parties of a legal marriage. In order for a marriage that takes place in the UK to be legally recognised, it must conform to the requirements of the law in the appropriate part of the UK.

This requirement applies where a marriage is conducted in the UK according to another faith in, say, a mosque or temple. The ceremony will marry the couple in accordance with that faith or custom and so long as the requirements of UK law are also met, their marriage will be a legal marriage under UK law. The couple will therefore be "spouses" for IHT purposes and will be able to transfer any unused nil rate. It follows, however, that if the requirements of UK law are not met, the couple will not be "spouses" and will not be able to transfer unused nil rate band.

Where a marriage ceremony has been conducted abroad, it must meet the requirements of the law in the country in which the marriage was celebrated if the parties to the marriage are to be regarded as "spouses" for the purposes of TNRB.

Similarly, a civil partnership in the UK must be registered according to the requirements of UK law in order to be recognised for TNRB purposes.

There is a style of marriage recognised in Scots Law by cohabitation and repute [IHTM11032]. If, on the first death, exemption under IHTA84/S18 has been granted, the survivor will meet the initial condition in IHTA84/S8A(1)(a) and any unused nil rate band will be available to transfer. Any case where TNRB is sought on these grounds should be referred to TG in Edinburgh.

Full details of the legal requirements for a marriage in England and Wales may be found at http://www.gro.gov.uk/gro/content/marriages/index.asp. For Scotland at http://www.gro-scotland.gov.uk/regscot/getting-married-in-scotland/index.html and in Northern Ireland at http://www.groni.gov.uk/index.htm.

IHTM43003 Transferable Nil Rate Band: divorce or dissolution of a civil partnership.

Where a marriage or civil partnership comes to an end by divorce or dissolution of the civil partnership and one of the parties to the relationship subsequently dies, any unused nil rate band on their death is not available for transfer on the death of their former spouse or partner. If the divorcee or former civil partner does not remarry or enter a new civil partnership, any unused nil rate band on their death will remain unused.

Unused nil rate band can only be transferred from one spouse or civil partner to the survivor when the relationship is brought to an end by the death of one party to the relationship.

IHTM43004 Transferable Nil Rate Band: the process to transfer unused nil rate band

Unlike most exemptions and relief for IHT, the personal representatives must make a formal claim to transfer any unused nil rate band from the estate of the deceased's spouse IHTA84/S8B. The claim is made using form IHT216 which should be completed and signed by the personal representatives of the surviving spouse and delivered with form IHT200 for the survivor's death. The personal representatives should include with their claim a copy of

- the death certificate,
- the marriage or civil partnership certificate
- copy of the grant of representation (Confirmation in Scotland)
- if the spouse or civil partner left a Will, a copy of it
- any Deed of Variation or similar executed on the estate.

Where no claim is made by the personal representatives to transfer unused nil rate band, perhaps because there is no need to take out a grant, any other person liable for tax on the survivor's death, for example, the trustees of a settlement or the donee of a gift, may make a claim – but only when the initial period for claim by the personal representatives [IHTM43005] has expired.

IHTM43005 Transferable Nil Rate Band: time limits

The claim to transfer of unused inheritance tax nil rate band must be made by personal representatives within the permitted period. That period is either no later than 24 months after the end of the month in which the second deceased died, or, (if it ends later) the period of 3 months beginning with the date on which the personal representatives first acted as such - IHT84/S8B(3)(a).

Under IHTA84/S8B(3)(b), an officer of Revenue & Customs has the discretion to extend that period where circumstances are appropriate. [IHTM43000].

Example

If the surviving spouse or civil partner died on 10 October 2007, the form would need to be received by 31 October 2009.

If no claim is made by the personal representatives, any other person liable for tax may make a claim within such later period as an officer of Revenue & Customs may allow, IHTA84/S8B(1)(b).

This means that technically, the trustees of trust that is liable to IHT following the death of the life tenant cannot make a claim until 2 years have passed. In practice, though, if there is no need to take out a grant, so that no personal representatives will be appointed, you may provisionally admit a claim by trustees (or other persons liable for tax) within the two year period and calculate the tax accordingly.

The phrase "first acted as such" in IHTA84/S8B(3)(a) follows the general law about acts done by executors and administrators before the grant. Whereas an administrator can do nothing until letters of administration are granted to them, an executor may undertake certain acts prior to the grant. Where an executor undertakes acts which show an intention on their part to take on the office of executor and which would preclude them from renouncing probate, that is the point when they have "first acted" as an executor. For example

- making an express claim to act as an executor, by bringing or defending a claim in that capacity,
- taking, using or disposing of goods; most often carrying on the deceased's business or trade,
- demanding, receiving or releasing debts due to the deceased.

This statutory extension to the period in which a claim may be made is most likely to be relevant where there is a dispute which must be settled before the personal representatives can be identified. In such cases, you should treat the three month period as commencing once the Court Order identifying the executors has been handed down.

Once a claim has been submitted IHTA/S8B(4) allows for that claim to be withdrawn no later than one month after the end of the permitted periods mentioned above.

IHTM43006 Transferable Nil Rate Band: late claims

Under IHTA84/S8B(3)(b), an officer of Revenue & Customs has the discretion to admit a late claim.

The most common example is likely to be where there is a dispute which must be settled before the personal representatives can be identified. If the dispute means that a claim cannot be made within the two year period, there is already a statutory extension to that period of three months beginning with the date the personal representatives first act as such [IHTM43005]. But where this is still insufficient time for the recently identified personal representatives to make their claim, you may admit a claim outside this three month period where the personal representatives can show that they or their agents have been actively pursuing matters since the Court decision.

Otherwise, you may admit a late claim in the following circumstances.

<u>An event beyond the claimant's control</u>

In general, we will accept a late claim if the claimant can show that an event beyond their control prevented them from making their claim within the permitted period. If the claimant was able to manage the rest of their private or business affairs during the period in question, we are unlikely to accept that they were genuinely prevented from making the claim on time. Examples of situations that we may consider as an event beyond the claimant's control include those where

- the claim was posted in good time but an unforeseen event disrupted the normal postal service and led to the loss or delay of the claim,
- the records necessary to make the claim were lost through fire, flood or theft and the records required to make the claim could not be replaced in time for it to be made within the permitted period,
- the claimant was so seriously ill that they were prevented from dealing with the claim within the permitted period and from that date to the time the claim was made. If an illness involves a lengthy stay in hospital or convalescence the claimant is expected to have made arrangements for completing and making the claim on time. But there may be circumstances where this is not possible and we may accept these as a valid reason.
- the serious illness of a close relative or partner will be regarded as a valid reason for a delay in electing only if
  - the situation took up a great deal of the claimant's time and attention during the period from the end of the permitted period to the date the claim was made, and
  - steps had already been taken to have the claim made on time;
- a close relative or partner died shortly before the end of the permitted period and the necessary steps had already been taken to make the claim on time.

<u>Other circumstances</u>

There may be cases where, given the overall circumstances, we will accept a late claim even where the claimant cannot show that the reasons for the late claim were beyond their control. Essentially, this will be where the claimant can show that they were unaware – and could not reasonably have been aware – that they were entitled to make the claim.

It is likely that such cases will involve a number of relevant features. The claimant or their agent should make the late claim and provide a full explanation of the factors that they wish to be taken into account.

In all cases where a late claim is made, you should refer the case to your manager to ensure that late claims are dealt with consistently.

See also [IHTM43034] sequential marriages where a claim was not made on the intervening marriage and [IHTM43041] legitim.

IHTM43007 Transferable Nil Rate Band: reviewing form IHT216

Form IHT216 is designed to obtain information that allows the taxpayer to quantify the chargeable value of the estate on the first death and then deduct that value from the nil rate band that was available to the death estate to quantify the amount of the nil rate band that was unused. The values used on page 2 of form IHT216 must reflect the chargeable value of the estate, for IHT purposes, at the date of the first death, not what the legatees actually received, accordingly no allowance should be made for costs.

Where property that was owned jointly with the surviving spouse or civil partner passed to chargeable beneficiaries, no joint property deduction should be made in view of the related property provision in IHTA84/S161 [IHTM09739]. Similarly, where a property wholly owned by the deceased is left between their spouse and child, exemption should be allowed for non-discounted half share.

IHTM43008 Transferable Nil Rate Band: action in risk assessment.

First death before 9th October 2007

On receipt of a claim for TNRB, you should ensure that the appropriate documents listed at IHTM43004 have been provided and if not, contact the taxpayer to obtain those documents. You should review the claim and correct any obvious errors, including collecting any additional tax due as a result, before releasing form D18/C1.

You will, however, need to bear in mind that where the death was many years ago, supporting evidence may not be so readily available. Provided the documents show the claim is valid and tax has been paid, you can release form D18/C1. You should then consider the risk to tax in deciding whether or not to accept the claim as offered.

Where the claim can be accepted at the outset, you should do so before referring the case on to PC&S [IHTM43009] or Compliance Group [IHTM43010] as appropriate. Where it is not possible to establish with certainty how much of the nil rate band was unused, perhaps because of the terms of the Will, or the availability of relief and the tax at stake is worthwhile, you should refer the case to either PC&S or Compliance Group to take up the matter with the taxpayer.

First death on or after 9th October 2007

Our published guidance has advised taxpayers to keep the following records from the first death to support a claim to transfer unused nil rate band

- a copy of the IHT200, IHT205 (C5 in Scotland) or full written details of the assets in the estate and their values,
- death certificate,
- marriage or civil partnership certificate for the couple,
- copy of the grant of representation (Confirmation in Scotland),
- copy of the Will, if there was one,
- a note of how the estate passed if there was no Will,
- a copy of any Deed of Variation or other similar document if one was executed to change the people who inherited the estate,
- any valuation(s) of assets that pass under Will or intestacy other than to the surviving spouse or civil partner,
- the value of any other assets that also passed on the death of the first spouse or civil partner, for example jointly owned assets, assets held in trust and gifts made in the 7 years prior to death,
- any evidence to support the availability of relief (such as agricultural or business relief) where the relievable assets pass to someone other than to the surviving spouse or civil partner.

We do not expect taxpayers to provide all this material in support of their claim, however, it will be much easier for them to make the claim with these documents to hand.

At the risk assessment stage, you should apply the same process as outlined above for deaths before 9th October, but where you are unable to accept the claim at the outset, you should either refer the case direct to Compliance Group, or provide guidance for PC&S to obtain the relevant supporting information to consider the position further.

IHTM43009 Transferable Nil Rate Band: action in PC&S

In the majority of cases dealt with in PC&S, any claim to transfer unused nil rate band will have been agreed by the risk assessors. Where, however, this has not been the case, you should follow the risk assessors' instructions to obtain further information or to have property valued. Upon receipt of this information, you should, if appropriate, amend the claim to TNRB and re-assess the case as necessary, following the relevant workaround for COMPASS. [IHTM43024]

Any case where the death is after 9th October 2007 and the taxpayer is unable to provide any additional supporting documents requested by the risk assessors should be referred to the Risk & Intelligence Team in CG for further research.

IHTM43010 Transferable Nil Rate Band: action in Compliance Group

Where a case with TNRB is referred to Compliance Group, the claim for TNRB, if not accepted by the risk assessors, should be investigated as part of an enquiry. This will be particularly relevant where, on the first death, relievable property was left to chargeable beneficiaries and it is now necessary to investigate the extent to which the relief was due in order to quantify the amount of nil rate band that was unused. You should always try to obtain our file for the first death, if one still exists.

You should investigate the position at the first death following current procedures, but you should always bear in mind that where the first death was many years ago, the information available may be very limited. Where this is the case and it is not possible to establish a conclusive position, you should discuss the matter with the taxpayer to try and arrive at a mutually acceptable conclusion.

The position is different where the first death is on or after 9th October 2007. Here, our published guidance [IHTM43008] sets out the documentation we expect taxpayers to keep. Where necessary, you should ask the taxpayer for the relevant documents to support their claim. Any case where nothing or inadequate documentation has been retained should be referred to your manager to consider the extent to which the claim should be admitted.

IHTM43020 Transferable Nil Rate Band: how the amount to be transferred is calculated

The formula expressed in IHTA84/S8A(2) is that a person has unused nil rate band on death if

$$M > VT$$

where M = the maximum that could be transferred on the first death at nil percent. M is therefore the nil rate band that applied at the first death, less the chargeable value of any lifetime transfers that use up the nil rate band first.

VT = the chargeable value of the transfer on death. This is the value of non exempt or relievable legacies passing under the Will or intestacy, assets passing by survivorship, gifts with reservation chargeable at death and any settled property.

Where M is greater than VT, that amount, expressed as a percentage of the nil rate band available on the first death, is the amount by which the nil rate band on the second death is increased. Where necessary, you should always take the percentage to three decimal places.

Example

The deceased died on 22 October 2002, when the nil rate band was £250,000 with an estate as below,

Net estate	400,000
Chargeable legacies	-100,000

Res to s/spouse	300,000

M is £250,000, being the nil rate band at the date of death, not reduced by any chargeable lifetime transfers and VT is £100,000. M is therefore greater than VT by £150,000, so there is an amount of nil rate band available to transfer from the first death.

The amount by which M is greater than VT is expressed as E in IHTA84/S8A(4). Having established that there is an amount of nil rate band to transfer from the first death, the percentage of nil rate band available is

$$\frac{E}{NRBMD} \times 100$$

where NRBMD is the nil rate band maximum at the first date of death.

So E is £250,000 - £100,000 = £150,000. The percentage of nil rate band available to transfer is

$$\frac{150,000}{250,000} \times 100 = 60.000\%$$

If, on the second death the nil rate band was £300,000, that would be increased by the amount available to transfer or

£300,000 + (£300,000 X 60%) = £480,000

If, in this example the chargeable legacies had been £300,000, then M would be £250,000 and VT £300,000. Therefore, as M is not greater than VT there is no nil rate band available to transfer.

IHTM43021 Transferable Nil Rate Band: how the amount to be transferred is calculated where there are lifetime transfers

Where the deceased dies with a cumulative total of lifetime transfers, the nil rate band is set first against those transfers. This reduces the amount of nil rate band that is available against the death estate and, in turn, that reduces the amount that may be available for transfer.

Example

The deceased died on 22 October 2002, when the nil rate band was £250,000 with an estate as below, having made lifetime gifts of £100,000 within 7 years of death.

Chargeable lifetime gifts	100,000
Net estate	400,000
Chargeable legacies	-100,000
Res to s/spouse	300,000

The nil rate band is £250,000, but this is not the maximum that could be transferred at nil percent on the first death, because of the chargeable lifetime transfers made. The maximum that could have been transferred at nil percent would be £250,000-£100,000 = £150,000. So the value to be used for M is £150,000.

The chargeable value transferred on the death £100,000, so VT is £100,000. E is M - VT or £150,000 - £100,000 = £50,000.

The percentage of the nil rate band available to transfer on the second death is then calculated

$$\frac{50,000}{250,000} \times 100 = 20.000\%$$

If, on the second death the nil rate band was £300,000, that would be increased by the amount available to transfer or

£300,000 + (£300,000 X 20%) = £360,000

IHTM43022 Transferable Nil Rate Band: how the amount to be transferred is calculated where first estate is less than IHT nil rate band on the first death

The process for calculating the amount of unused nil rate band where the estate on the first death is less than the nil rate band available at that time is no different from the normal calculation [IHTM43000].

Example

First Death on 16 August 2005		S.8A(2) calculation	
Net estate	250,000	M =	275,000
Chargeable legacies	-110,000	VT =	110,000
Res to s/spouse	140,000	M > VT by	165,000

S.8A(4) calculation
E (M > VT) = 165,000
NRBMD = 275,000
Percentage $\frac{165,000}{275,000}$ x100 60.000%

Second death on 3 December 2007

Nil rate band = 300,000 + (300,000 x 60%) = £480,000

Although in this example VT has been shown as a chargeable legacy, the same position would apply had it been property in a settled fund passing to a chargeable beneficiary, or a gift with reservation that is bought into charge upon death.

IHTM43023 Transferable Nil Rate Band: how the amount to be transferred is calculated where first estate is less than IHT nil rate band on the first death and with lifetime transfers

The process for calculating the amount of unused nil rate band where the estate on the first death is less than the nil rate band available at that time and there are lifetime transfers is no different from the normal calculation [IHTM43000].

Example

First death on 16 August 2005		S.8A(2) calculation	
PLCT	165,000	NRB	275,000
Net estate	250,000	PLCT	-165,000
Chargeable legacies	Nil	M =	110,000
Res to s/spouse	250,000	VT =	Nil
		M > VT by	110,000

S.8A(4) calculation
E (M > VT) = 110,000
NRBMD = 275,000
Percentage $\frac{110,000}{275,000}$ x100 40.000%

> 275,000
>
> Second death on 3 December 2007
>
> Nil rate band = 300,000 + (300,000 x 40%) = £420,000

IHTM43024 Transferable Nil Rate Band: how to reflect the increased nil rate band on COMPASS

The increased nil rate band replaces the single nil rate band available to the survivor on their death and is applied in exactly the same way. In other words, it is used first against lifetime transfers that fall chargeable as a result of the death and any balance is then available to set against the death estate.

COMPASS will be amended to record details of transferred nil rate band and to apply the increased nil rate band in this way. However, these changes will not take effect until the end of 2008.

To work around this the quick succession relief (QSR) box on the 'calculation of inheritance tax' window [IHTM31182] should be used, so that the benefit of the TNRB is spread across the chargeable components of the estate. To use this workaround it will be necessary to calculate the tax attributable to the increased nil rate band on estates where the total value of the estate is greater than the increased nil rate band. The following pages contain examples that show how this will work in practice.

An explanation should be added in the COMPASS notes box to the effect that "TNRB - the sum of £nnnnnnn deducted as QSR is the tax attributable to the transferred nil rate band".

If QSR is actually due on the case, you can add the QSR to the tax adjustment being made for TNRB, but it will need to be made clear in the COMPASS notes box what the individual figures are.

IHTM43025 Transferable Nil Rate Band: total value of estate, with no lifetime transfers, less than increased value of the nil rate band.

Where the estate is not taxpaying as a result of the increased nil rate band, a figure equivalent to the tax that would have been due, were it not for the increased nil rate band, should be entered in the QSR box on the 'calculation of inheritance tax' window [IHTM31182]

Example

The deceased died on November 2007 with an estate of £430,000, with no lifetime transfers or other aggregable property. A claim to transfer 60% of the nil rate band unused when the spouse died in 1999 is included.

The nil rate band on the deceased's death is increased by 60% from £300,000 to £480,000, so the estate is no longer liable to tax on the deceased's death.

The increased nil rate band is greater than the chargeable value of the estate, but COMPASS will initially show tax of £52,000 to pay, using the normal nil rate band. The figure of £52,000 should therefore be entered in the box for QSR to reduce the tax to nil, a note added to the calculation and the nil calculation raised, issued and paid.

IHTM43026 Transferable Nil Rate Band: total value of estate, with no lifetime transfers, greater than increased value of the nil rate band

In estates such as these, it will be necessary to calculate the tax saved on the estate of the surviving spouse or civil partner following the transfer of the any nil rate band from the estate of the first to die. This value should then be entered in the QSR box on the 'calculation of inheritance tax' window [IHTM31182]

Example

The deceased dies on November 2007 with an estate of £430,000 with no lifetime transfers or other aggregable property. A claim to transfer 25% of the nil rate band unused when the spouse died in 1999 is made.

The nil rate band on the deceased's death is increased by 25% from £300,000 to £375,000, so the estate is still liable to tax on the deceased's death. The amount by which the nil rate band is increased is £75,000. The reduction in inheritance tax on the estate of the second to die as a result of this increase is £75,000 x 40% = £30,000.

When raising the calculation COMPASS will use the normal nil rate band and will show tax of £52,000 to pay. The figure of £30,000 should be entered in the box for QSR to reduce the tax to £22,000, a note added to the calculation and the calculation raised and issued.

IHTM43027 Transferable Nil Rate Band: total value of the estate, including lifetime transfers below increased value of the nil rate band

As with estates with no lifetime transfers [IHTM43000], where the estate is not taxpaying as a result of the increased nil rate band, a figure equivalent to the tax that would have been due, were it not for the increased nil rate band, should be entered in the QSR box on the 'calculation of inheritance tax' window [IHTM31182]

Example

The deceased dies on November 2007 with an estate of £430,000 and a PLCT of £100,000. There is no other aggregable property. A claim to transfer 100% of the nil rate band unused when the spouse died in 1999 is made.

The NRB on the deceased's death is doubled to £600,000, so the estate is no longer liable to tax on the deceased's death.

The increased nil rate band is greater than the chargeable value of the estate, but COMPASS will initially show tax of £92,000 to pay, using the normal nil rate band. The figure of £92,000 should therefore be entered in the box for QSR to reduce the tax to nil, a note added to the calculation and the nil calculation raised, issued and paid.

IHTM43028 Transferable Nil Rate Band: total value of the estate, including lifetime transfers is greater than value of the increased nil rate band. The lifetime transfers do not exceed the single nil rate band

In these circumstances, it will be necessary to calculate the tax saved on the estate of the surviving spouse or civil partner following the transfer of the any nil rate band from the estate of the first to die. This value should then be entered in the QSR box on the 'calculation of inheritance tax' window [IHTM31182]

Example

The deceased dies on November 2007 with an estate of £430,000 and a PLCT of £250,000. There is no other aggregable property. A claim to transfer 50% of the nil rate band unused when the spouse died in 1999 is made.

The NRB on the deceased's death is increased by 50% from £300,000 to £450,000, so the estate is still liable to tax on the deceased's death. The amount by which the nil rate band is increased is £150,000. The reduction in inheritance tax on the estate of the second to die as a result of this increase is £150,000 x 40% = £60,000.

When raising the calculation COMPASS will use the normal nil rate band and will show tax of £152,000 to pay. The figure of £60,000 should be entered in the box for QSR to reduce the tax to £92,000, a note added and the calculation raised & issued.

IHTM43029 Transferable Nil Rate Band: total value of the estate, including lifetime transfers is greater than value of the increased nil rate band. The lifetime transfers are in excess of the single nil rate band

Normally, the benefit of TNRB is spread across all entries comprising the estate. But where the chargeable value of lifetime transfers exceeds the single nil rate band in force at the date of the second death, this will exhaust the amount transferred. In these cases, the chargeable value of the gifts need to be adjusted, to ensure the benefit of the transferred nil rate band is correctly set against the chargeable value of the lifetime gifts in the first instance.

Example

The deceased dies on November 2007 with an estate of £430,000 and a chargeable lifetime transfer of £350,000. There is no other aggregable property. A claim to transfer 80% of the nil rate band unused when the spouse died in 1999 is made.

The nil rate band on the deceased's death is increased by 80% from £300,000 to £540,000, so the estate is still liable to tax on the deceased's death. The amount of TNRB is £240,000.

Because the chargeable lifetime transfer exceeds the single nil rate band available on death, this should be reduced by the amount of TNRB. So the figure to include as a previous cumulative total of lifetime gifts in the 'calculation of inheritance tax window' [IHTM31182] becomes £350,000 - £240,000 = £110,000. When raising the calculation COMPASS will use the single nil rate band and will show tax of £96,000 to pay.

In this case, the note on the calculation should be along the lines of "TNRB - the cumulative total of lifetime gifts has been reduced by £nnnnnnn to reflect the transferred nil rate band", and the calculation raised & issued.

On sample cases selected for KAI, the lifetime transfer will have been data captured. To raise, issue and pay a nil assessment at the appropriate entry you should follow the process at IHTM43025.

IHTM43030 Transferable Nil Rate Band: survivor has been married to more than spouse, or been in more than one civil partnership

Where a surviving spouse or civil partner has been married more than once, or has been in more than one civil partnership and has survived both or all of their pre-deceasing spouses or civil partners the amount of unused nil rate at each previous death can be carried forward to the later death IHTA84/S8A(6)(b). This is limited to a maximum of 100% of the nil rate band at the death of the surviving spouse or civil partner IHTA84/S8A(5) [IHTM43031].

Appendix 4

Example

The deceased's first husband died on 7 May 2002 (when NRB was £250,000), with an estate as below

Net estate	400,000	S.8A(2) calculation	
Chargeable legacies	-100,000	M =	250,000
Res to s/spouse	300,000	VT =	100,000
		M > VT by	150,000
S.8A(4) calculation			
E (M > VT) =	150,000		
NRBMD =	250,000		
Percentage 150,000 x100	60.000%		
250,000			

So there is 60% of his nil rate band available to transfer to the surviving spouse or civil partner. The deceased married for a second time and again survived her husband who died on 7 September 2005, with an estate as below

Net estate	300,000	S.8A(2) calculation	
Chargeable legacies	-220,000	M =	275,000
Res to s/spouse	80,000	VT =	220,000
		M > VT by	55,000
S.8A(4) calculation			
E (M > VT) =	55,000		
NRBMD =	275,000		
Percentage 55,000 x100	20.000%		
275,000			

The deceased then dies in January 2008 and the nil rate band available on her death would be

£300,000 + (300,000 x 60%) + (300,000 x 20%) = £540,000

IHTM43031 Transferable Nil Rate Band: survivor has been married to more than spouse, or been in more than one civil partnership; limitation at 100%

Following the example from [IHTM43030], if the estate of the person dying in September 2005 had been as below

Net estate	300,000	S.8A(2) calculation	
Chargeable legacies	-55,000	M =	275,000
Res to s/spouse	245,000	VT =	55,000
		M > VT by	220,000
S.8A(4) calculation			
E (M > VT) =	220,000		
NRBMD =	275,000		
Percentage 220,000 x100	80.000%		
275,000			

then on the death of the survivor in January 2008, the nil rate band available on her death would potentially be

£300,000 + (300,000 x 60%) + (300,000 x 80%) = £720,000. Under IHTA84/S8A(5) this will be limited to £600,000.

IHTM43032 Transferable Nil Rate Band: survivor was married to or in a civil partnership with someone who was entitled to TNRB from an earlier death

Where a surviving spouse or civil partner was married to, or was in a civil partnership with, someone who had survived an earlier marriage or civil partnership and was entitled to transfer unused nil rate band from that earlier death, the amount of any nil rate band available for transfer on the death is survivor is calculated by reference to actual nil rate band that was appropriate on the intervening death IHTA84/S8A(6)(a). It follows therefore that on the intervening death, it was possible for the personal representatives to claim TNRB – in other words, that death must have been on or after 9th October 2007. This is limited to a maximum of 100% of the nil rate band at the death of the surviving spouse or civil partner IHTA84/S8A(5) [IHTM43033].

Example

The deceased's wife was the survivor from an earlier marriage. Her first husband died on 14 June 1996 with an estate as below

Net estate	200,000	S.8A(2) calculation	
Chargeable legacies	-150,000	M =	200,000
Res to s/spouse	50,000	VT =	150,000
		M > VT by	50,000

S.8A(4) calculation	
E (M > VT) =	50,000
NRBMD =	200,000
Percentage 50,000 x100	25.000%
200,000	

The deceased married the widow, but the widow pre-deceased him on 15 November 2007. On her death, her personal representatives are entitled to transfer the nil rate band from her first husband's death, so the nil rate band available on her death is

£300,000 + (300,000 x 25%) = £375,000

On her death, the amount of nil rate band unused, if any, is calculated with the value for **M** being the actual nil rate band available on the second death (less, if appropriate any chargeable lifetime transfers made by the deceased's wife). The value used for **NRBMD** is the nil rate band in force at the date of her death.

Net estate	400,000	S.8A(2) calculation	
Chargeable legacies	-105,000	M =	375,000
Res to s/spouse	295,000	VT =	105,000
		M > VT by	270,000
S.8A(4) calculation			
E (M > VT) =	270,000		
NRBMD =	300,000		
Percentage 270,000 x100	90.000%		
300,000			

So, although on this death, there were chargeable legacies of £105,000 against a single nil rate band of £300,000, the amount of nil rate band available for transfer is 90% because of the transfer from the earlier death.

When the deceased dies on 4 July 2010, the nil rate band available on his death is

£350,000 + (350,000 x 90%) = £665,000

IHTM43033 Transferable Nil Rate Band: survivor was married to, or in a civil partnership with someone who was entitled to TNRB from an earlier death; limitation at 100%

Following the example from [IHTM43032], if on the death of the widow there had been no chargeable legacies the calculation would look as below.

Net estate	400,000	S.8A(2) calculation	
Chargeable legacies	Nil	M =	375,000
Res to s/spouse	400,000	VT =	Nil
		M > VT by	375,000
S.8A(4) calculation			
E (M > VT) =	375,000		
NRBMD =	300,000		
Percentage 375,000 x100	125.000%		
300,000			

When the deceased dies on 4 July 2010, the nil rate band available on his death would be

£350,000 + (350,000 x 125%) = £731,250, but this is limited to £700,000 by IHTA84/S8A(5).

IHTM43034 Transferable Nil Rate Band: chargeable lifetime transfers by the second spouse or civil partner

Any available TNRB from the estate of the first spouse or civil partner to die can only be used against the death estate of the surviving spouse or civil partner. No TNRB will be available against any IHT due in respect of a transfer that is chargeable when made and above the inheritance tax threshold. However any TNRB available may reduce any additional tax due on the lifetime transfer as a result of the death, as the available nil rate band on the second death would be increased.

Example

The deceased's spouse died in June 2002 when the nil rate band was £250,000. His estate, valued at £950,000 was left as follows

Farm valued at £300,000 and qualifying for 100% agricultural relief to the son,
£10,000 to RSPCA
£50,000 to grandchildren
Residue to the deceased.

The chargeable estate is £50,000, so with the nil rate band at £250,000, the amount of nil rate band available for transfer is 80%.

The deceased makes a gift of £500,000 into a discretionary trust in July 2005 when the nil rate band was £275,000. This is an immediately chargeable transfer and the trustees pay tax at 20% of £45,000.

The deceased remarries in September 2005 and then dies in February 2008 when the nil rate is £300,000 and leaving an estate of £150,000 as follows

£25,000 to her grandchildren
Residue to her surviving spouse

The consequences on her death are as follows

1. The nil rate band applicable on her death is £300,000 + (£300,000 x 80%) = £540,000

2. The lifetime chargeable transfer uses up the nil rate band first. As the increased nil rate band is greater than the chargeable transfer, there is no additional tax payable as a result of the death – but equally, the tax paid in the lifetime is not repayable.

3. The nil rate band available against the death estate is £40,000. The chargeable death estate is £25,000, so that leaves £15,000 unused and available to transfer to her second spouse's estate

4. The amount of nil rate band available for transfer on the death of her second husband will be

$$\frac{15,000}{300,000} \times 100\% = 5\%$$

Note here that the percentage transferable is calculated by reference to the single nil rate band available on the deceased's death and not the uprated amount.

IHTM43035 Transferable Nil Rate Band: survivor was married to or in civil partnership with someone who was entitled to TNRB from an earlier death, where no claim was made on the earlier death

A claim to transfer unused nil rate band may not be appropriate in all cases when the surviving spouse or civil partner dies, for example, where their estate qualifies as an excepted estate. [IHTM43052]. However, if the survivor had remarried, the lack of a claim on their death may reduce the amount of unused nil rate band available for transfer when their second spouse or civil partner dies.

This is catered for by IHTA84/S8B(2) which allows the personal representatives making a claim on the last death to include an earlier claim, provided it will not affect the tax payable on the earlier death. It follows therefore that it was possible for a claim on be made on the earlier death – in other words the earlier death must have been on or after 9th October 2007.

Example

The deceased died in July 2010. He had been predeceased by his wife who died in January 2008 and she in turn had been predeceased by her first husband in 1997.

On the first death, the whole estate passed to the surviving spouse, so that 100% of the nil rate band was unused. On the second death, the whole estate, which was valued at £270,000 was left on discretionary trusts for the children of the first marriage. As the estate was below the nil rate band, there was no need to make a claim to transfer the unused nil rate band from the first death.

On the deceased's death in July 2010, the amount of unused nil rate band available from the second death alone is

$$\frac{(£300,000 - £270,000)}{£300,000} \times 100 = 10\%.$$

However, if the personal representatives had made a claim to transfer unused nil rate band from the first death, the actual nil rate band available on that death would have been £600,000. So the calculation becomes

S8A(2) calculation
M =	600,000
VT =	270,000
M > VT by	330,000

So the unused nil rate band taking into account both earlier deaths becomes

$$\frac{(£600,000 - £270,000)}{£300,000} \times 100 = 110\%.$$

Thus the nil rate band available on the deceased's death is capped at 100% of the amount available at that time, giving a nil rate band of £700,000.

IHTM43040 Transferable Nil Rate Band: simultaneous deaths

The rules that govern what happens when spouses or civil partners die at the same time (IHTM12191) are different in England & Wales to that in Scotland and Northern Ireland. As a consequence, the extent to which the nil rate band is unused on the first death varies.

In England & Wales, where spouses or civil partners die at the same time leaving Wills and it is not possible to establish who died first, there is a presumption that elder person died first. The couples' estates are treated for IHT on this basis and where the terms of the Will mean that there is unused nil rate band on the death of the first, it is available to be transferred to the estate of the surviving spouse or civil partner. IHTA84/S4(2) continues to operate on the death of the younger to exclude the assets from the estate of the elder. So in effect, the younger's estate could benefit from a double nil rate band and the assets accruing to their estate from the elder are excluded. If the couple had died without Wills, the presumption does not apply, so each person's estate would pass on to their heirs under intestacy. If the event that one spouse or civil partner had any unused nil rate band, it is available to be transferred to the estate of the other, if required.

In Scotland & Northern Ireland, both spouses or civil partners are treated as dying at the same moment, so neither can inherit from the other. Each person's estate will pass on to their heirs whether by Will or under intestacy. If the event that one spouse or civil partner had any unused nil rate band, it is available to be transferred to the estate of the other, if required.

IHT43041 Transferable Nil Rate Band: legitim

Legitim [IHTM12221] is only relevant in Scotland and applies to the one third of movable estate to which the children are entitled upon the death of a parent, in preference to the terms of the Will. A claim for legitim does not have to be made until the child is eighteen.

A new provision inserted at IHTA84/S147(10) provides that where an amount of unused nil rate band is transferred to the estate of the survivor if, following that death, a claim for legitim is made in respect of the earlier death, which uses up a portion of the nil rate band on that death, the amount of nil rate band transferred to the second estate may be amended to reflect the impact of the legitim claim.

Example

The deceased and her husband have one son. The husband dies when the son is 10 years old. His Will leaves his entire estate (£600,000) to the surviving spouse. An election is made for IHTA84/S147(4) to apply [IHTM35213] so that spouse exemption applies in full. The deceased dies when the son is 15 years old. Her estate, ignoring the potential legitim claim is £1.5m, and is left to son absolutely.

If the nil rate band, on the deceased's death was £450,000, a claim for TNRB would increase this to £900,000 leaving £600,000 in charge. A subsequent claim for legitim made by the son would allow him to inherit £200,000 from the first death (which would reduce the value of the second estate to £1.3m), thus potentially allowing £1.1m to pass free of tax. The revision to

IHTA84/S147(10) ensures we can reduce the amount of nil rate transferred. If, in this example, the nil rate band on the first death was £300,000, the amount available for transfer following the legitim claim would be 33.333%, so the TNRB claim is revised to £600,000. This would bring £700,000 into charge (£1.3m - £600,000), making the legitim claim unattractive.

As is clear from the example, it may be disadvantageous to claim legitim. The position may be different, however, where there are second marriages and split families.

IHTM43042 Transferable Nil rate Band : domicile of first spouse or civil partner to die

Every person, UK domiciled or not, is entitled to the full nil rate band that can be set against their UK assets.

The availability of TRNB on the estate of the first to die of a non domiciled spouse or civil partner is calculated only by reference to property that is potentially subject to an UK IHT charge. For a non domiciled spouse or civil partner, VT [IHTM43020] will be calculated only by reference to their estate in the UK. Assets held outside the UK, by a person not domiciled, or deemed domiciled in the UK, regardless of the devolution of those assets are not taken into account when calculating the available unused nil rate band.

Thus where the survivor dies in the UK and their spouse or civil partner, who held no UK assets, died abroad leaving all their all overseas assets to their children, none of the nil rate band was used on the first death and the personal representatives of the survivor may claim to transfer 100% of the nil rate band to the estate of the survivor.

IHTM43043 Transferable Nil rate Band : calculation where the domicile of the survivor at the first death is outside the UK

On the death of the first spouse or civil partner, exemption for assets passing to the surviving spouse or civil partner may be limited to £55,000 in accordance with s18(2) Inheritance Tax Act 1984 as the surviving spouse or civil partner was domiciled outside the UK [IHTM11033]

If the entire estate passed to the surviving spouse or civil partner, anything over £55,000 is a chargeable legacy. Where the net estate is above the nil rate band plus £55,000 there will be no nil rate band to transfer, as illustrated below.

Example				
First death in 02/03		S8A(2) calculation		
Net estate	450,000	M =		250,000
Exempt under s18	55,000	VT =		395,000
Chargeable residue	395,000	M > VT by		Nil

Where the net estate is less than the nil rate band plus £55,000, there will still be an amount of nil rate band available to transfer. This example shows how both the amount that the net estate is below the nil rate band, and limited spouse exemption combine to produce the amount of nil rate band available to transfer.

Example				
First death in 02/03		S8A(2) calculation		
Net estate	200,000	M =		250,000
Exempt under s18	55,000	VT =		145,000
Chargeable residue	145,000	M > VT by		105,000

Appendix 4

```
S8A(4) calculation
E (M > VT) =                    105,000
NRBMD =                        250,000
Percentage 105,000  x100       42.000%
           250,000
```

On the survivor's death in 2007/08, the nil rate band available on death would be

£300,000 + (300,000 x 42%) = £426,000

This approach will be appropriate on the death of the survivor when either

- they remain domiciled abroad and their UK assets exceed the single nil rate band, or
- between the first death and their own, they became domiciled, or deemed domiciled in the UK.

IHTM43044 Transferable Nil Rate Band: conditionally exempt property or woodlands in the estate of the first spouse or civil partner to die

When property is granted conditional exemption [IHTM04111] or woodlands relief [IHTM04121] on the first death, IHT is generally due on the sale of the property.

The charge is levied on the sale proceeds (or value at the time the undertaking is breached), which is added to the value of the estate on death (and any other sales/breaches that have taken place) and tax charged on a top-slice basis. Tax is charged using the nil rate band that applies at the date of sale.

These "recapture" charges are affected by TNRB and there are different rules about how this will affect the transfer of any unused nil rate band depending upon whether the disposal occurred before [IHTM43045] or after [IHTM43046] the second death.

IHTM43045 Transferable Nil Rate Band: conditionally exempt property or woodlands, recapture charge arising before the death of the survivor

If the property is disposed of before the death of the survivor, the original percentage of TNRB should be calculated. A further calculation is then made under IHTA84/S8C(2) to quantify amount of nil rate band that will be used by the charge on disposal. The original percentage is reduced accordingly, to give the revised percentage of nil rate band available for transfer to the estate of the survivor.

Remember, however, that if there was any IHT paid on the first death, or if IHT becomes due on the first death as a result of the recapture charge, there can be no nil rate band to transfer to the second death.

Example

The deceased survived her husband who died in 2002/03 leaving an estate shown below, including conditionally exempt property worth £125,000. This left 80% of his nil rate band unused.

```
Net estate                  550,000    S8A(2) calculation
Conditionally exempt ppty  -125,000    M =                 250,000
Chargeable legacies         -50,000    VT =                 50,000
Res to s/spouse             375,000    M > VT by           200,000

S8A(4) calculation
```

374

E (M > VT) =	200,000
NRBMD =	250,000
Percentage $\frac{200,000}{250,000}$ x100	80.000%

Before the deceased's death, the conditionally exempt property was then sold in 2005/06 for £175,000 when the nil rate band is £275,000. When the sale proceeds are added to husband's chargeable estate, the total becomes £225,000 – no tax is due, but the unused nil rate band is reduced. An adjustment is necessary to reflect this.

The calculation at IHTA84/S8C(2) is expressed as

$$\frac{E}{NRBMD} - \frac{TA}{NRBME} \times 100$$

E & NRBMD have the same meaning as they do in IHTA84/S8A(4) [IHTM 43020].

TA is the amount on which tax is charged in relation to the disposal and NRBME is the nil rate band maximum at the time of the event occasioning the charge. So in this example, TA is £175,000, NRBME is £275,000.

The s8C(2) calculation is therefore

$$\text{Percentage} \frac{(200,000)}{(250,000)} - \frac{(175,000)}{(275,000)} = (0.8 - 0.64) \times 100 = 16\%$$

On the deceased's death in 2007/08, the nil rate band available for transfer is only 16%, so the nil rate band available to her estate is

£300,000 + (300,000 x 16%) = £348,000

Where there is more than one recapture charge before the survivor dies, the IHTA84/S8C(2) calculation should be performed for each charge and the nil rate band available for transfer to the survivor reduced by each successive amount, IHTA84/S8C(3).

IHTM43046 Transferable Nil Rate Band: conditionally exempt property or woodlands, recapture charge arising after the death of the survivor

Where the disposal occurs after the second death, the unused nil rate band may be transferred to the survivor's estate in the normal way [IHTM43020]. In order to avoid recalculating the survivor's estate when the recapture charge arises IHTA84/S8C(5) adjusts the nil rate band available against the recapture charge on the deceased's death by taking account of the amount of unused nil rate band transferred to the estate of the survivor.

Example

The deceased survived her husband who died in 2002/03 leaving an estate shown below, including conditionally exempt property worth £125,000.

Net estate	550,000	S8A(2) calculation	
Conditionally exempt assets	-125,000	M =	250,000
Chargeable legacies	-60,000	VT =	60,000
Res to s/spouse	375,000	M > VT by	190,000
S8A(4) calculation			
E (M > VT) =	190,000		

375

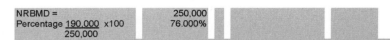

NRBMD =   250,000
Percentage <u>190,000</u> x100   76.000%
          250,000

The deceased died in 2007/08, before the conditionally exempt property was sold and left an estate of £450,000. The nil rate band available on her death was £300,000 + (300,000 x 76%) = £528,000, so no tax was paid. Not all the unused nil rate band was needed to keep the deceased's estate free of tax, so there remains an element of the nil rate band available on the first death to count against the liability that will arise when the conditionally exempt property is sold.

After the death of the survivor, the conditionally exempt property worth £125,000 on the first death is sold for £300,000 in June 2009, when the nil rate band was £325,000. Normally, the sale proceeds are added to the chargeable estate on the first death and tax charged accordingly. Here that would give a liability of £360,000 - £325,000 @ 40% = £14,000. But £150,000 of the nil rate band was transferred to the surviving spouse's estate in order to keep the survivor's estate free of tax, so the nil rate band available on sale is adjusted as follows

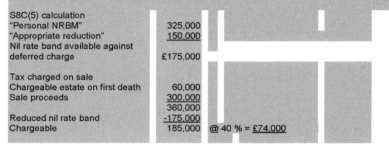

S8C(5) calculation	
"Personal NRBM"	325,000
"Appropriate reduction"	<u>150,000</u>
Nil rate band available against	
deferred charge	£175,000
Tax charged on sale	
Chargeable estate on first death	60,000
Sale proceeds	<u>300,000</u>
	360,000
Reduced nil rate band	<u>-175,000</u>
Chargeable	185,000 @ 40 % = <u>£74,000</u>

The "personal NBRM" of £325,000 is the nil rate band in force at the date of disposal. The "appropriate reduction" is the amount of the nil rate band that was needed by the survivor's estate to keep it free of tax. In these circumstances, it follows that you will need to know the chargeable value of the estate of the surviving spouse or civil partner.

IHTM43047 Transferable Nil Rate Band: deceased's estate includes funds in an alternatively secured pension

The IHT provisions for alternatively secured pensions (ASP) have been changed to reflect the interaction of an ASP charge will the transfer of unused nil rate band. Currently, a charge arises on left-over ASP funds once a relevant dependant's pension benefits cease and the rates of tax are those applying at the date of that event rather than as at the date of death of the scheme member. This rule will be modified so that, if the IHT nil-rate band was not fully used when the original 'owner' of the ASP died, the same proportion that was unused will be applied to the amount of the nil rate band in force at the date of the later event and be available against the charge on the ASP funds.

In addition, a similar procedure to that applying to recapture charges on conditionally exempt property and woodlands is appropriate to ASP charges, to recognise whether the ASP charge arises before or after the death of the survivor.

Detailed example to follow

IHTM43048 Transferable Nil Rate Band; application when the first death occurred under Estate Duty and Capital Transfer Tax

Both Estate Duty and Capital Transfer Tax, while having tiered rates at which duty or tax was payable, had amounts under which no duty or tax was due. This sum will be the equivalent of the nil rate band for calculating the TNRB available on the death of a spouse whose estate was subject to either Capital Transfer Tax or Estate Duty. The nil rate band in such cases is defined in FA08/Sch4/Para10.

When calculating VT [IHTM43020] on the first death, you will need to bear in mind that up until 21 March 1972 there was no spouse, or charitable relief available. From 22 March 1972 to 12 November 1974 spouse relief was limited to £15,000, charitable relief to £50,000. From then on, unlimited exemptions for spouses and charitable bequests were available. The effect of this will be similar to when spouse relief is restricted by IHTA84/S18(2).

This means that where, for deaths prior 13 November 1974, property was left to the spouse, an Estate Duty charge would have arisen. If the estate was large enough so that duty was paid, it follows that the equivalent of the nil rate band was exhausted, so there is nothing left to transfer.

Rates of business and agricultural relief applicable to capital transfer tax are set out on the IHT quick reference guide on the guidance page of the CAR homepage.

There was no equivalent capital reduction in the chargeable value of either agricultural or business property for the purposes of Estate Duty; where the equivalent relief applied, it was a relief against duty. It follows therefore that if the relief was in point, duty must have been payable and the nil rate band was fully used on the first death.

IHTM43049 Transferable Nil Rate Band: penalties for incorrect claim for transferable nil rate band

IHTA84/S247(2) has been amended so that the difference in tax on which a penalty is calculated can include the liability of another person, but only where s.8A applies in establishing that person's liability. This means that if an incorrect account is delivered on the first death, as a result of which there is an overstatement of transferable nil rate band on the second death, the tax underpaid on the second death as a result of the incorrect account is in point in calculating the penalty that is due in connection with that incorrect account. This change takes effect from Royal Assent, so it can only apply where an incorrect account in relation to the first death is delivered after that date.

Example

On the first death in August 2008, the executors – in the knowledge that there is no liability on that death – do not make full enquiries about the deceased's estate and as a result, deliver an incorrect account.

When the second death occurs in January 2009, those executors deliver their account and include a claim for transferable nil rate band based on the (incorrect) information contained in the earlier account. The nil rate band available for transfer is overstated by £100,000.

Our subsequent investigations reveal errors on the first death and the transferable nil rate band is corrected. This gives rise to an additional liability of £40,000 on the second death.

The executors on the first death are liable for a penalty under IHTA84/S247(1) for the delivery of an incorrect account. Normally, this is calculated by reference to the liability on the first death alone – which will be nil in these circumstances. However, because IHTA84/S247(2) has been extended to take into account the liability to tax of another person – but only where that liability is calculated through the operation of IHTA/S8A – the additional tax payable on the second death as a result of adjusting the transferable nil rate band can be used in calculating the penalty payable by the executors of the first death as a result of the delivery of their incorrect account.

IHTM43050 Transferable Nil Rate Band: settling the amount of unused TNRB at the first death

Our published guidance sets out the recommended actions to be taken by the personal representatives of the first spouse or civil partner to die. Because of the potential for the circumstances of the surviving spouse or civil partner to alter between the two deaths, in which case any work undertaken on agreeing the amount of TNRB may potentially be wasted, any requests to agree the amount on the first death should be declined.

Where the estate on the first death will not be taxable, but there are nevertheless chargeable elements, you should not seek to settle the chargeable estate on the first death. You should, however, note up any points that would be appropriate to take up had there been a liability so that when the file is reviewed on the second death, the issues can then be raised – if worthwhile at that time.

IHTM43051 Transferable Nil Rate Band: requests to revise values included on the first death

The introduction of TNRB will sharpen the focus on the value of assets included on the first death that pass to beneficiaries other than the spouse or civil partner. If the agents seek to revise values previously submitted <u>before</u> the death of the survivor, you should explain that there is no need to do so at this stage and decline any invitation to agree, say, the value of a house. If and when it is relevant on the survivor's death, you should ask the agents to use the revised values they consider should apply in submitting the claim on form IHT216, and to explain why they are using a value that is different to that used on the first death.

IHTM43052 Transferable Nil Rate Band: excepted estates and transferable nil rate band

The limit for excepted estates remains at the single IHT nil rate band available to every individual, irrespective of whether or not there is any unused nil rate band to transfer. Where changes in an estate mean that it is no longer excepted – but there will still be no tax to pay because of the transfer of unused nil rate band, you should proceed as follows.

You should continue to accept a Corrective Account delivered with an IHT205 as a full "account" for these cases [IHTM06034] and in addition, the prs should make a claim on form IHT216 [IHTM43004]. Upon receipt of all these documents, you should deal with the claim in accordance with IHTM43007.

IHTM43053 Transferable Nil Rate Band: the rate of tax on exit charges from relevant property trusts which include TNRB before the first ten year anniversary.

Where an amount up to the single nil rate band is settled on relevant property trusts by Will, there is no charge to IHT on any property leaving that settlement before the first ten year anniversary. This is because the rate of tax on such an exit is ascertained with reference to the IHTA84/S68(5)(a) historic value of the fund at the date of death. As this value was at, or below, the nil rate band at the date the settlement was created, and as it is most likely that the nil rate band will have either remained constant, or increased, between the date the settlement was created and the date the property leaves the settlement, the nil rate band at the date of the exit charge will almost always be greater than the historic value of the settlement.

However, where the Will of the surviving spouse or civil partner leaves a sum "that is equal to an amount that will not give rise to an IHT charge" on relevant property trusts, that amount will include nil rate band that has been transferred. When calculating the rate of tax under IHTA84/S68(1) that applies to any property leaving the trust before the first ten year anniversary, if the historic value of the fund is greater that the single nil rate band that applies when the property leaves the trust, there will be a positive rate of tax under IHTA84/S68(1) and a liability will arise on the exit charge.

IHTM43054 Transferable Nil Rate Band: valuing the first estate, ascertained valued for CGT

Where the value of an asset is not ascertained for the purposes of determining the chargeable value of the estate on the death of the first spouse or civil partner to die, on any subsequent sale, the acquisition value for CGT will need to be established. If that property is subsequently valued to find the percentage of the TNRB available on the second death, the value we adopt for IHT does not replace the value used in establishing the CGT liability IHTA84/S8C(8).

Example

On the death of the first spouse in January 2008, their share of the matrimonial home is left to the son. The value returned for the entirety is £300,000, so the half share chargeable on the first death is £150,000.

The property is sold in 2009 for £350,000 and the son's share is liable to CGT. As the value for his share was not ascertained for IHT purposes on the first death, it is necessary to agree the acquisition value to establish the chargeable gain. The value of a one half share in January 2008 is agreed at £127,500.

On the survivor's death in 2011, we need to agree the value of the house so that we can establish the amount of the nil rate band available for transfer. The value is agreed at £300,000, so the chargeable estate on the first death is £150,000, meaning that TNRB available for transfer is 50%.

As the value of £150,000 has been ascertained for the value of the half share on the first death, this would normally be the acquisition value for the CGT charge. IHTA84/S8C(8) prevents the normal rule applying and the CGT calculation is not adjusted.

This only applies solely in connection with TNRB; in all other cases, TCGA92/S274 applies to adopt the value ascertained for IHT purposes as the acquisition value for CGT.

IHTM43055 Transferable Nil Rate Band: effect of clearance certificates or clearance letters

IHTA84/S239(4) is amended by the insertion of a new paragraph (aa) which says that where too little IHT has been paid on the second death, because too great an increase in the nil rate band was allowed, the accountable persons remain liable for paying any additional tax that is due.

IHTM43056 Transferable Nil Rate Band: disclosure of TNRB calculations to other liable persons

The claim to transfer unused nil rate band is made by the prs and you should treat this in the same way as any other information provided by a taxpayer. Just as with aggregable property where we need to tell all those liable for tax on a case what the total value for each component of the estate is so that they can see how their individual liability is calculated; so we have to tell all those liable for tax what the revised nil rate band is. This will allow them to work out what the transferable amount is; but not how that amount has been arrived at.

Appendix 4

Any request from taxpayers other than the prs for information about how the transferable amount has been calculated should be refused and the taxpayers told that they should contact the prs for that information.

District probate registries and sub-registries

The contact details for all probate registries and sub-registries can be found at www.hmcourts-service.gov.uk/infoabout/civil/probate/registries.htm.

Index